HUMAN INSTINCTS, EVERYDAY LIFE, AND THE BRAIN

HUMAN INSTINCTS, EVERYDAY LIFE, AND THE BRAIN

A paradigm for understanding behavior

Volume Three

Specific behaviors in response to instincts, or feelings

Seeking Sex

Case examples: #2273 - #2890

A research series by

Richard H. Wills, University of Prince Edward Island

ISBN: 0-9684020-2-X

Printed in Canada

Distributed by

The Book Emporium
169 Queen Street
Charlottetown
Prince Edward Island
Canada C1A 4B4

Telephone: 1-902-628-2001

To everyone who participated in this research

CONTENTS

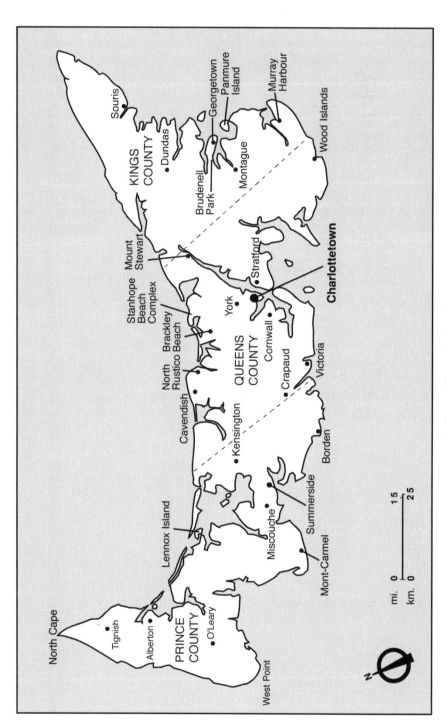

Prince Edward Island

Prince Edward Island relative to other locations

CANADA

NEWFOUNDLAND

Gulf of
St. Lawrence

Cape Breton
Island

QUEBEC

PRINCE EDWARD
ISLAND

Caribou

Dartmouth

Halifax

NOVA SCOTIA

NEW
BRUNSWICK

Cape
Tormentine

Moncton

Federicton

MAINE

Montreal

Ottawa

ONTARIO

UNITED STATES

Boston

New York City

Toronto

N

ix

1. INTRODUCTION

Volume One

Volume One in this series contains a list of implications; photographs; a theoretical introduction; five chapters on specific behaviors in response to instincts, or feelings; and a discussion of a) the study of behavior, and b) human perception of nonhumans. The five chapters on specific behaviors deal with seeking positive reactions; avoiding embarrassment, criticism, and rejection; and not hurting others. A short summary of Volume One is provided in the next few paragraphs.

Feelings act as instincts in humans and other species. Feelings are designed to help us obtain and protect resources. Feelings are a more reliable means of directing our behavior than are learning, memory, culture, and conscious thought. Instead, we use learning, memory, culture, and conscious thought as means to satisfy our feelings. We seek positive feelings and avoid negative feelings. Positive feelings occur in the form of pleasure, which is provided by a variety of sources, including positive reactions from others, pleasant stimulation, the achievement of goals, and sex. Negative feelings include loneliness; anxiety; envy; anger; and hurt from criticism, rejection, embarrassment, and self-criticism. Feelings involve an increase of tension or a release of tension. Tension and the increase of tension are experienced as hurt, and the release of tension is experienced as pleasure. People engage in specific behaviors in response to positive and negative feelings. The five behaviors which are dealt with in Volume One are seeking positive reactions, avoiding embarrassment, avoiding criticism, avoiding those who reject us, and trying to help others. Each of these is considered in turn below.

People want positive reactions from others, and try to get them in a multitude of ways. People seek positive reactions in order to avoid loneliness and to experience pleasure. When people receive the kinds of positive reactions they want from the individuals they want them from, they feel pleasure and they cease to feel lonely. People establish relationships in order to obtain a steady supply of positive reactions. Those who provide a person with positive reactions usually provide the person with resources. Resources include food, shelter, protection, help, money, stimulation, and sex. Those who do not provide a person with positive reactions usually do not provide the person with resources. Therefore, the ability to get positive reactions from a person serves as an early indicator that one is likely to get resources from the person. People provide others with positive reactions and resources in order to get both positive reactions and resources from them. When people experience pleasure they smile and laugh. Smiling and laughing are desired positive reactions, and people do things for others in order to receive smiles and laughs.

People are embarrassed when others know they have done something that is disapproved of. Embarrassment is a punishing experience because it hurts. People try to avoid embarrassment in order to avoid hurt. In order to avoid embarrassment, people a) avoid doing the things that others disapprove of, and b) try to keep others from finding out what they do that is disapproved of. When a person is disapproved of, others are less willing to give the person resources. Embarrassment acts as an early warning system. It notifies us that we are in a situation which is likely to cause others to cut off our resources. When we avoid embarrassment we avoid alienating others and losing resources.

People try to avoid criticism from others. Criticism hurts, and people avoid criticism in order to avoid hurt. When a person is criticized, other people are already reducing that person's resources or making plans to do so. Therefore the more sensitive a person is to criticism and the possibility of receiving it, the more the person tries to avoid criticism, and the better the person protects his or her resources.

People reject others because their own resources are limited. If they give their resources to everyone who wants them, they will not have them available for themselves and those they want to give them to. People usually do not experience hurt when they reject others. However, those who are rejected do experience hurt. Because of this hurt, people normally avoid those who reject them. This enables them to stop wasting time and energy continuing to try to get resources from those who are unlikely to provide them. Instead, people seek resources from those who do not reject them and are much more likely to provide them with resources.

When people hurt others, cause them to lose resources, or fail to help them, they often criticize themselves. Self-criticism, or guilt, is a punishing feeling. It hurts. Therefore people try to avoid hurting others in order to avoid feeling hurt themselves. People spend most of their time with a small number of people and receive most of their resources from them. It is very much in their interest that they do not damage these people or alienate them. When they take good care of their human resources they are likely to continue receiving resources from them. It is an expensive process to try to establish relationships with new people in order to receive the same resources that one was already receiving. When people feel hurt, they cry, cry out, or want to do so. When they cry they notify others that they are being hurt and need help. When they cry they are more likely to cause those who are hurting them, or who could help them, to feel guilty. Therefore crying helps people protect themselves from being hurt and enables them to get help.

Volume Two

Volume Two contains chapters on five other specific behaviors in response to instincts, or feelings. Volume Two also includes photographs and an updated and expanded list of implications. The behaviors which are dealt with are conserving time and energy, protecting self and resources, removing physical discomfort, taking precautions, and trying to get what others have. Each of these behaviors is discussed below.

People seek to conserve time and energy. They try to expend a minimum amount of time and energy in their physical and mental activities. The feeling which encourages them to do so is hurt. People employ tension in order to exert themselves (to act), and they experience tension as hurt. Therefore, people feel hurt when they exert themselves, and they try to avoid this feeling by exerting themselves as little as possible. This hurt is intensified by fatigue. People engage in activity because the hurt or pleasure they experience from other feelings overrides the hurt they feel from exertion. When people do exert themselves, they try to spend as little time as possible in an activity, because they feel hurt from exertion and they feel anxious about all the other things they have to do. As a result of hurt and anxiety, people employ numerous tactics to conserve time and energy. People experience hurt and anxiety when they first consider effort. This provides them with the maximum amount of time in which to conserve time and energy.

Introduction

People normally go to considerable effort to protect themselves and their resources when they are actually threatened. They seek to protect themselves from attack and mistreatment, and they attempt to protect their resources from being taken by others. The resources they try to protect include food and water, time and energy, property, possessions, jobs, money, reputation, sex, positive reactions, relationships, stimulation, and self-image. People view their resources as an extension of themselves. Therefore, when people protect their resources, they protect themselves. The feeling which encourages people to protect themselves and their resources is anger. Anger enables people to act aggressively. It helps them challenge and drive away others. As a result anger often enables people to protect themselves and maintain access to their resources. People feel anger as soon as they realize others are trying to attack them or take their resources. This often allows them to respond quickly enough to protect themselves and their resources. Signs of anger enable a person to communicate the message, "Don't mess with me, because I can get violent," to others. Anger is an activator. Anger frequently produces fear in those it is directed against that they may be hurt, and it often causes them to retreat. Another feeling, anxiety, also helps people protect themselves and their resources. People feel anxiety when they think they might be harmed or lose resources, whereas they feel anger when they are in the process of being harmed or losing resources or just after it has happened. Anxiety helps people avoid future threats, whereas anger helps people protect themselves and their resources from present threats. (Anxiety is considered in Volume Two in the chapter on Taking Precautions.)

People experience a variety of types of physical discomforts at different times. These include hunger, thirst, hot, cold, itching, soreness, aches, pain, and fatigue. They also feel irritation as a result of a clogged nostril or ear, a particle between their teeth, something in their eye, or an object which abrades or pushes into their skin. In addition, they feel discomfort when they need to breathe, urinate, or defecate. People feel bothered by physical discomforts and they seek to remove discomforts as they experience them. By removing physical discomforts, people prevent damage to their bodies.

People are very much concerned with taking precautions. They take precautions to protect themselves and their resources. People take countless precautions to better ensure that they get food, water, and shelter; conserve time and energy; protect themselves from various dangers; avoid accidents; obtain stimulation; protect possessions; avoid negative reactions from others; and keep their sources of positive reactions. People take precautions by avoiding threats, removing threats, and reducing threats. The feeling that drives people to take precautions is anxiety. Anxiety involves an increase in tension. It is a punishing feeling which often dominates a person's consciousness. People experience numerous anxieties, or worries, about threats to themselves and their resources. People take precautions in order to reduce anxiety and to prevent anxiety from occurring. As a result of anxiety and taking precautions, people better protect their bodies and their resources. A great many precautions are instituted by groups and societies to better protect their members and their interests. People experience anxiety as soon as they become aware of a potential threat. This provides them with a maximum amount of time in which to take precautions.

People frequently try to get what others have. This may be positive reactions, possessions, advantages, experiences, relationships, accomplishments, and anything else that others have but they do not. The feeling which motivates people to try to get what others have is envy. Envy motivates people to focus on resources which others have that they do not, and to endeavor to acquire these resources for themselves. They may try to take a resource from the person who has it, get the person to share the resource with them, get those who distribute the resource to give them a share, or find another way to obtain the same resource, such as buying it or making it. The feeling of envy notifies people that someone has succeeded in getting a resource that they would like to have too. Envy encourages people to obtain the same resources that others have and encourages them to exploit the resources that are available.

Volume Three

Volume Three, this volume, contains a list of implications and a chapter on an additional specific behavior in response to instincts, or feelings. This behavior is seeking sex.

Numerous quotes are given in the volumes in this series. These quotes were gathered from people on Prince Edward Island. A small percentage of the material deals with experiences that people on Prince Edward Island have had in other provinces and in other countries. The person quoted is not identified by age and occupation, because in most cases the person would not want this information known. Given the small size of the province, the amount of information that people know about each other, and the effort they put into learning more about others, facts such as age and occupation would confirm the identity of many of those quoted. Unimportant details in the quotes and case studies are sometimes changed to protect the identities of the subjects.

In this volume case examples are numbered consecutively starting with #2273 and ending with #2890. Volume One contained case examples #1 through #1155. Volume Two included case examples #1156 through #2272. An index of case examples is provided at the end of each volume.

2. IMPLICATIONS OF THIS RESEARCH

Contents

continued on next page

Implications of this research

Introduction

This is a partial list of ideas, or models, which have been produced by the research to date. These ideas result from the research reported in Volumes One and Two and from the research which is currently in process which has not yet been published. This is a working list which will certainly change as the research proceeds. There will be alterations, deletions, and additions to this list.

Feelings as instincts

1. Humans have biologically programmed feelings.

2. These feelings are present in all members of the species.

3. Feelings act as instincts.

4. Most instincts in humans and other animal species are experienced as feelings.

5. Responses to feelings in nonhuman animal species have been interpreted as instincts.

6. Feelings explain most of the behavior in humans and other animal species.

7. Feelings provide the motivational system of a species with voluntary movement.

8. Evidence that a species responds to any feeling, such as discomfort (hunger, thirst) or anxiety (running from threats, hiding from threats), indicates that the species responds to other feelings too.

9. Our behavior is directed by feelings, rather than by reason and learning. Reason and learning are used to help us satisfy our feelings. They serve as handmaidens of feelings.

10. Feelings encourage the individual to get and keep resources. Discomfort encourages us to find resources, such as food, water, and shelter, which will remove specific discomforts. Loneliness encourages us to establish relationships with friends and mates, who help us get resources, share their resources with us, and help protect us. Envy encourages us to get the same resources that others are getting. Anxiety helps us avoid threats to ourselves and our resources. Anger helps us defend ourselves and our resources. Guilt encourages us to take care of our human resources. The hurt produced by criticism, rejection, and embarrassment encourages us to avoid doing things which alienate other people, who provide us with most of our resources.

11. Feelings are activated at the first signs that resources are available or threatened.

12. Individuals act in response to feelings, or they act in advance of feelings to avoid or promote the feelings.

13. The three major types of feelings are the pleasures, the hurts, and the bothers.

14. The individual pursues pleasures while avoiding hurts and bothers.

15. Our lives are dedicated to trying to obtain pleasant feelings and avoid unpleasant feelings. Pleasant feelings are provided by the pleasures. Unpleasant feelings are provided by the hurts and bothers.

16. The pleasures are produced by sex, positive reactions, and stimula-

tion. In addition, the removal of hurts and bothers releases tension and produces pleasure.

17. The hurts are produced by physical and mental effort; negative reactions from others (criticism, rejection); loneliness; threats (anxiety); envy; self-criticism, or guilt; pain; and physical discomforts, such as hunger and not breathing.

18. The bothers are produced by phenomena which are not categorized, inconsistency, phenomena which are not oriented, and differences between models and reality. The bothers hurt also, but usually to a lesser degree than the hurts.

19. Humans can experience and act on feelings without being consciously aware of them. For example, humans take each breath in response to the feeling of increasing discomfort that they experience when they do not take a breath. Humans are not normally consciously aware of this discomfort or of their decision to act and take a breath in order to get rid of it.

20. A considerable amount of excess behavior occurs in response to specific feelings which fails to obtain and conserve resources.

21. Individuals respond to current feelings and live in the present.

22. Human feelings and responses are constant in different cultures and in different historical periods.

23. There is a common set of feelings which is shared by different animal species. For example, in many species individuals associate together in order to obtain positive reactions from each other. Their desire for positive reactions is so strong that they engage in efforts to obtain positive reactions which attract the attention of predators.

24. Various animal species employ different behaviors in response to common feelings. For example, humans smile, cats purr, and dogs wag their tails to express pleasure.

25. Specific feelings are tied to specific muscle groups. For example, humans feel anxiety in their diaphragms, hurt in their lower eye sockets, and pleasure at the raised corners of their mouths.

26. Different feelings are experienced at different locations on the body.

27. Feelings which are experienced at separate locations on the body are separate feelings.

28. Feelings which are experienced at the same locations on the body are the same feeling.

29. The same feeling can be tied to different muscle groups in different animal species. For example, humans feel pleasure where they smile, cats feel pleasure where they purr, and dogs feel pleasure where they wag their tails.

Individuals

30. An individual is designed to a) get and keep resources, b) compete with other individuals for resources, c) cooperate with other individuals to get and keep resources, and d) exchange resources with other individuals.

31. Feelings encourage individuals to get and keep resources, compete for resources with others, and cooperate and exchange resources with others. An individual is encouraged to get resources by the feelings of discomfort, loneliness, and envy. Discomforts, such as hunger, thirst, and feeling hot or cold, encourage one to obtain resources which will remove the discomforts. Loneliness encourages one to seek the company of others, who provide protection and other resources. Envy encourages one to obtain the same resources that others are getting. An individual is encouraged to keep resources by

the feelings of anxiety and anger. Anxiety encourages one to take precautions. Anger enables one to aggressively protect oneself and one's resources. Also, the hurt produced by effort encourages one to avoid exertion and conserve time and energy. Because individuals experience their own feelings rather than the feelings of others, they try to satisfy their own feelings. As a result, they compete with others to obtain resources. Individuals are encouraged to cooperate with each other and exchange resources by the desire for positive reactions and the desire to avoid both negative reactions from others (criticism, rejection, and embarrassment) and guilt (self-criticism).

32. An individual experiences his own feelings. He learns about the feelings experienced by other individuals, but he does not experience them firsthand. Therefore an individual experiences his own feelings far more vividly than he experiences the feelings of other individuals. As a result, each individual spends most of his time acting for himself, thinking about himself, and trying to communicate about himself to others.

Communication of feelings

33. The members of an animal species share a well-developed means of communicating certain of their feelings to each other.

34. Such feelings are communicated to each other through the action of the specific muscle groups associated with each feeling.

35. Simulating the actions of these specific muscle groups will enable humans to better communicate with other animal species.

36. Indicating one's feelings to others is costly in terms of a) the biological systems required to be able to do so, and b) the time and energy expended when one does so. Nevertheless, individuals

frequently make their feelings known to others by various means, including sounds, facial expressions, and the movement and position of body parts. Therefore, it must be advantageous to indicate what one is feeling to others.

37. Because feelings determine behavior, it is important to let others know what you are feeling in order that they can correctly predict how you will act and coordinate their behavior with your own. When others correctly recognize what you are feeling, they are more likely to act in an appropriate way at the appropriate time. When others correctly coordinate their behavior with your own, you have to exert less time and energy trying to get them to do so.

38. Because feelings determine behavior, it is important to know what others are feeling in order that you can predict how they will act and you can coordinate your behavior with their behavior. When you correctly coordinate your behavior with the behavior of others, you expend less time and energy dealing with them. Appropriate behavior expends less time and energy than does inappropriate behavior, and is more likely to be successful.

39. Signs of specific feelings carry specific messages which provide advantages. Signs of happiness (smiling, purring, tail wagging) provide others with positive reactions and enable one to obtain positive reactions and resources from them. Signs of discomfort and unhappiness, such as crying, enable one to obtain help and resources from others. Signs of anger warn others that one will aggressively protect oneself and one's resources. Signs of fear notify those one depends on for resources and protection that there are threats present. Signs of interest notify those one depends on about the presence of threats and opportunities.

40. Individuals experience their own feelings, but not the feelings of others. Therefore it is easy for individuals to fail to take into account the feelings of other individuals. When individuals show others what they are feeling, they notify others that they have feelings, they remind others that these feelings need to be taken into account, and

they reveal precisely what these feelings are. Only by revealing feelings can others take them into consideration.

41. In many species a tail is a device for communicating both visually and physically what one is feeling to others. Cats use their tails to indicate alertness, interest, enthusiasm, irritation, affection, fear, discouragement, and relaxation. Humans and apes use facial expressions instead of tails for this purpose. Tails are particularly noticeable because they are a distinct appendage, move independently of the rest of the body, make pronounced movements, are frequently banded in contrasting colors, and hit against other individuals.

42. Both tails and faces indicate the nature and degree of the tension that the individual is experiencing.

Activators

43. Individuals have *activators*, or specialized behaviors which activate specific feelings in other individuals. Crying, smiling, and anger are three examples of activators in humans.

44. Different animal species use different activators to achieve a common purpose. For example, humans smile, cats purr, and dogs wag their tails as activators to obtain positive reactions from others.

45. Activators are the first social behaviors expressed by the infants of many animal species. Mewing and purring are two examples of activators in kittens.

46. Individuals cheat, or use an activator without experiencing the feeling which produces the activator, in order to get others to respond appropriately. Cheaters employ various activators, including crying, smiling, and anger.

47. The presence of activators can be used to trace the presence and evolution of certain feelings in various animal species.

Behavior

48. The regular use of a specific social behavior by members of a species indicates that the behavior frequently evokes a specific feeling and a specific response in other members of the species.

49. The Parallel Feelings Hypothesis: If two different species a) use the same social behavior, and b) produce the same response in others, then c) the feeling which is evoked in others by the social behavior is the same in both species. For example, because infant humans and infant birds a) both "cry," and b) in both cases their parents respond by feeding them, then c) the same feeling is evoked in both sets of parents, i.e., a desire to avoid self-criticism, or guilt.

50. In accordance with The Parallel Feelings Hypothesis, when we can identify the feeling that is evoked in one of the two species, we can assume the same feeling is evoked in the other species. Therefore, when we know what the feeling is in humans (when humans are one of the two species), we can assume that the same feeling is present in the other species.

Association and extension

51. An individual recognizes what he thinks, does, says, and owns as extensions of himself.

52. An individual recognizes a positive reaction by others to anything he thinks, does, says, or owns as a positive reaction to himself.

53. An individual recognizes a negative reaction by others to anything he thinks, does, says, or owns as a negative reaction to himself.

54. An individual considers the other individuals he is associated with to be extensions of himself.

55. An individual treats negative reactions to those he is associated with as negative reactions toward himself.

56. An individual views the behavior of those he is associated with as though it is his own behavior. As a result, actions which would embarrass the individual if he did them himself, embarrass him when they are done by other people he is associated with.

57. When a person is familiar with another individual's experiences, he does not experience them as the other individual experiences them. Instead, the person experiences them as he would feel if the experiences had happened to himself.

58. People "adopt" others as an extension of themselves. Thus they adopt characters in novels and films, individuals in the news, and sporting teams and players. When something happens to someone or something that a person has "adopted," the person responds as though it is happening to himself. This is the case when those who are adopted (or their resources) are threatened, or when those who are adopted succeed and receive positive reactions. People have difficulty adopting a character when the character does things which they would not do themselves, such as things which they consider bad, incompetent, immature, self-centered, selfish, foolish, stupid, rude, inconsiderate, narrow minded, or a result of bad judgment.

Tense and release

59. Feelings involve an increase of tension or a release of tension.

60. Tension is experienced as hurt.

61. An increase in tension produces a corresponding increase in hurt.

62. Difficulty releasing tension, or the inability to release tension, prolongs hurt.

63. We try to minimize physical and mental effort because they involve tension and hurt. When we conserve time and energy, we avoid effort, and we avoid tension and hurt.

64. The release of tension is experienced as pleasure.

65. When we complete a task or achieve a goal, we release the tension that was driving us, and we feel pleasure. Therefore we feel pleasure when we complete a paper we are writing, pay off a mortgage, complete our income tax return, win a sporting competition, or get the positive reactions we want.

66. Sources of stimulation, such as movies, novels, amusement-park rides, and certain sports, produce entertainment by providing tension and releasing it. People seek out these sources of stimulation in order to experience tension, its release, and the resulting pleasure. The more tension experienced and the greater its release, the more successful the entertainment.

67. The more tension released, and the more easily tension is released, the more pleasure experienced.

68. Humans and other animal species seek to a) avoid tension, b) release

tension, and c) increase tension in order to release it and experience pleasure.

69. Warmth releases muscular tension, and this release of tension provides pleasure. Therefore humans like lying in the sun, hot showers and baths, hot tubs, whirlpools, saunas, hot drinks, hot food, smoking, heat lamps, hot-water bottles, and electric heating pads.

70. Many other species like lying and relaxing in the sun, which indicates that the release of tension also provides them with pleasure. This indicates that their bodies and minds operate on the same tense and release principles that human bodies and minds do.

71. Massage is pleasurable to humans and other species because it releases tension.

72. A living organism consists of an organized system of tense and release mechanisms. These tense and release mechanisms are able to perform respiration, circulation, movement, digestion, reproduction, nervous control, mental operations, and other activities, such as yawning and sneezing.

73. It may prove possible to explain all physiological phenomena and the origin of life with tense and release models.

74. The brain evolved to coordinate tense and release mechanisms.

Effort

75. People avoid physical and mental activity because activity requires tension. People experience tension as hurt. In order to minimize hurt, individuals a) tense as little as possible, and b) release tension as

soon as possible. As a result they exert themselves as little as possible, and conserve as much energy as possible.

76. People engage in physical and mental activity in response to their other feelings. They act when a) the pleasure they obtain from the activity, or b) the hurt they feel from other sources when they do not engage in the activity, outweighs the hurt they feel from exerting themselves.

77. People avoid activities in which the hurt they feel from exerting themselves is greater than the pleasure they experience from the activity.

78. People avoid activities in which the hurt they feel from exerting themselves is greater than the hurt they feel from other sources when they do not engage in the activity.

79. Something is boring or tedious because one does not obtain enough stimulation from it to outweigh the hurt one feels from exerting oneself to do the activity. Thus one finds it boring to reread the same material, to continue to eat the same food, or to listen to someone say something one is already familiar with, because these things no longer provide stimulation.

Models and behavior

80. Behavior is structured by mental categories and models.

81. Without models, behavior is random.

82. Each individual uses categories and models in order to act in a non-random fashion.

83.   When categories or models are changed, behavior changes.

84.   Individuals develop and use their own categories and models.

85.   Each individual employs models in order to deal with feelings.

86.   Most behavior can be explained in terms of feelings and the models employed to satisfy them.

87.   When models are inconsistent with reality, people experience tension.

88.   People act in order to rid themselves of this tension. When they act they change reality to be consistent with their models. For example, there is a glass on the left side of the table, and you want the glass to be on the right side of the table. Therefore reality (the glass is on the left side) is inconsistent with your model (you want the glass on the right side). Because of this inconsistency, you experience tension. Therefore, you act to rid yourself of this tension. You change reality (by moving the glass from the left side of the table to the right side) to be consistent with your model (you want the glass on the right side). When reality (the glass is now on the right side) is consistent with your model (you want the glass on the right side), then the tension is released, you no longer experience tension, and you no longer feel pressure to act.

89.   People act to remove their greatest sources of tension. The greater the tension, the higher the priority.

90.   People select the model and action which produces the least inconsistency with their other models, i.e., the least tension.

91.   Humans and other animal species develop models, select models, and act for the same reasons.

92.   The mind evolved to a) recognize categories, b) recognize inconsistencies, c) deal with feelings, d) produce models, e) select between models, and f) execute models.

Language

93. A shared language based on sounds is a means by which individuals coordinate their use of the same sounds with similar categories and models.

94. In a shared language, specific sounds (or other phenomena) trigger the specific categories and models in the minds of other individuals that the sounds are associated with.

95. A shared language allows individuals to exchange and pool information about their individual categories and models.

96. In human language standardized sounds were associated with the individual categories and models that pre-humans were already employing as an animal species.

97. Human language enables humans to discuss their feelings, behaviors, and mental operations, which they and the other animal species have in common.

98. Humans are animals who can tell each other what it is like to be an animal. Humans are talking animals.

99. If we want to know what animals feel and think, all we have to do is listen to humans talk about themselves.

100. Humans speak because they feel tension to say something. Once they have said what they want to say, the tension, or pressure, is released and is no longer there. When person A finishes saying something, and person B asks person A to repeat or explain what he has just said, person A finds it annoying to do so, because the initial tension is no longer there and person A has to force himself to comply.

101. Certain animals make sounds to other animals or to humans a) when they want something, or b) when they are bothered by something (have something to say). They stop making the sounds when a) they get what they want, or b) they have said what they wanted to say. This indicates that animals feel the same tension to make sounds that humans feel and release it in the same way. This indicates that their minds operate in the same way that human minds operate.

102. Animal species have to form categories in order to recognize phenomena, and have to formulate models and apply them in order to act non-randomly.

103. Human categories and models are primarily sensory images. Consider buying a loaf of bread, eating an ice-cream cone, or having sex with a specific person. You think about these things primarily in visual images, not in words. If I say, "A kangaroo buried a watermelon in my front yard," how do you experience this in your mind? You see your own visual images of a kangaroo, a watermelon, burying something, and a front yard, rather than collections of words in your mind which describe a kangaroo, a watermelon, burying something, and a front yard.

104. Members of a species use means such as sounds in an effort to communicate their feelings, categories, and models to each other. Thus cats use sounds for a variety of purposes, including calling, answering, indicating discomfort or pain, seeking positive reactions, trying to get others to comply with what they want (establishing consistency), criticizing, threatening, and expressing what is on their mind, such as telling about their experiences or complaining.

105. Many species use sounds in an effort to activate feelings, categories, and models in other individuals.

106. Human language enables humans to communicate in generalizations, or words, which individual humans relate to their own personal categories and models.

107.   Species differ as to how specific their communications are, i.e., the degree of detail in which they can describe their categories and models. Words communicate categories and models in greater detail than basic sounds. However, human language is severely limited when it comes to communicating the full detail and complexity of categories and models. Consider how difficult it is to use words alone to describe a person's appearance to someone who has never seen the person before, and to do so well enough that he would have no difficulty recognizing the person within a crowd of people. Consider also how difficult it is to use words to describe to another person all of the details and feelings that you experienced when you watched a film, read a novel, listened to a piece of music, or took a trip. Although words enable us to easily distinguish between "a chair" and "a couch" when we talk, it is difficult to use words to accurately describe a specific chair or couch to another person. When we want to communicate something specific to others we have to provide them with a visual image by showing them the item, showing them a photograph or a drawing of it, or using gestures.

108.   It is very possible that a species could evolve a language which enabled it to communicate categories and models in much greater detail than human language. Such a species could communicate more accurately and rapidly, could achieve a much finer degree of cooperation among its members, and would be much more successful than a species that relied on human language. In fact, the gap in ability between such a species and humans might be at least as great as the present gap between humans and other animal species on earth.

109.   Theoretically a shared language could be just as specific and descriptive as the personal categories and models held by individuals. Other things being equal, the closer the language of a species is to this ideal, the more successful the species.

110.   One can view a potential progression taking place from sounds, to words, to increasingly specific words.

Culture

111. Because each individual uses his own categories and models, no two individuals have the identical understanding of a situation.

112. Inconsistency produces tension, and people seek to establish consistency to remove this tension.

113. In order to establish consistency, people try to get others to adopt and comply with their personal models.

114. When we see someone do something, we behave as though we are doing it ourselves. We consider others as an extension of ourselves. If they do, say, or think something we would not, we view it as a mistake on our part and act to correct it by trying to change their behavior.

115. People use a) resources, and b) negative reactions, such as criticism, to get others to adopt and comply with their personal models.

116. People adopt the personal models of those who control resources in order to get a share of their resources.

117. Culture is the net result of individual efforts to establish consistency within a specific group.

118. Many individual and group models produce more negative results than positive results.

119. The ability of humans to communicate in greater detail through words has enabled human individuals to communicate their specific likes and dislikes to each other and to establish a much more elaborate repertoire of correct and incorrect behaviors in their societies than have other species. Although other species are concerned

with avoiding negative reactions, they do not communicate or understand criticism in as fine detail as do humans and therefore do not adjust their behavior to as fine a degree. Therefore other species do not a) wear clothes, b) hide their sexual activity and elimination from others, or c) stand up straight, cover their mouths when they yawn, and use napkins.

120.   A species which uses a language which is more specific than human language will have rules for correct and incorrect behavior which are more detailed than the rules used in human cultures. Humans will be unable to understand these rules or act in accordance with them, just as animals do not understand or act in accordance with human rules. Therefore, human behavior will appear as crude and uncouth to such a species as the behavior of animals does to humans.

Categories and models

121.   Categories are an efficient means of dealing with sensory phenomena.

122.   Phenomena which are not categorized produce tension and attract notice.

123.   Categories are formed by recognizing repetition. For example, when humans speak and write, they use synonyms in order to avoid repetition which will produce a second, competing, unwanted, distracting category in the mind of the listener or reader. In poetry and song, on the other hand, humans use repetition to produce additional rhythmic patterns in the mind of the listener. Music consists of repetitive sounds, sequences, and phrases which enable the listener

to establish categories. It is significant that music relies heavily on numerous forms of repetition, and to a much lesser extent on symmetry, to produce categories.

124. The organization of phenomena into a category releases tension and produces pleasure.

125. The quest for stimulation is the search for unfamiliar phenomena to categorize.

126. People use the arts, learning, entertainment, and travel in order to organize unfamiliar phenomena into new categories and thereby experience pleasure. The arts include music, painting, sculpture, literature, poetry, photography, film, architecture, crafts, fashion, and decoration.

127. Successful art is designed a) to be different than existing categories so that it is not already categorized and therefore produces tension and is interesting, and b) to be easily categorized so that the tension is released with little effort and pleasure is easily produced. Orientations are employed by artists to enable phenomena to be easily categorized, and orientations are violated by artists to a limited extent to produce tension and interest.

128. The fewer categories that are needed to categorize phenomena, the less effort is required, and the more attractive the phenomena. For example, lakes and lawns can be categorized with few categories and are peaceful and pleasing, and because younger faces have fewer features than older faces, they can be categorized with fewer categories and are more attractive.

129. Once phenomena are categorized, they are no longer stimulating. No tension remains to be released. No matter how attractive a specific phenomenon is initially, once it has been fully categorized, it is no longer interesting. This is true of art, literature, music, clothing, jewelry, other possessions, and a person's appearance.

130. The play activity of the young provides parents and other adults with stimulation, i.e., pleasure. Members of a species value, maintain, and protect their sources of pleasure.

131. Models relate categories together, and are an efficient means of dealing with categories.

132. Models are also used to explain unknowns. It is important for our survival that we be able to recognize and explain unknowns, because unknowns may constitute threats or opportunities.

133. Learning consists of the placement of phenomena into categories and models.

Orientations

134. Phenomena which are not oriented produce tension.

135. The orientation of phenomena releases tension and produces pleasure.

136. The more oriented phenomena are, the less tension is produced, and the more attractive the phenomena.

137. The less oriented phenomena are, the more tension is produced, and the less attractive the phenomena.

138. Humans employ orientations in order to reduce the effort the brain has to make to organize phenomena into categories.

139. The use of orientations enables humans to easily organize phenomena into categories. Examples of human orientations include

symmetry, repetition, rectangles, circles, lines, horizontal and vertical, parallel and perpendicular, consistency, centering, equidistant placement, simplicity, perfection, thoroughness, grouping on the basis of similarity, and the use of solid colors.

140.   An orientation can be approximate; it does not have to be mathematically perfect. Thus the colored designs on the individual members of a species can be approximately symmetrical, centered, or repetitive. An orientation only has to be close enough to perfect for the members of the species to be able to recognize the orientation. Humans use tools to apply their orientations with mathematical precision.

141.   The presence of an orientation in the appearance of members of a species indicates that members of that species respond to that orientation. For example, if the facial or bodily designs on members of the species are symmetrical, centered, or repetitive, then members of that species respond to that orientation.

142.   The symmetrical, centered, and repetitive designs on the faces and bodies of individuals are aesthetically pleasing to the members of that species.

143.   Individual differences in designs on faces and bodies result in individuals appearing more or less attractive than other individuals to members of their species.

144.   Specific orientations and violations of orientations are used to draw attention to specific areas of the body.

145.   Many other animal species have the same orientations as humans.

146.   The orientations that are used in the colored designs on nonhuman species are the same orientations that humans employ in their construction and decoration of clothes, vehicles, everyday objects, architecture, and the arts, and in their behavior.

147. The extensive use of repetition and symmetry in a) the designs on nonhuman species, and b) the designs that humans use for and on their clothes, vehicles, everyday objects, and architecture indicates that nonhumans and humans form categories in the same way and therefore their minds operate the same way.

148. Symmetry is a form of repetition. In symmetry, one half of the design repeats the other half, but from the opposite direction.

149. An individual's body maintains an approximate symmetrical appearance between the right and left halves as the individual develops and ages.

150. Humans apply orientations to their objects and behavior to produce the categories they want to perceive and want others to perceive.

151. Humans violate the orientations in order to produce tension and attract attention. In order to attract attention they use contrasting colors, off-center placement, diagonals, and inconsistency.

The mind

152. The fact that the mind and the body both a) resist effort, b) experience fatigue, and c) are better able to handle difficult tasks after a period of rest indicates that they operate in a similar manner.

153. The mind seeks to a) recognize inconsistency, and b) establish consistency.

154. The human brain gets humans to expend physical effort which enables the brain to reduce mental effort.

155. Humans can only focus on one category or model at a time.

156. When we focus on one category, we do not recognize other categories.

157. When we focus on a category, we have to give up our previous category. Therefore we often forget what our previous category was.

158. Other animal species also have single-focus minds.

159. Pack hunting is so successful because prey focus on one predator, or category, at a time.

160. Our progress in science is so slow because each individual has a single-focus mind. We can only focus on one category at a time. Therefore, when we consider one category, we can not consider others. As a result we only see what we focus on. Our single-focus mind can only perform one mental operation at a time. Thus we can only make one observation, develop one category (or model), or apply one category (or model) to data at a time. Also, we can not a) observe, decide, or act, and b) analyze at the same time. When we observe, decide, or act, we can not analyze; and when we analyze, we can not observe, decide, or act. Because we can not both do something and analyze what we are doing at the same time, we have little conscious awareness of what we are doing and why we are doing it. Because we have a single-focus mind, we have to do science through piecemeal accumulation, and add one bit of information or analysis at a time.

161. A species whose individuals have multiple-focus minds could deal with more than one category (or model) at a time, and could perform more than one mental operation, such as both observation and analysis, at the same time. Such a species could understand situations and behavior, respond appropriately, and develop science and technology at a much faster rate than a single-focus species. In comparison with a multiple-focus species, a single-focus species would be mentally retarded. A multiple-focus species could be produced through a) evolution in certain environments, or b) genetic engineering.

162. A group is a collection of individuals whose single-focus minds are focused in different directions. Therefore a group operates as a multiple-focus mind, which recognizes more opportunities and more threats than an individual would recognize alone.

163. The more individuals there are in a group, the larger the number of threats and opportunities that will be recognized.

Consciousness

164. Physical and mental activities require conscious attention when they must be learned or changed. They must be changed when it becomes clear they are inappropriate and when obstacles are encountered.

165. Conscious attention is required to examine and select alternatives. Examining and selecting alternatives requires much more conscious attention than monitoring routines.

166. Physical and mental activities which are repeated without change become routines. They can be executed very quickly because they require little conscious attention except to monitor their execution and their relevance.

167. Because conscious attention and selection involves more mental operations than does the execution of routines, it is much slower.

168. The more tension produced by a phenomenon, the more likely one is made consciously aware of the phenomenon.

169. One must apply conscious attention when a) one recognizes things, b) one tries to find something, c) one tries to understand what is happening, d) one tries to understand why something is happening,

e) one chooses between alternatives, f) one decides how to deal with a situation, g) one decides how to deal with changes, h) one decides what one ought to be doing, i) one sets objectives, j) one decides how and when to carry out objectives, k) one decides what one needs to have in order to carry out objectives, l) one establishes priorities, m) one decides whether to act, n) one decides what to do next, o) one decides what to do in the future, p) one thinks about what could happen, q) one decides why one should not do things, r) one takes precautions, s) one recognizes obstacles, t) one decides how to act when one encounters obstacles, u) one solves problems, v) one decides how to make improvements, w) one checks on one's progress, x) one recognizes that one needs to find an alternative, y) one realizes that the situation is different than one thought, z) one tries to change one's behavior, aa) one tries to change the behavior of others, bb) one imagines a possible outcome, cc) one imagines a desirable outcome, dd) one dreams, ee) one considers or decides what to do if something happens, ff) one recognizes when something significant happens, gg) one considers past events, hh) one thinks about what one should have done, or ii) one evaluates things and events.

170. Any species which does one or more of the activities mentioned just above has consciousness.

The study of brain and behavior

171. Rather than view each species as having a unique evolutionary past, unique mental operations, and unique behaviors, it is more useful to view different species as sharing a common set of mental operations and behaviors which have been modified for survival in particular niches.

172. We have assumed that the behavior of each species is unique.

173. However, the behavior that is unique to a species is a thin veneer over a common set of feelings, behaviors, and mental operations which are shared with other animal species.

174. By focusing on the differences between species and the differences between cultures we have overlooked the greater significance of the similarities between species. Differences between species and between cultures are inconsistent, produce tension, and attract our attention. Similarities between species and between cultures are consistent, do not produce tension, and do not attract our attention.

175. Feelings, categories, models, consciousness, and communication did not originate with humans. They originated with animals. Humans have them too because humans are animals.

176. Language and technology did not free humans from their animal programming, or feelings, but rather gave humans more power to implement their animal programming on each other and their environment.

177. Perhaps the biggest obstacle to understanding ourselves is our pretentiousness, or the belief humans are unique, special, and important, and more so than other species. This pretentiousness has interfered with and delayed our understanding of a) our location in space, b) our evolution, c) our mind and behavior, and d) the similarity between human nature and animal nature, and our realizing that e) other species have as much right to the environment as we do.

178. Every behavior of humans and other animal species can be understood in a scientific manner.

179. Each and every thing an individual does reflects the structure and operation of the brain.

180. An understanding of human behavior and the human mind will likely precede and produce a greater understanding of the behavior

and minds of other animal species.

181. We will find simple ways to accurately describe and explain behavior, the mind, and the brain.

Humans and other species

182. Human exploitation of other species is based on superior power rather than natural right.

183. Humans act like the Nazis of the animal kingdom, and treat other species worse than Nazis treated Jews.

184. Just as the Nazis envisioned a Thousand-Year Reich for their race, humans envision a long and glorious destiny for their species on earth and in space.

185. Humans do not act any better or any worse than any other animal species would act if it had moved into the dominant position.

186. The argument that "it is acceptable for humans to harm animals provided humans are benefited" is no different than the arguments that "it is acceptable for Europeans to harm Africans provided Europeans are benefited," "it is acceptable for men to harm women provided men are benefited," and "it is acceptable for Nazis to harm Jews provided Nazis are benefited."

187. Other animal species are so similar to us, that when we do something to another species, we might as well be doing it to ourselves.

188. Humans live as though they are the only species on earth that matters. They do not consider the consequences of their actions for the members of other species.

189. Humans consider each individual human precious, but each individual member of other species insignificant.

190. Humans show an almost complete lack of empathy and respect for members of other animal species, who are experiencing many of the same feelings and thoughts that humans would experience if humans were in their situations.

191. The food chain is cannibalism on a large scale. Animal species are so similar to each other, that animal-eating species are effectively eating themselves.

Humans and the environment

192. Humans are in the process of converting the entire earth to human use at the expense of other species.

193. Humans find the appearance of nature chaotic and irritating. Therefore they apply human orientations to nature in order to reduce the effort of looking at it. Thus they produce lawns, gardens, and parks which conform with human orientations. Human orientations include the extensive use of rectangles, circles, lines, parallel and perpendicular, horizontal and vertical, repetition, symmetry, consistency, perfection, and grouping on the basis of similarity.

3. SPECIFIC BEHAVIORS IN RESPONSE TO FEELINGS

Contents

SEEKING SEX

Brief contents

Detailed contents

Detailed contents

continued on next page

Detailed contents

Introduction

People engage in sex in order to experience pleasure. As a result of engaging in sex, people tend to procreate and maintain proximity to those they mate with. When they maintain proximity, they are likely to provide their mate and their offspring with resources and receive resources from them.

People seek to establish a relationship with a sexual partner in order to obtain a regular supply of resources for themselves and their offspring. These resources include food, shelter, money, help, and protection, as well as sex. Relationships also enable people to receive positive reactions and avoid loneliness. (See the chapter on Seeking Positive Reactions in Volume One of this series.)

People employ a variety of models to help them obtain sex and establish relationships. Certain cultural models are well established to help them do so. Two dominant cultural models are *A female should not appear promiscuous* and *A male should not appear effeminate.*

Efforts to obtain sex

Sources

Relationships

The majority of people obtain most of their sex from their partner in a committed relationship. People learn which techniques usually work to obtain sex from their regular partner. Such techniques are quite varied and include being affectionate, necking and petting, expressing desire for sex, wearing sexy clothing, giving the other person flowers, going out to eat in a restaurant, drinking alcohol, dancing, and causing the other person to feel guilty that he or she is not satisfying their partner's sexual needs.

When you have a boyfriend, everyone automatically assumes you are having sex, even if you aren't. #2273

I can have sex whenever I like with my steady girlfriend. But I still have to be very nice to her and spend money on her. #2274

I've been going with my boyfriend for four years, and all he wants to do is park. I want to go to a movie or go get a beer, and not spend my time on the back seat of his car. But he pesters me until I break down and say, "OK, let's go get it over with." #2275

I had this girlfriend, no shit, we would go through twelve rubbers in two days. What a girl she was! I had a lot of fun. #2276

When we were first going together we were just like rabbits, always at it. As time went on and we got to know each other better, we found we could do other things too. #2277

I find the frequency you have sex with your partner can vary a great deal. When you first start going together you have sex almost all the time. Later, when the relationship is more established and everything is more routine, sex often takes second place to work or school. When you are hanging out together, and are rested and don't have stuff you have to do, you are much more likely to have sex. Sundays and holidays are great times for sex. But when you are in a rush to go somewhere, have lots of stuff to do, are worried about things, or are tired after a hard or busy day, you don't have much sexual desire at all. #2278

Establishing relationships

People seek to establish relationships in order to obtain a regular supply of various resources, including sex, food, physical comforts, security, help, protection, and positive reactions from their partner and from the community. Relationships also enable people to prevent the feeling of loneliness. (See the chapter on Seeking Positive Reactions in Volume One of this series.)

There are many factors involved in establishing relationships. These will be illustrated through a variety of topics:

Courtship
School
Peer pressures on males
Roller-skating hall
Hanging out
    Hangouts
    The shopping mall
    McBurger's
    The beach
Cruising
    Yelling at people from cars
Dances
Objectives
    The search for Mr. Right
    Finding a boyfriend
    The male attitude
    True love
Dating
University
    Female status
    The gym
Community

Courtship

I grew up in a fishing community and observed and participated in the courtship patterns, or dating games, of teenagers and young adults. In my area guys and girls begin to show a serious interest in the opposite sex between the ages of thirteen and fifteen. However, the two sexes differ in their orientations. Guys work to build a reputation among their peers by sleeping with as many girls as possible, while not falling in love or sticking with any one girl. Girls, on the other hand, work to keep a good reputation and the respect of others by not sleeping indiscriminately with guys with whom they have no romantic or emotional attachment. Girls are expected to "save" themselves for the right guy.

At this age, it is very common for young people to begin experimenting with alcohol. Most have already been drunk at least once, but it now becomes the accepted practice for the guys to get drunk every

Friday and Saturday night, and for the girls to do so once every week-end or second weekend. In addition to providing status within their peer group, drinking gives young males the courage to pursue contacts with members of the opposite sex. In fact, alcohol is often used as an excuse for one's behavior. Guys frequently tease each other about having gone out with one of the less desirable girls. This might be an ugly or fat girl, or a girl one takes out to screw, but not home to meet one's parents. The usual reply to such teasing is along the following lines: "That just goes to show how drunk I was that night," or "I can't remember that at all. I thought you were with her. It's almost enough to make a guy quit drinking." Girls also use alcohol as an excuse; not for whom they've been out with, but to justify their receptiveness to sexual advances. One girl I know tried to defend herself for sleeping with a guy on the first date by explaining that she was too drunk to resist him.

The majority of the girls in this and neighboring communities have lost their virginity by fifteen to seventeen. In fact, there have recently been a dozen or so babies born to local girls fifteen and sixteen years old. Many girls begin to sleep with guys around the age of thirteen, although they aren't necessarily promiscuous. They often start to have sex out of curiosity, and will go out with a guy several times before they will sleep with him. In this way they can justify their actions to themselves and others by saying that they are going with the guy they have sex with. This makes it easier for them to protect their reputations. Although the girls like to believe and have others believe that they are going with one person, the opposite is true of the boys, who do not want to appear tied down.

Guys usually date the girls in their own community before they turn to neighboring communities. They are about fifteen when they begin to attend high school in town some twenty miles away. Then they start to go to town every weekend for high school dances, parties, and so on. It isn't fashionable for guys to go steady at this age, and they very seldom arrange dates. Instead guys try to pick up a different girl each time they go to social events in town. I can remember going to high school dances and watching the guys walk around the edge of the dance floor, where the girls were sitting, and look all the girls over a couple of times before they would ask one to dance. Most guys make physical advances toward the girl they are dancing with. The big thing to most of them is "Am I going to be able to make it with this girl?" and "Just how far can I get?" However, they aren't really persistent and if you aren't interested you can usually turn them off pretty quick by saying something or repositioning their hands a couple of times. I've also been promptly dropped back at my seat and replaced by another girl when I resisted physical advances. Guys tend to be looking for someone they can get to third base with on the first night. Sometimes guys try out three or four girls during the evening before they finally find one to go outside with or to drive home. It is important for many of the guys to have their friends think they are real hotshots and sexually successful, whether or not they actually are.

Guys often show little concern for the feelings of the girls. For example, I've heard the guys tease each other about a girl named Charlene. Charlene is very unattractive and slightly overweight. She comes from one of the poorer communities, which has a reputation for the promiscuity of its women and a high incidence of alcoholism. One guy told me that when he was fifteen or sixteen, he and a buddy went to a party. They were drunk and looking for someone who would sleep with them. They were sober enough, however, that they wouldn't just settle for anyone, but wanted someone nice looking with a fairly good reputation. During the night he or his buddy walked up behind Charlene on three different occasions and grabbed her, thinking she looked pretty good from behind. When she turned around, they quickly did an about-face and beat it. Guys often talk about such misadventures and laugh about them.

It is very unacceptable for guys to get hooked on any one girl at this age. This may in part explain why younger guys seldom arrange formal dates with girls, even after they've been seeing the same girl for quite a while. Thus they can indicate to other guys that they aren't emotionally attached to this particular girl, but that she just happened to be there and they could easily pick her up. Almost all the boys between fifteen and seventeen who regularly see a particular girl do occasionally take out others. This helps the males maintain an image of being unattached. The girl they see regularly either has to accept this or break up with them. Sometimes a girl will go out with another guy to pay back her wayward male, but this isn't that common. When a girl does so, the male refuses to let on he is bothered, which defeats the purpose of her action. Another advantage of not going out on set dates is that few guys in this age group have steady jobs and money is fairly scarce. When they simply pick up their girl at a dance, movie, or elsewhere, they don't have to pay the girl's way. I feel quite certain, however, that peer pressure to remain unattached exerts a much stronger influence than lack of funds.

The majority of those I know follow the patterns I've described. Guys spend their time and energy trying to let on they are playing the field, when in fact this may not really be the case. Girls, on the other hand, spend their time and energy trying to convince themselves and others that there is indeed an emotional attachment with the guy in question, and that it is reciprocated in spite of any behavior on the guy's part which suggests otherwise. Nevertheless, there are some girls and guys who see a different person each night they go out, and there are those who go out with many different individuals while they are attached to someone.

By the time they reach seventeen or eighteen most guys and girls have dropped the patterns I've described. By now they are either high-school seniors or in the workforce, and it is a sign of maturity to carry on a lasting relationship with a member of the opposite sex. Because this age group is applying for and holding jobs, the opinion of older people and employers in the community becomes more important and that of their peers less important. Everyone knows everyone else's business and reputation. Someone who has settled down with a girlfriend or with a wife and child is seen as more stable than someone who has a reputation for being a womanizer. Also, when you start to get into your twenties, it's viewed as time to settle down.

By seventeen or eighteen, boyfriends and girlfriends go places with each other and no longer arrive separately. Usually one of the couple has a driver's license and access to a car, which adds to a mature image. The girls tend to look down on younger guys who want to play the field, and make comments like "What a shithead. He's just out for what he can get." It is advantageous for guys to appear to be available for a serious relationship in the eyes of the girls. Girls do not want to get involved with a guy who is still playing around. Otherwise they may get a bad reputation, or, if they really like the guy, a broken heart. Steady dating, which begins about seventeen or eighteen, is usually continued until the time of marriage. A couple may go together for quite a while and then for some reason decide to break up. Although both parties may play the field for a month or so, they practically always end up back together or going steady with someone else. One steady relationship is very quickly replaced by another.

Even though the age of marriage varies greatly, a few years ago most of the young people I knew began to think seriously about marriage at twenty to twenty-two years old. They didn't necessarily get married at that time, but they did begin to make plans for the future. Thus if they didn't already have a steady job or trade of some sort, they began to search for one. Often they decided to remain in school, or if they had already dropped out they returned to high school or university. If they didn't get married right away, at least they set a target date to work for and announced their plans. Many young people decided they would get married after completing university, and the girl was given an engagement ring during her first or second year of study. I think things are changing somewhat today, because most people in my area are waiting until they are older and aren't getting married until they are in their late twenties.

Guys who drop out of school and stay out, seldom change the dating tactics they used when they were younger. As a result they are still not seriously involved with someone by the time they are twenty or so. A number of males from my community didn't finish high school. Instead they normally choose to work at fishing, either as a hired hand or with their own fleet (a boat and equipment). They are usually in their early twenties or older when they begin to have serious relationships with females, and then with girls from outside the village. Many are still not married at twenty-five or thirty. Local girls usually become seriously involved with high-school males from other communities. They normally marry earlier than males do in my community and usually to someone from outside.

It used to be a trend for couples to live together as common law husband and wife, or to "shack up" as it is commonly called. Quite often this arrangement was a trial marriage, and if it worked out for a year or two the couple would decide to be legally married. Sometimes the couple would decide to remain common law or to marry when they decided to begin a family. However, living together isn't considered as cool as it once was. Now most are remaining at home until they marry. After a couple have gone together for a long time, people start to assume they will be getting married. They will sometimes say, "I wonder when the wedding's going to be?" In any case most couples seem to give themselves lots of time before they make a final commitment. I don't know of any couple that married before eighteen or nineteen years old of their own free choice. If they marry earlier than this, it is because of an unplanned pregnancy. When people learn that two teenagers are getting married, it is common to exclaim, "She's pregnant?" They might have married eventually, but they probably would have waited several years.

Young people of this village and the surrounding area are very conscious of the stigma attached to illegitimate children, and often go out of their way to protect themselves and the child from it. A few years ago the attitude was that if you got yourself into this situation, then you got married, and everyone saw this as the right thing to do. One girl I know, Cathy, went out for about a year off and on with Larry, who was four years older and from another community. When Cathy became pregnant, she and Larry automatically got married in spite of the fact they were only having a casual relationship. The marriage took place just before Christmas, and before a year was out, Cathy, who was nineteen, was divorced with a five-month-old baby. Nevertheless, this was seen as much more acceptable than the scandal of having an illegitimate child. Also, marriage was a way for the girl to uphold her dignity. However, this is changing somewhat. I find many more girls today are not getting married when they get pregnant and have a child. Sometimes their relationship with the guy continues and sometimes it ends. Although this is certainly not considered to be a desirable solution, it seems people in the community do not view it as negatively as they did several years ago. When they know the parties involved, people say, "I hope she doesn't marry him just because she's pregnant." #2279

School

School provides an ideal location to meet and get to know members of the opposite sex. Young people try to attract attention by acting cool, wearing the current clothing styles, playing sports, and attempting to hang out with groups of the popular kids. Junior-high students attend parties and dances, stay out later, and talk on the telephone for hours. They begin to date, and as their confidence grows they begin to make sexual advances. Their friends ask them, "Did you kiss her/him?" or "How far did you two go?" They begin to fool around, which can involve necking, caressing, or petting, and some begin to have intercourse. If the female does not want to participate, the male is likely to resume advances the next time they are alone or seek another partner. After all, she is standing in the way of progress. "If you didn't give a guy what he wanted within a short period of time, ranging from one day to three weeks, you were tagged 'a tease' and no longer included in the in-crowd. This was a very strong motivator and most girls gave in."

In high school most males who have not yet had sex are no longer satisfied with just fooling around and become more determined to get laid. It becomes the primary ambition for some, and as their friends succeed they become increasingly desperate. Some get drunk every weekend, approach any girl they see, and blame their behavior on the alcohol. High-school parties are wilder and there is a greater choice of partners. When young people get their driving licenses they are able to drive and park. At any social gathering you are likely to find several smooth-talking young men who try various methods to get girls into their cars, such as "I want to talk to you," "Let's go for a ride," and "Can I drive you home?" Girls who have too much to drink quickly attract guys because they look like an easy conquest.

Most girls try to protect their reputations and prove they are not loose by limiting the number of boys they date and the sexual activities they engage in. In addition, there are students who tend to date for a short while and then stay together, or go steady. Often they do not rush into sex, and establish a mutually acceptable sexual arrangement. Nevertheless, although they enjoy the security of a relationship, they are inclined to feel they are tied down and not experiencing the active social life of others. When couples break up they are likely to become more active sexually. A girl may become involved with a number of guys to try to get back at her boyfriend for breaking up with her or for cheating on her. #2280

Relationships between males and females are an important part of high school life. This is particularly true for girls, who seem to define their worth based on their popularity with males, and constantly compare how popular they are relative to other girls. Boys, on the other hand, spend much less time talking about the dating game and evaluating themselves on the basis of it.

Males and females seldom display direct interest in each other in high school. They typically let someone know they are interested by sending an envoy. They tell a friend of theirs, who in turn tells another friend, and hopefully contact will be made. This method of establishing contact is used less often by senior students, but is considered quite reliable even by them.

Whenever a new couple is "created" news spreads quickly throughout the school. Girls are particularly adept at getting this information around and soon everyone is talking about it. Girls make judgments whether or not the new relationship is a good one, whether it will last, and so on. If the successful girl is at all unpopular or unattractive, others are sure to comment, "Well, if she got a guy there's hope for the rest of us. And he is kind of cute too."

Few high-school girls have a strong concept of confidentiality. Basically, they repeat everything they hear. Thus if a girl is having problems with her boyfriend, usually the whole school is soon aware of it. Many girls enjoy dispensing advice; all the while pointing out that their own situation is far superior to that of the girl with difficulties. "I don't have to deal with anything like that. But if I did, you can be sure that I wouldn't stick around for long."

Because so much emphasis is placed on having a steady relationship, girls who fail to establish one often feel left out. Many complain of feeling alienated and alone, although most are quick to point out that the relationships which their friends have are far from perfect. The social situations which occur in high school make having a steady person to date very important. Girls who have serious problems with their boyfriends will typically put off the task of discussing the problem or confronting the issue until after an important social event has occurred. "If we can just make it till graduation, we'll be OK. I'd hate to not have him to go to the prom with. We have to stick it out until then. I mean, I have my dress and everything. And how would I feel if we went together all this time and then were apart for graduation? It just wouldn't seem right." In fact, I've known girls to put up with some very unpleasant situations, such as infidelity or abuse, just in order to maintain a relationship through an important social event.

Relationships are much more important to females than to males in this age group. Girls definitely talk about their relationships more and usually try to shape them into something loosely resembling a marital relationship. They also tend to project the relationship further into the future than do their boyfriends, who largely prefer to live for today. As a result girls are willing to put up with a great deal to maintain their relationships. Even at this age females define their social status and their self-esteem very much in terms of the relationships they are able to forge with males. [#2281]

Peer pressures on males

Between the ages of fourteen and sixteen my male friends put a lot of pressure on each other to have sex with girls. We hung out in groups, and the most influential guy would boast about his terrific experiences with all the girls he'd laid that week. We all looked up to him. He was the first to get a driver's license and a stereo. If one of the others of us had a date, we could expect him to ask lots of questions and for others to join in. Things like "Did you go up her top?" "Did you get down her pants?" and "Did she moan or groan?" We'd say something to suggest we'd gotten somewhere, although we rarely did, and leave it to the others' imaginations. Sometimes when we went somewhere guys would make bets as to who could get laid the fastest. The money wasn't important. What mattered was the respect you'd get if you won. We used to kid any guys who were known to be virgins. If a group of your buddies was watching a sex scene on TV, someone might yell out, "Hey, Jerry, you'd better pay attention and learn something from this." Or if we were getting in a bus, someone would yell, "Virgins to the back of the bus!" When we went camping we'd say, "The guy who doesn't get a girl tonight has to sleep on the picnic table." Often guys felt they had to prove themselves and had sex just to escape these comments. Guys were also worried whether they could satisfy a girl, especially if she'd had sex with other guys and could make comparisons. You felt if you didn't deliver she might tell others you were "green," or inexperienced. #2282

In high school a male did not want to be labeled "green." Someone who is green, or inexperienced, was supposed to be scared of having sex with a girl. It was considered very uncool to be green. Guys wanted to be cool, because you need to be cool to be popular. You did not want to be associated with those who were considered green, because you didn't want to be considered green too. Some guys who were labeled green were also labeled gay. Being gay, or homosexual, was the worst label a guy could have, and the other guys would have nothing to do with you. Some guys who were considered gay would do anything in their power to disprove it. I saw a guy that others thought was gay screw a girl in front of ten other people just to try to dispel the rumor. #2283

Your male friends can put pressure on you to cheat. "It isn't safe to go out with the boys if you have a girlfriend. They all want to get you in shit with your girlfriend, either by getting you to cheat or by saying you did." "I didn't want to cheat on my girlfriend, but I felt so pressured by the guys. If I hadn't done it, they'd have looked down on me." "I once told a friend that I didn't want to cheat on my girlfriend, and he laughed. He didn't even believe me. He thought I was joking." #2284

Roller-skating hall

Skate World (pseudonym) is a roller-skating rink on the outskirts of Charlottetown. There are two skates on both Friday and Saturday evenings; one from seven until nine and the other from nine thirty to eleven thirty. Although there is skating every night at the facility, Friday and Saturday evenings are the only times when the crowd is made up almost entirely of teenagers. Usually between one hundred and fifty and two hundred teenagers attend each of these skates. On these evenings it costs $2.75 for admission, and an extra seventy-five cents to rent skates. Those who pay admission to the first skate can stay over for the second skate for an extra $1.25, skate rental included, and many do so. (Prices are in 1984 dollars.) Sometimes teenagers ask to come in and look around before they buy their ticket. These are regular skaters who want to see who is there before they decide on a night of skating. This is permitted at slow times, but is generally discouraged, because the teenagers tend to hang around inside and on a busy night they can quickly become lost in the crowd and end up skating for free.

Anyone driving past Skate World on a Friday or Saturday evening would think that few people were there, because the parking lot is largely empty except for the cars of the staff. This is because most teenagers are not old enough to drive. When they do have a driver's license, they don't have a car. As a result most are driven to the rink by their parents or neighbors taking their own children. Those who do not live too far away, walk. In the summertime about fifty percent skate to the rink. When they arrive the doorman tells them to use the automatic wheel wash, which costs twenty-five cents and prevents dirt, pebbles, and grime from being carried on to the skating floor. Skaters do not mind because no one likes to skate with dirty wheels. The doorman also gets those he sees chewing gum to throw it in a large garbage can by the door.

The same teenagers are present at Skate World almost every weekend. Most of those who attend are between thirteen and sixteen years old. Consequently there is an enormous variation between individuals in terms of size and physical maturity. The atmosphere at the rink is quite alive and intense. When off the skating floor the teenagers are very active and there is a great deal of talking, squealing, laughing, shouting, name-calling, physical contact, and horseplay between members of the same and opposite sexes. There are many groups and cliques present from different urban and rural areas. A single group may include members from different areas and schools, and friendships and dating relationships are frequently formed between teenagers from different areas. Teenagers eighteen and older are almost never seen at these skates because they prefer to go places where they are able to drink. Skate World serves several purposes for the teenagers. It provides them with something to do, allows them to participate in a fun activity, enables them to get together with their friends, and gives them opportunities to develop contacts and relationships with members of the opposite sex.

The teenagers are concerned with appearing "cool." This includes wearing the accepted style of clothes, and there is little discernible difference between the teenagers on the basis of dress. Practically all wear what is currently "in." Thus the girls wear similar sneakers, jeans, tops, and jackets. Both sexes are very much concerned with how they look, and no one wants to appear out of place. One teenage boy, Jerry, came to the rink on a Friday night wearing a Wayne Gretzky (a hockey star) shirt he had received for Christmas. When he took off his coat and skated out on the floor, a group of girls began to tease him. They poked fun at his shirt, called Wayne Gretzky derogatory names, and made clear they thought his shirt was stupid. Jerry is fairly independent and gave a typical response. He told them to get lost. However, a few minutes later he went into the office and called his father. Jerry explained that he had spilled something on his shirt, which wasn't true, and asked his father to bring him another shirt. Jerry waited in the office for his father, and told the cashier, who had known him for some time, that he couldn't go back out because the others made him feel too uncomfortable to skate. After he changed his shirt he joined the others and had a normal evening. Another aspect of being cool is attending the skate without one's little brother or sister. One of my cousins, Allan, has to take his younger brother along, and he spends most of the first skate trying to get away from him. However, his younger brother has to go home at nine o'clock, after the first skate. Allan is always glad, because then he is able to skate with his friends without the little guy being around.

Out on the skating floor, skaters circle counterclockwise. Lights are dim, special lighting effects are used, and a disk jockey plays the latest hit records for the skaters. People who are friends stick together, just like in a school yard or at a school dance. Girls come to Skate World in a group or with one or two friends. They almost never come alone. Within a group of girls, one or two appear to be dominant. These are probably the better-looking girls. In contrast, guys seldom come in a group. Most teenagers skate by themselves. However, girls are much more likely than boys to skate with several friends, while they chat, gossip, and giggle together. Boys usually just skate, which they do alone or with a friend. In order to introduce variation, the disk jockey occasionally tells people the next song is to be skated in a clockwise direction. This is unpopular, because most skaters are unaccustomed to skating clockwise, and a number leave the floor. I leave too, because I can't do crossovers in a clockwise direction going around the corners.

Although both sexes love to skate, guys tend to be more flamboyant than the girls. The girls are usually adept at skating forward and backward, but the guys also do turns, jumps, and spins. Guys are more daredevilish. They are willing to try something so outrageous that it is totally acceptable if they fall, and they are likely to get a bit of admiration for trying. Girls, on the other hand, would be too concerned about messing up their hair or makeup to try. If a guy likes a girl, he may whip around, do a "360" (turn), and end up skating backwards just ahead of her so he can talk to her.

Once every hour there is a couples' skate. This is equivalent to a "waltz," or slow dance, at a dance. It consists of two slow songs during which each couple skates around the rink holding hands or in waltz position with one person skating backwards. Certain lights are shut off to make the rink darker at this time, and single skaters, who constitute the great majority, are required to leave the floor. Who skates with whom during a couples' skate is very important to the teenagers and is a frequent subject of conversation among them. Often other teens are involved in bringing couples together. A male may not be interested in asking a particular girl who likes him to skate, but her friends can put a lot of pressure on him to "Ask her! Ask her! Ask her!" until he gives in. Or, if a boy wants to skate with a particular girl, he may first tell her friends, they in turn will tell her, her reaction will be conveyed back to the boy, and then the boy knows whether or not to ask her. This enables the male to avoid rejection by the girl herself and to save face. However, not all such couples are arranged by others and sometimes boys and girls approach the potential partner directly.

Because these skates are dating grounds for many young people, one commonly sees signs that courting is not proceeding smoothly. From time to time a girl will leave the floor to have a good cry in the women's washroom. There will be all this concern among those who know her. "What's wrong with Susan?" they'll ask. When this happens I sometimes feel the girl wants the guy to think that she doesn't want him to see her cry. However, she does want him to know that he has hurt her so badly she has gone off to cry alone. One overhears friends talking about breakups and sometimes they tell staff members about so-and-so and so-and-so who have been going out for perhaps two weeks and have just broken up. Occasionally a girl who is upset will take off her skates, put on her coat, and sit down to wait for her ride home or even call a taxi. Skate World is on the outskirts of town, and many would find it difficult to walk all the way home.

On Friday and Saturday evenings the two pay phones at the rink are almost always in use. The younger teenage girls seem to phone boys more often than their male counterparts phone girls. It is not uncommon to see two or more girls gathered around a pay phone. Frequently the one who is least shy phones a boy to find out "Who do you like?" and "How come you're not here?" Sometimes the girl who has called will tell the boy that a certain girl likes him. If that girl is present she will act upset by this, leave the group, or deny the whole thing. When the call is finished the girls will excitedly gather around the caller to find out just what the boy said. Boys also phone girls from the pay phones, but there is seldom a crowd gathered around and for the most part the call goes unnoticed.

There are also many incoming calls on the office phones on Friday and Saturday nights. Teenagers who are not at the skate call to ask their friends who is there and whether or not they should come out. On a very busy night there are just too many calls and staff will not call people to the phone or relay messages unless it is a parent calling. At such times staff members may tell the caller that the rink is too busy, but that if it is an emergency they will deliver the message. Frequently callers will respond, "Well, it is," and then make up an emergency. Some say something like "I'm calling for his mother (or father)," but staff know it's untrue because they can hear kids laughing in the background. Some are foolish enough to say, "Tell Tom to call Buffy." Big emergency! But staff members sometimes do their best to relay such a message because it probably is an emergency to Buffy. Teenagers also try to use the office phone at times when the call does not require much privacy. For example, they may call home to arrange a drive or to ask for permission to stay out longer. They like to get into the office to mingle with staff and the phone provides a good excuse.

There is a great deal of interaction between skaters and the staff, who are between twenty and twenty-five years old. Staff are expected to act mature, set a good example, and be nice to each skater. At the same time they are supposed to be firm when dealing with various difficulties which arise. Nearly every skater knows each staff member by name. Some skaters seem to idolize the staff. According to one office worker, "Once when I was shopping in a store downtown, I heard several twelve-and-thirteen-year-olds giggling nearby. I looked up and didn't recognize any of them. Just then one of them said, 'She works at Skate World.' They followed along nearby whispering and giggling for a few minutes, and then were gone. I felt like a celebrity." Some of the kids would give anything to work at Skate World. Sometimes one will proudly say, "Ron (the manager) said I can get a job here when I'm sixteen," and then count off the years he or she will have to wait.

In addition to female office staff who handle cash and plan schedules, there are usually one or two male floor guards working at the rink. Floor guards circulate about the skating floor and help those who fall back on their feet before someone skates into them. When the rink first opened there were really big crowds of poor skaters present and pileups were common. Now the rink is less crowded and people have become much better skaters. Floor guards also make sure no one goes around tripping people or skating too fast. They frequently have to slow guys down because their speed can confuse and upset the other skaters. If a boy fails to skate slower, the floor guard will kick him off the floor for fifteen minutes. Some of the girls appear to be infatuated with the floor guards, and you often see several girls huddled around them asking questions. However, floor guards seldom date these girls, because the girls are so young and the guards usually have girlfriends already. Various boys also tend to hang around the floor guards. The floor guards are very good skaters and the boys get them to show them how to do different tricks.

The management is concerned that parents define the rink as a proper place for their children. Therefore they are quite concerned about preventing practices which might upset parents. Some parents enter Skate World when they drop off and pick up their children, and sometimes they just stand and watch what is going on. In addition, kids frequently report to their parents what has happened during the evening. Many parents expect the staff to look after their children while they are at Skate World, and from time to time an irate parent will call to give the management hell.

At a recent meeting, it was brought to the attention of staff that on a few occasions young people were observed necking in the seating areas. The manager pointed out that the rink was for recreational skating, not necking, and urged staff to put a stop to it whenever it happened. Management felt this just wouldn't look good to parents. Subsequently the staff obliged, although some staff members found it very embarrassing to have to confront two necking adolescents and did so quite hesitantly. Since then it has become common knowledge among the teenagers that necking is not acceptable and for the most part it has been stopped. However, some still neck when they skate together to slow songs in waltz position and are at the far side of the rink where it is hard to see them.

On another occasion the management scheduled a contest between "air bands" during the evening skate. Several different "bands" of teenagers pretended to sing and play instruments in accompaniment to a hit song by a leading rock group. They acted out various movements of the rock group which they had observed in music videos. During the contest, however, certain actions by the teenagers in the better air bands were considered quite improper by management, such as sticking the neck of a guitar between the legs of the lead singer to produce a phallic pose. Therefore, when prizes were awarded, management felt compelled to express disapproval. "I want to say something before I give out the prizes to the second-place and first-place groups. What they did almost got them kicked out. They knew damn well, ah, darn well, that they weren't supposed to do that. OK, so the guys were pretty close to getting kicked out."

Teenagers are also forbidden to smoke, drink, and fight on the premises. When Skate World first opened there was a lot of smoking in the washrooms. However, everyone caught was kicked out and this pretty well eliminated the problem. Another difficulty occurs in connection with drinking. Teenagers frequently experiment with and use alcohol, which can result in obnoxious behavior. This is not as big a problem at Skate World as it is at other locations where teenagers go, such as school dances and McDonald's Restaurant, because Skate World has very strict rules prohibiting the use of alcohol. Anyone who is found drinking or drunk on the premises is expelled and not allowed to return for up to five months. There are no exceptions. This is very effective, because someone who is barred for a few months has nowhere to go on Friday and Saturday evenings when all of their friends are roller skating. A list is posted in a prominent place displaying the names of all rule breakers and the date when they will be allowed back in. Those who are punished in this fashion act very cool and don't appear upset. However, I think they must feel bad and disoriented. Some come back and suck up to the owner to see if he will let them back in. However, he sticks to the rules. On the other hand, those who seldom attend Skate World have less to lose if they are kicked out. When this happens, they seldom return. If anyone leaves the building to go outside they have to pay the regular entrance fee again to get back in. This is also quite effective in preventing teenagers from going outside to smoke and drink. [#2285]

Hanging out

Hangouts

Hanging out was a very important part of my adolescence. Hanging out is getting together with other people for no specific reason other than to get together. It normally occurs in a public area, such as a park or a restaurant, rather than a private place, such as a home. For the most part, it is a passive activity in which one sits, talks, smokes, eats, and waits; but sometimes people also do active things together. In order for a place to function as a proper hangout, one has to be able to stay there for long periods of time without being forced to leave. Charlottetown has only a limited number of hangouts for young people. I am going to describe those we used when I was growing up. Since then, fast-food restaurants, like McDonald's, and shopping malls have become popular hangouts for young people.

I began to hang out with a number of other people in my last years of elementary school. During the warm months we would go to Victoria Park, ride our bicycles, and play hide and seek and "kiss and chase." In kiss and chase, kids chase a member of the opposite sex and kiss them if they catch them. Most members of our group lived in the same suburban neighborhood and attended school together. In winter we went to the YMCA (Young Men's Christian Association) for gym and swimming classes, or to the rink to skate. Classes at the "Y" were segregated by sex, but we could still get together with members of the opposite sex on the way there and back.

The "Y" had youth clubs that were also segregated by sex. I can remember having to spit out my gum during the Friday night meetings and planning the occasional sock hop. Our activities were closely supervised, and early signs of rebellion began to appear. For example, some kids had started to smoke, which was certainly not permitted by the "Y" supervisors, who even checked washrooms. By the eighth grade some of the youth were moving on to new hangouts to escape personal supervision. Many others, however, seemed content to frequent the "Y" right up through grade twelve. Those who remained at the "Y" tended to come from good neighborhoods and often had an interest in sports.

Kids who drifted away from the "Y" were looking for something less respectable and a little more exciting. The spot that met these requirements was a diner across from the skating rink. It was basically an all-night "greasy spoon." The diner was in a poor neighborhood and most patrons lived nearby. The clientele had the reputation of being very tough, and would not have been accepted by the mothers of those who moved there from the "Y." Although kids from the "Y" were from residential suburbs, the two groups mixed in the diner. A real advantage of the diner was that no one knew your parents or cared what you did, so you could smoke openly.

Contrary to public opinion, things were usually very quiet in the diner. The diner contained a long counter with stools, and four booths. Kids preferred the booths, which were sometimes very crowded. We spent our afternoons and evenings there drinking Pepsi and playing the jukebox. The ages of those at the diner ranged from under thirteen to over twenty. However, people hung out with those who were approximately the same age as themselves. Because we lived at the other end of town, and none of us had access to a car, we had to spend a considerable amount of time walking to and from the diner. We often made the trip there and back, a distance of over a mile each way, twice a day. There was also a loose arrangement of couples, who spent a great deal of time walking around in pairs. For some of us, the diner became a second home.

Eventually we found that more exciting things were happening elsewhere, and the diner began to seem a little dull. One spot we started to frequent in the summer was Stanhope Beach. Kids would hang out down on the beach and up in the parking lot by the canteen. We would sit or lie on the beach, smoke, listen to the radio, and talk to people who came by. Up at the canteen we wandered around, chatted, ate ice cream, and drank pop. There were many strangers present at the beach. During the day our groups were seldom large. Usually two or three friends would hitchhike there together, share the same space on the beach, and interact only casually with other friends. This changed in the evening, however, when a large group of people would gather at a huge tent. The tent could hold several dozen people, there was no charge, and there were none of the restrictions one finds in a restaurant or a recreation center. The owner of the tent was frequently told to move, so the tent made the rounds of all the campgrounds in the area. A great variety of people turned up every evening. This included kids from middle-class suburbs in Charlottetown, some of whom had hung out at the "Y" and the diner; transients and budding hippies; a few country kids from the local area; and an older motorcycle and car crowd. Behavior at the tent was often uninhibited. Drinking and tearing around on motorcycles and in cars were very popular. One of the biggest attractions was the unpredictability of events when one hung out there. Transportation to and from the beach was a major problem, however, and many of us had to hitchhike to and from Charlottetown. Getting back home in time for curfew around midnight was often difficult. Our second summer hangout was the Confederation Centre in the center of Charlottetown. This is a complex of buildings, which includes theaters, an art gallery and museum, and a library, with numerous broad steps and ample outside seating. Tourists and transients had no trouble finding this location, and often made up the majority of those hanging out. This area was unsupervised and people could sit there for hours.

By fall most of our crowd had moved back to Charlottetown to hang out. We began to spend our time at the Catholic recreation center, which contained a gymnasium, bowling lanes, ping-pong tables, and a coffee shop in the basement. The major gathering place was the coffee shop, which had a counter with a few stools and ten to twelve tables with lots of chairs. There were about fifty regulars, most of whom attended the same high school. Regulars could be divided into two groups. One group numbered about twenty and was composed primarily of Catholic males from central Charlottetown who were comparatively clean-cut. They usually congregated near the pop machine and the counter, or played cards in a side room. The other group of about thirty was more varied in composition. Some were Catholics from the local neighborhood, some were from the residential suburbs, and some were transients. Much of our cohesion came from seeing ourselves as an avant-garde group. However, we did not spend our time in philosophical discussions. Instead we sat, smoked, drank pop, and waited for things to happen. We rarely if ever bowled, played ping-pong, or made use of the gym. By the early 1970s there were more drugs available, such as hashish, marijuana, LSD, and later speed. People began wearing anti-establishment clothing, such as jeans and army surplus items, and boys let their hair grow long. We tried anything new, and seemed to feel we were taking part in a North American revolution. This added significance to each happening and gave legitimacy to hanging around.

Those who hung out at the rec center did not exist as a real group outside the coffee shop. People would start arriving late in the afternoon after a long walk across town from school. Small groups of friends often came together. The most influential members would have seats nearest the tables, and others would group around them. These influential members would lead the conversation, which was oriented toward gossip and school happenings. Some people always had cigarettes, and others never did. If you gave yours away too readily you were considered a sucker. If you held on to them you were thought to be cheap. The influential people always expected to be given cigarettes. There were few serious couples in the group, and those who did date usually blended into the larger group. Kids who didn't live nearby would have to leave early to get home for supper. After supper on weekday evenings the groups around the tables would be smaller and a wider variety of topics were discussed. Few kids would miss weekend nights at the coffee shop.

Occasionally there were dances with live bands upstairs in the gym on a weekend night, and this was exciting. Sometimes on weekends when there was no dance, we would drink in cars. However, most of the time we just hung around. Few of us seemed to have any special skills. The exception were several guys who started a rock group, and this became everyone's interest. Sometimes we would use the coffee shop as a meeting point before leaving for a party or somewhere else. Occasionally we would go out to a restaurant for coffee or hot chocolate and a change of scenery, but local restaurants usually discouraged our being there for any length of time. In the summers, people often sat outside the rec center. The rec served as a hangout for most of our group all through high school, and for some even after they began university.

Gradually members of our group stopped hanging out. We gained access to cars, formed serious relationships with members of the opposite sex, developed other interests, or went on the road ourselves. When I look back at hanging out, I am shocked at the amount of time we seem to have wasted. I could have been taking piano lessons, figure skating, or learning to play tennis. Time spent in organized activities certainly keeps kids out of trouble, but it does restrict their experience. We were interested in experiencing new things, and exploring behavior that our parents disapproved of. Hangouts provided a comfortable home away from home in which we could try to learn how to deal with the world around us and the changes in ourselves. [#2286]

The shopping mall

Shopping malls are a major hangout for many teenagers who are too young to get into clubs and lounges. Most of those who hang out at the mall fall into two groups. The first group are those in junior high or younger and are from eleven through fourteen years old. The second group are those in high school or older, and include those from fifteen through eighteen. Those in the first group are too young to drive and depend on their parents or older siblings for a ride to and from the mall. Members of the second group either drive themselves or get a ride from their friends. Those in the second group can leave or go to another location whenever they want without having to call home to arrange a ride. Although teens tend to hang out with their own age group, the two age groups are not mutually exclusive. If a fourteen-year-old girl has a boyfriend in the high-school group she is likely to hang out with his group. Also, a group of older teens will sometimes talk to younger teens if at least one member in each group knows the other. It will be simpler to refer to the two groups as younger teens and older teens. Very few young people who are nineteen and older hang out at the mall.

Groups of younger teens usually include both sexes and may number as many as ten individuals. They normally travel to and from the mall with members of the same sex, except when siblings are included. When girls go into female clothing stores most boys wait outside or go off on their own and arrange to meet the girls later. In places like the video-game arcade boys outnumber girls. Girls don't like going to the arcade unless they are looking for a friend, and they go somewhere else when boys want to go there. Younger teens are usually present in the mall between seven and eight thirty in the evening.

Groups of older teens tend to be smaller and seldom include more than six individuals. Guys and girls at this age stick together more, although the guys are still reluctant to enter "girly" stores. They spend a shorter amount of time in the mall, because the mall serves as a jumping-off point to meet people to go elsewhere with. Older teens are normally present between eight thirty and ten o'clock at night, when the mall closes.

A typical Friday night for Tara, a thirteen-year-old girl, begins with two or three girls meeting together at one of their homes to get ready for the mall. Getting ready can take more than an hour and includes choosing what to wear and doing makeup and hair. The perfect outfit is preferably one that hasn't been seen before and definitely one that wasn't worn to school that day. Clothes are really important, and the girls usually try on two or three outfits before deciding what to wear. The girls have fun dressing up. They like wearing tight black pants or bell-bottom jeans that cover their black high-heeled shoes, and a dressy shirt or a nice T-shirt with a saying or picture on the front. They are roughly the same size and trade clothes back and forth. They also like to do each other's hair and makeup. One friend is so good with hair that the others want her to fix theirs for them. Another friend knows great techniques for covering and concealing blemishes.

Some parents consider the clothes that the girls want to wear to the mall too sexy or too dressy for girls that age. Therefore some girls go straight to the bathroom as soon as they get to the mall and change their clothes and apply more makeup, so their parents won't know how they look. Then before returning home they wash their faces and change back to what they were wearing when they left home.

When Tara and her friends get to the mall the girls walk from one end to the other to see who is there. When they don't run into anyone they sometimes go into stores to try on clothes. Most of their time is spent on "their bench" in the main hallway outside a specific store. Most people walk through this area, so it is the perfect place to see who is at the mall without having to do a lot of walking. There is lots of room here for their friends to stand around and talk to them without blocking the passage of other people. They also go to the tables at the back of the food court near the arcade. One of Tara's friends has a boyfriend who is usually found playing arcade games and pool there. The girls often leave their bulky winter coats with him so they don't have to carry them around. This area is very loud and smoky, and they don't like to spend much time there. They have their best times when they run into friends from school and can relax and talk. They also enjoy shopping. Sometimes they need to buy a present for a friend and spend the whole night going in and out of stores until they find the perfect gift. Tara likes to get the opinions of her friends so she can get something that really suits the person. Most of Tara's friends get their allowances on Saturdays. So they look for things on Friday that they can buy the following evening. They usually buy things for themselves right after Christmas and their birthdays when they have more cash.

When Peter, who is eighteen, comes to the mall, he usually comes with his younger brother and a male friend or two from their neighborhood. Unlike the girls, they do not put much time into getting ready. They may change to a nice shirt or sweater and wear the pants they wore to school earlier. At the mall they stop at the CD (compact disk) store to see the latest music albums. They also go to the mall three times a week to exercise at the health club. On Friday nights they usually have no plans. They normally run into a friend who is going somewhere and make plans to meet him later. Otherwise they make their own plans to do something with any friends they meet. If all else fails they go to the food court and get coffee and smoke cigarettes, or they go to the electronics store and look at new video games. Sometimes they wait around the liquor store until an older friend or a stranger agrees to buy them some alcohol. Otherwise, they may have to walk through the mall to find an older friend who will get liquor for them.

There are only three liquor stores in Charlottetown, and one of these is in this mall. The legal age for purchasing liquor was eighteen, and is currently nineteen. Liquor is an important source of fun and status for teens who are too young to buy it legally. A large number of minors obtain and consume liquor over the weekend. If they do not know someone old enough who will buy liquor for them, they have to get a stranger to do so. Some of the teenagers wander through the mall carrying their liquor in a plastic cup for soft drinks, and security has detained kids as young as eleven years old for drunkenness.

There are more teenagers in the mall on Friday and Saturday nights, and some come every weekend. They walk up and down the mall, and hang out on benches in the main corridor and at tables in the food court. They are usually in groups of four or more individuals, and as the night progresses the number of these groups increases. The security guards will ask them to move when they block the paths of shoppers. When customers complain that the teens are blocking their entrance into a store, clerks will ask them to move or ask a security guard to do so. Clerks report that some of the youths respond with bad language. However, most teens move when asked without causing any trouble and end up gathering again further down the hall. Shoppers sometimes complain about the large number of teenagers hanging out. "You can't get away from them anywhere. I had to push my way through a group of them in the corridor. I can't believe they didn't know that they didn't leave any room for others to get by. And once tonight I was almost pushed over. A boy about fourteen stole his friend's bag as a joke and then ran down the hall while she chased him. Both were laughing loudly and yelling to each other. The mall is just like a playground at recess. I hope my own son doesn't act this way when he leaves home." Clerks also have complaints about the teenagers. "It drives me crazy. A group of girls will come in

The shopping mall

the store and try on a huge amount of clothes, and then leave without buying anything. So I'm left with a pile of clothes to fold back up and put away." In the past there was more concern about teenagers congregating in the malls and "taking over." At that time security guards would tell them to keep moving anytime they sat or stood in one place, and most stores discouraged them from entering unless they planned to buy something. Parents were asked not to let their teens hang out there. The phrase "mall rats" is sometimes used to refer to people who hang out at malls.

There are additional factors which determine the number of teens in the mall. There is a movie complex in the mall which shows eight or more movies a night. There are more older teenagers in the mall an hour or so before and after movies begin. Younger teenagers are usually dropped off by their parents just before a movie starts and picked up soon after it ends. Because the malls are close to the high schools, students also go to the malls at lunchtime. Many more young people hang out in the malls during the school year than during the summer. In the summer there are more things to do outdoors, such as go to parks, walk to the fast-food restaurants, and go to the beach. Also, more teenagers work during the summer. Many kids also come in to the malls from nearby towns and suburbs, and some hitchhike to get there.

Most parents fail to understand the attraction of the mall for their teenage children. Aside from the malls and the fast-food restaurants, teenagers do not have many places to hang out with their friends. "There aren't many places in Charlottetown where my fourteen-year-old daughter can go. The mall is really close by, so I don't mind dropping her off. That way she can go see her friends, and I know where she is in case I need to get hold of her. Also the mall is relatively safe. As long as she stays in the mall, there are people who can look out for her. Ideally, I would like for her to bring her friends home or go to her friends' houses, but I know this isn't always possible." Her daughter says, "It's too complicated to have my friends come over to my house. First I have to ask Mom and then arrange to have someone drive them over and pick them up. Also some of the things my parents and younger brothers say and do are embarrassing. If we are watching TV or in my room, my brothers are always coming in and don't leave us alone. After my brothers go to bed at eight o'clock we have to be really quiet. It's easier just to meet at the mall and not have to worry about waking them up." Malls offer many attractions to the teens. Teens can get out of the house and do what they want with those they want to be with. They can meet and get to know other people their age without the supervision of their parents or the interference of their siblings. They can browse in the stores and look at the latest items. Nevertheless, sometimes the teenagers find the mall boring, and the fact they don't have much money prevents them from buying things. For older teens the mall is a great place to meet and kill time before going somewhere else. They can make plans with others, find out what is going on, and tag along with friends who have plans. #2287

McBurger's

McBurger's (a pseudonym) is a fast-food restaurant and a major teenage hangout on Friday and Saturday nights. "Many kids start hanging out at McBurger's when they are thirteen or fourteen years old and continue until they are eighteen or nineteen." "You can always go to McBurger's on a weekend and meet people, talk to friends, eat, and just feel part of something." "McBurger's is the place to go after a dance or a sports event, just to see other people and see what's happening." "It's where you go to find out what else is going on." "Charlottetown can be pretty boring. If you want something to do, you can usually find it at McBurger's. There's often something exciting happening." "McBurger's is great on the weekends. Everyone and their dog goes there. It's the only place my parents let me go." "There's no other place to hang out with all your friends." "We can watch all the young stuff and hope to pick up someone." "It's the place for teens. It's their place." "It's the cool thing to do when you're a teenager, because everybody is doing it."

Teenagers reach the restaurant in cars and by foot. It is in the middle of the main cruising strip, or University Avenue. Most of Charlottetown's fast-food restaurants, video-rental stores, shopping malls, liquor stores, and movie theaters are located along this strip. McBurger's is located within about half a mile of two shopping malls. There are also several residential areas nearby. McBurger's is much more popular as a week-end hangout during the summer months than during the winter. "It is more fun to hang out there in the summer." The warmer weather, and lack of snow and ice, makes it possible for more teens to walk to the restaurant and to stand around outside the cars in the parking lots. "Staying inside your car is too boring, and staying inside the restaurant is too expensive." However, many parents do not want their kids to go to the restaurant on weekend nights, because of its reputation as a rowdy and dangerous hangout with numerous teens involved with smoking, alcohol, recreational drugs, fights, and cars.

At lunchtime many teens from local schools also prefer to eat at McBurger's rather than their school cafeteria, and the air around their tables is often thick with cigarette smoke. The girls and guys sit apart and try to look at their favorite person when he or she isn't looking. Girls say, "I come here for lunch because everyone else does. It's the thing to do," "I like the food and all the guys are nice," and "I usually come to make sure the guys notice me." Guys say, "It's better than eating at school," "If you didn't come, you'd be lonely back at school eating cafeteria food," "I come because most of the other guys do and it's cool," and "I come because all the girls come here."

McBurger's offers many attractions to teens. It has a large seating capacity. It also allows patrons a good view of others who are present both inside the restaurant and outside in the parking areas. There are glass doors and large plate-glass windows. The restaurant provides fast-food items, such as French fries, hamburgers, sundaes, and pop, which are popular with teenagers and affordable, even on a small allowance. It also provides teenagers with a legitimate reason for being there, i.e., "I was hungry," which they can give their parents, who are well aware of voracious teenage appetites. When teens are at McBurger's they are more likely to find out if anything is going on, such as a party, and to see anything exciting, such as a fight. The restaurant has large parking areas surrounding it. The parking lots provide an ideal meeting place for teens driving around town and up and down the strip. These areas enable teenagers with and without cars to socialize, drink, smoke, use drugs, and fight. They provide enough space for teenagers to hide from enemies, act foolish, and do and say things not permitted in the restaurant. Some teens come to McBurger's practically every weekend, except when there is a dance or a house party. Many come after the shopping malls close, after seeing a movie, or after a dance or sporting event is over. Younger teens, aged thirteen through fifteen, are present from before nine o'clock until about ten thirty. Older teens, aged sixteen through eighteen, are present from about ten thirty until twelve thirty. Older teens are more likely than younger teens to arrive in a car. Some brag about their cars, even though most cars belong to their parents. Teens dress up to hang out at McBurger's and are probably better dressed than they are at any other time of the week. "Many girls look like they are in a fashion show instead of a fast-food restaurant."

"Before you go to McBurger's you meet at the shopping mall and walk around for a couple of hours. Everybody looks for people who are old enough to buy them liquor in the liquor store." Many minors wait outside the liquor stores on Friday and Saturday nights. Adults entering a liquor store may be asked to buy liquor as often as three or four times by teens they do not know. "After you get some liquor or meet someone else who has gotten some, you leave to have a few drinks." "Once I saw six kids, fifteen years old or less, with a case of twenty-four beer and a couple of pints getting into the back seat of a compact car. The funny thing was they did it right in front of the liquor store where everyone could see them." When the mall closes at ten at night the crowds start for McBurger's. "Teens often drink or smoke up beforehand so they will be buzzing when they get to the parking lots at McBurger's." "We get drunk at the hockey games and head into McBurger's afterwards."

Teens usually arrive in a group of three or four. Four is the maximum number who fit comfortably into a car so that each gets to sit next to a window, and four is the maximum number that can sit comfortably in a restaurant booth. The first thing you see when you arrive at McBurger's is the horde of cars. Typically a group of guys will arrive in a car and first drive around the restaurant to check out the other cars. They recognize whom most of the cars belong to. They may park close to other teens who are hanging out in the parking lot and talk, smoke, and drink for a while. "You park beside your friends, roll down the windows, and yell back and forth. Then you go inside to order food and a pop." If there is a big crowd inside the restaurant, they will usually enter and take a look around to see who is there. A typical group of girls arrives in a car or on foot. They may get an older brother or sister or a parent to drive them to a nearby shopping mall under the pretext of going shopping or to a movie. Then, after being dropped off, they walk to McBurger's or another fast-food restaurant. A group of guys is less likely to arrive on foot. Having access to a car is important for the status of the males. Many guys will not go out unless they have use of a car. Those with a car often drive through McBurger's four or five times a night to see who is there. Teenagers frequently squeal their tires, but no one is impressed unless the squeal is unusually long and smoky. "Every clown with a fast car wants to squeal his tires or just race around the restaurant until his gas runs out. It's a miracle no one has been hit."

Girls arrive in close-knit groups and immediately hurry off to the bathroom to double-check their appearance. Inside the bathroom they freshen up their makeup, straighten their hair and clothes, and perhaps drink some alcohol. Girls are more confident about themselves when they exit the bathroom. They buy something at the counter, usually fries and a pop, and occasionally a cheeseburger or an ice-cream cone. Next they find a seat. Once they sit down they are more likely to take off their jackets than are the males. A girl's status is based on how attractive she is, the number of friends with her, the number of guys that she knows there, the quality of her clothes, her access to a car, and whether or not she smokes, drinks, and is sexually experienced. Girls say they come to McBurger's because of the boys. "I never went to pick up a guy. They would pick me up."

Groups of guys stride into the restaurant, very relaxed and nonchalant, and stop to case the joint. They want to make a good impression and look assertive. Guys usually find a place to sit and then go up to the counter and place their order. This allows them a good look at who is there, including friends, enemies, and interesting girls, and enables them to "strut their stuff." If a male is wearing a team jacket he almost never takes it off, because it is a status symbol. Girls are most attracted to guys with team jackets, cars, and alcohol. They are also attracted to older guys. Junior-high girls are attracted to high-school guys, and high-school girls are attracted to university guys. Guys say they come to McBurger's because everyone else does, there is nowhere else to go, and to watch the fights. "My friends and I go there to check out the girls and try to pick them up." "My girlfriend never likes to go to McBurger's; she's into going to movies or parties. Sometimes I'll say I have to be up early the next day, drop her off, and go to McBurger's to see what's going on. Usually a bunch of my friends are there, and of course they have beer and tokes. I catch a buzz, drive around with them, and hang out until the place closes. Then I go home."

After people sit down, they look around and watch attractive individuals of the opposite sex. They talk, drink their pop, and eat what little they order. Girls often make many trips to the bathroom to comb their hair. Guys stand by the counters and watch the girls go by. Girls and guys sit in separate groups. "Eventually after some looks and laughter are exchanged, one or two daring souls venture away from the security of their friends to visit a group of the opposite sex. Some just walk by and make a short comment. Only the bravest, most secure souls do so. Others just watch and listen. Some hide in corner seats, happy enough to be part of things. Girls use more body language, especially with their eyes. Boys use loud and sometimes rude language and gestures. For the girls, the sweeter the smile the better. For the boys, the louder the burp the better." "Guys pull the old 'ignore them' trick. Then as the night wears on they gradually notice some girls and talk to them for a while." Many groups leave within half an hour and then return again later in the evening.

"When you eat you save your pop. Then you take your liquor from your purse or your jacket and pour it into your pop. Sometimes you mix them in the bathroom." Alcohol helps teens feel confident about approaching others, by removing their anxieties about being rejected and how they appear to others. "Many kids come up and talk to you like they've known you all their life, but in reality you don't have a clue who they are. They are too drunk to know or care who they talk to. The crowds of kids are unbelievable. Some hang out inside, mainly because they are hungry or too drunk to move, but the majority hang out outside." Management does not want the restaurant to become a hangout. They want to maintain the image of McBurger's as a family restaurant and not scare adults away on the weekends. Often groups of teenagers are asked to leave by the store manager or a security guard after about fifteen or twenty minutes. "When a group is kicked out they try to act cool and laugh it off, but their faces look like they are ready to kill." "Getting kicked out is a source of prestige. The more often you are kicked out the cooler you are."

McBurger's also provides easily accessible bathrooms, where people can use the toilets and mirrors, mix liquor with pop, and smoke drugs without much threat of discovery. The bathrooms usually become dirty, messy, and full of smoke. "Once I walked into the girls' bathroom and saw a girl sitting on the floor almost passed out with a cigarette in one hand and a bottle of rum in the other. You even see girls arguing in the bathroom; not really fighting, just bitching back and forth." "If you are out drinking with your friends and you need to use the bathroom, you go to McBurger's." Sometimes McBurger's locks the bathrooms after eleven or twelve o'clock, and kids use the bathroom at the neighboring coffee and donut shop.

When they leave the restaurant teens frequently hang out in the parking lots and stand around in small groups talking and joking. Or else they walk to another fast-food restaurant nearby and often return to McBurger's later. The dark night helps to hide what people do. The favorite place for people to hang out is in, on, and around a car in the parking lot, and preferably a car whose driver they know. "It's a boost to be in a car and have lots of people gathered around you." Groups of up to thirty guys and girls mingle in and around their cars, talking, laughing, dancing to car stereos, and acting foolish. In addition to the dark, they have the security of their cars revved up and standing by. Periodically people get in a car, leave McBurger's, and cruise up and down University Avenue. After about fifteen minutes of this they go back to McBurger's and start over again. The outside area for hanging out extends to include a coffee and donut shop on one side and a convenience store on the other. There they drink and buy cigarettes and rolling papers. Some guys and girls roll joints and smoke them. Smoking, drinking alcohol, and taking drugs enable teenagers to get favorable attention from other teens. The police keep a close eye on the teens in the parking lot and drive through the grounds several times a night. At other times teens control the area. "If you try to drive past them they only move out of your way when they're ready and usually with some comment. On one occasion two girls sat down practically in front of my car and pleaded with me not to run over them. They were showing off to a crowd of onlookers."

Outside is where everything usually happens. The drunk kids get in the most trouble. They are easy to spot because they carry the same cup of pop around for hours. The brave ones just drink their beer which they carry in their jackets. The really drunk ones try to make friends with the policemen who patrol the parking lots and the restaurant. They stagger up to the police and say stuff like "Hi! How are ya? Cold out, isn't it?" or "Look at those dopes over there. Aren't they stupid?" Then they stagger away feeling damned proud that they've just conquered the police. "You can usually see some clown who's drunk, trying to impress everybody by showing how far he or she can go mouthing off at a cop. Sometimes the cop gets fed up and puts the teen in the back of the patrol car or paddy wagon." When kids are drunk their voices get louder and they start yelling. "You don't want people around you yelling. When voices are too loud the police come over to tell them to shut up and also try to catch underage drinkers. One time a drunk friend of mine saw me and starting yelling my name and running toward my car. We quickly shut her up. Eventually she calmed down and passed out." "The worst I've ever seen it at McBurger's was one evening when we pulled in and saw a teenage boy in the middle of the parking lot urinating on the pavement. It was disgusting. He was staggering all over the place. When we entered the restaurant we were hugged to death by friends from school who were drunk. Then we ordered our food and sat down to watch the fights." Normally police ignore the drunk and stoned kids in the parking lots, unless they get a little wild. "Two young girls had too much to drink and were shouting obscenities at the female manager of the restaurant. She told them to leave, and having challenged her authority, they eventually did. The two girls were quite loud and obnoxious when they left the restaurant. As they blended into the safety of the night and the crowd of kids, a police cruiser pulled up. The crowd broke up without a word. Every group has its limit, and the authority of the police was the limit. The teens know that the police can take them to a place more horrible than any jail cell; home to Mom and Dad."

There are fights on weekend nights at McBurger's. These range from shouting matches to large brawls. "It's quite funny when you are sitting inside eating and someone yells, 'There's a fight outside!' All of a sudden a gust of wind blows past you as everyone runs to look out the doors to see who is fighting and how bad the fight really is. When the fight is over everyone returns to their seat and talks about it. Then everyone waits for the next fight to start." Fights break out because some guys want to fight or else they are too drunk to care. Alcohol helps provide the confidence to fight by removing anxieties over the consequences. Fights can start over little issues like one drunken teenager bumping into another followed by insults, such as "Jerk!" "Asshole!" and "Shithead!" Usually everyone crowds around to see the fight. "Fights start off with the customary ritual of insults and swearing. Then the fighters push and shove each other while their friends shout encouragement. Sometimes it stops at this point, but more often it escalates into a real fight, with each guy trying to pound the snot out of the other." When the police see the crowd they rush over to break it up. If there is a big crowd, additional fights may start. People push to see the fighting and those who are pushed can take offense. "Gary and I were in town after a party. We were on shrooms (magic mushrooms). Soon as we got to McBurger's, we saw a big crowd in the middle of the parking lot. So we parked the car and ran over to see the fight. I guess Gary freaked out on all the commotion, because the next thing I knew he was having it out with this other fellow. Somebody jumped him from behind and I grabbed hold of that one and started beating on him. You know, to help Gary out. But then somebody jumped me from behind too. I ended up with a fat lip and a bruised face. Gary did alright though, because he put one guy's head through this other fellow's car window. Then somebody yelled, 'Cops!' and we all scattered. Nobody was charged because we took off out of there and never went back for the rest of the night." Fighting may continue until the police show up, but the police may be too busy elsewhere to come soon. It isn't unusual for the fighting to start again after the police leave, and they have to be called again. Sometimes the fight gets bloody and a police van takes the worst offenders away. Most fights break out between older teenagers, and police are called more often later in the night after the older teenagers arrive. Fights occur periodically through the night until the main troublemakers are kicked out of Mc-Burger's and off the parking lots. Fights also start inside the restaurant. "One night I was sitting in McBurger's with about seven or eight of my friends. In walked one of my worst enemies and he was drunk. As soon as I saw him I knew we were going to fight. When he saw me he flicked the cigarette he was smoking at me. I picked it off the floor, said, 'Thanks for the smoke,' and smoked it. Two minutes later he asked if he could have a drag and I gave the cigarette back to him. He returned to his two friends, laughed, and flicked it at me again. I told him to back off and he came over and grabbed me by the neck. We started fighting and it ended with me knocking him on the floor. The security guards separated us and sent us out opposite doors. Outside I realized my sweater was ripped. This really pissed me off and I walked back through McBurger's to the other door where he was standing, and I sucker-punched him. I was a hero at school the next day because the guy wasn't liked. He never bothered me again after that." "I work at McBurger's. I'm there all the time, and I've never been attacked. I've never seen or heard of anyone getting jumped or beaten up who was minding their own business and not looking for a fight. You may get insulted, but if you ignore it, you should be fine. Despite all the crowds and all the fighting and drinking, there is very little damage. Occasionally a garbage can gets kicked over. Most of the crowd are friends hanging out together and people who want to see the fights, not participate in them."

At times the restaurant hires security guards and off-duty police-men to patrol the restaurant and the parking lots. Otherwise, they call the city police when there's a fight. Security is there to maintain control, but not ruin the fun. According to one guard, "There isn't much drinking done. Most are still too young to obtain alcohol. If there is any, we have a hard time spotting it because of all the cars. Generally the kids are well behaved and just want a little fun. Sure there can be times when they get out of hand, especially hockey teams from rival schools, but most of them straighten up when they see the badge."

Kids hang out in cliques. Members of the same clique sit together at a table or gather around certain cars outside. "The snobs are with the snobs, the normals with the normals, and the scum with the scum." "Groups can be labeled preppies, jocks, normally dressed, queers, head-bangers, and druggies. The preppies are sharply dressed in expensive name-brand clothes. They don't hang around much and often drop in on a night there is a school dance. The jocks are athletes on the hockey and other teams. They stop by to talk to friends and show how popular they are. After a game they drop in to find out where the parties and their girlfriends are. The normally dressed is the everyday group. They are not too popular, but know a lot of people. They come and go frequently during the evening. This group contains a lot of drunk teenagers making asses of themselves. The queers are guys and girls dressed all in black with strange haircuts. They look like social outcasts and are in a world of their own. They are not there as often as some of the other groups. They take a lot of abuse and park away from McBurger's so their cars won't be damaged. Headbangers are males with long hair and jackets with heavy metal patches. They are very unpopular, but enjoy hanging out most of the night in the parking lot around their souped-up cars and slutty girlfriends. The druggies, or potheads, can usually be found in dark corners of the parking lot around several cars. Their stereos are blaring and there is a haze of smoke around them. This group includes high-school dropouts. They are frequently chased off the lot by the police, but are back a few minutes later. Inside the restaurant the headbangers and the druggies sit in separate corners away from the other teens. They are also more isolated on the parking lot." There is limited interaction between the cliques. Some mixing occurs when kids are too drunk to care who they talk to.

McBurger's is also staffed by teens, who enjoy dealing with their friends and other teenagers. When they are working in the dining area and the parking lot they frequently see people they know and stop and talk to them. Often the manager has to tell them to get back to work. "When a good-looking guy or girl goes up to a cash register at the counter, let's say register number two, an employee will yell out, 'Grill on number two!' The other employees all turn to look at the customer when they hear this. The same thing is yelled if the customer is exceptionally ugly."

The activities carried out in fast-food restaurants are similar to the activities in a club or lounge, except that clubs have more music and dancing. In both locales groups of males and females hang out together and attempt to establish contact with members of the opposite sex. Relationships are started and ended. Use of cigarettes, alcohol, drugs, and cars adds to the adult image. "Hanging out at McBurger's is a stage of life most of us go through. It's a place where kids can have fun with no parents or teachers around to hassle them. It's true there are fights, booze, and drugs. But kids seem to enjoy a bit of wildness in their lives. They need something to excite them over the weekend, so at least they'll have something to talk about in school on Monday." "Kids don't do these things because they go to McBurger's. All over town you see kids in cars and walking around who are smoking cigarettes, drinking, and getting stoned. McBurger's is just where the kids gather. And because they do these things anyway, naturally they are going to do them at McBurger's too." When kids become older they can get admitted to clubs and lounges. "A club provides you with a better place to drink than a field, someone's backyard, or a car. I can remember many times walking around in the rain or snow with a pint stuffed inside my jacket just trying to find a place to drink. Now that I'm old enough to get in, clubs provide me with shelter." #2288

The beach

In the summer, many young people hang out at the beach. Many work for businesses and the government dealing with tourists in communities near the beach, and they go to the beach when they are off work. Others travel to the beach from communities a half hour or more away. The beach is one of the greatest places to meet others. "I'm always lucky when I go to the beach. Several times last summer I was able to get a date or at least meet some real good-looking babes at the beach. Why else would one go?"

You want to look good when you go to the beach. "In March you start thinking of the beach, swimming, and tanning. But then your mind fills with a dark cloud as you visualize your present physical condition. You feel considerable pressure to get off your fat ass and get in shape for the summer months. The deadline draws closer and you feel more and more pressure until you start working out. As summer approaches the number of people hanging out at the gym increases." A tan is also important, and sunbathing requires little energy. "All you do is lie down and close your eyes, and you've mastered the basics. People use sunscreen lotions so they won't burn. But others get their base tan and then just live to get as much color as they can. They don't worry that their skin will look like an alligator's by the time they are fifty."

People use various items to help them connect with others at the beach. First, one must wear the latest styles. "Guys wear popular beach wear, and girls wear the skimpiest bathing suit they feel comfortable in, which catches the sideways glances from guys that they want so much." Sunglasses are a must. "I always wear my shades to the beach. They come in real handy when someone points out a hunk. Guys don't realize we are checking their bodies out. Besides, I do look good in sunglasses."

77

Another helpful piece of equipment is a radio or ghetto blaster, which helps to pass the time, creates a party atmosphere, and attracts others. "One day Gwen and I went to the beach around noon and had the music blaring five minutes after we got there. It's amazing how many people sit near you. By two o'clock, thirty or more people had moved in around us. It was great. We made plans to meet a couple of the guys at a club that night. Did we ever have a good time that night and the rest of the weekend." "George and I always bring a radio to the beach whenever we go. We set up beside these two girls, one thing led to another, and we ended up spending a lot of time with them that week. We were on vacation and so were they." People also use other equipment. "I go to a campground at the beach, get a campfire going, and start to play my guitar. Girls come over and I can simply take one to my tent. Girls from out of town are so easy. If two girls are equally attractive, and one is local and the other is from out of town, I always go for the one from out of town. She's much more likely to go to bed with me." "If somebody at the beach is 'from away' (from off Prince Edward Island), it doesn't matter to them what they do or how they act. They figure, 'Who's going to know anyway?'" #2289

Cruising

University Avenue is the major street into Charlottetown. It consists of a two-kilometer stretch which begins past the university and ends at the heart of downtown. It is known by several names, including the strip, the alley, and tin-can alley. Along this stretch are many of Charlottetown's fast-food outlets, shopping malls, restaurants, and gas stations. The stretch constitutes the primary cruising area for teenagers in cars. Cruising begins in spring, when it is warm enough for numbers of people to walk along University Avenue, and continues until winter. As a result of cruising, traffic is heavier on Thursday night and quite heavy on Friday and Saturday nights when it can be bumper-to-bumper from one end of the strip to the other.

The majority of those who cruise the strip are between sixteen and eighteen years old. This is because the age at which they can begin to drive is sixteen and the age when they are allowed to drink is presently eighteen. As soon as the kids turn eighteen, and earlier if they can get away with it, they start to go to clubs and no longer have to cruise the strip. The main reason they cruise is because the other kids their age are walking or driving along the strip too.

Cruising

Males who cruise the strip frequently hope to make contact with females. However, skills at this age are rather undeveloped. Often we tried to evoke reactions from girls we saw by abusing them verbally. We would yell things like "Hey, slut!" and "The best part of you was left on your mother's leg" (implying that any good genetic characteristics, such as looks, were left behind in unused sperm). We'd also yell, "You're a fucking dog," (implying she looks as ugly as a dog) and then we'd bark, "Ahr! Ahr! Ahr! Ahr!" Girls would ignore this, tell us to "Go fuck yourself!" or give us the finger. We didn't feel offended. Instead we usually laughed our heads off. It's much more fun when you go cruising if you can find someone to yell at. At guys we would yell "Faggot!" and "You're a fruit." Acting like this didn't help us meet many girls. A much more successful approach was to find a carload of girls and follow them wherever they went. After following for a while, we would try to get them to pull over somewhere like McDonald's, Burger King, or a parking lot so we could meet them.

The type of car you cruise in is very important. The most common car that you see cruising on a Friday or Saturday night is the family car which is owned by the driver's parents. These cars are usually nice, late-model cars, with four doors, normal tires, and attractive interiors. They are quiet and well-looked after, and because they are built for comfort, they can be quite luxurious. The cars are roomy and normally have the most people in them, because everyone likes to cruise when a car is available. Girls tend to be favorably impressed with these cars because they can ride in luxury. Their drivers usually drive much more cautiously than do those who own their own cars.

Another common type of car is the souped-up, or homemade, sports car. These cars are usually jacked up, have wide tires, are loud and fast, and are often falling apart. Drivers of these cars usually drive reckless-ly. For example, they will roar up to a stoplight, slam on the brakes, and when the light turns green squeal their tires taking off again. This causes quite a racket and everyone within hearing distance turns to see what is happening, which is the reaction the driver wants. Apparently most males who own such cars think that driving this way shows how masculine they are and impresses the females. In my experience, only a minority of girls are impressed with this behavior, and most girls consider the drivers assholes. These drivers also seem interested in impressing other guys with the power of their cars, because when they pull up beside you at a red light, they always seem to want to drag to the next intersection. I find that if you win when you drag, you feel pride; and if you lose, you don't look at the other driver. If you decide not to drag, the other driver squeals away just to show he could have beaten you anyway. There are usually two or three people in these cars, but sometimes there are so many males inside there would be no room for any females. Souped-up cars are usually uncomfortable to cruise in and depending on how the guy drives, a girl may be very nervous about riding in them. Having a car like this may be a disadvantage when it comes to impressing a girl and picking her up.

Another type of car is the factory-built sports car, such as a Trans Am, Firebird, or Corvette. Because of their cost they are seldom owned by people between the ages of sixteen and twenty-one. When you do see these cars cruising the strip there are usually only one or two people in them. People feel these cars are built for no more than two, and it looks bad to have a whole pile of people crammed inside. Such cars are seldom driven crazily or dangerously. They are worth so much that the driver doesn't want to risk smashing one up. Also you don't have to drive fast and loud to get people to notice you. Everyone notices a car like this anyway and wants to see who is driving it. Such cars imply that the driver has a lot of class, and girls like to be driven around in them because it raises their status. Most people assume the driver of the car is the girl's boyfriend and that he must be rich. Guys and girls who own these cars take very good care of them because they are a major factor in their success in the dating game.

Ideally when cruising the strip one has a nice fast car with only one or two guys in it, and a nice loud stereo. A nice car impresses the girls, and the best car is a factory-built sports car. However, your family's car is quite acceptable if it is a recent model, because it is attractive to ride in. The worst cars are worn-out older models. The most important feature of a car's stereo is how loud it is. A loud stereo attracts attention to your car and to yourself, which is one of the main objectives while cruising the strip. When we went cruising we would roll down all the windows even if it was cold and turn the stereo up really loud. It would sound terrible inside the car, but to people outside it sounded OK. Best of all is to have a stereo that sounds nice as well as loud, because if you do pick up a girl she will hear it inside the car. I remember one guy who cruised the strip in a recent model car with a nice loud stereo. He was the envy of everyone on the strip and he always had girls in his car.

When I first turned sixteen, I seldom had use of the family car. However, I would never think of walking up and down the strip. It would have been very degrading because everyone would know that

Cruising

I didn't have a car or use of one. A friend of mine had a car to use anytime he wanted. He wasn't a very good friend, but my friends used to get around with him just so he would take us cruising on the weekends. There was some competition between us, because only three people were allowed to ride with him in the car and more than three of us wanted to. His car would actually seat six people, but that meant three in the front seat and three in the back. You never wanted to be the middle guy on either the front or the back seat, because it was hard to see who was walking around, you couldn't yell out the window, and it didn't look cool. Another reason you didn't want a full car was that if you happened to succeed in picking up girls, you needed a place to put them.

It was difficult to borrow the family car if all you wanted to do was to cruise the strip. Parents always wanted to know where you were going and how long you were going to be out. You could tell them you were taking a date to a movie, and this would guarantee you the car. The problem occurred the day after if your dad noticed you had put some one hundred kilometers on the speedometer. He would walk in the house and demand to know, "Where the hell did you go last night?" and you knew you were caught. One excuse I used was that I had picked up my date early, driven around a little before the movie, and tried to find someplace to eat afterwards. If this failed to pacify him, I could always add, "I'll pay you for the gas. I didn't realize we drove around so much." Sometimes to avoid this problem you would sit in your parents' car in a parking lot on the strip and watch the others cruise up and down the street. This wasn't quite as much fun, but at least you were still part of the action. All along the strip you find people sitting in cars doing this. Not only does it save gas, but it's a good way to meet girls who are just walking up and down the strip.

There was a very good reason why the other kids and I would go through so much shit with our parents about how much gas we used going to a fictitious movie with a nonexistent date. We were willing to do what we had to to get the car because girls this age were very impressed when they got picked up by someone driving a car. It meant they could cruise the strip with class and not have to walk. The girls who got picked up were always interested in the driver of the car. He was the one behind the wheel and the one who had made the final decision to pick them up. Girls this age always wanted to go out with guys who either owned a car or had use of one to take them out.

While cruising the strip many people would also pull off and cruise around McDonald's Restaurant. McDonald's is a fairly good spot to meet girls, or at least see some ugly ones to yell at. There are two sides to McDonald's. The north side has the fewest people hanging out. If you are going into McDonald's you usually park your car on this side so it won't get damaged. On the south side one usually finds groups of people standing around. These include the kids who like to fight on weekends with anyone they know they can beat up. Many gang fights between the high schools start on this side of McDonald's or move here from inside the restaurant. Because none of the guys I got around with fought very well, we usually went around this side of McDonald's faster than we did the other side and were very discreet when looking to see who was standing there.

Despite all the times we went cruising, probably our best night was the one in which my friend and I parked the car and just walked up and down the strip. We saved gas and money, met a great many people, picked up two girls who were also walking, and partied in the Dairy Queen parking lot with two guys who also picked up two girls. The night was a huge success. #2290

Yelling at people from cars

The car is frequently used as a safe area from which to abuse people outside the car. Occupants of a car may taunt, insult, and threaten pedestrians and those in other vehicles. This is usually verbal, but gestures, spitting, throwing objects, and the physical threat of the car itself are also used. Because the car is normally moving or can quickly be put to flight there is reasonable safety for the occupants of the car, regardless of what they say and do to others.

Drivers of all ages and both sexes express their irritation at obstacles which interfere with their smooth progress, whether it be pedestrians, traffic lights, potholes, construction work, or other vehicles. Normally comments are kept to the confines of the car, but sometimes they are delivered to those held responsible. For example, if you get stopped at a red light, you can still turn right. Usually drivers get annoyed, because although it's their chance to get going, that is always the time pedestrians cross the street. When you're really in a big hurry, you are likely to encounter shoppers coming in bunches of twenty or thirty. I've leaned out of my window and yelled, "Why don't you walk a little slower? I'm in no rush anyway." I've heard one old man yell, "C'mon! C'mon!" at women, and others roar, "Hurry the Christ up!" and "Get the hell out of my way!" Other people just lay on the horn to try to hurry them by.

Yelling at people from cars

People usually ignore irate drivers, but not always. One taxi driver said his car was stalled at an intersection and he was unable to start it, but the driver behind him continued to honk his horn. Finally he got out of his taxi, walked to the car behind him, and told the driver, "You go forward and try to start the car. I'll stay here and honk the horn for you." The driver drove off in a huff. Usually the greater one's hurry, the more impatient one is when held up.

An additional form of abuse is used by certain males between the ages of sixteen and twenty-five years old. Often they taunt pedestrians that they drive by and call them names, such as "Fruit!" and "Slut!" They also pick on physical characteristics, such as "Hey, baldy!" or simply curse them, "Goddamned son of a bitch!" Occasionally they throw objects from the car, spit on a person, intentionally splash them with water from puddles, or purposely drive very close to them. Such behavior can happen any time of the day or night. However, it is particularly common on a Friday night when you are likely to have a carload of teenage males bombing down the street roaring out things you can hardly make out. Then they turn around and come back to do it again. Each tries to get off a better comment than the others in order to get the most laughs out of their friends. I can imagine the other guys in the car saying, "Oh God, Christ, that was a good one." I've never yelled these things at people from cars myself. I'd be too embarrassed. It's just not my nature; it's not me. I tend to think that people who do the yelling don't have much going for them in the first place.

One of the most popular forms of abuse by males of this age consists of making sexual comments to females. Although this often involves just a comment or two, occasionally the interaction is quite elaborate. One Friday night a friend and I were walking down the street of an Island village. A girl was approaching in our direction on the other side of the street. A jacked-up car drew alongside the girl and three guys with beer cans and cigarettes in their hands leaned out of the windows and shouted such things as "How good are you in bed?" "Why don't you come over and I'll show you something that'll widen your eyes?" and "You want to make out? I don't think a girl with your looks goes to bed alone." They appeared to be sixteen-year-olds who had been drinking. The girl became upset and told the guys to "Go fuck yourselves!" and "Go to hell!" The guys used gestures such as flexing their muscles, grabbing their crotches, and "mooning," or pulling down their pants and showing her their asses. The girl became intensely angry and picked up a large rock which she threw into the car. The guys began a long chorus of cursing and calling her a dog and a bitch while she ran off. Finally they drove away. Two of the three guys I'm sure she didn't know, because I'd never seen them in the community before. But the third had grown up with the girl, and she acted as though his actions were particularly upsetting to her. A couple of weeks later I saw the girl fly into him at a party and demand to know, "Why were you putting on this big show in front of the other guys?" It was clear she was still mad about it. I observed another occasion when seven girls were walking down the street together. As they approached the local rink an old Dodge drove up and five guys in stylish shirts began yelling at them. They asked individual girls, "Are you on the pill?" "Have your breasts always been that big, or have they been tugged on a lot?" and "Are you on your period? You've been walking around town all night bull-legged." The guys told the girls they could give them a whole new definition of sex. At first the girls were angry but then they began to play along by making gestures to torment the males such as clutching their breasts. The males responded by unbuttoning their shirts a bit and sticking out their chests, and by grabbing their crotches. The girls laughed at them and said they would have to be desperate to be seen with such crude, ignorant, and sick people. The guys laughed until the girls started calling them wimps, fruits, and homely. Then when the girls decided to ignore the guys, they finally drove off. Afterwards the girls laughed over their victory.

Although it is much rarer, occasionally girls in a car will make sexual comments to males. One evening I was sitting outside across from a parking lot in a large Island town. A friend of mine came through the lot on foot and behind him was a carload of females. The girls weren't from the local community. They began yelling at my friend, wanting to know if he was going to meet his girlfriend or his boyfriend. He responded that he was as much a homosexual as they were lesbians. They laughed and asked, "Do you know any other guys as good looking as you?" He replied, "I don't know. I don't make it a hobby to look at other guys' bodies." This banter continued. Then the girls started shouting things such as "You sure fill out a pair of pants nicely," and "Given the size of your body, you probably get a bigger erection than most guys." This was one of the few occasions I have seen females make such statements publicly to a male. My friend's behavior was very different than that of females I've seen in the same situation. Instead of acting insulted, he looked flattered. He stood there smiling at the girls for a long time. One could see he was really pleased by all the attention he was getting, particularly when they said he was good looking and "a hunk."

Yelling at people from cars

Insults from cars generally lead to hurt feelings. Often people are minding their own business when the abuse occurs. People yelling out of a car normally direct their comments at one person, who may be standing in a crowd of cars and people. I've been yelled at when alone and when in a group. It's so loud, everybody hears it. I feel other people stare right through me, and I feel like dirt. It's intimidating and embarrassing, and I go, "Oh, my God." I just turn around and almost pretend I don't even hear them. I consider it ignorance. A person with any standards would come over and talk to you, not shout their loud mouths off across the area.

Sometimes people being abused respond aggressively. Some friends and I were sitting in a car at McDonald's with the windows rolled down. Nearby were three guys and two girls in a car who began to talk loudly about the two guys standing a few feet away next to the restaurant door. Those in the car called the two "wimps" and "fruits," which are common insults. The two guys gave them dirty looks and told them to "Shut the hell up!" They asked why the guys in the car were being so ignorant (rude) and suggested it was because they couldn't get it up to satisfy their girlfriends. The guys in the car replied, "At least we know how to have fun with members of the opposite sex." One of the girls called, "Hey, queer! I heard your father shot himself hunting the other day. Maybe he decided to do it when he found out what you do with your younger brother." This soon led to a fight in which the two guys hurt two of the three guys in the car and gave the girl who made the crack about the hunting injury a punch in the mouth. The hunting incident was a suspected suicide, and I was really surprised the girl used it.

There are a variety of factors involved in verbal abuse from cars. One is that people make comments from cars that they would be less likely to make if they were on foot. Apparently the car provides a greater sense of security and independence, and this permits people to engage in less acceptable behavior. An important factor appears to be the number of people one is with in the car. Although drivers who are alone sometimes abuse others when they are annoyed by delays, sexual comments are usually made when there are a number of other people in the car. They are seldom made by a single occupant. It appears that one needs additional social support to make comments which are even less acceptable socially. Another pattern is that males are much more likely than females to engage in verbal abuse and verbal abuse of a sexual nature. If a teenage male makes these comments, others see it as normal and may just laugh. Females, however, are not as aggressive in this way or as outspoken about sexual matters. If a girl were to make such comments, I can just see people asking, "What kind of girl is this?" and the word "slut" would come to mind. It appears that males are not as upset by sexual comments from girls as girls are by sexual comments from males. I think if a female were to show pleasure from this type of attention she would be labeled loose or a sleaze. Females do not want to be thought of and talked about in sexual terms. Also, it appears that one of the most effective defenses for ending this abuse is to ignore it. Nevertheless, the abuse does provoke violent feelings and on occasion a violent response.

Willingness to yell at others seems tied to both anonymity and immunity. Probably in many cases the person making the comments is not known to those he is abusing, but in other cases he is recognized or will be identified on the basis of those he is with. However, being in a group probably adds to a sense of immunity from retaliation. Finally, such yelling does not only happen from cars, because I've heard similar comments yelled by a group of young males on bicycles, a group of young guys dashing out of a public washroom, and males in the windows of university dorms. The other day I heard a guy yell at a girl from a dorm window, "Why don't you come on up? Test out the (bed)springs." [2291]

Dances

The regular Wednesday night dances for teenagers are very popular in Riverdale (pseudonym) and the surrounding area. Dances are the high point of teenage social activity, and attendance at them is a badge of social acceptability. In addition, the Wednesday night dances break up the monotony of the school week. Those who attend are fifteen and older. Although the dances are ostensibly for teenagers, a majority of those in the area who are in their early twenties also attend.

Riverdale is a rural community, and the dances are held within the Riverdale Royal Canadian Legion building. Inside the building, the dance area is separate from the drinking area, or lounge. Separate entrances are maintained for the dance and the lounge on Wednesday night. Parents worry that without separate entrances alcohol will be served to minors.

The dance is held in a large room. The band is located at one end of the room, there is a dance floor in the middle, and chairs are placed around the dance floor. Sufficient space is left between the chairs and the dance area so that people can pass by. During the dance two or three bouncers walk around the room to keep order. As the dance proceeds, the room becomes quite warm and full of cigarette smoke. This encourages people to leave the room and stand around outside. People socialize a great deal just outside the entrance.

There are many groups within the room. Most groups are composed of friends of the same sex from the same area or from the same school. Other groups are made up of two or three couples who stand together talking and show little interest in talking to passersby. Many of those who drink alcoholic beverages form groups with their drinking friends. Younger drinkers seem to get together with those who drink the same amount they do. For example, Claire, a sixteen-year-old girl, hangs around with peers who drink roughly as much as she does, and doesn't associate with those who drink much more or much less. Within each group of teenagers at the dance, there is usually at least one person who is eighteen years old or older, who can legally buy alcohol. It is easier for those who are underage to enter the lounge without being stopped when they are together with those of legal age. There is normally a friend of legal age in Claire's crowd, and because of the presence of this friend, Claire rarely fails to get into the lounge. The ability to get into the lounge while underage is a source of status among most of the younger teenagers. Those who are prone to cause trouble also stick together at dances. As they drink they become rowdy and start fights. When one gets into a fight the other members of the group soon join in. Very little marijuana is smoked at the dances, but those who do smoke usually hang out together and rarely include nonsmokers in their groups. In the case of cigarettes, most groups at the dance include both smokers and nonsmokers.

One sees certain patterns repeated every dance. Thus many people sit in the same location in the room. When one walks into a dance one can almost count on seeing the same people in the same seats they were in at the last dance. Nevertheless, people do leave their seats to talk to others they know. There are also similarities from one dance to the next in regard to who dances and when they do so. One particular set of girls never fails to be the first group of girls on the dance floor. There are also the people who never get up to dance until later in the evening.

Most guys at the dance try to act "cool." They want to look like they know everything and are always right. Most of the time they stand around the edge of the dance area near the doorway. Here they watch other people, especially the girls. They also spend a great deal of time walking around the dance area and talking among themselves and to people who are sitting down. Most guys spend about half their time in the room where the dance is held and the other half in the lounge. Many guys and some girls drink in order to have a good time. The guys spend more time in the dance area if they are interested in or dating a particular girl. Charles, for example, is eighteen and regularly goes to these dances with his girlfriend. However, he does not spend all his time dancing with her. He also goes in the lounge with his male friends and walks around the dance area with them.

Most girls show that they are definitely interested in guys at the dance. Thus a group of girls will laugh very loudly or otherwise carry on to attract the attention of guys nearby. When a girl is interested in a particular guy, she usually makes sure she sits or stands near him. If this doesn't get his attention she will make a point of passing near him and smiling at him repeatedly. Other girls can be seen imitating the behavior of the most popular girls and staying near them. Girls seldom spend the entire night waiting for a guy to ask them to dance. Instead, if they don't attract the males they are interested in, they often get up with their female friends and dance in a group. As a result they have more fun, and they become highly visible to the males.

Most of the music played by the band is fast music and the dancers stand and face each other without touching. Periodically the band plays a slow dance, or "waltz." When this happens many girls sit down and impatiently wait for a guy to ask them to dance. Some girls smile at every good-looking guy who walks by, hoping he will ask them. Many other girls take off for the washroom. Meanwhile guys walk around the room searching for someone they want to dance with. When there is a good band and good music, there are more people up dancing. The more the band is liked, the less drinking and fighting there is at the dance. [#2292]

Objectives

The search for Mr. Right

I think every little girl dreams of her wedding day and having a husband, children, a dog, and a home with a white picket fence. This will be a blissful life, where no one is unhappy or gets divorced and you live happily ever after. In order to achieve this dream you must find the perfect man. But is there one right person for everyone, and if so is there only one? What happens if you never find this one amazing person? Are you then doomed to a life of unhappiness? Or does every male have the potential to be the perfect man? And also, what is love and how do you know when you've found it? These are just a few of the questions I hear others ponder. Also, what kind of male would be right for you? Some people have very clear ideas as to what kind of appearance and personality they want, but others are not so sure. "When people pick out their lifetime partner, so many factors have to be considered. Even though I am young, I try to look for guys I could marry, not just go out with. Dating people I have no real interest in is a waste of their time and mine. I'm at the point where I have to give my head a shake and figure out what I want in a mate. Do I want someone who is perfect in terms of public appearances and money, and then worry about love and companionship later? Or do I want a real old-fashioned love-based relationship? Ideally, I want both. But am I ever going to find my perfect mate?"

There is an ongoing struggle among females to try to figure out the opposite sex and what makes relationships work. Girls never take the initiative to discuss difficulties with the males involved, but instead they debate them endlessly with their friends. These conversations focus on problems and hopeful outcomes or the lack of them, while listeners offer their opinions and suggestions on the latest revelation or crisis. Discussions include playing every event over and over again in the hope that some sort of divine plan or piece of advice will arise which will solve all of the relationship woes. Usually this is to no avail, and people remain confused as to why something happened and unclear what to do.

It is difficult to define love or to describe being in love to someone else, even when you are in love yourself. It is depressing how many women give up on love after a few or no relationships. Some hold very strong negative opinions about it. One girl stated, "Love is an idealistic phenomenon which was thought up in the 1960s when everyone was stoned. It was probably invented by men to rationalize having pre-marital sex. You know, 'It's OK baby, cuz I luv you.' Yeah, right! Love and true love don't exist today. Instead, we all compromise and convince ourselves we are 'in love.'" The girl made the quotation marks around "in love" with her fingers to indicate her disbelief. Then she pretended to gag and retch. Another stated, "Love is a stupid idealistic theory developed by greeting-card companies and flower shops in cahoots with whatever morons thought up Valentine's Day and New Year's Eve." Others are not so negative. Many believe they have been in love at one time or another in the past, but looking back are not sure if what they experienced was really love at all. Still others, who can be characterized as hopeless romantics, believe in true love. One woman, who has been in several relationships, expounded, "I've told guys that I loved them, because that's what I believed at the time. But I think love is bigger than anything I've ever experienced. I'm not sure if it's something instantaneous that hits you so hard it nearly knocks you over, or if it's something that grows gradually over time, like the song that says, 'One day you wake up and realize you fell in love.' Either way, it's going to be great and someday it's going to happen to all of us. We'll all be bitten by the lovebug."

Once you've decided, or have been convinced by your friends, that Mr. Right is out there, the next big question is where to meet him? Suggestions range from the library and supermarket to the bar and pool hall. "Looking for Mr. Right is never easy for a girl. A boy doesn't just appear wearing a name tag with 'Mr. Right' written on it." Girls are taught that the man is supposed to take the initiative. "We are expected to just wait for Mr. Right, I suppose." "I don't really look for him; he looks for me." But many girls grow impatient and fear that they'll end up with no one if they don't do something themselves. There are those who are constantly on the lookout for Mr. Right. "Several girls in my university dorm belong to an elite club in which members must say hello to at least one new boy each week. This is a boy they've never met before, and they record when and where they spoke to him and what the boy looked like and if he replied. The club started with the requirement to speak to one new boy each day, but this proved too difficult. Most of those who hear about the club think it is weird and that this is not the way to go about meeting new people." Some girls find a boy they think would make a good Mr. Right and follow him around until he notices them. One girl went into this wholeheartedly. A friend of hers explained, "It's almost scary how much she likes this boy. She's never had a relationship with him and just between you and me, she probably never will. She does things completely out of character to impress him. She used to have fun and party and drink with the gang on the weekends. But she's stopped drinking because he doesn't drink. He is studious and spends most evenings in the university library. Now she spends her evenings wandering aimlessly through the library carrels hoping to run into him. She has also developed a keen interest in hockey and freezes her butt off at the rink to watch him play. She has really changed, and if you ask me, it isn't for the better. And for what? A few idle conversations with him about nothing? It's just a little too whacky if you ask me." Then there are a few girls who have a very precise vision of where they are going to meet their Mr. Right. One seemingly mature woman predicted, "I will be driving down a busy street and stop at a traffic light. Next to me is another car, and there he is staring back at me. When our eyes meet, it will be magic. Wham! Love at first sight, no questions asked."

Dating different guys can help you find Mr. Right. But first you need to get dates. So the story is not so much how to find Mr. Right as it is how to attract guys, get dates, and get a boyfriend. If you get a boyfriend you can decide if he is Mr. Right or not. But none of these things are easy. "Finding Mr. Right or just a date is almost impossible. I went to a club several times. The few good guys I saw were taken, and the rest were jerks. I tried talking to guys in my university classes. Well, that never leads to much either. The only method I have is to sit in a club and look pretty and hope I get asked to dance." "In order to find someone for a potential date you have to be 'looking,' or willing to meet new people. You can not be antisocial. You also have to seem to be available, but not desperate. Your initial conversation should be laid-back and stimulating to the other person. During your interaction with a prospective date you should watch for signs that reveal your initial success or failure in attracting the other person. For example, does the other person maintain eye contact with you, or does he fail to face you, look past you, focus on something else, pay little attention to the conversation, or start talking to someone else? But this isn't foolproof, because some people are extremely bad at giving signals or taking a hint." "It's pretty hard to get a date really. You have to meet guys through mutual friends mostly. I made a few new male friends this year that way. Double dates can sometimes work out too. I go to pubs with groups of girls, but for the most part we talk only to guys we know. I usually dance with guys who are just friends." Then there is the problem that girls often do not want to waste time with dates and boyfriends who are clearly not Mr. Right. "I don't want to have a boyfriend if it is not going to last." "I don't want to go out with just anyone. I'm thirty years old and I've had my fun. It's time to settle down and have a family. I'm not sure how I'll know when Mr. Right comes along, but I figure he'll knock my socks off. He must be loving, kind, considerate, trustworthy, nice looking, muscular, helpful around the house, and free from bad habits, such as drinking and smoking." Finding Mr. Right is a difficult task. "I've kissed many toads, but never my prince." "You have to compete with all the other girls for dates and boyfriends. It is definitely not easy. You have to be lucky and smart to find Mr. Right."

Efforts to obtain sex

Most people turn to clubs in their search for Mr. Right. Many are convinced that bars and clubs are "where it's at," because that is where one can always find numerous available males. There are girls who go to clubs three or four times a week hoping to find a boyfriend. Some seem to spend most of their paycheck buying clothes just to look good. It is common to find an apartment or dorm room full of girls "getting all slutted up for a night on the town." They do each other's hair and makeup and try on each other's clothes in search of the perfect outfit. "Most girls dress up fancy and wear makeup to attract a male. If they are lucky, someone will ask them to dance." "It's like you're getting all done up to meet the man of your dreams. And I know it seems wrong to be something you are not. But if I went into the club in track pants and a T-shirt with my hair back in a ponytail, which is the real me, do you think I would get a second look from a guy? No way!" Still, people differ in their opinions as to how successful going to clubs will be. One who feels positive said, "The club is a great place to meet people. There are lots there in your age group who are looking for the same thing you are. Alcohol takes the edge off, and makes meeting people that much easier." Another looks at clubs differently, and argues, "Alcohol not only impairs your judgment and makes you attracted to people primarily on the basis of looks, but it also makes you do things completely out of character. You'll do something stupid you normally wouldn't even consider, like go off with a stranger God knows where and have sex with him." After a night of barhopping one girl found she was physically attracted to a particular boy. He wasn't giving her the attention she wanted, so in order to look cool she downed five shots of tequila. This was on top of what she had already drunk and she became violently ill. The guy was not impressed and she was tactfully escorted out the door by the bouncers. The next day she couldn't remember a single detail of the boy's appearance. Girls report finding a telephone number written on a napkin or matchbook in their pocket the next day and can't remember how it got there. Or someone may phone them that they must have given their phone number to, but they don't have a clue who it is.

When you find a potential Mr. Right and start dating him, you might think things would get easier. On the contrary, this is when things get analyzed to death and very troubling questions arise. Questions like "How do I feel about him?" "How does he feel about me?" "When does dating become a relationship?" "Is this a relationship yet?" "Where is our relationship going?" and "Is this the person I want to spend the rest of my life with?" These and a thousand other questions produce great confusion. People have more worries about relationships than you could ever dream of. Many girls with long-term boyfriends are far from certain about them. "My last boyfriend was a disaster. While we were dating he got another girl pregnant. I've been going out with my present boyfriend for three years. He gave me a ring for Christmas. It was supposed to be an engagement ring, but I decided to call it a pre-engagement ring. We fight a lot. One day he told me I was good for nothing, so I always bring that up when we fight." "A friend of mine has been living with her boyfriend, Bob, for two years. When I asked if she was going to marry him, she said, 'It's too soon to know if we're right for each other.' She has an engagement ring, but she's still not sure of Bob." Does anyone know if she really has Mr. Right? #2293

Finding a boyfriend

Finding a boyfriend is a great concern for many females. As teenagers, girls feel considerable pressure to get a boyfriend. Some girls always have a date, while others never have one. With a boyfriend one is usually assured of a date. Although it often seems that only the popular girls in high school have a boyfriend, girls who go through high school without one often think there is something wrong with them. The time of the high school prom can be very upsetting for many girls. There are always people who go around asking everyone, "Are you going to the prom?" If the girl replies in the negative, she is often asked, "Well, why not?" This kind of question can almost drive a girl over the edge. It is really difficult for many girls to admit, "Because no one asked me." Quite often the girl will say something like "I don't have a dress," or "There is really no one I want to go with." The fact a girl is young and pretty can also lead people to assume she has a boyfriend. This is true for my friend Gail. She works as a waitress and people often make remarks such as "What are you doing working on a Friday night? You should be out with your boyfriend." When Gail tells them she doesn't have one, they say something like "Well, why not? You should have a boyfriend." Comments such as these often increase a girl's anxiety over getting one.

As a result, many girls go to considerable effort to get a boyfriend. Often they try to become more attractive to males. They will get new hairstyles, go on diets, exercise, tan, and wear makeup. In addition, many use a variety of other methods to try to help things along.

If a girl has a particular guy in mind, she will often go places where the guy hangs out. Rachel had had her eye on Mike for quite a while.

Efforts to obtain sex

She met him in one of her classes, but never got an opportunity to get to know him better. She figured out what time he was usually in the student lounge and thereafter would make sure she arrived a short time after him. Rachel would sit beside Mike in the lounge and start a conversation. After they got to know each other Mike asked her out. In another instance, Lori had liked Wayne for about four months. She would sometimes go to nightclubs in the hope she would run into him there. However, she didn't know which club he went to or what night he usually went out. One day she ran into him and they stopped to talk. During their conversation she found out he usually went to the Tradewinds on Tuesday night. Once Lori knew this you could be sure she planned to go to the Tradewinds every Tuesday. Subsequently she often saw him there, and they would talk and dance together. Some girls who like a certain guy will become interested in his activities. Thus girls who like a hockey player will often go watch him play. They may never have gone to a hockey game before in their lives. You would not believe how many girls get dressed up to go to hockey games. Instead of putting on the usual attire for a cold rink, they wear dress pants, pantyhose, and high-heeled shoes. They must be trying to catch someone's attention. Some girls who are interested in a guy on a sports team will frequent the bar where members of the team usually go to drink.

Many girls depend on their friends to help them get a boyfriend. Doreen had her eye on Ralph, who was in her university biology class. Doreen thought he was really cute but didn't know how to meet him. The weeks passed and Doreen was too shy to sit beside him and initiate a conversation. Jill, Doreen's friend, kept trying to think of a way that Doreen could meet Ralph. Jill found out that Cynthia, another friend of hers, knew Ralph. Jill explained the situation to Cynthia and Cynthia knew the perfect opportunity for Doreen and Ralph to meet. Cynthia and Ralph belonged to the same youth group. The youth group had a party coming up and each member was allowed to bring along a couple of friends. Cynthia invited Doreen and Jill to the party and during the party introduced them to Ralph. Doreen and Ralph exchanged only a few words, but it was a start. To Doreen's surprise, Ralph, who normally sat on the opposite side of the classroom, sat right behind her during the next biology class. They started talking before class, and this continued for weeks. One day in class Ralph's friend asked Doreen if she was going home for the long weekend. Doreen replied loudly enough for Ralph to hear, "I'm staying in Friday night and going home Saturday afternoon." She hoped Ralph would get the hint. When she left class she

Finding a boyfriend

walked slowly enough for Ralph to catch up. He did and asked her if she had plans for Friday night. Doreen said she didn't and Ralph asked if she would like to go to a show. Of course she said yes. Doreen and Ralph have been going out for about a month now. Without friends she might never have met him. Sometimes a girl's best friend has a boyfriend, and the two of them will help her find someone. Carol and Tina are best friends, and Tina has a boyfriend. Tina and her boyfriend, Bill, decided to try to get Carol matched up with one of Bill's friends. Carol and Bill's friend didn't know each other, but Bill and Tina felt they would get along great. Tina asked Carol if she was interested, and when Carol agreed, Bill asked his friend to invite her out. About a week later his friend called Carol, everything went well, and now they go out regularly.

Some girls will not wait for a guy to ask them out, but will take the initiative themselves. They figure the only way to get a guy is to let him know they are interested. In many situations this works. My brother's girlfriend, Pauline, used this approach to meet my brother. Pauline had heard a lot about my brother, Terry, but she had never met him. One night she saw Terry at a nightclub and decided to ask him to dance. He accepted her invitation and after the dance they sat down to talk. At the end of the night Terry asked Pauline if she would like to go out the next week. On their first date they went to a movie and then out to eat. Terry is very shy, and when he dropped Pauline off he didn't have much to say. Pauline, on the other hand, is not the least bit shy and was not going to let Terry get away without making another date. She piped up and said, "So, when are we going out again?" That was about two years ago, and now the two are engaged. Pauline says that if she hadn't made the first move, they probably never would have met. She says girls just can't sit around and wait for the guys to come to them. After hearing this advice, I passed it on to my friend Corinna. Corinna had liked Martin for about a year, but they had never gone out. She only ran into him occasionally, but after talking to me she decided the next time she saw him at a nightclub she would ask him to dance. Finally one night she saw him at the Tradewinds. Corinna was shy and found it very hard to ask him. However, she managed to do so by the middle of the evening. To her surprise it worked, and by the end of the night Martin had asked her over to his apartment the next week to watch a movie. Also, from time to time there are special events when girls are expected to make the date and ask a guy out. One such occasion is the coed dance at the university. Lori frequently encountered Wayne at the Tradewinds on Tuesdays (see above), and they would often talk and dance together.

However, even though she had the impression he liked her, Wayne did not ask her out. As the time of the annual coed dance approached, Lori realized this was her chance. She was a touch leery, because she had never asked a guy out before. But she finally worked up enough nerve, and Wayne said yes. After the coed they started going out on a regular basis.

Some girls adopt the opposite approach and pretend they are not interested in the particular male. Heather and Garth had been really good friends for three years. However, Heather wanted to be more than friends, but didn't know how to get Garth interested in a serious relationship. One night while they were having a serious talk, Heather let it all out and told Garth how she really felt about him. Garth was taken by surprise. He had an idea Heather liked him as more than just a friend, but he didn't expect her to tell him so. However, Garth wanted his freedom, and told Heather he really liked her but wasn't sure if he was ready for a serious commitment. At the end of their talk, they both decided to have their relationship remain as it was before. Subsequently, however, Garth didn't visit Heather as much as he had before. Heather got pretty mad and figured she would try to forget about him. She decided not to visit Garth anymore and that she would turn her attention to Neil, one of Garth's friends, who had shown some interest in her. She began to visit Neil more often and one evening while she was there, Garth came over to see Neil too. Heather made every effort to ignore Garth, and directed all her attention to Neil. This was enough to make Garth start thinking he might lose Heather. A week later Garth came to see Heather, they went out to dinner and had a long talk, and Garth indicated he was interested in more than just friendship. In order for Garth to realize this, Heather had to ignore him and act interested in Neil.

In their efforts to get a boyfriend, some girls will go out with a guy before they know much about him. This may work out well, but sometimes the outcome can be quite upsetting. My sister is twenty-five and still single and wants a boyfriend very much. She feels she is getting old and doesn't like the idea of remaining single for the rest of her life. One night her roommate had a party, and as usually happens there were some people present they didn't know. During the party my sister met Ian, who seemed like a very nice guy, and they talked for about an hour. Ian asked my sister to go out the next week, and she accepted. My sister thought she had finally found the right man and was on cloud nine. Everything was perfect. Ian was pleasant to talk with and smart, handsome, and rich. His home was in Nova Scotia and he was working on the Island for three months. Ian and my sister went out a few times, and then all of a sudden she quit hearing from him. She asked one of Ian's friends where he was and the friend said he didn't like to see my sister hurt so he would let her in on the secret. Ian was married and his wife was in Nova Scotia. Naturally my sister was very upset. She was just thankful the relationship hadn't become too serious. She says the next time a guy asks her out she'll make sure she knows more about him.

Getting a boyfriend is a serious concern for most girls without one. Many girls go to considerable effort to obtain one, even to the point of taking the initiative, which most females find very difficult to do. "I haven't been involved with anyone for over a year. I've tried to meet someone through friends and work, but things just never worked out. I've gone out to clubs and even took a vacation to Florida hoping to meet someone, but still no luck. I go out of my way to look nice and be friendly, but so do all the other girls out there. Most of my co-workers are married or involved and this just makes me feel more desperate to find someone. I've tried just about everything to find the right person, but I'm not ready to give up yet. These clothes and trips are bound to pay off someday." "One twenty-year-old girl has tried different ways to find a suitable companion, but without result. She finally became so desperate she answered a newspaper ad from a gentleman seeking correspondence and friendship. She met him but was disappointed once again. She seems to think it's the end of the world because she hasn't found a boyfriend." Some girls feel that getting a boyfriend is so important that they would even be willing to move off the Island to do so. A friend of mine, Joan, says it is just too hard to meet guys here. Joan makes it quite clear that if she is still single by the age of twenty-four, she is going to leave Prince Edward Island and go somewhere where it's easier to get one. Unless a girl succeeds in getting a boyfriend, she has little hope of eventually getting married. #2294

The male attitude

The male attitude is frequently discussed by females, but rarely by males. In fact, once females get started on this topic, they can go on forever. Anyone who has ever been involved with a male will have encountered the attitude. It is the enemy of every female. For no apparent reason a male will do something completely out of character and give no explanation for it. This attitude appears at an early age and continues well into the forties and the midlife crisis. Little boys on a playground will suddenly stop playing with little girls, who were good enough before, but now are icky. As males get older the attitude gets worse. Female experiences with the attitude are very similar. Basically, boy meets girl, they fall in love, boy suddenly changes, girl gets dumped, and girl chalks it up to the male attitude. Often the male states he doesn't want a big commitment, or that he's not ready for marriage. Then he adds that he is being pushed too far and needs to be independent to experience other things and other people. One male reported, "We were too serious and we were fighting some. We would have ended up married or hating each other, and I didn't want either." Or else the male suddenly feels that one girl is not enough, no matter how wonderfully she treats him. Instead, the more girls he has, the merrier he is. Another problem is male bonding, which males call "time with the boys." These are dreaded words in the ears of females. Time with the boys consists of drinking, acting like idiots, picking up women, and losing all self-respect. One guy I know told his girlfriend he wanted to break up because it wasn't fair that his friends could go out and pick up girls all the time, but he couldn't. In other words, he felt left out. It's hard to believe that he let his need to be part of the gang ruin a good relationship. We don't understand why guys would prefer other guys instead of their girlfriends. Do they feel they need to be with guys in order to be themselves? Whatever the reason, the outcome is always the same. The male decides to sever all ties with the girl so he can do his own thing. So another breakup occurs for no apparent reason. A certain amount of attitude can be tolerated, but some guys just go right off the deep end in wanting to be independent. Do the males want to prove they don't need anyone? Do they want to hurt the girls before the girls hurt them? Are they trying to prove something to their friends? We're not asking that males be perfect, just a little easier to understand. Many girls think the male attitude is the easiest scapegoat, because men are impossible to figure out. Others conclude, "All guys are the same; insensitive jerks," or "All males are sluts." I've decided there is no way to explain the male attitude. Even the men I talk to can't explain it. Men will probably never change, and neither will women. All we can do is keep getting back up and hope we won't be knocked down again. #2295

True love

Many females and males want a relationship based on true love. "I want so desperately to find true love in order to love and be loved." "I want to love someone and to be loved unconditionally. I want to be able to share everything with my partner." "There is nothing better than true love." People believe true love would provide for all of their emotional needs. "My true love would be my best friend and my lover combined." "A true love would be like a mother, father, brother, sister, lover, and best friend all rolled into one." "It would be everything I need." "The person would be someone I could live with forever."

People have various beliefs about the nature of true love, which they sometimes refer to as "love" or "real love." People believe that true love involves total commitment to the other person. "True love is a decision. I choose to love without conditions and to commit myself to a person." "Love is a commitment that requires deep and intense caring, responsibility, and fidelity from both parties. Barbara and I share such a commitment. I trust her with my life and know she loves me with all her heart. She is the true love I am destined to spend the rest of my life with. I am not the least bit afraid of the idea she is the last girl I will ever be with. In fact, I am quite ecstatic about it." True love requires sharing. "If you have true love you want to share." "You share everything; sorrow, happiness, achievements." Both parties should be willing to make sacrifices for each other. "It is putting the other person first." "It's wanting and really trying to make the other person happy." It means being willing to compromise with the other person. "It involves a lot of give and take." Both parties also need to be able to communicate with each other and talk honestly about what is important to them, as well as about their feelings, problems, and fears. Each needs to understand what the other person says and does, and to be supportive. "I would be happy having someone who really understands me and who I can really understand as well. I want someone I can be happy with." "I want to be listened to, not ignored. I want to have a secure relationship with someone I can really talk to. Someone who is my mate and my best friend all at the same time." Each person also needs to accept the other. "You need to understand each other's imperfections and excuse the mistakes each person makes." "Real love is caring for someone despite their inadequacies." "Knowing that someone loves you the way you are is a very comforting feeling." Each needs to treat the other with kindness and respect. "You need to be sensitive to each other's feelings and never deliberately insult the other person. I mean don't hit below the belt."

True love also provides protection and security. "It gives you security that you can't get from anything else." People want security and protection for themselves, and they also want to provide security and protection to their partner. "I believe I've found the man who was made for me, because he makes me feel safe, protected, and understood, and he loves me for who I am. This is important to me." "Real love is constant support and service to ensure the other's well-being." "You feel protective about your partner." "You can't stand if anything hurts them." "You don't want to take any chances of something happening to the other person, because it would be a devastating loss. You would lose the very person who provides you with your love, security, and happiness."

People say that when you are truly in love you know it. "It's hard to express in words. But you know by the way two people approach each other, talk, and look at each other." "It's in the air when you are together." "It's in your heart. You just know it; you realize it." "I definitely believe in true love. I couldn't possibly think of anyone but Tommy. It's true love for me." "My girlfriend is my true love, even though that sounds corny. She is stuck on my brain with superglue. She is kind, warm, loving, ready to do anything for anybody, and the most beautiful girl on the face of the planet! That's why I'm so crazy about her. She wants to get married as much as I do and we plan to as soon as I finish university. Right now I am trying to get a temporary job so I can buy her an engagement ring. If any relationship is based on true love, it is ours." "I've seen lots of relationships where either one or both of the individuals are not in love. Those are the ones that suck. If you are in love with your partner, then it just seems so right. Everything goes along great. You are happy all of the time and nothing goes wrong. It's almost like you are in heaven. But watch out if it ends. That's when the fireworks start."

When you have true love, the other person takes a major position in your life. "Dave and I are in love and the love grows stronger every day. When I look at other guys I don't see in them what I see in Dave. Dave is my whole world. When I'm with him I feel so special." People who experience true love feel a unity with their partner. "You feel a part of the other person." "In some ways, it's like you are one person." "You want to be together forever." "If she left me or died, part of me would die too." True love is fulfilling. It provides completeness. "You feel content. You're not searching for anything, so you are much more relaxed." "I can be myself around him." "You feel happy, totally happy. It's like nothing else." Each feels they can fully trust the other. "Love is built on friendship and trust and without these elements a relationship will not work." "It's complete trust. You never have to doubt your partner." True love also provides great depth of feeling. "The emotions you feel are deeper than in any other kind of relationship. You love the person so much that they can make you feel happier and sadder than anyone else can." Each wants to spend a great deal of time with the other person and be together as much as possible. "Most people in love want to see each other every day, or else they feel something is missing in their lives. Then when they get together they want to show some affection for each other." "I love seeing my wife after we have been apart for most of the day. As long as she is nearby I'm really happy. When she goes somewhere I often want to go with her." "I feel the need to be with my girlfriend constantly. When we are together it doesn't matter what we do or where we are. All that matters is we are together." "You cherish being with each other so much that everything else becomes secondary." "I'm just happy to be with him. Even when we're having a rough time, it's still good. I can't explain it."

True love is considered different from other types of love. "Everyone experiences various kinds of love during their lifetimes. But no love is more intense and consuming than the love you feel for your true love." True love is not the same as infatuation or longing for a person. "People are infatuated with someone who is unattainable or unsuitable. But those who find true love are looking for someone suitable and compatible. Infatuation is based on single characteristics, such as appearance. Love, however, grows out of knowledge of many characteristics of the person. When you are infatuated you usually ignore problems. But those who are in love try to work out their problems in ways which are mutually acceptable." "Infatuation lasts for a brief period. When you are infatuated you are unable to see any undesirable qualities in the other person." "When there is true love, there is no way you can forget or replace the other person like you can with infatuation." True love is also different from falling in love and love at first sight. "It is a different kind of love than the feeling you have when you first meet." "It's not as exciting as a romantic fling. But it is better in many ways." "True love is beyond romance. It can last forever." "Love at first sight is a strong physical attraction between two people. Before true love can exist one must see into the soul of a person and beyond their physical qualities. True love is a very deep bond which takes time to mature."

Finding true love can be difficult. "True love is hard to find." "True love is a dream for all of us. We may have to suffer great heartache before we eventually receive it. It is a gift more precious than gold or diamonds. It is the one thing money can't buy. It can only be achieved through respect, devotion, and time. Some individuals may never find their true love." There are those who believe that there is one true love for everyone on earth, and the problem is finding that person. "There is someone for everyone out there." "If you haven't found your soulmate yet, keep on looking. He or she is out there somewhere." "Some people have been hurt before or can not find that special person anywhere. True love is hard to find, but it is worth the effort. It gives you a companion for the rest of your life." There are also some who believe that true love occurs only once, and if a relationship does not work out then it was not actually based on true love. "True love can only happen once. The feelings in other relationships are just strong likes." "People often jump into a relationship too fast, and find out later they were not really in love." But there are others who believe you can experience true love more than once. "I was in love twice and both had equal amounts of love. Circumstances can cause you to separate, but if you are lucky you can love someone else."

It often takes time for true love to develop and for people to realize they are in love. "It takes time to feel comfortable enough with another person to share your feelings and fears." "She just grew on me. I loved her before I realized it." "One night it just dawned on me that I truly loved him and wanted to spend the rest of my life with only him." "It took me a long time to realize I was in love. I couldn't stand the jerk at first."

True love requires effort. "It's not easy; it takes work." "Love is very demanding and one has to be willing to give as well as take." "There are problems, but they can be fixed if you work at it." "I believe God gives everyone a mate. But it's up to you to want this and to make it work." True love also requires forgiveness. "You need to forgive the other person when they hurt you."

It is believed that a relationship which is not founded on love will either fail or be an empty shell. "Love is very important in a successful marriage." "When a high-school friend of mine became pregnant, her boyfriend talked about getting married and luckily she rejected the idea. A year later they broke up and weren't speaking. Their relationship didn't contain that special ingredient needed for a marriage to work; true love." "When people marry for financial security the marriage will fall apart in a short time. They soon realize something is missing. Their eyes, as well as their bodies, start to wander away from their partner. They turn to others to search for what they lack in their lives, which is true love." "In my small town many people have to settle for less than the real thing. If a girl doesn't have a boyfriend early in high school she is likely to go through her late teen years alone, because most of the eligible young men are taken. So she'd rather go out with just about anyone, and I felt this pressure. One night at a dance I got together with a guy two years older than me and I continued going with him for the next two years. During that time he cheated on me, talked about me behind my back, and lied about everything. It was the biggest mistake of my life, and one that took a long time to get over. I felt I couldn't trust another guy again. Then I met my present boyfriend, who with understanding and time has shown me what love is all about." "If people married only when they were truly in love, we wouldn't have this tragic divorce rate."

Many relationships experience difficulties. In a relationship one person may feel more love than does the other. "In most relationships there is usually one partner who loves more than the other does. This partner will give his whole being for the other. The other person may love their partner, just not to the same extent. If the relationship breaks up, it is usually the person who is most in love who gets hurt." "Allyson has been going with Joe for five years. She thinks she has found her true love and that things seem great. In fact Joe gave her a hope chest for her birthday. However, Joe is having second thoughts. He wants to see other girls and picks up girls at clubs. Nevertheless, Allyson still takes him back." When people do not act totally committed to the relationship or when difficulties are encountered people frequently wonder whether their relationship is actually based on true love. "I love my boyfriend. But I still look at other guys; everybody does. So I guess it's not true love." "I've been in love twice. But it wasn't true enough to want to marry either of them." When relationships are not working out well, when there is cheating, or when relationships break up, people may feel disillusioned about the existence of true love. "I don't believe in love. I've had a couple of relationships and they have gone bad. All men are after one thing, which is sex. Love is just a quick rush to the genitals. I don't plan to get together with another guy, and I don't want to get married and have children." "To some, true love is everything, and to others it is a fake." Some people feel so hurt by a breakup that they do not want to take the risk of being hurt again. "Love can bring much happiness, but it can also bring heartache. One of the partners may fall out of love or destroy the trust between the two. Many people never recover from such a heartbreak and never find true love again. Because they are afraid they'll be hurt again, some people never let their emotions show, while others never let themselves love as strongly as they did before." "I thought Ted and I could be together forever, until he broke the trust between us. I was devastated. I cried myself to sleep for months afterwards. If it weren't for my friends, I don't know what I would have done. Although I will always love Ted, I have found someone else whom I care a great deal for, and he is helping me cure the wounds. But in this relationship I will try not to make the same mistake as before. I'll hold part of me back so I won't get hurt again."

People often believe they can recognize the presence or absence of true love in other people's relationships. "One couple I know have been married over fifty years. They act like a couple of kids; always sitting together, holding hands, and smiling at each other. They are always together, helping each other through the door, and laughing and giggling. I challenge anyone to find a cuter couple. They couldn't act this way unless their relationship was based on true love. But I know another couple that is very different. Except for the legal arrangement, their marriage lacks a firm foundation. The husband works from eight to five and then goes to the gym to work out every night. He is rarely at home and spends little time with his wife. His wife stays home and takes care of the children and the house. There must be some reason why they got married and have stayed together, I just don't see what it is. They must love each other, or they wouldn't have been together for thirty years. But who would want a marriage like this? True love does not exist in this relationship. It never has."

Individuals differ in how they define true love and in what they expect from it. For example, some define true love simply as getting married. "When a person gets married they accomplish their idea of true love." "Just to be able to walk down the aisle means that true love must have flourished before the wedding day." Some have more stringent requirements which they expect their partner to meet. "My husband provided me with the love and relationship I needed. He made me feel secure and he loved me for myself. But there are other things I need from a partner. My husband has listening and supportive skills, but I also need him to communicate both his feelings about himself and his feelings for me. He doesn't want to take the risk of learning new skills so he can learn more about himself. I no longer consider him my true love. True love is directly proportional to the degree both parties are aware of their feelings, needs, and motivations. True love is diminished to the extent that each individual chooses not to grow within the relationship and within himself or herself." #2296

104

Dating

I find first dates are very stressful experiences. Before you can make the phone call you have to get the girl's phone number. If you are brave enough, you can just start up a conversation with the girl and ask if you can call her sometime. Her response will tell you how interested she is. If she says the number is in the phone book but she's pretty busy for the next two months, then it's clear you are wasting your time. Her facial expressions and body language are also good indicators of how interested she is. Asking her directly is the riskiest method, but it does show you have confidence in yourself, which makes a good impression. A safer and more popular approach is to check the idea out first with the girl's friends or roommates. This way you don't have to experience rejection directly from the girl herself. It is important, however, to make a good impression on her friends. It is best to approach the situation casually, and not seem overanxious or pushy. The third method is simply to use the phone book to get her number. This method leaves me with the unpleasant feeling I am a stalker. It is always better if you get the number from the girl or one of her friends, because it gives the girl some time to think about you and decide whether or not she wants to go out with you.

The phone call itself is a critical part of the date. An important factor is what your prior relationship is with the girl you are calling. If you call a girl you've never said more than a few words to and you sound like a moron on the phone, then she is obviously going to think you really are a moron. On the other hand, if you have known the girl for a long time and make an idiot of yourself over the phone, it probably won't matter. She will already have determined what you are like and whether or not she would like to go out with you. The time you place the call is also significant. It's best to call anytime from early evening to ten o'clock at night. Calling a girl at one thirty in the morning from a bar when you are drunk is a bad idea.

I cannot call a girl for the first time unless I'm by myself in a room. It's bad enough having to worry about making a fool of myself in front of the girl, without having to worry about looking like a fool in front of other people too. I usually try to seem like I'm pretty casual about the whole thing and just spontaneously decided to give her a call. I also like to have music playing in the background. Not very loud, but loud enough so that I can hear it. It relaxes me and puts me more at ease before the phone call. I have actually started to sweat because I was so nervous about calling up a girl. When I'm nervous I have to psych myself up before I can pick up the phone. One time I debated over making the call for about an hour. Then when I called I dialed the wrong number and had to deal with an annoying old lady asking me over and over again why I was calling her and who I was looking for.

If you have really good chemistry with the girl on the phone, it makes asking her out a lot easier. There is nothing worse than those long awkward silences which result in her starting to whistle and then saying she has to go. If the conversation is going nowhere, it is best to just ask the girl for a date and then get off the phone as quickly as possible.

If the girl accepts then the preparation begins. You have to get ready for the date. The age-old objective is to try to make yourself look good without looking like you put any effort into it. You should always shower and probably shave. Personally, I hate shaving, but most girls just do not like facial hair. I once asked a girl what the big deal was whether or not the guy shaved. She compared it to a girl not shaving her legs, which I find disgusting. So I guess it's fair. I also hate to brush my hair, and just run my fingers through it after I get out of the shower. Most of my friends put gel in their hair, but I don't because it makes my skin feel greasy.

What to wear is also a tough decision. It is best to wear something you would normally wear that makes you look really good. I know deep down it does not really matter how a person dresses, but it is one of the first things I notice about a girl. If there were two beautiful girls and one was an amazing dresser and the other wasn't, I would ask the first one out. I should add that dressing nicely does not mean dressing expensively. A lot of people wear really tacky clothes just because they are expensive.

The most important part of getting ready is your smell. Smell is one of the most important factors in attraction, although people have their own preferences as to what smells good and what doesn't. The safest bet is to just smell clean. If you are going to wear a cologne or after-shave, you want to make sure it isn't overpowering. You don't want to smell like you bathed in the stuff. It's also a good idea to have some chewing gum or breath mints with you, especially if you smoke. Nothing turns a person off more than bad breath.

The amount of preparation depends on one's personality. One friend of mine goes to great lengths. He usually washes his car inside and out, buys the girl a rose, and then spends an hour or two planning the date.

Dating

There are two possible outcomes to this. One is that the girl will be totally impressed and think you are the best guy in the world. The second possibility is that she will think you are a sappy cheeseball who hasn't been out with a girl for quite a long time. The Mr. Romance routine works for a lot of guys because they have the disposition to go with it. I myself am pretty pathetic when it comes to preparing for a date. I usually don't start thinking of what to do on the date until I'm on my way to pick her up. I'm open to anything except going to the movies, because it doesn't give you a chance to talk. I have actually done the rose thing before, and I felt like a huge dork while I was doing it. After that I decided it was not my style. You basically just have to be yourself.

There are so many little rules that apply to first dates, it's hard to know where to begin. First there is the question of who pays. It's pretty stupid to make a big deal over it. Just use your common sense and remember that nobody likes a cheapskate. There is also the question of opening and closing doors. Some guys trip over themselves trying to do this. I think you should always be polite, but the main goal of the evening is not to ensure that your date never touches a door. Also, you should make sure you have a car for the night. One girl told me she went on a date with a guy who didn't have a car and they had to walk to the movie theater. Also, when you drive up to the girl's house you should get out of the car and go to the door. Sitting in your car honking the horn makes a very bad impression. Another thing, you should never seem overanxious. A girl I know went out with a guy who laughed at everything she said. At first she thought it was pretty cool that the guy laughed at all her jokes, but he carried it too far. He laughed at everything. He also kept telling her how much he liked her and how glad he was to be going out with her. It is not a good idea to tell the girl on the first date how much you like her. It makes you look like a weirdo who might be a stalker and hard to get rid of. The biggest blunder you can make on a first date is to ask the girl if she wants to go parking, or to drive to a known make-out spot and turn off the ignition. The night is not going well when you sense fear.

The last obstacle is the good-night kiss. This depends on the couple and the chemistry between them. Some make it a rule never to kiss on a first date, while others wing it. Whatever the case, always make sure the signs are there before you make your first move. If you do kiss, do not inhale her mouth and shove your tongue down her throat. It should be just a little kiss at first and you can proceed from there. It will usually take some time to adjust to the other person's style of kissing anyway, so don't rush into it. Reading your date's body language is very important. If she gets out of the car as soon as you pull into the driveway, then she obviously doesn't want you to kiss her. If she stays in the car to finish a conversation, but keeps one hand on the door handle the whole time, do not try to kiss her! If she invites you inside, it is usually a positive sign, but not a definite one. Always read her body language. Where does she sit in the room? If she sits beside you on the couch, then you usually can kiss her. This raises another issue. How far should you go on the first date? I don't think it is wise to let your level of physical intimacy exceed your level of conversational intimacy.

The next question is what do you do after the first date? How long do you wait until you call her again? How do you act the next time you see her? What do you tell your friends? All of these issues are sources of stress. When do you call again? It is usually best not to call the very next day, because you'll look too eager and too desperate. If the date went great you might call the next evening just to say hello, and you might tell her where you'll be with your friends, in case she is out with her friends too. It isn't wise to wait for her to call you. A friend of mine actually waited by the phone for two days for a girl to call. He even carried a cordless phone around with him while he was cutting the grass. It was pretty funny and we teased him terribly. The next time you see the girl you should act pretty casual. Running down the street screaming for her to wait up makes you look like a fanatic. If you see her in a bar, go over and say hello, but not right away. Make sure she sees you there first, but don't be obvious about this. If you are loaded when you see her, try to avoid saying too much. Nine times out of ten you'll make an ass out of yourself and regret it later. What do you tell your friends? It depends on what kind of friends you have. You don't want the things that your date told you in confidence to get back to her through other people. Her friends are important too. If you are going to start seeing her, you almost have to make friends with her friends. If her friends don't like you they will almost surely convince her not to like you too. Dating is usually not as difficult as it sounds. Most of the dos and don'ts are simply common sense, and therefore not hard to remember. #2297

People date for various reasons. "Everyone else is dating. You're left out if you don't." "People will think something is wrong with you if you aren't going on dates." "You need someone special." "It's the only way to get a relationship started." "I'd never go out with someone I couldn't see myself married to." "Dating is the best way to get to have sex with girls." Whatever the reason, the first date is the crucial one, because it determines whether you'll have subsequent dates, or whether you'll never see each other socially again.

First dates involve many different feelings. They are almost always exciting and often romantic. People have numerous hopes and expectations, and a first date may end in success or failure. Nevertheless, it is the first step in determining whether two people can communicate and work together, share experiences, and make each other happy. It may even lead to a permanent bond which lasts the rest of one's life. "The first date is the crucial one. It determines whether there is sexual attraction between you." "All people want is to find love. Half of the meaning of life, and maybe all of it, is to find your other half, or soul mate. For every person in the world, there is someone out there who completes them. It all starts with a first date, which is why I value them highly." "First dates can be the beginning of a wonderful relationship or a hellish evening you'll never forget. First dates make big impressions on people. There is only one way for you to find out if someone is right for you or not. You can't send someone else for you or depend on hearsay. Everyone has different tastes in people, and personal experience is the only way to know for sure. You have to take the chance."

The male is expected to ask the female out on the first date. "If I am interested in someone, then I will ask them out. We guys have to do that sort of thing, that is if we ever want to have a date. Even though I have been turned down by several girls, I still find the courage to ask girls out. Because, you know, I don't want to spend the rest of my life alone." "If he wants to go out with me he has to ask me. There's no way I would ever ask a guy out." At the same time many guys would like to have the girl take the initiative. "I wish girls would ask us out. It would sure take a lot of stress out of the whole thing. I mean, then you'd at least know she was interested." Most girls agree that the guy should initiate things, and many people think it looks bad for a girl to ask a guy out. "It would be really hard for me to ask a guy out. Even if I knew he was interested, I'd rather give him signals that I was interested, and let him do the asking. I'm really old-fashioned that way." "If a young lady asks the boy out, it means she is fast and cheap." "If I ask him out, he'll think I'm some kind of slut." Nevertheless, some girls say they are willing to take the initiative. "If I'm attracted to him, sure, I'll ask him out. Why not?" "We are not living in the 1950s. There's nothing wrong with a girl asking a guy out." "If I liked a guy and wanted to date him,

I would most certainly ask him out. People are equal, and I wouldn't regret it. It's not as if society would turn against me if he turned me down." "When I ask a guy out I do so indirectly. I get one of my friends to let him know I'm interested."

There are many indications whether you are likely to get a positive or a negative response if you ask someone out. "If the girl avoids making eye contact with you, isn't interested in your conversation, tries to blend into the crowd when you enter the room, insults you, or pokes fun at you in front of her friends, then don't bother asking her out. But if she smiles at you, joins in your conversation, asks you questions, laughs at your attempts to be funny, or jokes around in a suggestive way, then consider asking her out."

Most males find it difficult to ask a girl out on a first date. "For me the hardest thing about a date is asking someone out. Even if one of her friends says she'll say yes, I am still not sure that she will. I always have to get my courage up to ask." "The easiest way to ask a girl out is to phone her. That way if she rejects you she doesn't see your reaction. It takes a lot more guts to ask her face to face." "I get quite anxious before I phone a girl for a date. But I know I'll be pissed off with myself if I don't go ahead. Also, if I don't call her now, I know I'll continue to go through this torment until I finally do make the call, so I might as well get it over with. Finally, I take a deep breath and make the call. If she accepts the date I feel great and start to imagine how nice it would be if she were my girlfriend. If she turns me down I feel hurt and demoralized. But I usually get over it after a good night's sleep." "I don't know whether girls understand just how much apprehension a guy goes through when he ponders whether or not to ask a girl out. I try to live by a simple principle, which is 'go for it.' I mean, a guy should not be afraid just to ask a girl out. If she says no, at least you tried. You really have nothing to lose and everything to gain." "I met this girl at the student union. I knew who she was, but I didn't know her well. We talked for about two hours, and I think it went very well. I got good vibes from her. I decided to wait two days. You have to play it cool and make sure you wait at least two days before you call. If you call the next day you seem too anxious or desperate. I was very nervous before I called because I was worried she might refuse. It's not just the fear of being rejected. It's also the fear of everybody else finding out I was rejected." Some males are unable to muster the courage to ask a girl out. "I have never had a date because I can't find someone I like enough to ask out. I hope that when I find her she likes me. I don't want to get turned down." "If a girl asked me out and I knew who she was and she seemed cool, I'd say yes. God knows I'd better say yes, because I don't have the nerve to do it myself." "A girl asked me out, and it took a lot of pressure off me because I wanted to go out with her, but didn't have the courage to ask. I didn't mind paying for the date, because she did the hard part and asked me out. We went to the movies and dinner and enjoyed both, and we are still going out today." "I wanted to ask this one girl out whose name was Terri. Terri was one of the prettiest girls I ever laid eyes on. I was just in love with her but I couldn't bring myself to ask her out because I was so afraid she would say no. I figured I never had a chance with her so I kept making excuses to myself. I kept saying, 'I'll wait until then.' I never asked Terri out and I was always mad at myself because she is so friendly to me. However, she has a boyfriend, who I think is a jerk, and I have a girlfriend. I know Terri deserves a nicer guy like me. I kept using excuses and I never asked her out. But I still think she is the prettiest girl I ever laid eyes on."

People experience anxieties and other feelings before going on a first date. They may feel apprehensive, uncertain, scared, pleased, or excited. They aren't sure what to expect, if they will make a good or bad impression, or if there will be subsequent dates with this person. "The two elements of a first date are nervousness and a lot of bravery." "A first date is one of the most nerve-wracking experiences you can have. You worry about everything; what to do, what to say, and when to say it." "After she accepted, I had a week before the date. I thought about where I would take her, the way I would make my first impression on her, how I would act, and whether I would know what to do in certain situations." "I'm kind of excited because I like the girl a lot. But I'm also nervous because I don't want to screw up and ruin my chances with the girl." "When a guy I like asks me out my initial reactions are happiness and self-praise. But from that time on until we actually go out is nerve wracking. It is like a roller-coaster ride of emotional ups and downs. I am overcome by many things. I don't have a clue what I'll say to the guy. I worry I'll sound stupid or be so nervous I'll blush when I talk to him. Also, a major problem is what I am going to wear. I just hope the date isn't a total washout." "When a man goes out on a first date with a woman his heart is racing. Believe me, I know from experience. Many guys I've talked to have many mixed feelings about the first date. They really want to get to know the girl. But they'd probably rather just get to know her in some other way. Perhaps by meeting her somewhere with more people around, rather than all alone." "For a male, a first date is more of a necessity than something he really wants to do. It's not that they don't like the girl or want to be seen with her. Men would rather not have that whole awkward first date. There are many horror stories about first dates and men always worry that the worst may happen. What if I trip and fall and embarrass myself? What if I spill my drink on the girl? What if I don't have enough money in my wallet to pay for things? The whole date consists of trying to prevent such things from happening." "I was at a really nice restaurant once and the guy I was with dropped a glass of red wine in my lap. I wasn't too happy, but he looked like he was going to die right there on the spot. That's got to be one of the worst things, when you really make a fool of yourself." "I know I've gone on a lot of dates, but this one is really making me nervous, man. I have liked her for a long time now, and I finally got the nerve to ask her out. And can you believe it, she said yes! With other girls I was just goofing around. But this time I want to make something happen and be with her for a long time. I hope I don't screw it up." "First dates? I hate them. The whole time you have knots in your stomach because you don't know how to act. You're so nervous trying to please the other person that you don't have any fun. It's a hassle." "My stress begins about noon on the day of the date. It can be so great that I think of phoning her and cancelling with the excuse that I have had a sudden attack of the flu. This is simply fear and has to be overcome. I have to remember what I went through to get this far." "The worst date is the first date. I would just as soon skip right to the second one." Some people deal with their anxieties by taking precautions. "I've never had a bad date, because I won't go out with strangers. For my own peace of mind, I insist that a friendship be established first. The guys I go out with are usually very nice. The worst that has happened is that the movie was terrible." "I always drive when I date a new guy. That way I have a certain amount of control. One wrong move and he can find himself flying through the windshield. I don't put up with shit like that. If I'm in danger, it's going to be him in the hospital." Most people say they have more good dates than bad ones, and that they start to lose their nervousness once they arrive at their destination.

An important factor is how well one already knows the person one is going on a date with. There is less apprehension when one is familiar with the other person. There is less concern about trying to make a good impression, hide flaws, or be something one is not. "I'm not as nervous when I already know who they are. There are fewer surprises." "I had known this girl forever. When we went on our date, I felt very comfortable with her. We already knew a lot about each other." "In the twelfth grade I began to date Troy, a guy I'd known since we played together in kindergarten. Over the years we'd always talked about the people we had crushes on and wanted to date. At first it felt weird to go on a date together. But I was more at ease with Troy than with anyone else I've been on a first date with. There was no conflict over which restaurant to go to, because we already have the same favorite one, and we always had something to talk about." At the other extreme are blind dates which may be arranged by a friend or relative, a dating service, or in response to an ad in a newspaper. "By far blind dates produce the most stress and tension. I really admire people who go on blind dates because you have no idea what to expect. You don't know what this person will look like, act like, and even be like. I think people who go on blind dates are adventure seekers." "When you know what your date looks like beforehand, there is some physical attraction. But you don't even have that advantage on a blind date." Many people feel their blind dates are awful. "My friend told me the guy was perfect for me, and we arranged to meet at this little place downtown where all my friends go. First of all, he was bald. Bald! Now, there's nothing wrong with that, it just wasn't what I was expecting. After that initial shock, I thought, well, OK, my friend's an idiot, but the guy might be nice. Wrong! He had no personality. He is one of those guys who is really snotty with the wait-ress, who is a friend of mine. After he complained to her about every-thing from the cutlery to the service, I knew the whole thing was going nowhere. I said, 'Oh my, I forgot I promised Mom I'd help her with some stuff tonight. Bye!' and I left. I went home, called my friend and gave her shit, and never had a blind date again." "My blind date was 'the date from hell.' The guy was really sleazy and tried to take advantage of me. I immediately ended the date and called the night quits." "A friend arranged a date for me and her female friend, but neglected to tell the girl that I'm gay. During the date I became uncomfortable with her attentions, and I finally told her, much to her embarrassment. Both of us were very irritated with the friend who had set us up." But there are blind dates that are exceptions. "My blind date met me at the door loaded down with a dozen red roses. Then he tucked me gently into his sixty-thousand-dollar Corvette. He was easygoing and intelligent, and swept me off my feet. We had a fabulous dinner of lobster flambé washed down by the most expensive bottle of wine on the menu. Then we had a deep discussion into our souls during a moonlit drive through the park. We stopped only for a hand-held stroll along the waterfront lit by the full moon. He had me home before midnight and held my hand as he walked me to the door. He gave me the tiniest of tender kisses and promised to call me the next day. I was amazed at all the thoughtful and loving ways in which he pampered me. For me, it was love at first sight."

People differ in the amount of experience they have had in going on dates. Some frequently go on dates, but others are having their first date ever. "I was so excited to be going on my first date. I wanted everything to be perfect. I bought new clothes, and I wore makeup for the first time. The guy was older than I was and I wanted him to think I was older too, so I tried to look and act older. At the end of the date though, he tried to go too far and I ended up crying and running to my older sister like the little girl I was." Still others are beginning to date again after ending a long-term relationship. "I forgot what it was like to date. The only person I'd gone out with before was John, and we were together for five years. If I needed a date for anything, John was there. But now if I need a date, I have to hint around to someone I want to go out with and hope he asks me out. If he does I have to hope we'll have a good time together. It's not a sure thing like it used to be. I just get so scared. But I don't want to open up to guys anymore either." "After you separate or get a divorce and start to date again you have to learn a set of skills all over again. When you're together in a marriage you develop good skills at getting along together with one person, and you forget what it was like to be dating. You are used to being completely involved with your spouse. But when you start dating again you have to learn to deal with lots of very different individuals. Things seldom work out well, and you have to deal with a great deal of rejection and disappointment. You have to learn to keep your emotions in check and only get superficially involved. No matter how much you like another person, they aren't likely to feel the same way about you. A good rule to try to follow is 'Don't get more emotionally involved than the other person is with you.'" Another difficulty is the tendency to compare the person you are just beginning to date with your previous partner. "She was fun and everything, and she is real cute. But, man, she just isn't like Sandra." Single parents carry a lot of baggage which can complicate the dating process. "It doesn't matter who I go out with, on that first date I always get twenty questions from my mother about the guy. She thinks every new guy I go out with might be Mr. Right for me and my son. But that's not what I'm looking for right now. I had a child when I was young, and I want to be able to date like my friends do. I know it isn't totally possible, but I want to try. Another problem I have is my son's father. Every time I go out with a guy he sticks his nose into my life. At no other time does he do this. Just if he hears that I have a date with someone new."

People want to make a good impression on their date. "The first impression is important, because people find it hard to change their first impressions." "You only have one chance to make a good impression." "This is your first date together. The guy should try and impress you, and you try and impress him. You can slack off later. If you don't put a little bit of effort into it, why bother going out? May as well stay home and watch TV, and get to know each other that way." "The more you like the guy, the more it affects the way you act, because you want to make a good impression." "If the girl is really special you are very careful not to offend her. But if the date is just putting in time, then you don't worry too much about what happens." "Nervousness is the most common feeling in dating. The female is anxious and doesn't know what to wear. The male is anxious and doesn't know what to do to impress the girl. The male acts cool even though he is sweating. The female smiles several times hoping he is not looking at the big zit on her forehead. They both feel one way, but act another in order to make a good impression." "Women I talk to are more worried about what to wear than they are about the date itself. They fret over different outfits from the time they are asked out until their date arrives. If the woman considers the date an important one she may buy a brand new outfit for the occasion." Most women devote considerable effort to looking attractive. "I think all week about what I am going to wear and how I'll present myself." "I started to get ready that morning when I got up, and my date wasn't even picking me up until eight thirty at night." "It took me hours to figure out what to wear. It was a total waste of time because all I ended up wearing was a sweater and jeans." "When I go on a date I want to look dressed up but not too dressy. I usually wear a sweater and a nice pair of jeans or dress pants. By looking a bit more dressed up than usual, I am ready for wherever my date takes me. A friend of mine wore a skirt because she wanted to look attractive for her date. However, when her date came, he told her she looked really good but was a bit overdressed for Burger King. She quickly told him she would change. She felt awkward for the rest of the night and embarrassed for thinking they would be going to dinner at a fancy restaurant." "A girl doesn't want to look trampy. Often she chooses a blouse which shows she has a figure, but isn't too revealing. She also wears a pair of dress pants or a skirt, but nothing too fancy." "Brenda, our roommate, was asked out and spent an entire week talking about what she was going to wear and what they would do on their first date. Finally the night came, and none too soon, because we were getting a little sick and tired of listening to her worries about her date. Getting dressed seemed to be the hardest decision of her life, and she tried on eight different outfits. Then she waited upstairs for her date to arrive so she could make a grand entrance by walking down the stairs to greet him." "When I go out with a guy the first time, I want to knock his socks off. I don't want him to be able to take his eyes off me. If it means taking a little extra time to get ready, so be it." Some are less willing to go to extremes. "If he liked me before he asked me out, why should I change myself and the way I look to impress him, just because we're going on a date?" Males are also concerned about their appearance. "If I really like a girl, I'll spend more time trying to look good so she'll be impressed. She's looking good for me and I'm looking good for her. It's a respect thing." "Guys put added care into choosing their clothes for the evening, and they spend an extra long time in front of the mirror." "I start with a good, long, hot shower with loud music to rid my mind of nervousness. Then I have a very close shave and try to avoid cutting my face. I use a lot of deodorant and I use a mild cologne with a nice fresh scent that isn't overpowering. Then I study myself in the mirror to make sure everything is in order." People frequently concern themselves with more than personal appearance. "Often a girl will straighten her house or apartment so it is neat and tidy. She may do something out of the ordinary, such as put fresh flowers on the table or a plate of cookies in the kitchen. A guy is likely to wash and polish his car and to clear all the junk and mess out of the inside." People try to emphasize their best qualities and hide their bad ones. "People show their best behavior in the hope their date will think they are special." "The last thing Mom told me before I left with Donnie was not to slouch, and to smile a lot because I have beautiful teeth." "I wanted to impress the girl and look smart, and when we first talked I told her I was interested in politics, but I'm not really. Then when we went out she wanted to know my views on Island political problems. I just ended up looking really stupid." Many people are very nervous on the date itself. "A first date is full of sweaty palms, stuttered and misused words, and many other things that embarrass you." "When I was in the tenth grade a guy asked me out on my first date, and I was so nervous I went cold and didn't know what to do. I even forgot how to dance." Some people are more nervous than others on a date. "I drove my two young male cousins on their first date. They and their dates were all thirteen years old. The boys had saved their allowances for two weeks so they could treat the girls. Eddie was doing

116

his best to hide how nervous he was as the time approached to go get the girls. He was pacing around, brushing his hair, eating candy, and applying his third layer of cologne. Ray, on the other hand, was cool as a cucumber. This unnerved Eddie even more. The fact he was nervous and Ray wasn't was killing him. Ray is just your typical smooth-talking, easygoing kid. Eddie is louder and tries too hard to seize your attention. When we arrived at the house to pick up Eddie's date, I could actually see the sweat running down the side of his face. He made it to the door and only tripped once, falling into the stairs and hitting his head on a light. When we got to the movie theater, I sat a couple of rows behind them. Before the movie was over Ray was holding his date's hand and had nonchalantly placed his arm around her. The only thing Eddie spilled on his date's lap was his popcorn. She caught his coke before it splashed over her. Everything went smoothly after that. Ray kissed his date on the cheek, and Eddie shook his date's hand. Afterwards Eddie openly admitted he was scared out of his wits. On Ray's second date he gave the girl a little picnic on the beach. Eddie and his date watched professional wrestling. Both of the boys had a good time and were looking for ways to wow the women."

Another source of discomfort, anxiety, and embarrassment occurs in regard to family and friends. Family usually want to know everything about your date, even before you know these things yourself. If the girl is still living at home, it is often necessary for her date to meet her parents and be vetted by them. Often both the guy and the girl hope this can be avoided. Ideally parents and siblings are absent when he picks her up. "I hope my parents will be out on the night of the date. But if I'm unfortunate, they're home, and I have to introduce my date to them so they won't worry about me. Both my date and I feel we are on display. Once my father has finished asking him questions, we can leave." "When I drove up to her house to pick her up for the movie, she came right out the door. That was a bonus. I'm glad I didn't have to go to her door, because her dad might have answered." "After my date picked me up, he stopped at his grandmother's house to drop something off. He took me in to meet his grandmother. She looked me up and down and said I wasn't as pretty as his last girlfriend. When we left the house my date apologized profusely and promised I'd never have to meet another member of his family. Needless to say, that was our last date." "My little brother is too young to get a driver's license. He got me to drive him because he felt our parents would embarrass him in front of his date." Friends can also be a problem. "When a girl is asked out on a date, the first people she tells are her friends. They ask where she is going on the date and then they gossip about the guy. They usually give advice about what to wear and what to say, and after the date is over they want all the details." "It always seems that within a couple of days after you've set up a date everyone else finds out about it. They start to talk and the gossip begins. Often the comments are not very flattering, such as 'Doesn't she already have a boyfriend?' 'He just uses girls,' and 'She's been around the block.'" "Often a guy keeps quiet about his date until it is over. He may tell his friends about it if it went well." "One of the biggest reasons why males don't like first dates is their buddies see them and try to embarrass them in front of their date." "Afterwards everyone wants to know everything about the date. They ask where you went, how you got along, and if either of you did anything stupid or embarrassing."

People frequently try to reduce their anxiety by going on their date in the company of their friends. "We went to a community dance. What happened was our friends set us up. It took the pressure off me to ask her out." "We all went to a pizza parlor with a couple of our friends. It was nice that way because there was less tension for both of us." "A double date with another couple is ideal. It's a lot of fun and there is less chance of awkward silences." "When I was younger I would bring friends along on my dates to talk to the girl because I was too nervous to talk to her myself." "Some people prefer to go on a date with friends. If they are your date's friends you get to know what their friends are like, and you get to see how your date acts with them. However, you can feel like an outsider and be overwhelmed by everyone. Often they tell you facts and stories about your date. These may be embarrassing and can be attempts to get a rise out of your date. When you are with mutual friends the evening may not feel like an actual date, but more like a party." However many people prefer to avoid other people when they go on a date. "I wanted to get to know him as he really was. So I didn't want his friends around. I was afraid he would act differently with his friends there." "I would never want to go on a date in the company of other people. Initially, I don't want to know how my date relates to other people. I want to find out how she relates to me, and how compatible we are. When other people are around there is little opportunity to really talk to your date about the things that matter. A date is a lot like a job interview in which you try to determine how well you'll work together."

There are all the problems about where you go on your date. Common destinations are a coffee shop, a movie, dinner, a dance, a concert, a park, miniature golf, bowling, and the beach. "If you asked a girl what her ideal date would be she is likely to say a picnic or a walk on the beach. This is because girls are romantic. They watch soap operas on TV and they read romance novels in which women are swept off their feet and treated royally. A guy, on the other hand, is likely to say his ideal date would be going to see a sporting event and getting dinner at a fast-food restaurant, because these are the things he likes. He feels most comfortable at a game, and it doesn't matter at a fast-food restaurant if he accidentally does something wrong." "I try to take my date somewhere special, like to a good restaurant or a performance on stage. Maybe I want to make a good impression. Or maybe I feel she's more likely to accept the date." Probably the most common destinations are the movies and dinner. "If you decide to go to the movies, there are lots of factors to consider. First, you have to decide which movie you are going to see. Often it is difficult to decide, because neither person wants to make a decision. You ask her which one she'd like to see. She says, 'It doesn't matter to me. You pick.' And you say, 'No, no. You decide. Really, I don't care.' Then there are the questions as to who pays. Most guys expect to pay, but they don't want to upset the girl if she wants to express her independence and pay for herself. But some-one has to pay for the tickets and any popcorn and drinks you get be-fore the movie. Then there is the question of where each of you likes to sit when you see a movie. Some people like to sit up close, while others like to sit in the middle or further back. After you are seated you have to worry about not saying stupid things or asking idiotic questions. Once the movie begins you can start to relax." "Going to a movie is a customary first date. It's ideal if you don't know each other well. You can simply enjoy being in each other's company and neither of you has to speak because the movie is the focal point. Afterwards you can al-ways discuss the movie if you haven't got anything better to talk about. Another common first date is dinner. Dinner is bolder and more daring than a movie. This is the ultimate one-on-one dating experience and you have to be ready to converse. During dinner there is so much time to be filled up with conversation, and the two of you come away knowing quite a lot more about each other. You usually discover whether or not you've connected and whether you plan on seeing each other again." "Women I've talked to don't like going to dinner on their first date, because they are scared the man might find something wrong with the way they eat. Also many are worried they might get some food between their teeth, on their face, or on their clothes, where it can produce a noticeable stain."

Sometimes one person is more concerned with the activity than with getting to know the other person. "I took this girl bowling. Once there, she wouldn't stop talking. The worst thing was she was a lousy bowler." "When I was thirteen I took a girl to the movie and she wouldn't stop talking. So I turned to her and said, 'Will you shut up?' She didn't say another word. I walked her home and she went in the house and that was it. Not another word."

As people talk they reveal details about their lives and learn more about the other person. They volunteer information and ask questions about family, childhood, places they have lived, work, and school. "Women spend the evening trying to find out what they don't already know about the man." "We talked so much that people in the movie theater told us to be quiet. We got to know each other very well." Talking also enables you to find out if you have common experiences and interests, and if you like and dislike the same things. "As soon as we found out we both loved scuba diving, we talked about diving for most of the evening." "My date and I got along so well we decided not to go to the movies. Instead we went back to his house to get better acquainted." "I got to know my date better during dinner and decided he wasn't for me. I could tell he felt the same way, so we decided to end the date." When you have little in common and lack common interests you can have difficulty conversing. Long, uncomfortable pauses can help one or both of you decide you aren't meant for each other. "We didn't talk at all. It was really uncomfortable. I think I watched the whole movie and that doesn't happen very often." "Once I realized that Donnie was only interested in sports and all he wanted to talk about was football, I knew I probably wasn't going to see him again." "I had the worst date last week. The girl was so boring. We had many awkward silences, and I felt very uncomfortable with her. After the first hour I just wanted to end that date right there. She's the biggest dodo I ever met. The whole time I was wondering where her brain was. I kept trying to find something we had in common to talk about, but I came up with nothing. I would ask a question like 'How is school going?' Then she would say, 'Good,' and that was it. She gave a short answer to every question I asked. She'll be lucky if I even talk to her again." But perceptions can change. "We had an awful dinner, but really hit it off after a funny movie. We realized we were just nervous during dinner, and later relaxed during the movie." Sometimes the problem is a very different outlook on life. "You find out right away whether guys are sweet or just plain jerks." "I took this girl to the movies when I was in high school. I was into comedy, but she was more into romance. I knew right off there would be trouble in deciding on a movie. Well, I let her pick the movie, but I was not happy at all. I really wanted the date to be over." "I thought she was pleasant and attractive. But she said nothing really mattered to her and she wasn't serious about anything. Now, I care a lot about a number of things, so that was it for me. I knew I didn't want to waste any time on her." "I asked her out because she was quite attractive, easygoing, and nice. But I learned her family was originally from France, she had spoken French at home, and she was studying French in graduate school. I decided she had taken the easy way out, and didn't like challenges. What could be easier than specializing in your own native language? I didn't ask her out again." Dates are learning experiences. "I think you learn much more about your own likes and dislikes through your interaction with the other person. There are things you originally thought were important that aren't that important to you when you get along well with the other person. And there are things that you really react to when you encounter them in your date. You never realized before they were so important to you."

People may decide beforehand or during the date to adopt a specific orientation toward their date. "Often one person tries to make their date feel as special as possible and that he or she is the only person in the world." "If I'm on a date and I know it is right, I make the guy feel really good about himself." "Someone twisted my arm to go on a date with a girl I found unattractive. I went ahead and was pleasant and considerate, but there was no way I was going to encourage her to think I was interested in her."

Who pays has become a big issue, and has introduced additional uncertainty and anxiety. "I didn't know how much money to bring because I didn't know if he was going to pay or not." Traditionally the man is expected to pay for everything. "If I ask a girl out, then I am expected to pay. The girl may offer just to be nice, but it is my responsibility." "I always pay when I take a girl out. Maybe I'm just an old-fashioned kind of guy. How would a girl feel if I asked her out and left her with the bill? It wouldn't be right for the girl to have to pay." "I always offer to pay. I don't want to hear later how cheap I am." Some women today still expect the male to pay. "If a guy asks me out, I expect him to pay my way. It's not as if I asked him out. I guess things would be different if I had a steady boyfriend. But when I date casually I never offer to pay. Besides, the guy usually grabs the bill first anyway." "It wouldn't be a date if the guy didn't pay for everything. He should treat the lady to whatever she wants if he wants to impress her. I mean should-n't the guy always have to pay? It's common courtesy. He won't get a second chance if he doesn't!" However, other women today want to pay for themselves. "I work at a restaurant and bar, and I see many couples each week who fight and bicker over who pays the bill. Often both of them grab for it. It is a very unpleasant and unfortunate way to end an otherwise enjoyable evening." "I've learned to be extremely flexible. I'm out for a good time, not a good fight over who is going to pay. If a guy seems gung-ho about paying, I'm certainly not going to make a big deal out of it. But I'll make sure that everything works out fairly in the end. If he pays for movie tickets, I'll go ahead and buy popcorn or the first round of drinks at the bar afterwards. I don't think it is necessary to di-vide the bill down to the exact penny. I feel a lot more at ease when he lets me pay half of the time without making a big deal out of it. This way we can both have a good time and nobody is stuck with the entire bill." Some men are pleased with this arrangement. "I don't mind pay-ing, but I really do appreciate it when she offers to help out. Don't get me wrong; I certainly don't want to sound cheap or anything. I just think it's only fair if we both share the cost of an evening out." Many women want to maintain their independence and avoid any sense that they are obligated to the male and owe him something, such as sex. "I feel much better if I split the costs on dates. That way I don't feel like I owe him anything." "I never let a guy pay for me when he takes me out. I never want to feel as if I owe him anything. Like when we go to a nice restaurant and the guy spends a lot of money, I feel as if he expects something at the end of the evening. As long as I pay my own way, I never have to worry about feeling guilty or anything." "I never let a guy buy me a drink at a bar. It's my number-one rule about going out. If a guy does buy me a drink, I always feel kind of obligated to spend time with him, or at least stand and talk with him for a while. My solution is to pay my own way all the time. That way there are no strings attached." "Older women may still expect the man to pay for everything. But women in their teens and twenties usually expect to pay their half, and some get quite upset if you try to pay for them." "On a first date I'd prefer if he took me somewhere where there are no questions about money and who should pay. The ideal first date is taking a drive out to the beach and just talking. Maybe if you don't feel comfortable enough with him for that, then just going to his place to rent a movie." Many males recognize the need to adapt to their date's perspective. "Who pays can be very awkward. Each is hesitant to say, 'I'll pay for it,' or 'Let's split the check,' and neither wants to feel cheap or to act controlling." "I always ask my date if she minds if I pay. I don't want her to think that I'm anti-equality or something." "I always offer to pay on the first date. It seems to make a good impression on most girls. If she doesn't want me to, that's fine. I'm not going to make a scene insisting on it." Many people feel that a male should pay the expenses on the first date and the girl should help with expenses if the couple continues to date. "When a guy asks me out for the first time, I will often offer to pay. But it usually ends up that he pays since he was the one to ask me out. Then once I've gone out with the same guy for a number of times, I make it known that it is only fair for me to pay half the time. He shouldn't have to pay for everything, especially if we are seeing each other on a regular basis."

People have different kinds of dates. Some dates are rather ordinary. "I had just finished playing a basketball game, and started talking to one of my female friends. We didn't want to go home yet, so we went out to the movies." "I met a girl and couldn't get her out of my mind. So I called her up and asked if she would like to go for a cup of coffee. She said she was swamped with work, but it would be nice to go out for a while. We went to a coffee shop and talked about everything under the sun. I learned a lot about her and we discovered we had a lot in common. We both hated school, liked to sail, and loved to watch *Survivors* on TV. We only spent two and a half hours together, but I feel we really connected. We decided we'll get together again when we aren't as busy."

There are dates which are quite memorable. "One day out of the blue a friend of mine asked me out on a date. It was a beautiful summer day and he picked me up in his new convertible. We headed for the beach and had a picnic. He had thought of everything. He had a blanket and sunscreen. In his cooler he had fresh fruit and a bottle of my favorite white wine. We sat and laughed all afternoon and had a swim. Afterwards we looked at the shops near the beach. We got some ice-cream cones and drove to town for supper in an excellent restaurant. We talked late into the night and drove home with the top down. It was the best day ever and we have been together ever since." "I was quite excited because my date said he would pick me up at seven but wasn't going to tell me anything more because he wanted it to be a surprise. When he arrived he told me to put on a warm coat. When we stepped outside there was a horse and sleigh and a man at the reins waiting to take us on a tour out of town. I was really impressed and it was a lot of fun. We traveled around for an hour and a half, drank hot chocolate, and watched the stars. We hoped to see a falling star but didn't have any luck. My date explained that our driver was his uncle and he had promised him a couple of Saturdays of barn work in exchange for the ride. No one had ever been so creative in planning a date for me before, and I was really flattered. After the sleigh ride we went to my date's house, ordered a huge pizza, and talked for the rest of the evening. When he drove me home I leaned over and gave him a kiss. He said he was caught off guard but really liked it. I told him to give me a call and we have been happily dating since then." "I was only sixteen when I met Terry at a party. We started to talk and hit it off from the start. Later that evening he asked if I would consider going on a date with him. I accepted and wanted to scream. I couldn't get over that an older guy was interested in me, a little sixteen-year-old. The next morning I called my girlfriends and they were excited but warned me to be careful, because you know what most males are like, all they want is sex with a virgin. But I didn't listen to them and went on the date anyway. When he picked me up he met my parents and they loved him. We went to a nice quiet restaurant and were the only ones there. The lights were dim and there was soft music playing in the background. The waiter gave me a single rose and said it was from a secret admirer. I was ecstatic. Terry asked for a bottle of their best wine. I didn't have the heart to tell him I wasn't old enough to drink, but it was good. When supper came it was my favorite dish. I asked him how he had known and he said that someone as pretty as me deserved the best. It was the sweetest thing anyone had ever said to me. After dinner we went for a moonlit walk along the beach. It was so perfect. We could hear the ocean waves hitting the rocks. Everything was going great until he mentioned he wanted to go to his favorite spot. All I could remember was what my girlfriends had warned me, that all he wanted was sex with a virgin, and I started to panic. We drove down a dirt road to this bluff over the water. He had a blanket, candles, and more roses. We sat on the blanket and talked for hours. To my surprise he never tried a thing with me. I was in love. That was three years ago and we are still together. Terry is still very romantic and considers every time we go out like a first date."

There are also dates which go overboard, or are too extreme. "I went on a very romantic date. The guy picked me up early in the day and drove me to a secluded beach for a picnic. He produced a checkered picnic blanket, and had a complete lunch for us, including potato salad, wine, and brownies. By the end of the date he was almost proposing marriage, and when I arrived home I found roses and a poem on wooing women. He was more serious than I had expected. I found the date uncomfortable, because I didn't know him very well. It would have been wonderful if this were the tenth date with a guy I was really interested in. But in this case, I turned down a second date."

A few dates are unusually bad. "My date took everything so seriously. Everything had to be perfect, from the clothes he wore to the place we ate. When we arrived at the movie he planned for us to see, they were already sold out. He flipped out and took me home. He said if the date couldn't be perfect, there was no use in continuing. Needless to say, that was our first and last date." "A friend arranged a date for me. I wasn't worried because I was assured the guy was really nice and when he called me up he was very polite. But when he showed up, I was surprised. My friend hadn't warned me that he had green hair and a nose ring. When we arrived at the movies and went to get our tickets, he turned to me and said, 'How about you pay for the movie and I'll get the treats?' I'd just assumed he would pay. When I arrived at the concession stand, he had bought a large buttered popcorn, a box of chocolate-covered peanuts, a large soft drink, and a small soft drink. He handed me the small soft drink, I thanked him, and we went to sit down. During the movie he was nice enough to share his popcorn, but he didn't offer me a single chocolate-covered peanut. When he ran out of napkins he wiped his buttery fingers on his pants. Later he leaned closer and started to put his hand on my knee, but I crossed my legs to move them further away, and he must have caught the hint. When the movie was almost over he let out a huge belch, but was nice enough to excuse himself with a smirk on his face. Before we left he picked up the popcorn bag he had placed on the floor, which contained a few leftover kernels, and said, 'Late night snack.' During the drive home I kept thinking how to get from the car to the house without inviting him in. We were talking about how expensive it is to live on your own and he said he saved money on toothpaste by brushing his teeth no more than three times a week. I decided I didn't need an excuse not to invite him in. As soon as the car came to a halt, I said, 'Thanks,' and ran inside the house." "I was asked out by Gene, a member of a varsity team. He said he would pick me up around eight. He arrived at nine thirty with the smell of liquor on his breath. I was very offended, but decided not to say anything. Gene said he didn't have anything planned and asked if there was anything in particular I wanted to do. When I said it didn't matter, he said some of his friends were hanging out at an apartment and would I like to stop by? I agreed because I thought it would be fun to meet some new people and get to see who Gene's friends were. When we arrived, the music was so loud I could feel it pounding beneath my feet before we entered the apartment. As we entered the heat and the smell of booze hit me in the face. The living room was full of guys, who began to cheer when we walked in. I felt out of place, but didn't want to be rude, so I put on a forced smile. Gene took the last seat available, so I sat on the floor next to him. One of Gene's friends passed him a beer and offered me one, but I declined because I don't like beer. When I said I didn't want a beer, the guys all booed. I blushed, but wouldn't change my mind. As the night progressed, the topics of conversation ranged from sports to who had the biggest breasts on a popular TV program. The guys, including Gene, made no attempt to include me in their conversations. But I didn't mind, because I was just chalking up the reasons why I would never go out with Gene again. After I had spent four and a half hours with Gene and his friends, I decided it was time I went home. I had had my worst date ever, and did not enjoy any of Gene's friends. In fact I found the sight of them repulsive. I stood up and told Gene I was ready to go home. Gene looked at me and said he wasn't ready yet and wanted another beer first. I told him I was leaving and he could stay if he wanted. He made no effort to help me find my coat and didn't offer to walk me home, which didn't surprise me. As I walked to the door, Gene yelled from the living room, 'Give me a call sometime.' I kept on walking and never looked back. When I passed Gene and his friends a couple of days later, I pretended I didn't see them. But I made sure to tell all my friends about Gene and his friends so they would think twice if they were ever asked out by one of them." (Author's note: Perhaps Gene is trying to prove to his peers that he would never let a female take control of his life and "wrap him around her little finger.") "I asked a girl out and we became rather close at her place. I knew she had recently broken up with her boyfriend, but I didn't know how recently until he walked in on us. I got dressed while he stood there yelling at me. I'm not really the violent type, so I just said, 'Get it over with. Hit me.' She was really nice. She made sure I was OK before she kicked him out. We didn't go out again."

Some first dates go well, but turn sour based on what happens subsequently. "I went out on a date and the date went fine. We arranged to get together a second time at his place to watch movies. When I got there I found he had kept everything from our first date, from my gum wrapper to the napkin I used to wipe my mouth after dinner. I freaked out and left." "One night when I was out with my friends I met a guy named Robin, and we hit it off right away. He asked me to go out on a date, and I accepted, of course. Later that week I received a dozen roses from Robin with a card which won my heart. The card said he couldn't wait to see me and our date would be a night I'd never forget. The night of the date he picked me up in his new car, and we went to a fancy restaurant. Afterwards we went to a hotel where he had rented a VCR and a romantic movie. A week later I was at a bar and saw Robin there with his friends. I went over to talk to him and he yelled out that I was an easy lay and all the guys had to do was wine and dine me and I'd put out. I was so embarrassed and humiliated I left the bar and never went back."

As the date nears an end and often beforehand, each person considers whether or not they are likely to get together again. "Most people know by the end of the first date if they want to pursue the relationship." "After the first date you know how comfortable you are with the person." "You want your first date to be fun and memorable, not dull and boring." "I like it if we have a really good time. It gives me the initiative to ask her out again." "I like to be treated well on a date. A kind word and a simple compliment can do wonders to stroke the ego." "I like for him to make me feel wanted and special, and to pay me nice little compliments." "I like to be treated with utmost respect when I'm on a date. No one deserves to be treated like dirt." If first impressions were good and both feel they "connected," then a second date is likely. "My date took me to the beach. He had brought a blanket and a stereo and gave me a long-stem rose. I was so surprised, I cried. No one had ever done anything like that for me before. We talked and danced all night. It was the best date I ever had. When he took me home, he asked for a second date. I said yes, and he kissed me good night." "It was really good; I had a lot of fun with him. He's a real sweetie! I know we are going to go out again. He was much cooler than I expected. We have a lot in common, and he seemed interested in all of my hobbies. I love to go hiking and he told me some time in the future we could go on a hiking trip to Cape Breton. I'm really glad we got together." However, if one or both did not feel the date went well, then chances are slim that there will be a second date. One may try to clear up the uncertainty by trying to find out how the other feels about getting together again. "So what do we do next?" "Can I call you tomorrow?" Or one may state how one feels about the situation. "Well at least we gave it a try." "When the date goes well then I tell him that I hope to see him again and I tell him to call me or something. If the date was awful then I won't say anything at all and I just ignore him." "I don't usually expect a lot from the first date. I would never rush or force my date into a second date, even if the first date went really well and we both had a great time. If my date is interested in continuing the relationship then it would be greatly appreciated if she gave me a good, strong sign. It could be a kiss at the end of the date, or something more subtle like brushing against each other as we walk. I find these signs very important."

At the end of the date there are various anxieties regarding a goodnight kiss. "One thing that is always on my mind is going in for the kiss at the end of the night. A lot of guys are too shy because they don't want to look too forward. I agonize about this all night. If the date is going well I can usually get a kiss." A kiss is usually initiated by the male. Some males consider a kiss on the first date to be too pushy, and do not want to alienate the woman. Other guys feel a kiss after a successful date is a must. "The date isn't complete unless I show her my affection." "If you still feel as positive about the girl after your date as you did before it, then you are forced to make a tough decision. Do you kiss her good night, or would a kiss be inappropriate? If you decide you want to kiss her, you have to be very cautious. Once again, you have to put your neck on the line. You have to try to read her thoughts, because she may not have had the great time that you did. If she doesn't look at you, has little to say, and has her hand on the door handle as she waits for a break in the conversation so she can dart out of the car, then you'd better rethink your plans. But if she makes no attempt to leave, maybe she wants to kiss too. It is a tough call, so be very cautious." "Women are very nervous whether the man is going to kiss them or not. We send out signals when we want to be kissed, but men never pick up on them." Most guys who do kiss on the first date agree that the kiss should be on the girl's cheek as they part company. Many women feel a goodbye kiss on the cheek is a perfect ending to a first date. However, they have little control over what kind of kiss they get. "I agreed to go on a date with a guy I'd always flirted with. However, the movie was boring. Also, because you can't talk in a dark theater it was more like being with a friend than a date. Afterwards I told him I was tired and had a headache and just wanted to go home. When he dropped me off he leaned over to kiss me and covered my entire mouth with his lips and slobbered all over my face. It was the worst kiss ever. I was repulsed and pulled away, but he must have thought he did a wonderful job, because he had a big smile of satisfaction on his face. I couldn't get out of the car fast enough."

Then there are all the issues concerning physical involvement.

"When people start dating there may not be any sexual involvement, but there is an enormous amount of curiosity about each other's body." Some have no desire to get intimate on a first date. "I was working with this girl and we got along well together. I asked her if she'd like to watch some movies at my house and she said yes. I fixed dinner for us and everything was going great because we had lots in common. After dinner we watched a movie and I leaned over and tried to kiss her. She got mad, asked me to take her home, and said she never wanted to talk to me again. I gave her time to cool down and asked her out again. She turned me down and I regretted asking her out." "You really can't be too careful. With all the sexual diseases you have to take longer to get involved with a person, and even then you need proper protection." "If I slept with a guy on the first date, I would be a big slut. No way! If I like him and he likes me, there should be no problem with waiting a while. How long is up to the individuals, but I don't know anyone who would on the first date." "If you have sex with a guy on the first date, he won't stay interested in you for long." "Many guys would like to know how far they can go with their date. But they don't dare try to find out, because they are afraid the girl won't go out with them again. Also, they don't want to get a bad reputation among the other girls." Others plan to get as physical as they can. "The girls are the goalies and the guys are on a breakaway. It's the girl's job to stop us from scoring. But if she doesn't stop us, then she's not the type of girl I want to date, and I move on." Some males feel that a girl owes them sexual favors in exchange for the money they spent on the date. "If I take a girl out for dinner and then for drinks, I certainly expect more than a kiss good night."

Once the date is over there are all the reflections about what you did and didn't do, and what the other person must have thought. "Many guys and girls leave a date not knowing whether they made a good or bad impression and not knowing where they stand. They frequently worry that they gave the wrong impression." "I just hoped he still liked me after the date." "The success or failure of the date is totally in your hands. If you both enjoy the night then chances are she will want to see you again. If things don't go as well as planned, chances are you've blown it. Most dates are a one-shot deal." "I didn't really want to go out with him, I just felt bad saying no. I didn't even offer to pay for anything. I felt really bad after the night was over when I realized what a bad date I was." If the other person doesn't want to get together again, you try to determine what you did wrong. "At the end of our date I parked in her driveway. She waited in the car for a minute, and I knew she wanted me to kiss her. But I froze and didn't do anything. We never had another date. If only I had kissed her, I'm sure we would be together today." "Once the date is over you judge for yourself how the evening went. If you feel the date went smoothly, then you are usually happy and wonder why you were so uptight over the whole thing. You start to wonder if the guy will call you and want to go out with you again. If he does, then you can start worrying about the next date. If he doesn't, or if you don't want to go on another date with him, then you have to start over, meet someone else, and go on another first date." #2298

Going on a date is a wonderful way to find out what a person is like. You get to see and know the person better than you ever have before. There are many things you notice and reach conclusions about which help you decide that you do or don't want to spend any time with the person in the future. For example, is the person stupid? Is he obvious and boring? Is she exciting? Is he verbal or does he have nothing to say? Does she know enough about different topics to carry on a decent conversation? "Is it too much to ask for a guy to have an average IQ, or some intelligence? I'm not looking for an Einstein, but I don't want the mind of a five-year-old either! Of course, there's the extreme opposite, the know-it-all kind of guy who can tell you anything about nuclear war and outer space, but can barely write his name. As they say, 'There's a thin line between a genius and a fool.'" Are alcohol and drugs important to the person? Does she have hang-ups or mental problems? Does he have his own car? "It's nice to go out with a guy who has his own car. It's even better if it's a nice car, not some old beat-up jalopy." Does he have a responsible job? Is he independent? Does she have her own mind? Does he have any ambition? "I like somebody who wants to do something with their life." "I don't like a guy who sits home and does nothing all day except drink beer and watch TV." Can he support a wife and children? Is he generous? "You have your cheap kind of guy, who always runs out of money on the days you go out with him. He can play pool all day long and drink till he drops, but he can't pay your way into a show." Is he responsible? Is she reliable? Is she pleasant, or is she moody and depressed? Does she constantly complain? Does he feel down about most things? Is he rude and obnoxious? Is he confident? Is she vindictive? Do you have common interests and concerns? "Does she want to be out partying all the time, or is she comfortable staying home reading a book?" Do you agree on lots of the same things? Is the other person easy to talk to, fun to be with, and do you laugh together?

"My perfect guy has to be my best friend." Does he have a sense of humor? Does he read, dance, like sports, or like the same kind of music you do? Is he romantic? Is she open to trying new things? Can he take adversity in stride? Does she only talk about herself? Is she conceited? Is he considerate? "I like someone who opens doors for me and treats me as someone special." Is he respectful and caring? Is she a good listener? Is he understanding? Is he kind, patient, and loving, and would he make a good parent? Does she have empathy for others? Does he go to church? Is she a giver, or a taker? Can the person admit being wrong and apologize? Can he tell you what he feels? Is he faithful? Does she flirt with other guys? Does she lie? Can she accept me as I am? "Does she get grossed out if I burp or fart?" Does he have good manners? What are the person's friends like? How does he act with his friends? How does she treat other people? How does he treat animals? Is he sensitive to women's concerns and issues? Is she an ardent feminist? Is he controlling? Does she nag? Is she possessive or jealous? Is he looking for more than sex? Is he sexually aggressive? "I like to be treated with respect and romanced, not pawed over every time I go out with him." Is he violent? Has she had successful relationships before?

Then there are the qualities of the person that you ask yourself whether you can live with. Is the person attractive enough? "Looks are fairly important to me. If we're going to spend a life together, I want to wake up to a nice-looking lady and not a dog." Is the person's facial appearance and body type acceptable to you? Do you like their eyes, lips, and nose? Does she have nice breasts? Is he in shape? "I like a muscular guy, because I feel protected and like to feel the muscles." Does the person have bad health or a handicap? Is their racial and cultural group acceptable to you? Is the other person ugly or dirty? Does he smell? Is she too fat or too skinny? Does he eat like a slob? Do you like the other's smile? Are her teeth unattractive? "I hate crooked teeth." "I was flirting with this really hot guy. But when he smiled and I saw his teeth I took off." Does he care about his appearance? "Clothing is important to me. When I see a guy who is well dressed I know he takes pride in himself and looks after himself." Can you live with his tattoos? Is she taller than he is? Is he younger or much older than she is? Can you tolerate the fact she smokes? "I avoid smokers, because they smell and taste like an ashtray." Is she clean and neat enough? Does he have any mannerisms, such as a high or squeaky voice, a raucous laugh, or bad posture, that bother you? Is the person presently married?

Then there are the person's behaviors during sex, and whether they are acceptable to you. Is the person disinterested and unresponsive? Does she switch to baby talk? Does she claw your back? Is the person a screamer or a biter? Does he try to help you reach orgasm? "I like a man who can go for long periods of time." Does she dislike sex in different positions and oral sex? Are you physically compatible, or do you get sore every time you have sex?

The sooner you find out whether or not there are things that would prevent you from having a successful and comfortable relationship, the better off you are. However, it is always a disappointment if the person doesn't work out. Initially you look at the person in a very positive light and hope this is the perfect person for you. "Usually when I meet a guy I say this is the one I want to marry. Then it wears off after a couple of days." "I wanted to marry Albert for about three weeks. Then I realized what a jerk he is." "Demi was really attractive. But as she talked about all the vindictive things she was doing to her ex-husband I knew I wanted nothing to do with her." "I found out she is a real nut case. She went back and forth from hot to cold and blew everything I said way out of proportion." "She's the most outgoing person I know. She loves being around people and loves to party. She has to chat with everybody we meet. This would be great if I were the same way, but I'm not. I'm a quiet guy who likes to relax with a girl. She thinks dinner and a movie are boring and clubs are fun. It's starting to piss me off." #2299

Two big questions in dating are "When do you start to get physical?" and "How physical do you get?" Some people have clear rules on the matter. Many women feel they should wait a week or longer. "The first couple of dates should be strictly platonic. You want to spend the time getting to know the guy before any sexual activity takes place." "I would never do it with a guy on the first date. Never." Some think they shouldn't have sex before they are married. "I want to wait until my wedding night." "I'm saving myself for marriage. If a guy truly loves you, he'll wait." Some guys believe in waiting a while too. "I think it is kind of tacky to kiss a girl on the first date, unless you really hit it off. It makes it look like your only interest in her is physical. If things work out between you, you'll get physical sooner or later anyway." Other people are more flexible. Many think it depends on the people, or "whenever it feels right." "There is a time and a place." "I wouldn't mind having sex on the first date, but I wouldn't push it. I'd feel bad putting a girl in an uneasy situation." "If the timing is right and he's someone I want, then why the hell not?" "It just happens." "If there is no passion on the first date there never will be." Often when two people start dating, they find they have no real interest in the other party and they stop dating. But when the first few dates are successful they usually continue seeing each other and establish a relationship. Sex is likely to fall into place and become an integral part of the relationship.

Then there are people who see dating strictly as a means to get physical. "The guys I talk to go on a lot of dates to increase their chances of getting sex." "Not many guys would pass up the opportunity to have sex. It wouldn't matter if it were the first, second, or third date, as long as they get it." "I try to get sex as often as possible." "I try to create a good mood and humor my date. I don't try to hide the fact I'm interested in sex with her, and I'm successful about twenty-five percent of the time." "I only take a girl out on a date if I think there is a very good chance of sleeping with her. I'm not going to spend all that money on someone who is not going to put out. I especially like it when a girl shows interest in me first. That way I know I have a very good chance of sleeping with her. Girls are no different from guys; all they really want is sex too, they just can't admit it." "If I get nothing in return from my date, I have to decide if she is worth the effort to take out again." "I enjoy dating lots of girls. I think if guys want to get more sex they have to be more patient. I don't mind if I have to date a girl for a whole week before I sleep with her, so long as I do. Usually after that I don't want to date her anymore. It's time to move on to the next one. I do like to try and stay friends with them, but that doesn't always work. Either way I guess all I'm really looking for is sex with as many different girls as possible. I'm proud of what the other guys think of me. They think I'm a real stud and I enjoy the reputation. It really doesn't matter to me what the girls think."

There are many misunderstandings which occur because people have different agendas as to whether, when, and to what degree to get physical. "I don't mind being the one to initiate a conversation or even go so far as to ask a guy out, but sometimes problems arise. One guy in particular assumed because I asked him out I would sleep with him. I didn't. I only wanted a chance to know him better. And did I ever get to know him better. He took offense to this and now he won't even talk to me, not that I really want to talk to him. Why can't guys realize that girls need to get to know them better and feel more comfortable with them before we will consider sleeping with them? I will be a lot more careful about who I ask out, that's for sure. Some guys can be real assholes." "What do men want nowadays? A roll in the sheets in exchange for a coke and a movie?" "A guy I had been dating for a short time planned a special evening for us. It consisted of flowers, dinner, dancing, and finally, after I had been swept off my feet, a visit to a local hotel. I ended the so-called special date by phoning a friend to take me home." "I had known him for a little under a year. We had been friends, dating on and off during that time. One afternoon he came over to go for our usual walk and a coffee, and we had an excellent time as usual. I honestly felt that I loved this person. Later we ate supper and ended up sleeping together. The next morning I told him I loved him. His response was 'Don't be crazy.' That was our last so-called date." #2300

University

University provides you with freedom that you didn't have when you were living at home. You live in dorms and apartments where no one interferes with what you do or who you do it with. Everywhere you go you are surrounded by members of the opposite sex. There are an unlimited number of young, single people who are interested in sex and relationships. You meet new people and see others you already know in classes, the cafeteria, snack bars, study areas, the student union, student organizations, and at sporting events, dances, parties, and movies. "The easiest place to meet guys is in the university because you have things in common, such as classes, teachers, and whatever is happening." "Lots of underclassmen join the Freshman Orientation Committee to meet the incoming freshman girls." Most students meet other people through mutual friends and acquaintances. They also meet others by asking questions like "Have I met you somewhere before?" "Are you in my English (business, math, biology) class?" "Didn't I see you at the party last night?" or "Do you play basketball?" In order to meet a person in one of their courses they may ask about an assignment or what their professor said. Students also meet and hang out with those who share their interests, such as sports, a particular program of study, or a hobby (computer games, cards, chess, debating, skiing); with those in their dorm room, apartment, or dormitory; or with those with the same lifestyle, such as preppy dressers, drug users, or smokers.

Most students are surprised at the number of unattached members of the opposite sex there are to choose from. "Talk on campus is primarily concerned with members of the opposite sex." Each one mentally picks someone they would like to meet. The majority of these choices are based on appearance. When students see individuals they find attractive they ask others if they know them, what they are like, where they come from, if they are going out with someone, and what their reputation is. Guys tend to rate girls on the basis of looks, personality, reputation, and intelligence (in that order). Girls, when they see a nice-looking guy, ask around to find out if he is a good guy to be seen with. They want someone with good character traits. If he has a bad reputation, most girls soon forget him. After meeting and finding out what the person is like, looks don't matter half as much. Getting to know a person determines whether the interest remains. Often the one you want to meet does not come up to expectations and the attraction disappears. People frequently attend campus activities, particularly parties and dances which are regularly held at the student union building. Often people attend hoping to see the person they have had their eye on during the week. When alcohol is available the atmosphere is more informal and people find it easier to meet and talk to strangers. In addition, people ask others for dates and go on dates arranged by their friends. Many girls feel they have accomplished a goal when they get a date.

Most females are interested in finding the man they want to marry. "Girls are brought up to consider marriage their most important decision and goal." "University is the place where you learn and grow, and where most of us expect to meet the love of our life. On any given night of the week and usually at any hour you can find some girl in the dorm deep in conversation about her love life." "Guys rarely arrange a date with a girl that they know is more intelligent than they are. Therefore girls will often pretend that they aren't as smart as they really are. They don't want to show up the guy and make him feel stupid, or to get a reputation for being a brain and scare off potential suitors." Most males are interested in having sexual experiences. "The whole idea of our having this toga party tonight is sex. I mean why else bother with the togas, right? All of the guys here tonight are out for one thing." Many guys make drinking and sex a top priority. "Going on a date with a university guy is kind of an adventure, because most of them only have one thing on their mind." "A lot of guys turn into complete assholes when they get to university. Some of them were the sweetest guys in high school, but once they get here they transform into sex maniacs." "Guys are always hoping to get sex. In male residences you commonly hear, 'Got any rubbers? I've got a hot one tonight.'" There are female students who are just as interested in having sexual experiences. "Eventually I'd like to settle down with a guy, but I'm having too much fun now." "One woman I know has a reputation for frequent sexual encounters. She says she likes the company of males, enjoys sex, doesn't mind saying so, and isn't bothered that the other girls see her as inferior and avoid her. I often see her at a male dorm flirting with many guys." "I like sex, but because I am a woman I can't openly invite sexual encounters. Otherwise the girls in my dorm would look down on me and show they didn't approve of me. I tell the other girls I've had fewer sexual encounters than I've actually had in order to be accepted by them."

There is not much that happens that doesn't become widely known. "If a guy and girl are seen talking together at a social function for more than fifteen minutes, others assume they are involved and probably going together." Many students quickly get reputations based on their sexual activities. When a guy is mentioned girls may say, "He's pretty fast," "He's European (Russian hands and Roman fingers)," "He likes to have a different girl every night," "That guy is nothing but a skin hound," "He's out for tail tonight," or "He's all talk and no action." Guys may say, "She's Slut of the Year," or "She's green. I stopped the car in the park and dropped my pants and she refused to do anything." "Rumor can be an excellent source of information. Two of my friends are dormitory dons. They give me the scoop on who is putting out and who is vulnerable to a few romantic words. Therefore I spend a lot of time at the dorm. But I don't even tell my best friend what I'm doing. When you have a good thing going, who needs competition? The only guys who brag about the previous night are those who only get it once a month or practically never." People befriend and avoid others based on their reputations. "If a girl gets a reputation for being easy, her circle of friends seems to diminish one by one." "If a guy is known to be really fresh or to brag about his conquests, many girls won't talk to him." Girls are often warned to stay away from certain guys. People usually avoid those with a bad reputation so they won't be hurt, or so they won't be tarred with the same reputation. "Ironically, guys with bad reputations have a lot of dates, mainly because they have a really polished line and go out with those who don't know much about them. Girls with bad reputations get a lot of dates with guys who want to get in their pants." #2301

Female status

I am fascinated by the means female university students use to try to win status. My observations are based on female students living in a university dorm. About half the girls in the dorm come from farms or small towns; a third from larger towns on Prince Edward Island, such as Summerside, Montague, and Souris; and the remainder from off the Island. Students from Charlottetown, where the university is located, normally live at home with their parents. I find there are four primary means which the girls use to attempt to gain status. These are having a beautiful appearance, attracting members of the opposite sex, being a "fun" person, and achieving academic and career success. I will use actual cases to illustrate each of the four types.

Elaine is "a beautiful person." She is nineteen years old and a mediocre business major. Her academic standing doesn't worry her much, because as she says, "I was never the brains of the family, and my parents never expected me to be." Instead, her time is dedicated to her appearance. She often takes over an hour to get ready for such mundane events as walking from the dorm to the cafeteria for brunch. She showers, shampoos her hair, and then dries it in the first fifteen minutes. The next forty-five minutes are spent curling her hair, giving herself a full facial, applying complete makeup, carefully choosing a color coordinated outfit, filing and polishing her nails, picking out jewelry and suitable accessories, and then making sure everything is properly in place. One might become irritated watching her go through her routine, if she did not carry it out so solemnly, and if the result did not seem so vital to her. I have seen her deliberate for ten minutes over which pair of shoes to wear. As she says, "It's important to look your best. I'd die if anyone ever saw me with a brown suit and gray shoes! People look up to you when you're well dressed and attractive. They think, 'She's in control of herself. She knows what she wants.' And I like that. I mean, I probably wouldn't go to all this trouble if it didn't matter."

Elaine is also preoccupied with her weight. She eats very little bread and no desserts, and would rather die than touch pizza. She weighs herself religiously every morning, and if the scales tip upward, she lives on salads for two or three days. She confides that the one thing she fears most is getting "fat and ugly." Elaine admires her mother more than anyone else. "Mom always manages to look so perfect, no matter what happens. I mean, nothing ever upsets the woman. She's great!" Elaine's mother buys her own clothes in Halifax and Montreal and has her hair done every other week. She is also slim and wears a considerable amount of makeup. While Elaine may be a little extreme, her behavior is by no means unusual. Many of the other girls do seem to admire her, and go to her for advice on hair, clothes, and makeup. However, I have often seen her sitting alone in the library or cafeteria, appearing a little aloof. This impression is a result of her air of perfection and her shyness.

Success in attracting and holding a member of the opposite sex is another source of status. Girls who attract many suitors, often as a result of attention to their physical appearance, are envied by the other girls. This is also true of those who can maintain a long-term relationship with a desirable, eligible man. Mary is one of the latter. Quiet and serious at twenty, Mary comes from a well-to-do family in one of the larger Island towns. People invariably express disbelief and respect when they learn that she has been going out with Barry, a good-looking, athletic engineering student, for five years. Mary doesn't mention this fact to others herself. But she admits she doesn't mind when others bring it up. "It sort of makes me proud, I guess. Especially when someone I don't like is told. I'm too smug, I know. I just feel like saying, 'Yeah, I can hold a man, and you can't.' Of course, don't get me wrong, I'm really fond of Barry. Being with him really makes me happy, and we have a lot of fun. But why shouldn't I enjoy the prestige of it too?"

Mary is not alone in her attitude. Time and again I have heard girls talking about their boyfriends to less fortunate young women, and there is often a slightly patronizing tone to their statements, though it usually seems unconscious. Girls with especially nice, good-looking, or generous boyfriends are generally more respected. But even someone dating an insignificant male gains status in the eyes of someone who isn't dating at all. Mary states, "I don't even want to think about being without Barry. I've been going out with him since I was fifteen. Every girl is looking for a man. The successful ones, the girls who find one, are the elite. When you lose that position, there's just one thing to do, and that's to start looking again."

A third source of winning status is the ability to be the life of the party. Those who shine at social functions, chat brilliantly, and infect others with their enthusiasm are highly respected and sought after as friends. Many others imitate them, with varying degrees of success. However, only a few seem to be able to be genuinely outgoing and get along with everyone without appearing to overdo it. I find the floor supervisors of the dormitories are usually picked at least partly on the basis of having these qualities. These girls are almost always in the midst of a laughing group and are seldom alone. They are the first to be nominated for house elections and social committees. Their status relative to the other girls is definitely high.

Donna entered the university at seventeen from the western part of the Island. At that time she felt the best way to be popular was to go to all the parties, get as drunk as possible, and be as much "fun" as she could. "I was always trying to impress people, and worrying about what they thought about me. Boy, was I young! I think a lot of freshettes believe that's the trick, especially if they live in residence, where there's always a party somewhere. For most of them, that's their first shot at that kind of life. And there's always a crowd who really believe you *can* get status that way. So they chug beer and make idiots of themselves every second night, skip classes and don't turn in assignments, and think they're doing great."

A fourth means of seeking status is employed by Sharon, who is eighteen. She is a biology major headed for medical school, and spends most of her time studying and in afternoon labs. Sharon believes it is your achievements that win you status. "Your accomplishments, the awards you win, the success you have in reaching your career goals; this is what makes the community look up to you and admire you. They've got to give you credit if you do what you say you're going to do. Positive actions are what give you status."

Earning high grades, getting awards at sports or for community service, finding a good summer job or part-time job, and working responsibly toward a worthy career are all actions in this direction. But do such things actually provide one with status in the eyes of one's peers? On the basis of my observations in the dormitory, I would say less than one might think. Perhaps such accomplishments are secretly admired. However, they are usually ignored when the group hierarchy is decided. Perhaps the rewards remain largely personal. Most of the girls I've talked to agree that studying hard for an exam and doing well provides a personal victory, but not an increase in status. As Sharon says, "I continue working hard for my own satisfaction. I don't care if I don't get any recognition from the other girls, because I know what I'm doing will result in success in the future. Who knows where these girls will be then?"

There is an additional factor involved which applies to all of the above forms of seeking status. People who pursue any one of the four types are likely to be far more successful in winning positive recognition from others if they have a friendly, open, sympathetic personality. Niceness gives them added rank. In contrast, girls who are snobbish, brusque, selfish, or cruel may find themselves friendless, even if they sport dazzling clothes, are never seen without a male on their arm, party riotously, or win all kinds of honors. The fact they are disagreeable can undermine their efforts at success. [#2302]

The gym

Many people go to the gym with the hope of finding their future partner. On a university campus the gym is one of the primary social centers. Others are the student center, the library, and the cafeteria. When you enter the local campus gym you see people talking to others and hanging around the front desk, sitting on the desk, and standing by the water fountain. Many are dressed in street clothes rather than sports gear. When you ask what they are doing, they tell you, "I'm just waiting to meet someone here," "I just finished working out," "I'm on my way to a workout," "Well, I was going to work out, but now I don't feel like it," and "I just thought I'd pop in here on my way to the car, to see who's around." It is hard to get in or out of the gym without talking to a friend for at least ten to fifteen minutes. You chat and gossip about everything going on around campus. There are rumors and news about who's dating whom and who just broke up.

Many women who go to the gym say that they go to see and meet males. "We just go to see all the hunks." "I don't do very much; I never even sweat. I just come here with my friend to talk to the guys." "I like to find my males at the gym. You can see what they've got when they're wearing spandex." "I mean, what could be better than checking out half-naked sweaty guys. When a guy frequents the gym, at least you know he's concerned with his physique." Many women wear makeup at the gym and do not work out enough to break into a sweat. What they wear is an important consideration. "If I feel good that day I'll wear a tight Lycra outfit. That's usually what I wear, and I have about five outfits. But if I feel a little fat then I just wear Lycra shorts and a regular T-shirt, because I'm just not confident in the whole Lycra outfit. I don't want anyone to think I'm fat." Women often spend a great deal of time in the locker room making sure they look good before they enter the exercise areas and then they look in the mirrors and adjust their outfits several times during their workouts. Men notice the women and what they are wearing. "I enjoy seeing the girls at the gym and talking to them. Girls that are in shape wear skimpy clothing. One girl works out at the same time I do. After about five minutes on the step machine her breasts become quite noticeable through her tank top, which is spandex. Most of the guys working out in the room comment on this. She makes many trips to the water fountain, which gets her even more attention." Women frequently use eye contact to get men to notice them. A woman may try several times to establish eye contact with a man during a workout so she can start a conversation with him either that day or in the future. When two female friends work out together they may spend some time laughing at the television program while on the step machine. This attracts attention and lets the men know they have a sense of humor. One male commented, "It's kind of funny to watch actually. They aren't wearing radios, so they can't hear the TV set, but they laugh anyway." Men also try to impress women in the weight room. Men will flex their muscles in front of the mirrors and look to see who is watching. When there are several attractive women in the room, the extra-heavy weights come out and the grunting and groaning begins. "I've done that a few times. All I end up doing is hurting myself. I pump higher weights than normal, hurt myself, and the girl I want to notice me doesn't have any idea what I'm doing. The worst thing is your friends, who know exactly what you are doing. They tease you about it for days." Most of the time it is women who make the initial contact and carry on a conversation with the male. The majority of women say the best place to meet guys in the gym is in the weight room, which is a predominantly male area. For example, they may ask a guy to spot for them when they lift weights. This lets them start a conversation and introduce themselves, and then get to know him better during the next few times they see him at the gym. "It's definitely not an overnight thing. You may see him on Monday, then not again until Friday, and then again on the following Tuesday. It takes a while to get close enough for him to ask you on a date or even for you to ask him. It all takes time. Because this is a relatively small town, usually what happens with me is I see them at the gym a couple of times, talk to them, and then I see them out at the clubs and I talk to them there. That tends to speed things up." People say the worst place to try to talk to someone is on the track, because people are too busy running to talk. Some women try to do as little exercise as possible. "Sometimes I go with my friend and spend a few hours at the gym, but we never really work out. We sit in the sauna long enough to get a good sweat on so it will look like we've been working out. Then we spend the rest of the time walking around, chatting, and checking out who is there that day. We look for the least strenuous exercise we can find. We don't really want to exert ourselves, unless we are looking for help from a big strong boy."

Another common place to meet others is intramurals. Some women often go to the gym on days when intramural games are scheduled, hoping they will be asked to play on a team that doesn't have enough players. This works best if the woman is athletic, because the guys do want to win. However, sometimes they will ask a girl to play just to get to know her. "I've seen my friends ask some girl to play so they can talk to her. Usually my friends will only do this when they happen to be good at the game, so they can impress her. Sometimes a guy asks a girl to play, expecting to impress her, and she ends up being better than he is. I've seen this happen a couple of times, and it's just hilarious." "Many of the women who enjoy playing sports, like I do, don't want to intimidate the men by playing too hard. I probably play better than half the guys on the intramural teams. But if I think I'm intimidating them, I don't play as well as I can."

Many students who work out at the gym eventually end up dating someone else who works out there as well. There are a lot of phone numbers exchanged and dates arranged. "I've given out my phone number to what feels like a lot of guys at the gym. Occasionally they call and I've gone on a couple of dates, but nothing has really worked out yet. Sometimes it's discouraging, but I keep going. Obviously I don't only look for guys at the gym. I still go to the clubs every Saturday night. But at least at the gym I feel like I'm getting a good workout while I'm there. It's kind of like killing two birds with one stone." Others have succeeded in finding someone steady. "My reason for starting to go to the gym was to get in shape, and also to get to know some new guys. I thought this would be a decent way to find guys that I had something in common with, and it was. I met my current boyfriend while playing racquetball. Once I started playing regularly in the racquetball loop, I met all kinds of guys. At first Vernon was really shy about talking to me, but then I just kept making racquetball dates with him and we had a lot of fun playing. We played almost every day. One day he cancelled on me, and I thought he wasn't interested in me, or as interested as I was in him. But then the next day he was waiting for me at the gym when I showed up to see if I wanted to play. The girl who was working here said he asked her what time I usually showed up and then he waited an hour for me. I was pretty excited to hear that. Finally, after a month of just playing racquetball and getting to know each other, he asked me to go to the movies with him. I have to say I was really glad that I decided to start playing racquetball. Anyway, that was just over six months ago, and we still play racquetball almost every day." There are also some who are primarily interested in sexual contacts. "I look for girls with the tight outfits on who aren't really doing much of a workout. They just kind of stand around." "Meeting a guy at the gym is easy. Just start talking about how you don't know how to use the equipment and ask him to help you. Then introduce yourself and you're in. Time it so that you're leaving at the same time he is, or wait up at the front desk until he goes by. Complain about having to walk home or tell him you're afraid to walk home alone at night and ask if you can bum a ride home. Then you just invite him up and that's that."

Many people who go to the gym are seriously involved in exercise and sports. They often hope to find a partner who shares their interest in physical activity. "Women who are into sports are a lot of fun to date. They enjoy doing outdoor and sporty things, instead of just wanting to go for dinner and a movie." "I spend three or four hours a day in the gym. I just work out and run for two hours. Then I spend the rest of the time playing squash and hanging out and talking at the front desk. I think I'll eventually meet the right guy who loves the gym as much as I do." Varsity athletes are frequently present in the gym because they have to practice every day during the playing season and stay in shape during the off-season. It is common for varsity athletes from different teams to begin dating. Often relationships develop between members of brother-sister teams. There are a number of couples who play on the men's and women's soccer teams, or on the men's and women's basketball teams. "It's much easier dating someone who is also involved in sports, than someone who is not. Because we practice every day, it's nice to have someone who supports you, and who understands that sport is an important part of your life, because it's also important to them." "We see each other after practice, but we're both pretty tired by then and don't feel like doing much. We rent a lot of movies." There are more difficulties when someone who is not involved in athletics, such as a student employee at the gym, dates someone who is. "The only reason I got to know her is I have a job here. She came in every day for practice and we would talk for a while. It didn't last too long, because she was always at practice or with her team, and she was out of town almost every weekend." There are also many people who are seriously interested in exercise who are not interested in using the gym to find a relationship. They often come when the gym isn't as crowded, frequently wear earphones and listen to a cassette player during their workouts, and seldom talk to anyone other than the gym employees. "It's silly to come to the gym to look for a guy. It's insane. I know it happens; my friends do it. But that's not why I'm here. I come, I work out, I go home." [2303]

Community

When you want to meet people for sex and relationships there are a variety of things you can do. The best thing is to get out of the house and hang out in public areas. These include restaurants, coffee shops, bars, clubs, stores, shopping malls, libraries, museums, parks, and gyms. You can also attend concerts, dances, and festivals. Personally I find the local farmers' market a good place to go on Saturday, because people have time to kill and buy snacks and meals, and there is a crowded eating area where it is very easy to meet strangers and friends. There is also a local building for the Arts Guild, where they regularly hold concerts and dances. It is cozy and crowded and an easy place to meet and talk to people. I find that the problem with running an ad in the personal column of the newspaper is you get too many responses, and almost all of these are from people you do not find attractive. When you choose who you talk to in a public place, you can select those you find attractive. I make it a rule to get to know at least one new person a day. Meeting people and chatting them up isn't easy, but you get better at it. Even if you find you aren't interested in a person, that person may hang out with someone you are interested in. Also, when possible pursue one of your strong interests, like a hobby or sport, if this will bring you into contact with those you want to meet. Because you are enthusiastic, knowledgeable, and confident about your interest, this makes you more attractive to those you are interested in. [#2304]

When you are a single male you have to be intelligent about meeting single females. You learn quickly which strategies are more productive than others. For example, most bars in town are for the very young or for blue-collar workers. There are only a few bars for professionals. However, most of these are filled with tables and the girls sit at the tables with their girlfriends. Unfortunately, it is psychologically impossible to cross a room to a table of strangers to talk to a girl you don't know who is surrounded by a group of her girlfriends. However, there is one bar in town for professionals which gets so crowded, it is basically a stand-up bar. This makes it much easier to get close to a girl you want to meet. When girls are at the bar you simply go over and stand next to them while you order a drink. It's never easy to start a conversation, but it is easier when you are already next to a person. You spend more time with those who are responsive to your attempts to talk to them and who ask you questions about yourself, because they appear interested in you. If you learn the girl is married or has a

144

boyfriend, then she isn't really available and you don't waste much time with her and you start looking for someone else. One also learns to go out on Friday evenings after work, when most of the people in bars are singles, rather than on Saturday nights when most are couples. Sometimes you'll enter a bar and there are almost no females present or they all appear to be with someone. I think you'd be crazy to stay there and I turn right around and leave. You also avoid social situations where everyone else is a couple. These situations are quite boring because there are no singles present for you to get to know. They are also frustrating because they eat up the time you could be spending in a different setting with other singles.

A very different strategy is to get the couples you know to introduce you to their single female friends. Often you can arrange to have your friends invite the single person over to their apartment or arrange to meet her at a coffee shop. Then you can happen by and join them at the right time. Because the single girl doesn't know you are there just to meet her, there is none of the awkwardness which occurs on a blind date. Once you join the party, you talk with your friends, so you are more relaxed and confident than you would be with strangers. If it turns out you aren't interested in the girl, you can leave when you want and no one's feelings are hurt. I find this approach is much more productive than the bar scene, because you have little in common with most of the people you meet in bars. However, I suspect your friends actually tell the single girl you are interested in meeting her, in order to get her to come. But they don't let you know this. #2305

Relationships and sex

It is frequently difficult to separate efforts to obtain sex from efforts to obtain a relationship. Sexual, or physical, attraction is often a minimal requirement in selecting a partner for a relationship. A relationship normally provides positive reactions and other resources, as well as sex, and people often seek to establish a relationship in order to fulfill these needs. People have many different perspectives on relationships and sex.

All I want from a relationship is communication, understanding, and good sex. #2306

I sleep with lots of guys because I think it will lead to something better. Love, I guess. #2307

I find that many of my longer relationships begin with a sexual contact. First you get sexually involved, then you find out what kind of woman you are involved with. Also, sex is a good indicator of how interested the other person is. If she doesn't want to get sexually involved, she doesn't want to get emotionally involved. #2308

I feel people should live together before they get married. I think that sex is an important part of a relationship, and a couple should make sure they are good in bed together. It's like buying a car. You get to check under the hood to make sure all the parts will fit. I mean, what if you get a dud? #2309

It's nice to think of sex as a deep statement of love for each other, but I think it satisfies a basic biological drive. People place too much emphasis on "the glory of love" and "the ecstasy of sex with love." Even in a love marriage, sex is often not satisfying to both partners. No matter how much you love the person, sex is simply sex. It can be good or bad, but it is usually independent of love. I don't see how loving someone can make bad sex any better. Someone is still left unsatisfied. If you really love each other you can overcome the awkwardness and inhibition and get some enjoyment out of it, but it's no big deal. Glorious sex is going at it for an hour, ending in both coming at the same time. I am looking for a man who can teach me to really love and enable me to have glorious sex. #2310

Love is just another word for sex. #2311

There are three types of girls: greenies (inexperienced), cock-teasers, and your basic loose sluts. Right now I want someone who will give me tail and satisfy my needs without the hassle of feelings or commitment. #2312

When I was sixteen or seventeen, I thought you had to be in love with a guy before you slept with him. Now that I'm in my early twenties, I think it is more special to be in love when you sleep with a guy, but it is not a must. #2313

All of us have heard the saying, "Sex is a way of showing your partner that you love them." But I think love should exist first, before sex, and then you can use sex to express love. #2314

Relationships and sex

I'm not really into the whole celibacy thing. But I do believe it's best to be in love with the person you choose to have sex with. I waited until I was completely in love with my girlfriend before we decided to have sex. It's more special that way and it gives me a good feeling. [#2315]

I have been in a serious relationship with a girl for a few years. Sex is not as important to me as establishing a relationship. Once a relationship is established, then sex comes when both partners are ready. The stories and bragging of the other guys about their sexual escapades don't interest me. I have a good relationship and the emotional benefits go deeper and are more important than physical satisfaction. [#2316]

Sex isn't everything. It's nice, but the best feeling is the closeness you feel when you wake up next to your woman. It makes you feel wanted. Sex is not love, though. There is a difference. [#2317]

If two people can not talk about their problems and feelings, then no amount of sex will make the relationship work. [#2318]

Women are conditioned to associate love with sex. They are less willing than men to engage in sex solely to obtain physical pleasure. They consider a love relationship a prerequisite to sexual intercourse. Also, if a woman is in a love relationship, her partner is less likely to exploit her and to gossip about her, and this gives her protection from getting a reputation for being loose. [#2319]

Girls and guys look at it very differently. A girl likes to be romantic, whereas guys only have one thing on their mind, sex. Why can't guys realize that before a girl will have sex with a guy, she must feel something for him? It doesn't seem to mean as much to a guy as it does to a girl. That's why it hurts a girl more when a guy is just being nice to her in order to obtain a one-night stand. "Why can't guys be more patient? A girl likes to be romanced before she jumps into the sack. Most girls I know usually fall in love, if only a little bit, before they will have sex with a guy. But most guys are not sensitive to this and usually turn out to be assholes." "Girls give sex for love. Guys give love for sex." [#2320]

This was the first time either Allan or I had been this involved. We were both too young, too inexperienced, and too afraid to face our feelings.

Allan had great physical needs, and because of my insecurity, I couldn't satisfy them. I needed a deeper commitment, love I guess, in order to reassure myself that I was doing the right thing. But Allan wasn't willing to give me a commitment at this time. When I expressed my feelings, which ran deeper than his, Allan was frightened away. I couldn't understand this, and I still can't. We broke up, and I still love him. I always will. Maybe he'll come back when he gets his head straight. I hope so. #2321

There is a time in a girl's life when she is willing to engage in sex. But she has to try to justify this in terms of her previous attitudes. Previously she judged girls who engaged in sex immoral, and now she has to consider how others will respond to her. Often she uses love to justify sex. #2322

Most guys don't want to tell a girl they are in love with her until they are sure they are willing to make a full commitment to her. Most girls don't want to have sex with a guy until he makes a full commitment to them and tells them he loves them. If you think about it, guys are fast, or easy, when it comes to sex. They want to have sex right away and wait about falling in love. Girls, on the other hand are fast, or easy, when it comes to falling in love. They can fall in love right away, but they want to wait about having sex until they are in a committed relationship. In a sense, girls exchange sex for commitment, and guys exchange commitment for sex.

Many males think when you fall in love with a girl, you marry her. They don't want to fall in love or tell a girl they love her until they are ready to get married. "I'm young and I just want to sow my wild oats while I can. I think that most guys my age are only looking for sex. We don't want to fall in love. We're too young to be thinking of marriage." "When you say, 'I love you,' it should be to the girl you want to marry. You don't say it to every second girl you date." "Now love is very tricky. When do you know that you're in love, true love that is? All the other males I talk to, who are between seventeen and twenty-one years old, feel they've never been in love before. They agree that maybe the more sensitive guys fall in love quicker. But they say that they won't fall in love and get married for at least five to ten years. As for now, they just date and have fun." #2323

We were both drinking a bit. I was lonely and she seemed to be too. So I invited her back to my place. That doesn't mean that I automatically wanted her to be my girlfriend, which is what she figured. I mean it was nice, but I don't want a relationship with her. I didn't like to hurt her feelings, but I thought she understood. Why do women have to put meaning into everything? They just don't understand. I mean even now she still bothers me. #2324

Eric is in Ontario, and I'm here in Prince Edward Island. I've only seen Eric twice in the last year and a half, once at Christmas and once during March break. It wasn't for sex that I started going out with Steve; at least I don't think it was. I just missed having someone around; a man to do things with and pay attention to me. Steve knows all about Eric anyway. #2325

A good rule of thumb is don't get sexually involved with anyone you don't want a relationship with. Once they've had sex with you, there are all kinds of entanglements and problems with people you don't want a relationship with, and you don't want to feel guilty about hurting their feelings. But even though this is a good rule, it isn't easy to follow when you have an opportunity to have sex. #2326

It is important to make a distinction between making love and plain sex. Sex is just a way to satisfy a physiological drive. Making love with your marriage partner, on the other hand, is the highest form of sharing. It is the deepest promise of commitment with the person you love. My religious friend says Christ is present in each such loving sexual act. #2327

Frequently when people are not in a relationship, they assign a higher priority to establishing a relationship than they do to simply obtaining sex. However, if it becomes clear to them that they are with someone they do not want to have a permanent relationship with, they may seek temporary satisfaction of their needs by obtaining positive reactions or sex from that person.

Occasionally I've gotten sexually involved with someone I know I'm not really interested in. What I really want is to find someone I want a relationship with. However, it always takes time to find them. So someone I consider unsuitable can help stave off the loneliness and provide sex and other needs until the right person comes along. When I feel lonely, I'll often call this person up and suggest we get together. We usually do so and end up having sex. I try to be honest and tell the person I'm not really interested in a permanent relationship, but the person often hopes I'll change my mind. I suspect the only reason the person is available is that they define me as someone suitable for a serious relationship. [#2328]

Cheating

Those in a committed relationship may also seek sex with people other than their regular partner. Most people fantasize about having sex with individuals they are not sexually involved with, and many would like to have sexual experiences they are not having.

I was sitting in a café talking to several female friends. Marjorie, a girl in her twenties, was telling us about the past weekend. "What a weekend! Roy left for Toronto on Friday afternoon. I was so cool girls; you wouldn't believe. I drove him to the airport and everything. It was hilarious; telling him I'd miss him, the whole bit. As soon as he was out the gate, I was history. I immediately went to get Daisy and we hit the liquor store for a two-four (a case of twenty-four bottles of beer). We drank at my place and headed for the bars. The men that were out were unreal. Everywhere you looked, there were gorgeous men. Anyway, I picked up Grant, again. What a night! Thank God Roy never finds out about him." I asked her why she stays with Roy. "Money, my dear. Roy always has a pocket full of money, and besides that he's totally in love with me, which makes him a pushover. Actually, I'm thinking of breaking up with him. Grant's been wanting to take me out for quite a while, but the time just wasn't right." Several minutes later Marjorie left us to return to work. No sooner had she left, when Daisy, who was also sitting with us, said, "Boy, if Marjorie only knew the half of it." We asked Daisy to explain. "Well, Roy's always screwing around on her. He's put the moves on me several times. If she only knew, she would shit. He's not as in love with her as he lets on. Peter was telling me that Thursday night he and Roy went out partying and picked up two girls and went back to Peter's place. I guess what Roy didn't do with his girl was unreal. And Peter said it wasn't the first time Roy has done this. I'm going to wait until Marjorie and Roy break up. Then I just might tell Marjorie about him fooling around on her all the time. What a laugh that would be." [#2329]

Cheating

Somewhere down the line I have cheated on most girls that I went out with for any length of time. I'm not bragging; it's just I can't help myself. I always thought, "What she don't know won't hurt her." It was never pre-planned, and I was usually drunk when it happened. The only time I felt guilty or sorry was when my girlfriend found out. Of course she would break up with me, but then I'd usually get back with her. I would think of some excuse to tell her, and she'd usually believe me. Another thing, I find if I'm not seeing a girl, there are less opportunities to meet girls. But if I'm seeing someone steady, there are more opportunities than you can shake a stick at. I could love my girlfriend, and I would still cheat on her. It's probably the way I was brought up. In junior and senior high the more tail you could get, the better. You were considered a stud. However, in order to make a relationship last, I should learn to be faithful. It seems to me that if a girl ever cheated on me, I would probably break off with her. As far as I know no one has ever cheated on me, but hey, I could be wrong, but I don't think so. As for cheating on my girlfriends, well, that's another story. #2330

All of my relationships have ended because of my desire to sleep with other girls. I never mean to hurt my current girlfriend, but I have no control over my urges, and fooling around with someone else just seems to happen. For example, I had a flirtation going on with a friend of my girlfriend from the time we were first introduced. One night this friend and I had too much to drink and one thing led to another. When my girlfriend found out she was extremely hurt. She broke up with me and severed her friendship with her friend. #2331

When I'm not in a relationship, my primary interest is in finding a good relationship. But once I'm in a good relationship, I start to think about having occasional sexual adventures on the side. It adds a lot of spice to life. #2332

For most men sex is a hormonal thing. They often can't get what they need from their girlfriends when they want it, so they go out and get it elsewhere. Guys can have sex with other girls without guilt, because they still have all the feelings they originally had for their girlfriends. Doing it is just doing it, that's all. It's detached. Men cheat because they need to. Women cheat because they find out their boyfriends are cheating on them. #2333

I think women cheat because it is flattering for them to have guys all over them. Even when they have one good guy, it's not enough. They need to have all the guys around wanting to take them home. #2334

Cheating is a big adventure. It is exciting to see what and how much you can get away with. Many women get bored being with the same person all of the time. Doing the same old thing becomes very monotonous and tiresome. Getting involved with someone new is very stimulating. #2335

Cheating on my boyfriend gives me lots of excitement. I don't do it just to be mean. It's fun trying to keep the secret, and I love the thrill of living on the edge. It's not a nice thing to do to him, but I feel it improves our relationship. #2336

The reason I cheat on my guy is because I see someone good looking and interesting. I get caught up in the moment. It's just plain lust. #2337

I don't think there was any factor which made me do it. I just met a beautiful girl and we got it on. #2338

If I find some girl who is attractive and my girlfriend isn't out with me, then I have to make a move. It's hard to resist someone who is attractive and gets me real hot and excited. I just have to go for it. I always regret it in the morning. I feel obligated to regret it. #2339

What is a girl to do if there is a nice-looking guy with blond hair, blue eyes, and a body that just won't quit, and he expresses interest in you? Who in their right mind would pass up an opportunity like that, especially since opportunity usually only knocks once? Some girls send their boyfriends home from a club just to go out with another guy they meet. They put the main man out of the picture until the cheating task is completed. #2340

I was having a coffee with a friend of mine when a group of guys walked in. My friend jabbed me in the side with her elbow. "Quick, see the guy in the faded denim jacket? One night I was loaded, Shawn and I were fighting, and I picked him up." I was shocked, and told my friend I didn't think she was the kind to fool around. "Yeah, I know what you mean. But sometimes I like a little variety in my life. That guy is really good in bed, too. I figured I'd try him out, and I had no complaints,

Cheating

let me tell you." I asked if she wasn't afraid Shawn, her boyfriend, would find out. She replied, "Oh well, the secret to success is to be discreet. It's worked so far." Then she laughed. #2341

I didn't mean to go out with my best friend's boyfriend; it just happened. We were joking around, getting along great like we always do. Then I guess we started flirting with each other. He asked me to dance when a waltz (slow dance) came on and one thing just lead to another. When the night was over we went home together. What am I going to say to Vicki? She'll never understand. #2342

I had clues that my boyfriend was probably fucking around, so I wanted to do it too. I didn't want him to put one over on me. #2343

I cheated on my boyfriend once when I was drunk. This guy had been chasing me for quite a while. He was always there when I needed a friend. But he was giving me a hard time and always pressuring me. One time I was totally wasted and slept with him hoping to get him off my back. #2344

Being scared of falling in love can actually cause you to cheat. If you were previously dumped by someone you loved, you may be afraid when you fall in love again. You may cheat on your partner just to prove to yourself that you aren't really in love. This is a stupid idea, but unfortunately it does happen. #2345

The fact the other person is already involved with someone else doesn't cause much hesitation for many people. Most males don't let the fact the girl has a boyfriend or husband get in the way. "A man asked me if my friend is married. When I told him that she is, he asked, 'Is she bound by it?'" "The phone rang at work today and a male's voice said, 'I think you are really beautiful. I'm thirty-six years old. Would you like to have lunch together?' I had no idea who it was. I was caught by surprise and blurted out, 'I'm married.' 'So am I,' said the voice. 'I have to go,' I said, and hung up. I felt really uncomfortable not knowing who it was. If this had been face to face I would have known who I was dealing with. Then I could have seen the person's facial expressions, and would have a better idea what to say." Many males say, "If I like her bad enough I'll do anything to get her." Some qualify this, "Unless her boyfriend is really big." Many females act in a similar way. "Women

153

are no better than men these days. I think there is a shortage of men, and no man is safe. You go out to a club and all these women come on solid to the men. They don't know if the men have girlfriends or not, and it wouldn't stop them. I think they even like it better if they know the men do." #2346

I've been seeing a married man for the last year. So far it's been pretty easy. I mean, we can't go out or anything like that, but I live by myself so it makes it a little easier. He comes over to my place and we either talk, watch TV, have dinner, listen to music, or whatever. No matter what we do though, we always end the evening by going to bed. He makes me so happy that I wish I could tell everyone, but I can't or his wife will find out, so we keep it real quiet. I know that some people would think it's terrible, but right now, for me, it feels right. I think that part of the attraction is the fact he is married. It seems to add an air of mystery to the whole thing. #2347

I had a terrible marriage for fifteen years. It was awful living with Donald. He screwed around with so many women, and some of them I knew quite well. He just didn't care at all. About five years ago, after our two kids had started school, he was having an affair with one woman. He would do the evening farm work, come in the house to get cleaned up, and then head out to spend the night with her. Then early the next morning he would return and work all day on the farm. This went on month after month, and he knew I knew what was going on. I lost all my feelings for him, and eventually I began stepping out too. I figured, why not? #2348

Many married men in Vietnam obtain a mistress for sexual purposes. She is usually pretty and doesn't have much money. The man will supplement her income, or provide her with a house or apartment and living expenses so she does not have to work. The man expects to have exclusive sexual rights to his mistress, and this relationship can continue for years. The woman pretends to care for the man, but only until he can no longer support her. The community does not respect the woman, and they consider the man foolish because he is giving his money away instead of spending it on his family. Couples marry for life, so it is not considered proper for a wife to leave her husband because he has a mistress.

When I last visited Vietnam, a relative of mine told me about the case of a wealthy businessman who supported a young mistress for years. She lived in a nearby village where he bought her a house. One day when he traveled to visit her, they went out to a bar, and she encouraged him to drink until he was drunk. Afterwards as they were walking along the road he was struck by a passenger bus and killed. His mistress pretended he was her husband and acted very distraught. The bus company compensated her with a sum of money and she buried him on her property. Meanwhile, when the man did not return home, his family began to search for him. Eventually they found his mistress and she told them the man was like a father to her and she had looked after him. His family believed she pushed him in front of the bus, but could not prove it, and they took his body home. They believed she was tired of him and wanted him out of the way. #2349

There are about one hundred employees at my place of work, and I would estimate about fifty percent of them have been sexually involved with their co-workers at one time or another. People work different shifts and have lengthy periods between shifts so they have ample opportunity to get together when they want to. Also, the work is frequently stressful, so people become emotionally closer as they cope with shared experiences. Temporary employees, such as summer trainees, often see work as an opportunity to have numerous sexual experiences. One young female told me she wanted to have sex with as many male co-workers as she could while she was there. I get e-mails from female employees which say, "Let's get together tonight," "You said you were going to call. I'm ready," "I'll cook you that meal I promised. Breakfast, if you know what I mean." However, I believe you shouldn't dip your pen in company ink. Some employees are looking for a steady girlfriend or boyfriend, but others want as many sexual liaisons as they can get. Many of these employees are married and their spouses are not aware of these involvements. In certain cases the involvement is like a second marriage. One case, for example, has lasted twenty years and includes one or two children which the woman's husband mistakenly believes to be his own. In fact, I commented to the woman that one of her children looks more like her partner at work than like her husband. She pointed out that she has been involved with her co-worker practically as long as his own wife has, so she has as much right to be with him as the wife does. I know of about fifteen cases of couples who got together at work and eventually married. A quarter of these left their original spouse to do so, and there have been a number of ugly scenes at work produced by rejected spouses. Management is well aware of some of the ethical problems produced by sex at work, but doesn't want to touch this with a ten-foot pole. They don't want the negative publicity, which could result in losing their jobs. Also, individual managers at various levels are having sexual relationships with employees too. #2350

Why is it that people feel so threatened when their partner cheats on them? I think it's because a committed relationship is an agreement to work together to obtain resources of various kinds. A couple co-operates so that both parties get more resources than they could get on their own. When a person seeks sex outside of their relationship, he or she frequently provides the new partner with various resources which their original partner expected to receive. This may be attention, emotional support, sex, money, or help. As a result the person has less resources available to give their original partner. Another factor is that a person often becomes emotionally involved with the individual who provides him with sexual pleasure. If a person's emotional and sexual needs are provided by a third party, he or she no longer needs the original partner to provide them. Therefore the need for and the commitment to the original partner is weakened. #2351

Many people feel a desire to tell their partner afterwards that they have cheated. They may feel guilty, or they may feel uncomfortable, want to get it off their chest, and want reassurance from their partner that everything is OK. Knowledge that one's partner has cheated normally weakens or destroys the relationship. "I find that there are three reactions when one's partner finds out. One, the cheater is dumped. Two, the couple stays together for a while but there is a loss of trust and the relationship falls apart. Three, the cheater is forgiven but the act is brought up from time to time when the couple fights." #2352

Temporary separation from one's partner brings one into contact with other potential sexual partners and removes certain constraints. Temporary separation occurs when one partner is away from the other for purposes of work, education, visiting family, shopping, sightseeing, conferences, conventions, sports, or other reasons. When partners are separated, both parties are available for sexual opportunities with others.

I was with the girl's basketball team on a trip and met a guy from a university in Halifax. I couldn't get over how nice looking he was and how nice he acted to me. I spent most of the weekend with him and the whole time my boyfriend's name never entered my mind. But on the way home I started to feel guilty. I made the other girls swear they'd never tell. #2353

I went to visit my family in Ottawa and when I was there my sister and I decided to go get a beer. While we were sitting in a club I noticed this great-looking guy. Then to my amazement he came over and asked me to dance. I said yes without any hesitation. I left with him that night and spent many more nights with him while I was in Ottawa. I didn't feel guilty or even think about my boyfriend the whole time I was away. When I got home I told my friends what a great time I'd had. My boyfriend heard about it and broke up with me. #2354

I've cheated on my girlfriend from time to time. For example, one weekend my soccer team played out of town. After the game we went looking for loud parties, beer, and women. I met this girl with skintight jeans and a low-cut sweater at a club, and the two of us went back to my room for a good time. When we returned home I told my girlfriend I had spent the weekend in my room watching TV. #2355

I went to a dance when my girlfriend was out of town. I was fucking toasted and picked up a bitch I knew. I don't think I'd have done her if I wasn't drinking. #2356

I've cheated on all my girlfriends. I would feel guilty and tell them, and they would stick around. But now with Karla, my current girlfriend, we've gone together for two years and I've cheated on her four times. I was drunk each time and it usually happened when I was out of the province. I feel really guilty and I want to tell her what I've done, but I can't. She told me that if I ever cheated on her, she would drop me. And she would too. I don't want that, because I love her too much. Once a girlfriend of mine cheated on me, and I dropped her like a sack of potatoes. I don't want anyone fucking around with my girlfriend. If she agrees to have sex with someone else while she is going with me, then I want nothing to do with her. #2357

Our whole neighborhood gets a big charge out of this particular couple. When they first moved into the neighborhood, everyone thought they were the perfect couple. I swear to God! You should see them. When they are together you couldn't imagine a couple being more in love. But the husband goes away a lot on business trips. Every time he is away, his wife entertains, and usually somebody different. What a string of guys she has going in and out. I'm dead serious; everyone's beginning to think she's a housewife hooker. I bet she makes a fortune. [2358]

I estimate that fifty percent of the girls between the ages of seventeen and twenty-five step out on their boyfriends by going off on trips for sex. Males never even ask about the trips. They just assume we are shopping, sunning ourselves, and hanging around the other girls. One time I went to Florida and met a guy I really liked. We spent the night together, but I didn't sleep with him. But the girl I went to Florida with spent the night with a guy and there is no doubt in my mind they slept together. She has since gone back to Florida again. [2359]

Trips out of town

When you are off the Island, you don't have to worry about other people recognizing you and ruining your reputation. One thing a girl can do is take trips to another city in the Maritimes for a weekend with one or more girlfriends. Usually I and a few girlfriends will plan just to get off the Island and have a good time. It's never explicitly said we are going to pick up guys. Some of the ladies use the guise we're going for a shopping tour, which is fine, because most of us go shopping during the day. But at night we go clubbing. It doesn't matter if my girlfriends have husbands, are going steady, or are completely single, they are usually interested in seeing what the men are like off the Island. Usually the married ladies will come out to the clubs and might dance, but they're not really up for running around. But I find the single ladies, even if they're going steady with someone at home, are often up for a good time, meaning a sexual relationship. Usually the men you meet don't try to contact you afterwards, so there are no repercussions.

I first started taking trips off the Island to meet guys when I was eighteen. My girlfriend sort of clued me in, and I thought, "Jeez, this is great. Nobody is going to know about it." At the time I was interested in getting together with a particular guy at the university. If he had heard I was having anything to do with another guy, especially having a wild weekend, he wouldn't have wanted to have anything to do with me. Therefore I couldn't chance doing anything like this on Prince Edward Island.

Girls don't take trips for this reason much before they are eighteen. If you were younger than eighteen, you couldn't get into the clubs off the Island. I think girls continue to do this until they get married, and would guess a third of the single women between eighteen and twenty-five do so. Most of the ladies I know just do this once in a while. Some years I have taken a couple of trips for this purpose; other years I haven't done so at all.

Although I have gone on trips with as many as five girlfriends, I usually go with only one other girl. It's a lot easier to maneuver the weekend that way. You want to have a girlfriend you are compatible with who is interested in the same thing. Usually you make sure you go with a relatively attractive girl, who is on a par with you. If she's an ugly, the guys won't come around.

Pubs and taverns are the best pickup joints. But I like a better class, so I go to the nightclubs. When you go to the club, you sit at the bar or at a table close to the bar. These are good places to get picked up, because lots of guys hang out at the bar. Then you just look around at the guys. I find it's really easy to make eye contact with guys and start up a conversation when you are out of town, because you don't care what they think of you. It just doesn't matter. You're there for a good time, and you're darned determined to have one. You can't get a bad reputation, because they don't know who you are. If a girl sat at the bar and acted available in Charlottetown, she'd be labeled a slut or whore. People would say, "Look at that hussy."

Once when a girlfriend and I went to a club in Halifax, we both decided we would make the first move ourselves and not wait for the guys. So we each picked out a male we liked. "Have you picked yours out yet?" my friend asked. "Yes," I replied, "have you?" "Yes. How long do you think it will take?" "Less than ten minutes," I predicted. So we each got up and approached the male we had chosen. I told mine I was from out of town and interested in having some fun. The two males were really surprised and enthusiastic about it. We spent the whole weekend together and had a grand time. They took us out to dinner and everywhere. But I've never approached a male like that again. I want the male to choose to be with me.

When you are at a club, it's the usual gambit. You go out for four or five hours and you dance with the guys. Whoever buys you the drinks automatically becomes your date for the night. Afterwards you usually go with the guy to his place. Some ladies will return to their hotel room around three or four in the morning if they don't want the other girls to think they stayed overnight with the guy. Others don't give a damn, and will just stay away all night. If you hit it off with the guy, and he learns you are in town for the weekend, he will usually make a date with you for the next night too. If you really get along well, you just stay the whole weekend with the guy. This is what you want in the first place, because most of the single ladies go over for a weekend. Often my friends and I use fake names, because we don't want them to know who we are. I tell guys my name is Janet. Otherwise, I'm usually pretty honest. I tell them where I'm from, and what my profession is. I really don't expect them to show up in my life again anyway.

You don't have to worry about any consequences at home. No one knows that we were away or what we were up to. We usually go with very dear girlfriends, who keep what we do mum. Females will ruin your reputation even faster than males, and one has to be very careful who one talks to about one's sexual experiences. It's understood no one talks about what we do on a trip when we get back home. However, you often tell each other the intimate details of what went on. It's just like a boast session. You'll say something like "This is what I did and I picked up a six-footer who had one this long, and balls like you wouldn't believe." You talk like they are pieces of meat, because that's all the guys really mean to us. It's basically for the sex of it.

You don't succeed in getting together with someone every time you go on a trip. Everyone in your group may succeed in connecting with a guy, but other times a trip is a real bummer. You spend the money going to the city, get all dressed up and go to a club, but then don't meet anybody you'd want to do anything with. We've never had any problems with men approaching us. Guys always come along and ask us to dance. But sometimes they are either unattractive or else they don't come across well personality-wise as you talk to them. We aren't just going to pick up anything that comes up to the table. A trip where I don't meet anyone I'm interested in is my kind of bummer. On some trips I've gotten together with a male friend I already know and gone clubbing all night. We have a good time, but nothing sexual takes place. I don't want it to, so that's OK.

Sometimes all the ingredients are there for a successful trip, but something interferes and things just don't work out. One time a girl-friend and I took a trip to Halifax for the weekend. Halifax just abounds with clubs and bars, so everybody goes there. We were both students in university together and didn't have much money. The first night we shared our hotel room with a male friend of ours. Although my girl-friend found a guy and brought him back to our room, she wasn't willing to do anything sexual with him because our male friend was in the

160

room. The next night she and I had a hotel room to ourselves and we each found a guy. I met my guy in a club. He was just in from Vancouver, didn't have a place to stay, and wanted to stay with me. My girlfriend met a guy in a band. The guys in the band were from Ontario and were all sharing rooms together, so she couldn't go to his place. So we took our two guys back to our hotel. However, the security guard saw us come in and asked if he could please see our keys. We only had two keys between us, so he said, "I see two keys and four people. I'm sorry, two people will have to go." Now what we should have done is send one couple off to find someplace else. But we were klutzes and not used to this. So we sent the two guys away and went up to our room alone. That weekend there were all the men around and we had all the right intentions, but we just couldn't get a place to go to. Normally girls on a trip share a room together, and go to the guys' apartments to have their fun.

The best trip I ever had was with three other ladies. One was married, another was living with a guy, and the third was separated and has several kids. We went to a convention in Halifax. I went over there with absolutely only one thing in mind; I was going to pick up some guys. So we dolled ourselves up one night and went off to the Royal Canadian Legion of all places. I'd never been to the Legion in Halifax, and I thought, "Good God! I'll never meet anybody here." So this turd came along and asked me to dance, and I said, "No." He asked everyone at our table to dance and we all said no. He was atrocious looking. So I was really getting mad. I wanted to go to some posh clubs; that's where I usually go to meet guys. But here we were at this stupid Legion.

Then this really attractive-looking guy with blond hair came over and started talking to us. He was nicely dressed in a three-piece suit, and he and I really hit it off well. He asked me to dance and he had some class. Sandra, my married friend, was older than the rest of us and she was quite impressed with him for asking her to dance. She thought he had very good manners. She is a very friendly, lovely lady, and had come out for a few drinks and dances, and that was it. She wasn't out to run around. In the meantime Diane, my girlfriend who was living with a guy at home, was asked to dance by another very attractive guy. After she danced with him he asked her to go out to dinner. This was at two o'clock in the morning. Sandra had to practically break her arm to get her to go, and Diane accepted with great hesitancy. My guy asked if I would like to go out to a club with him, and I thought that was great. His buddy had joined us and he was interested in my third girlfriend, who is separated.

161

Efforts to obtain sex

My guy was really spiffy. He had a great big evening cape and a cane. It was great. I love classy guys. He asked if I had ever seen a burlesque show, and I said no, because there aren't any on the Island. He told me, "Look, if you would like to go, I'd be really pleased to take you." This place we went to was really swanky; it wasn't sleazy at all. This beautiful lady came out and did her strip act on a bear rug. I got rather embarrassed and asked him, "Why are you watching me?" He said he was more interested in seeing my reactions than in seeing the broad on the stage. He was really nice, and holy jumpers, he was really pouring out the dough buying me drinks.

Afterwards he and his buddy took me and my girlfriend back to their apartment. My girlfriend had her eyes on the guy I was with. She is separated with several kids and doesn't have much male companionship back home. So she was up for a little bit of a good time. But when her guy got down to brass tacks and wanted to go to bed with her, she wanted to go home. She could have ruined the evening for us, but my guy and I didn't let that deter us. We were getting along fine, we were having fun, he was treating me wonderfully, and we were going to go to bed together. So we went upstairs and had our evening of fun. He didn't want me to leave, but I felt I should join my girlfriends at the motel. This guy got a cab and escorted me home, instead of letting me go back through the streets of Halifax alone in a cab. That was really nice. Then he returned home. By now it was six o'clock in the morning. As soon as I got in the door of the motel room, Sandra, my married friend, looked at me and started laughing. "Did you get a piece of tail?" she asked. "Did I ever," I grinned. She thought that was great. There was no pretense; she knew exactly what was going on.

I was impressed with this guy and really liked him. Even though I initially used a fake name, I ended up giving him my real name and address. I was a tiny bit scared to start with, because I didn't know the guy, but he turned out to be really nice. I don't regret it; we had a ball. That was Saturday night, and I didn't see him again after that. He said he was going to write to me and really wanted to keep in touch, but he never did.

After my guy and I left them at the Legion, Diane, my friend who is living with a guy at home, went out to a Chinese dinner with the guy she met. They invited Sandra to go with them. After the dinner he drove them back to the motel and Diane wanted Sandra to stay with them, but Sandra said, "Oh, no," and got out of the car. She figured they'd go do whatever they wanted to. But Diane was really mad at her for leaving them alone in the car. Then she and the guy started necking and she got quite upset because she felt this was wrong. Here she was living with a guy and at the same time carrying on with this other guy in Halifax. The next day Diane was in a bitch of a mood all the way back to Charlottetown. I asked her, "What's the matter?" and it all came out. She had thought she was very happy in her relationship at home. Therefore she felt she shouldn't be attracted to anyone else or want to have anything to do with them. However, she was really turned on by the guy in Halifax and wanted to go to bed with him, although she didn't. She felt extremely bad she had allowed herself to get into such a compromising situation.

Most women who are seriously involved with guys at home are reticent about having a fling when they go away. Quite a few girls would think they'd committed a mortal sin if they stepped out on their guy at home. A girlfriend of mine was living with a guy in Charlottetown and went on a trip to Montreal with a girlfriend. She met another guy there and spent the weekend with him. When she came back she felt really guilty and felt she had to tell the guy she was living with about it. She figured this happened because she didn't really love her guy enough, and they ended up splitting up. As for myself, I have been going seriously with a guy on Prince Edward Island for some time now, and have no intention of sleeping with anyone else. Therefore, when I travel to another city in Canada in connection with my work, I don't go clubbing. But if I weren't going with anyone, I would go to clubs every night to get picked up. I meet guys who are interested in me when I travel, but I'm not going to let them get anywhere. Of course, this depends entirely on the person. Other girls think, "What's a weekend?" As long as the guy at home doesn't find out, it's not going to harm anyone. Certain girlfriends of mine take this attitude, and I don't judge them for it. It's their own business. I'm certainly not going to tell on them and harm whatever they have at home. #2360

Other sources

Many people are not in a committed relationship and must seek sex from other sources. Such sources may include friends, acquaintances, relatives, colleagues, employers, subordinates, strangers, and prostitutes. A sexual interest and connection may develop when people are together talking; working; shopping; commuting; traveling; vacationing; exercising; eating; drinking; dancing; dating; gambling; pursuing hobbies and interests; or attending conferences, classes, exhibits, performances, parties, or sporting events.

When you play sports, you get lots of opportunities to have sex. You attract lots of attention, and people come to see you play. Because you attract attention you are sort of a local celebrity, and many girls would like to be seen and be involved with you. Also, you are an athlete and in good physical shape and are attractive to other people. "There was this really hot babe on the hockey team that I just had to have. I went to every game he played, both here and out of town. I would wait in my car to see him leave the rink. After two months of this I saw him at a club. He came over and said he'd noticed me at the games. It pays to be patient." "There are girls who literally throw themselves at athletes. Athletes accept what the girls offer, just like any other guys would. I heard of one jock who rejected a lot of the girls and they decided he must be homosexual. The funny thing is after they have sex, the girls think the guys won't be interested in anyone else. When they learn that the guys are going to continue seeing other girls they still keep coming around. Sometimes no matter how badly a guy treats a girl, she's not going away. Most athletes do a lot of sneaking around on their girlfriends. Often they leave their own apartment late at night and return early in the morning. One jock was quite open about taking other girls home. When he was confronted by his girlfriend, he simply denied it. Then he sat down with the boys and laughed about it. Few seem serious about one girl, and most are friendly to at least six or seven different girls." Because you travel out of town to play other teams you meet women who aren't looking for anything more than a sexual encounter. "When we are on the road we sleep two to a room. A veteran gets first rights to the room when he gets tail and expects the rookie to disappear if he asks him to. But some of the girls we meet are willing to have sex with more than one guy. Sometimes other guys watch, join in, or wait their turn." Guys who aren't athletes are often jealous of the success of athletes in attracting females.

When athletes go out to clubs they often try to draw attention to themselves. "Jocks tend to make a lot of noise drinking with their buddies. They wear clothes which indicate they are athletes, such as team jackets and rugby sweatshirts. They often have unusual hairstyles and dance flamboyantly." "The loudest group of males in the club are the athletes. Maybe because they are the most popular. They never worry about what others in the club think of their actions. They are only concerned with what their buddies think, or some girl they are interested in." "It was Monday night in a campus bar. When I entered there were twelve guys and eight girls in the bar. Six of the males were jocks, and they sat together at a table in front of the TV. Although there was a special feature on TV that evening, the set was switched to a football game. The jocks were sprawled in the chairs. They were boisterous and laughed and kidded around. They toasted the football players on TV and were having a very good time. The other guys in the bar were much quieter. They mingled with others, watched the jocks, and also seemed to be having fun. The females were sitting two or four to a table. They tended to watch the guys, particularly the jocks. One of the guys who was not a jock went over to talk to a girl at a table. She responded with a smile and talked to him, but her head was turned toward the jocks throughout their conversation. As he left she turned her head to look at him for the first time. Some of the girls made a special effort to walk by the jocks as often as possible. Other girls, when they made their way to and from the washroom, shied away from the table with the jocks as though they were intimidated by them. Whenever another jock entered the bar there was a loud chorus of hellos from the jocks. When a girl entered the bar, particularly a girl they knew, the jocks would whistle and make remarks such as 'Hi, sweetie,' and 'Hey, not bad!' The other guys in the room just sat there, let the jocks do their stuff, and made no effort to copy them. It seemed perfectly natural for the jocks to behave this way. They ruled the roost. The waitresses were friendly with everyone, but more so with the jocks. They passed by their table more often than they did other tables, and were very prompt in taking their orders. They would joke and laugh with the jocks and react to their teasing with pleasure. Whenever the jocks whistled a waitress would flash a smile and add a wiggle. She wasn't flirting, just being very friendly. I've noticed that campus police are more lenient with the jocks than they are with other students. They let them get away with more, rarely give jocks a hard time, and are much more likely to throw a regular guy out of the bar than a jock." "Since the varsity athletes attract a lot of girls, for two years I hung around them so I could meet more girls. Afterwards, I concluded it's all bullshit! The athletes always go to clubs together and sit around talking about the last game or season, or the next game or season. Who cares? Then they all stagger out the door together. I don't know if they walk home holding hands. That's one thing I forgot to notice. They meet a few girls, but most of the girls have a large vacant area between their ears. Most girls who follow varsity boys around are freshettes and sophomores. They are usually silly and teases. You only work for your meal so long before you decide to hell with it. It's just a stage the girls go through. By their junior and senior years the girls are involved with their studies and their real friends, and have come to realize the athletes are spending Saturday nights at home watching hockey, football, or baseball on TV and telling their girlfriends, 'Get me another beer, and don't talk to me or touch me until the game is over.' This isn't true of all athletes, but it is true of many of them." #2361

There are special situations where a girl is anonymous on Prince Edward Island and can have sex and protect her reputation too. One is Halloween, when people frequently wear costumes which completely hide their identity. Often they try to cover themselves up completely, and they are careful not to wear shoes or jewelry or coats that someone might recognize. One Halloween I dressed as a clown and went to a club. I met this really good-looking guy there and we went out and necked in a car. I wouldn't take off my mask or any of my clothes. I could see he was really aroused, so I gave him a blow job. I've never viewed going down on a man as being that significant. If a guy has a hard-on, why not service him? You aren't having intercourse with him, and I don't believe in being a CT (cock-tease). Afterwards I was dancing with all these guys in the club and the guy I had been with in the car kept trying to arrange a date with me for the next night. But I wouldn't go along with it. I didn't want him or anyone else to know who I was. #2362

Divorced women attract a lot of sexual attention from males. I think there are a number of reasons for this. One, there is no question that divorced women are sexually experienced, or "saddle broken." In contrast, males are never sure how much sexual experience a woman has had who has never been married, unless she has a bad reputation. Two, a woman who is divorced no longer has a husband to guard her from the interests of other males. In other words, she is a sexual resource that is both available and unprotected. A divorced woman I know was approached by a male friend of her ex-husband, who dropped by to see how she was doing. This friend told her how much he wanted her and had always wanted her, and he assumed she would never tell his wife what he was saying. Three, another reason why a divorced woman attracts sexual attention is that in order to find a male for a committed relationship, she has to attend social functions, meet various males, and date, which is to say act like a single woman. All of these things indicate her availability. Four, divorce is often demoralizing, particularly when her husband leaves her for another woman, often younger than herself. As a result a divorced woman may have a poor self-image and try to prove to herself that she is attractive by having sexual encounters with a number of males. "Divorce is a form of rejection. It is a blow to the ego and some women try to compensate for their loss of self-confidence by dating extensively in order to prove they are still attractive and sexy. A friend of mine, who is thirty-five with one child, dates anyone, anytime, anyplace. She is currently dating both a twenty-two-year-old and a salesman. When I asked why, she replied, 'Because I can't get anyone better.' I think that low self-confidence causes divorced women to become promiscuous. They have to prove they are still desirable and can attract the opposite sex. At the same time they are scared they can not attract a desirable male, because it takes a lot of time and work to find one, and they have to compete with all the other single females."

Males have the idea that a divorced woman is sex starved. "I am female and was working at the bar on New Year's Eve in a local community. One of those present was a divorced woman about forty years old who was dressed in a figure-hugging black dress, black heels, and fishnet stockings. She looked very well dressed, not sleazy at all. She danced with all who asked her and accepted drinks from those who bought them for her. The men flocked to her side for dances. Some of the men, both married and bachelors, commented while they were waiting for their drinks that she was 'quite a number' and 'She's newly divorced, so you know what that means. She hasn't had a man for a while. So which one of us good gentlemen is going to help her bring in the New Year properly?' The woman made no sexual overtures, but people commented she was 'very' divorced and 'on the prowl.' The only ones who seemed to mind her presence were the wives of the men she danced with. I've noticed that at parties wives keep their husbands far away from divorcées, because they consider the divorcées on the make."

"I am Vietnamese, female, and divorced. My impression is that among Vietnamese it is the husbands who want to keep their wives away from me. The husbands fear I may influence their wives to get a divorce too." #2363

People will sometimes seek sex from someone they have had a previous sexual relationship with. This may be someone they have dated in the past, or a previous girlfriend, boyfriend, or spouse. Often it is easier to have sex with someone one has been sexually involved with before, than it is to develop a sexual relationship with someone new.

> I was drinking at a club and saw an ex-girlfriend. I asked her to dance, and we hit it off from there. #2364

> Some girls use sex to keep a guy interested in them. If a guy can get it, he'll keep coming back. Women yearn for love, but most guys just want sex. #2365

In addition, many people masturbate. In fact, masturbation can be their primary or only source of sex.

> When my husband is asleep, I often masturbate quickly in the bathroom. When he isn't home, I take my time and do it in the bathtub. I stretch out and let a gentle spray from the shower rain on my stomach and between my legs. And sometimes I masturbate after a shower while I'm creaming and perfuming myself. I wish he took time to enjoy me more than once or twice a week. #2366

People may create a frame of mind for masturbation by fantasizing, reading a book with erotic passages, looking at pictures of someone they consider physically attractive, going to see a strip show, or looking at a pornographic magazine or video.

Males from out of town

> When a girl doesn't want to get a reputation of being loose she can get together with men who are only here on Prince Edward Island temporarily. Because they soon leave they can't talk to everyone else who lives here about you. One group are the sailors who are in town when their ships dock here. Just the uniforms attract women. Sometimes a lot of ladies will be invited to parties at the ships. It can be quite a novelty. They have food and booze like you wouldn't believe, and are lots of fun. If you act like a lady, they treat you like one. And if you want to be a whore, they treat you like a whore. It is as simple as that. I've never

had anything to do with the sailors myself, and just went to the parties for a fun time.

Another group are the traveling salesmen. There are an incredible amount of salesmen who come over to the Island from New Brunswick and Nova Scotia to sell everything from car parts to copier paper. Many want a one-night stand or a regular lady when they come over, and a lot of women on PEI pick them up. If you are in a club or bar you can spot them in a minute. They always wear a three-piece suit when they come in the door, so they stand out. As soon as you see them, you know that's the salesmen. You get together with them if you want a one-night stand or a couple of dates for dinner and dancing and to have somebody spend money on you. A traveling salesman is not known here, and he's not related to everybody. Because he's not here very often, people don't see you with him regularly, and they don't know what you are up to. You aren't known to be having a relationship with him, so there's no harm to your reputation. Some girls will have an ongoing steady relationship with a salesman, just so they can have a good time, say once a month or so, when he's here. It's a way of playing it safe and still getting your hanky-panky once in a while.

I've met a lot of salesmen and so have my girlfriends. I've had many opportunities to get together with them, but have only done so with two. I didn't really feel like a one-night stand, and was also concerned with watching my reputation. There's still a bit of risk of having others guess what you are up to. One salesman I met in a bar of a motel one night. He was really nice, and I went to his room with him and we just had a drink and talked. There wasn't anything to it, and he asked if he could see me again. I gave him my name and phone number and he lost it. The next time he was in town, he went to considerable trouble to trace me down through my work. I thought that was really nice. The next day I went with him on his route around PEI, and that night we got together. After that we would see each other once in a while. I had his number at work in Halifax and was to call him anytime, which I did. Then it just sort of drifted off. I enjoyed seeing him and there wasn't anything else to it.

The other salesman I got together with was also from Halifax. I was in a club and saw him come in. I don't usually stare at guys, because I'm too shy. But I mistook him for a friend of mine, so wherever he went in the club he saw me staring at him. He got up from his seat and came right over and sat at our table. I apologized and explained, "I thought you were somebody I knew." "Well, I hope I'll be who you want me to be," he replied. He was a very attractive man with a great personality, so we spent the evening together. I didn't stay the night with him, but he invited me to be his date when he was coming over again two weeks from then. He called from Halifax to confirm our date. He brought a friend along, and I brought a girlfriend with me. We all smoked dope and had a grand time, went out to a club, and then back to their motel room, where they had a suite of two rooms. At first I said I wasn't going to do anything, but then we got onto the bed and were having our little fun. His friend took my girlfriend home. But then when his friend got back he came bouncing onto our bed without a stitch on. My guy just lay there while this guy climbed right on me. I must have had superhuman strength, because I heaved him right off me. "What are you doing?" I demanded. I got really upset and started to cry. My guy told his friend to get out of the room and then went and talked to him. He told me his friend wanted to apologize, and the guy came in, apologized, and then attacked me all over again. I was really freaked out by then. I got my clothes on and took off. That had never happened to me before, and it just wasn't my cup of tea at all. The guy I was with never called again. #2367

Unattractive females

Zoo dating is the practice of picking up very unattractive women, or zoolies, for purely sexual purposes. These are girls who don't look any better than a cow, pig, or sheep. Many males participate in zoo dating, and they do so for a variety of reasons, ranging from acquiring sexual experience to getting back at their girlfriend after a fight. However, the most common reason is that they don't have access to a more attractive girl at the time to have sex with.

I feel you take what you can get, and when the zoolies give it, you take it. Cuter girls can act more respectable and still attract males. But because the cuter girls aren't screwing around, guys go for the sure thing. Often you are pretty direct with zoolies about wanting to have sex, and you can get them to do all sorts of things sexually. You can get away with a lot more because they don't expect to be treated like princesses. One explanation why zoolies are so willing is that they are desperate. There are a lot more single girls than guys around, so the ugly ones really have a hard time. Maybe they think the only way they can get somebody is if they fool around. Sometimes they seem to want everyone to know they got picked up. Another explanation why they act this way is that they lack self-respect, but it's hard to keep self-respect if no one is attracted to you. Although one often contacts zoolies in bars and clubs, one can get together anywhere. One guy I know picked up a girl in the library, signed out a private study room, and screwed her there in many different positions. Alcohol provides a convenient excuse for both parties. As one person said, "If you're not drunk, you fake it; and if she's not drunk, she does too."

A common feature of zoo dating is that you don't want others to see you with the female. Because she is so unattractive, your buddies are likely to kid you unmercifully about her. Sometimes this kidding can go on for years afterwards. Guys who know you and see you leaving with the girl may make comments like "Where are you moooving to?" and "She looks pretty baaad." Barry told me he was sitting with some friends at a club next to some zoolies. When his friends left the zoolies started talking to him, and he thought, "What the hell; a fuck's a fuck." He left with one of the zoolies to get a cab home. However, his friends were outside the club and although he tried to take the zoolie in the other direction, they saw him and yelled, "She's a pig!" Mark, another guy I know, said he was taking a zoolie from a club to the parking lot when he encountered three of his buddies. He said the sex wasn't worth it, because he was verbally abused by the guys for weeks afterwards.

Many males lie to the zoolie about themselves. They often give her a fake name, address, and phone number, so she won't be able to contact them later. This is what I did when I was visiting a university campus in Halifax last summer. While I was sitting under a tree, two zoolies walked by, and I whistled. I caught the attention of the uglier of the two and we began talking about sex. She had spiked hair which was dyed three different colors; definitely not the kind of girl you'd take out anywhere. She was fat with enormous tits and what appeared to be a tight ass. She agreed to meet me at the room where I was staying and we had a real good time together. I used my real name, but she also wanted to know my address. She said she was coming to Prince Edward Island in about two weeks, and I figured you give her your address and you're in a lot of trouble. So I gave her the address of a guy who lives near me whose name is the same as mine. I also gave my best friend her address so he could call her if he ever went over to Halifax. While in Halifax, I met a couple of other girls on the same campus who were really cute. Then a month and a half later I got a letter from a girl in Halifax asking me over. I figured it was one of the two cute ones I had met there, and made plans to go over for five days. I spent about $50 getting the train there and another $100 drinking in the bar car. Then I got roses and chocolates and showed up at the dorm and knocked on her door. This beast comes out I've never seen before, and I near shit. The guy with the same name as mine must have gotten her to write me. He was getting back at me, because the zoolie I had given his address to must have gotten in touch with him. Well I took the girl out and we had supper at a restaurant. It wouldn't matter in Halifax anyway, because no one knows me there. I spent the night in a bar and got the train back first thing the next morning. I must have spent $400 that weekend. It was funny afterwards. I know the guy with the same name as mine must have done it, but what could I say? I'd already done the same thing to him. #2368

Holiday trips

On a holiday you usually go for a week or two out of the province somewhere which is totally new and different. If you're not involved with anybody at home, you're usually up for having a few sexual experiences at the time, because you don't have to worry about somebody carrying a tale home. You have more freedom to do as you please. For example, when I am on holiday I can wear bathing suits which are much more revealing. But on the beaches on Prince Edward Island, I have to wear a more conservative suit which doesn't expose too much so people won't think I'm loose.

One problem is that single girls often take their holidays with their parents or visit relatives elsewhere. This makes it almost impossible to have any sexual experiences at the time. Can you imagine going out to a club with your mom and dad hoping to pick up a guy for a one-night stand? However, I have had a couple of holidays which didn't involve my relatives.

One holiday I was lucky enough to have two guys in a one-week period. That was extraordinary for me, because I've never had that many guys in that short a time before. One was the conductor on the train, of all people. I was traveling overnight to meet a guy in Ontario, and it was like a straight pickup. I was sitting there in the train car and the conductor gave me the eye as he was going down the aisle. He just looked at me and said, "Oh, baby," and he kept coming back and making comments. Finally he struck up a conversation and we started talking. There was obviously a physical attraction between us. He suggested we go down to the night part of the caboose, but I felt a few reservations about it. Later the other conductor, who was a grandfatherly type, just looked at me and said, "Look, dear, you only live once. Have a good time while you're young," and winked at me. So I thought, what the hell, I'm going to have a good time. So I went down to the end of the train and we had a jolly time swaying to the music of the tracks. When I got to Toronto I met a friend who used to go with my girlfriend. He was interested in having me as his girlfriend, but I told him, "No way!" He could be a friend and that would be it. I didn't want to be second fiddle. He'd had my girlfriend, so he wasn't going to have me too. After I visited him I went to see a guy elsewhere in Ontario I was interested in, and he and I had three days of fun. Afterwards I came back home to Charlottetown, and no one ever knew anything about it.

Another time I went on a holiday to Florida with my girlfriend, Nancy. I had just finished several years of advanced training in which I'd had to spend my time studying and had little time available for men. So I was really ready for meeting some guys and having a few one-night stands. I didn't care what we did as long as we met some men. Nancy is going with a guy here, but it isn't anything serious. Unfortunately we went down after the regular tourist season. Usually the single male tourists are interested in having a good time too, but there weren't that many tourists around. However, I found the local men were pretty direct. They can spot the tourists right off. You come in with your white skins, and stand around looking at everything with an expression on your face that says, "Wow! Isn't this great?" They naturally assume you are up for a good time, which I was, and after a drink or two they want to know if you are game. If you're not there for sun, surf, and sex, why did you bother going?

But I didn't get to have a good time, because Nancy was such a wet blanket. She likes her guy at home and didn't want to have anything to do with the guys down there. Guys got the message she wasn't interested, and they wouldn't come around our table. Also she is kind of unattractive in some ways. Because we weren't giving the guys the come-on, I didn't have a selection of guys I would have wanted to get involved with. I also had to be careful about what I did. Nancy and I work together and she is an awful gossip. If she had been willing to have some fun with the guys, I wouldn't have had to worry. She wouldn't dare spill the beans on me when we got back to Charlottetown, because I could have done the same to her. But as it was, if I were to do anything by myself in Florida, she was likely to mouth off about it to everyone at work. I was ready to throttle Nancy. She's one hell of a milksop to take on a holiday.

I had a couple of offers in Florida and rejected them both. The first night Nancy and I went into a nightclub at the motel and met this really pleasant guy who was also from Canada. He and Nancy were really talking away, but you couldn't get me to open my trap. I was overwhelmed with all the hustle and bustle and the crowds. At home I'm used to going somewhere and knowing half the people there. But when I looked around the club, I didn't see a single face I knew. I was in culture shock and really scared. I finally got myself together and was able to yap a little bit with the guy who'd joined us. After we'd yapped for about an hour and a half, he asked me to dance. Once we were dancing and away from Nancy, he asked if I would like to go back to his room. I told him no, I didn't think I would. I was really tired that night and wanted to go back to my own room. But I think Nancy really got in my way of doing things. If she hadn't been there, I probably would have gone with him. Even though I knew the guy was married, it was just going to be a one-night thing and he was really nice and seemed to be a really kind person. You can usually tell if someone is going to be an ogre. He had a very nice personality, probably would have been quite good company, and wasn't making a real come-on either.

Another night we met this crazy ass, who was a big business tycoon and down for a convention. As soon as he saw Nancy and me, he moved right over to our table and bought us drinks for the evening. We all talked and talked. He thought he was really something, and gave the impression he could get anybody into bed. I thought, "You're a big crazy, because you're not getting this lady into bed." Later I went off to the washroom, and when I got back to our table neither Nancy nor the guy were saying a word. You could have heard a pin drop. Finally I asked Nancy, "What's wrong?" "Oh, nothing," she said, "I'm tired. How about you?" So as we were walking back to our room, I asked her, "What in the hell was going on?" Nancy explained, "He wanted us to go to a party of conventioneers with some other girls. And I told him we certainly weren't interested in that. He wanted to drop you off once we got to the party and for me and him to go to his room for some fun." The guy had become quite upset when Nancy turned him down, because I guess he figured that by paying for the drinks all night he was going to get us to give him a good time. I don't think I would have wanted to go to the party anyway. You don't know what kind of guys you'd meet there. They might get out of control and be really dirty with you if they wanted to. We also met a couple of broads who were going to the party, and believe me they were not my kind of people. They looked like paid whores.

As our trip continued, I got to feeling that Jeez this is one hell of a bummer of a holiday. I really wanted a rip-roaring hot time and wasn't having it. I was getting desperate and really, really mad. Then the last couple of days of the holiday we met a married couple at the pool. Nancy and I were suntanning when the guy struck up a conversation with me. He then introduced his wife to us. She was a sweet lady and she and Nancy got along well. So we decided we'd all go off to a club together that night. Nancy told me that from talking to his wife she had the impression the guy was a bit of a swinger or something. We all had a lovely dinner together, and while Nancy and his wife were off at the washroom he and I started talking about our favorite topic, which is sex. I looked at him and said, "You've fooled around, haven't you?" He looked kind of surprised and said, "Yeah. How did you know?" "Just the way you act." I didn't tell him it was because of what Nancy had told me. Then he asked, "Would you fool around with me?" "Yeah, I guess so," I told him. He got really charged up over that and got quite a hard-on. It was really funny. He said, "Oh, babe. Boy would I ever like to nail you right now." I told him, "For God's sake, will you keep your voice down. Your wife is right across the room."

I liked the guy. He wasn't gorgeous, but he wasn't bad looking, and he had a really nice personality. I always like people who are really outgoing and chatty and make you feel at ease, which he did completely. Later that night we made our plans about getting together. He said he didn't know how to make things work, but I told him, "It's easy. You take off and meet me somewhere tomorrow at one of the motels. Make an excuse and I'll make an excuse and nobody's going to know a thing." And that is what we did. We both took our cars and met at a Burger King up the road and went and got a motel room. We had a lovely time, let me tell you. And my God we were good. Usually when you just meet somebody like that, the sex part is not that great. But with him it was just as if we had known each other all our lives. Oh we had a fantastic time. He was really, really taken with me, which was nice. He said if he saw more of me he was sure he'd fall in love. I told him it was a good thing he didn't, because he was married and didn't need anything like that. We talked and chatted away and laughed. After about two hours we just had to tear ourselves out of the room to get back. That night the four of us went out together again. It was our last night in Florida, and the next morning when Nancy was out of the room he came to see me. "What are you doing here?" I said. "You're going to get in trouble, boy." "I couldn't leave without saying goodbye," he told me. And we ended up having some more fun in the bedroom. But there was no way I was going to let Nancy know that the two of us had anything going with each other. #2369

Asian sex centers

I know a number of males from Prince Edward Island who travel to Thailand and the Philippines for the women. Some of the males are single and some are married. I am middle-aged and single. I go about twice a year myself for this purpose and have done so for more than ten years. I and the others go to places like Bangkok and Pattaya in Thailand and to Manila and Angeles in the Philippines. These places have districts with many bars for foreign men, and I see lots of males there from Germany, Australia, England, and the United States. Most of the guys go for a visit lasting from ten days to three months. They have to travel so far to get there, and the airline tickets are costly, so they plan to stay for some time. The foreign males are from eighteen to seventy years old, and about forty years old on average. The girls in the bars are between eighteen and twenty-six years old. A few are as young as sixteen, but the average is about twenty-one or twenty-two.

Even though I prefer the culture and scenery of Thailand, and there are more gorgeous girls in Thailand, I go mostly to the Philippines. This is because the girls are more caring in the Philippines, and they look after you and show they really like you. Years ago the girls were this way in Thailand too. But today the Thai girls are no longer as caring as they used to be, although they are still nice and friendly. I think they are more interested in the money and perhaps they would rather marry a Thai man. There are other factors why I prefer to go to the Philippines. For example, there is a higher incidence of AIDS in Thailand and most Thai girls don't speak English, whereas most Philippine girls do.

Usually you find a hotel in or near one of the districts with many bars for foreigners. Often you return to your favorite hotel and the staff remember you and your name. Bars are clustered together, and you normally walk into a bar, take a quick look at the dancers and bartenders, who are female, and stay if you find any of them cute. Otherwise you leave and go check out another bar. I find about fifty percent of the girls are acceptably attractive and about two or three percent are gorgeous. It is difficult to judge how attractive a girl is in a bar with black lighting. You have to be careful, because black light hides wrinkles and stretch marks. It's like comparison shopping. Sometimes you see someone attractive but keep looking in other bars to see if there's someone you like better. Then if you decide there isn't anyone, you return to the bar with the cute girl, but sometimes someone else has already paid her bar fine and taken her out. The bars open between noon and four o'clock in the afternoon and close between two and three o'clock in the morning. Lots of the girls who have children work the afternoon shift so they can return home at night. Because they have had kids their bodies aren't as perfect. Their breasts aren't as firm and they may have stretch marks.

When you decide to stay in a bar, you watch a cute dancer and make eye contact with her. She smiles and comes over during a break. You might initiate contact by buying her a drink, but you definitely buy her a drink when you talk to her. The mama-san, who manages the bar and keeps accounts, often makes introductions and encourages you to buy drinks for a girl. On a busy night the ratio of girls to foreign men is about three to one. On a quiet night the ratio is about ten to one. Philippine and Thai men do not go to these bars. I find ninety to ninety-five percent of the dancers are available for sex. A few are virgins and not available. Sometimes the dancers get physical with you to get you to buy them a drink or take them home. I don't get physical in the bar unless the dancer initiates it.

The dancers make money dancing, getting customers to buy them drinks, and going home with customers. In the Philippines the bar pays the girl about $2.50 a day for dancing. Your drink costs 65 cents to a dollar, and her drink costs $2. In Thailand drinks are $3.50 to $4.00 both for you and the girl. The girl receives about half the price of the drinks you buy for her. My guess is that on average a girl might have men buy her 50 drinks a month. I buy lots of drinks for the girls. The dancer can decide she doesn't want to leave the bar with a specific customer. Each bar has its own rules for their dancers and expects they won't make a regular practice of turning men down. In Angeles the bar fine is $20 for taking the girl out. Half of this goes to the bar and the other half to the girl. After you pay the bar fine you don't pay the girl anything more unless you decide to tip her, and I normally tip about $5. In Bangkok you pay the bar $9 and pay the girl from $30 to $40. I think that the average girl is bar fined about twice a week, but the most popular ones are probably bar fined every night. You can see that by local standards this is a high-paying job for the girl. In fact many of the girls have cell phones, which are quite expensive by local standards. Most girls come from the poorer regions of the Philippines, such as Samar, and many tell their parents they are working in a hotel or department store. In contrast, I talked to one woman who works in a local supermarket and is paid less than $1 a day. I've been told that the girls in brothels for the local men cost from $1 to $5 and have to service large numbers of customers. All of these prices are in US dollars in the year 2000.

Efforts to obtain sex

After you pay the bar fine the dancer leaves with you for your hotel unless you two decide to get something to eat first. The dancer stays with you for either "a short time" or "a long time." A short time is an hour or two, and a long time is overnight. When you pay the bar fine you are paying for a short time. The dancer decides if she wants to stay with you for a long time, depending on how much she likes you. A long time doesn't cost any more than a short time; it's the same price. The girl expects to have straight sex with you. Most of the girls are not interested in oral or anal sex. The arrangement is much like renting a girlfriend, and the girl does what she is comfortable doing sexually and stays with you as long as she wants. I am pleased that the girls I take out from the bar normally want to spend the night with me. If a man is violent with a girl he is likely to be blacklisted in the bars and charged by the police. Most of the girls are interested in getting married, and they ask if you are married. Some of the girls, my guess would be ten percent, do marry foreign men and go to live in Australia, or Hawaii, or elsewhere.

I have my favorite bar where I spend most of my time and do most of my drinking. The bar lets me run up a tab and bring in bottled cokes that I prefer to drink. I spend more time with the bartenders than with the dancers. The bartenders are female and most are in their early twenties. They speak better English, often have more education, and are more fun to talk to. Also they are more of a challenge. In some of the bars the bartenders are sexually available and willing to be bar fined. However, most of the bartenders in my favorite bar are not willing to become involved with customers. They are very choosy and have to really like you. I'm proud that I've been sexually involved with two of them. Some of the other western men I've talked to in this bar have never been able to get together with one of the bartenders.

During my visit I go through a few girls until I find the right one, and then I stay with her the rest of my trip. In a two-week period I may see from one to three different girls, and I may have sex about four times. I often look for a favorite girl from a previous visit. I find there is a turnover of about twenty to twenty-five percent of the girls in a specific bar each year, but people will tell you where they are. A girl who leaves may be working in another bar, may have gotten married to a local man or a foreigner, may be working at another job, or may have gone back to school. You also have to worry about jealousy in the bars. Once you get together with a girl from one bar she is likely to be upset if you see another girl from the same bar. She does not take the fact she sees other men into consideration. I did see a fight between two girls over a tourist.

Some trips I don't have sex with anyone the whole time. I enjoy drinking and talking to the girls and often I just feel too tired and decide to go back to my hotel alone and go to bed.

I find the big attraction of going to these places is that because you have so much more money than they do the people treat you like a millionaire or royalty. Everything is inexpensive, including hotels, liquor, food, and women, and you can live like a king while you are there. If I could retire, I would spend a number of months a year there. Young, gorgeous girls at home are not attracted to a middle-aged man like myself. And there is an unlimited supply of young, gorgeous girls in Asia. Also, there is little commitment to the girls. If I get involved with someone at home there are all kinds of expectations. More than ninety percent of the sex I have is with girls in the Philippines and Thailand.

It is no problem meeting attractive young women in these countries who do not work in the bars. Many are interested in marrying western men and are willing to get sexually involved with you, and some of these are professionals, such as teachers and psychologists. Women want security, and security means money. Most people in the Philippines think all westerners are rich. Women in the Philippines tell me they are less interested in the local men because even after they get married the men want to have as many girlfriends as they can and to have children with all of them. The women also think an older man like myself is more likely to settle down with one woman. But I am not interested in marriage unless I fall in love. I find the fun is in the chase, but after you catch someone she becomes boring. #2370

Obtaining sex and relationships

People use various methods to obtain sex and relationships. These include trying to be more appealing, obtaining the right facilities, using alcohol, and employing certain strategies and tactics. Each of these is considered below.

Appeal

People make numerous efforts to be more appealing to potential partners for sex and relationships. These efforts include improving their physical appearance by dieting, exercising, wearing a hairpiece, undergoing plastic surgery, using makeup, and wearing clothes which are attractive, interesting, and/or physically revealing.

Guys and girls are very prejudiced when it comes to appearance. It really doesn't matter how nice you are as a person, because if you're not physically attractive, no one is going to bother trying to get to know you in the first place. [#2371]

People try to emphasize their attractive features and hide their unattractive ones. "If a girl has it, it doesn't hurt to flaunt it, and there are lots of girls who aren't scared to flaunt it. They wear short, tight miniskirts that show the most leg and emphasize the ass." "I'm proud of my large breasts, and most guys really seem to appreciate them. Every summer when I go to the beach I wear a small bikini because I like the looks I get." "Girls tell me I have a cute butt, so I dress to show it. I wear a snug-fitting pair of pants without any back pockets." "I think girls like a guy with lots of hair because it reminds them of their teddy bears." "I wear baggy sweaters to hide my fat stomach, because girls would find it very unattractive. I also have fat legs, so I wear baggy casual pants." "See this stupid birthmark? I use a foundation to cover it when I go out, because I'm afraid it would turn girls off. If I could afford it, I'd have cosmetic surgery to get rid of it." [#2372]

Trying to look sexy doesn't mean you want others to think you are "a sure thing" or "an easy make." It just means you want to look attractive to the opposite sex. Most women like to wear appealing clothes, ones that fit snugly and give them a shapely appearance. They try to emphasize their legs and bust. They like to wear an alluring perfume and continually moisten their lips to signal they are in the mood for a romantic kiss. A little extra wiggle here and there and a bit of cleavage doesn't hurt either. All these things make women feel attractive. When they look and feel attractive women are more confident that they can pique a man's interest and keep his attention. A woman wants to be noticed and then she can proceed from there in whatever fashion she is comfortable with. [#2373]

People watch you at the beach in summer, so you have to watch your weight. A lot of people refuse to go to the beach because they are too fat or too skinny. Instead you see a lot of muscular men and slim, attractive girls there. You also have to have a tan. I know one girl who starts lying in the sun in May, when it's still pretty chilly, so she'll have a tan before she goes to the beach. [#2374]

Appeal

I never found it very easy to talk to girls until I started working out really hard with weights. Now I'm really well built, and I know this body draws attention. #2375

If you look slim and trim, more males will be attracted to you, want to talk to you, and ask you out or to dance. The opposite is true if you're fat. It seems that all females, no matter how slight they are, think they are overweight. Therefore, it isn't surprising we try all kinds of techniques to look thinner. I'll mention some of the techniques that I and other females I've observed use to hide our weight.

Choosing the right clothes is crucial. Many females wear tight clothing, and some pants look so tight you'd think the girl jumped into them from a high-rise building. But I think tight clothes show everyone exactly where the lumps are. I find that loose clothing does a better job. Loose clothes are not molded to your body, so they don't reveal the troubled areas. One girl I know always wears loose-fitting clothes. If you study the shape of her body you can see she has excess weight, but her clothes conceal it well. Another girl repeatedly wears sweatpants. Sweatpants are baggy, comfortable, and hide weight well. A different technique is to wear skirts and dresses rather than pants. These hide the lower half of the body, especially the hips and thighs. Many short women wear skirts and dresses to hide their excess fat and to look taller.

Accessories are great, because they draw attention away from the body itself. The bigger and flashier they are, the better. For example, if you wear a shiny necklace over a dark top, you draw the viewer's eyes to your neck, and the lower body is left unnoticed. One girl frequently wears a bright silk scarf around her neck tied in a fancy bow. This does the trick, because you are less likely to see she is bottom heavy. When you wear a belt around your hips, rather than your waist, you can hide a thick waist and make your body look longer. I wear a belt around my hips to hide the fact I have a short waist. High heels make legs look longer, and help you look taller and therefore slimmer.

The face is so important for appearance that it is an asset if it looks thin. I find that long hair makes the face look round or squared off. But when your hair is cut short and is away from the face, your face looks more defined and slimmer. Blush used the right way can emphasize the cheekbones and make the face look thinner.

Also, how you carry yourself can make or break you. If you slouch, you'll look dumpy, no matter what you are wearing. If you walk heavily, instead of gracefully, you will also undermine your efforts. #2376

Other attempts to appeal to others include trying to appear wealthy, successful, confident, interesting, young, pleasant, fun, charming, talented, intelligent, agreeable, and interested in the other person and what the other person is interested in.

Money always seems to draw people like flies. I made the mistake of hauling out my credit card at the bar last night. I spent two hundred and fifty dollars buying drinks for others, but I almost think it was worthwhile. I had a great time and the girl I met is incredible. #2377

Guys with an expensive or fast car get a great of attention from females. As one girl stated, "Look at that guy with the Corvette. He must be loaded to own a car like that. That would be a good fellow to grab on to." I've been told by guys who drive a nice car, "We always spend Friday or Saturday night cruising around town. It's really surprising how many girls flag us down looking for a ride." #2378

When you go to hockey games, you always see lots of puck bunnies standing around giggling. Puck bunnies are teenage girls who attend hockey games because of their infatuation with the players. They usually wear a leather jacket or baggy sweater; skintight jeans; pointed shoes; no socks, which makes little sense in the chilly rink; perfect makeup; and a hairstyle which is sprayed solidly in place. They frequently support the local team "with the cutest players." Most have a favorite player, but know nothing about him other than his name and the information in the program. One told me, "I liked the same player for three years and was totally infatuated with him. I never missed a game and even traveled out of town to see him play. But I never did meet him." Another went so far as to call up "her player," but was too nervous to speak to him and hung up. Most have very little knowledge about the game of hockey and attend simply to watch "the boys," who are "dreamy." You often see them in a group wandering around the rink or standing next to the glass giggling. They hardly ever miss a game and some even show up for practices. They hope to marry their favorite player and giggle to each other whenever a player looks their way. In contrast with the puck bunnies, there are girlfriends of the players, who dress more casually and are more knowledgeable about the game. They express their sentiments about the puck bunnies, which range from "They don't really bother me. After all, they're only kids. Some are only thirteen years old," to "I hate those girls. They come here looking like sluts, and don't even have a clue about the game. They give us a bad name, because people call us puck bunnies too." #2379

Trying to look attractive

Shelly is an attractive and well kept twenty-one-year-old. She was born and raised on a farm. She finds outdoor work inviting and invigorating because "it gives you a healthy glow." I've observed her efforts in our apartment to look attractive for university classes, work, dates, and clubs.

Shelly showers and washes her hair every day. She washes her hair with Halsa shampoo at present, but says she is willing to use any kind of shampoo. She conditions her hair at least twice a week and shaves her legs every other day, "otherwise they are unbearable." Shelly likes to use soft-shave soap and Daisy razors, otherwise she gets razor burn.

Shelly is in the shower for seven to ten minutes, and occupies the bathroom for seventeen to twenty minutes altogether. While in the bathroom she washes her face with Phisoderm soap and applies Sea Breeze antiseptic skin cleanser. She flosses and brushes her teeth and rinses her mouth with mouthwash. She uses Secret deodorant and puts on her contact lenses. After she leaves the bathroom she does her hair. She combs it and applies a handful of mousse to the front and sides. Then, placing five clips in her hair to keep it up and off her face, she blow-dries it. The clips "help add volume to my hair." When her hair is dry she removes the clips, curls her bangs, and sprays her hair with Aussie Sprunch Spray. She prefers this spray because "I love the smell of it." Shelly maintains her hairstyle by having it trimmed every six to eight weeks, and by having a body perm every eight months or so. During the summer months Shelly often spritzes lemon juice on her hair in order to achieve some natural-looking highlights. This tends to dry out her hair; therefore she conditions it more often. Shelly prefers to wear her hair down and have it frame her face. However, for special occasions like Christmas and New Year's Eve she will wear it up in a French braid or a twist.

Shelly hates to be seen wearing her glasses. She often wears contact lenses because she doesn't like hiding her eyes. She likes her blue eyes and chooses makeup carefully to accentuate them. She refuses to wear any mascara other than blue-black mascara by Covergirl. Shelly curls her eyelashes in order to make her eyes stand out even more.

"It just gives your eyes a little more oomph." The most important of all her cosmetics is "my eyeliner pencil." Her teal blue eyeliner is a must. "I don't like people to see me without it because my face looks rather washed out."

Shelly files or trims the jagged edges of her nails a few times a week. She only applies nail polish if there is a special occasion, and even then she only wears soft colors, such as pearly white or soft pink. "It must be the country girl in me, because I just can't see myself wearing candy-apple red on my nails." She never applies polish to her toenails, but does use a pumice stone on her feet to remove layers of dead skin. She also applies peppermint foot lotion to keep her feet soft. This lotion has "a natural cooling effect and helps soothe tired feet."

The smile is especially important for looking attractive. Shelly maintains her smile by going to the dentist once a year for a checkup and fluoride coating. Shelly believes flossing is essential for a healthy mouth. She has never worn braces or a retainer on her teeth. She considered getting braces a few years ago until she discovered this would require having her jaw broken. She decided to leave her teeth as they are.

Shelly's wardrobe is a major factor in her appearance. She wears certain colors which bring out the color of her eyes, such as emerald green and teal blue. Fuchsia and red are other colors that are compatible with her skin tone. She enjoys shopping, particularly at stores which carry designer clothes. Shelly spends an average of two hours a week shopping for clothes. She has particular tastes and buys clothes that accentuate her tall, sturdy build. She is five feet eight inches tall and weighs one hundred and forty pounds. She enjoys shopping at stores such as The Jean Connection, Esprit, Drifters, Eatons, Christopher's Beach Club, Dalmys, The Lady Slipper, Henderson and Cudmore, and Seasons. When she is off Island she shops at The Gap, Bootlegger, Cotton Ginny, and La Senza Lingerie. "I like to be in fashion, but I also like to have some things that everyone else doesn't have."

Shelly's wardrobe consists of the following:
Pants: Two pairs of Guess jeans, and one pair each of Levi's jeans, Esprit jeans, Esprit cotton pants, gym pants, and leggings.
Tops: One Polo shirt, eight T-shirts in various styles and colors, four blouses, two cable-knit sweaters, three cotton-knit sweaters, and three sweatshirts.
Skirts: One each in blue, brown, pink, and a floral print.
Dresses: Two.

Coats: One Park City, one Helly Hansen, one trench coat, one denim jacket, one blue blazer, and one leather coat.
Shoes: Flats – one pair each in blue, black, beige, white, burgundy, and brown.
  Pumps – one pair each in white, black, brown, and beige.
  Nike Air – one pair.
Accessories: Purses – one each in brown, black, and white.
  Leather backpack – one.
  Handbags – one in denim and one in straw.
  Belts – one each in blue, black, and beige; two in brown.
Undergarments: All Vogue designs in either white or peach.

Shelly often changes her mind about what she will wear. She takes much longer deciding when she goes to clubs and other social events. It takes her an average of seven minutes to get dressed for class, and anywhere from ten to thirty minutes to choose an outfit when she goes out on a date or to the clubs. When she gets ready for a date she changes her outfit two or three times before she decides what is appropriate and looks best. She is more indecisive when she prepares for a date than when she goes out to clubs.

Shelly's jewelry is a must. She never leaves the house without it. She almost always wears sterling silver jewelry. Her everyday jewelry includes five rings, one bracelet, one bangle, two chains, earrings, and a Gucci watch. For special occasions she wears her gold jewelry, which consists of a watch, a bracelet, earrings, and two rings. But she thinks that her silver jewelry looks better on her.

Shelly also uses perfume to be attractive. Her favorite perfumes are Lauren by Ralph Lauren and Eternity and Escape by Calvin Klein. All of these perfumes have "a subtle, soft, and elegant scent." She tries to find perfumes that will attract attention from males. She thinks that women's perfumes are specifically designed for male senses. She sprays or dabs her perfume on her wrists and neck. Shelly also has matching body lotions to go with the perfumes. Most of the men she dates comment positively on her perfume. Only once did a date say that her perfume was "overpowering." She buys her perfumes at a local department store and at duty-free shops at the United States border.

Shelly does her laundry with great care in order to keep her clothes in good condition. She washes all delicate articles by hand with a liquid soap and then places them flat to dry. She irons all her shirts, sweaters, skirts, and pants (including denims). Shelly likes to be recognized for looking neat, and clothes that are ironed give her "a polished look."

Shelly watches what she eats in order to maintain her figure and to try to lose a few pounds. Some of her favorite foods include pasta, rice, soup, salads, fresh fruit, vegetables, chicken, steak, ice cream, and Pepsi. She absolutely refuses to drink coffee or tea. She limits herself when eating chocolate, sugar, eggs, or deep-fried food. She insists on drinking diet soda. When eating in a restaurant she asks for a straw for her drink in order to ensure that her lipstick lasts the duration of her meal.

Shelly exercises two or three times a week. Her exercises stretch and tone her muscles. They include situps, pushups, leg lifts, toe touches, jogging on the spot, and occasionally going for a ten-to-fifteen-minute jog outdoors. The main purpose of her exercises is to slim down and tone her thighs and buttocks. She refers to this region as "my weak spot" and claims this is where all her calories go. About once every two weeks Shelly goes for a swim at a local health club. She finds she gets a good workout in the water, and then she relaxes in the whirlpool and sauna. She considers the sauna particularly good "for cleaning your pores." Once she tried an aqua-fitness class at the YMCA. She enjoyed the class but was rather shocked to find the average age of the other participants was about sixty-eight.

Shelly likes to keep the entire apartment tidy, particularly her bedroom. She always makes her bed within twenty minutes after waking up. She likes to have the dishes done, and not piled in the sink. She dusts the furniture and waters the plants. She hangs her clothes in their proper places or folds them and places them neatly in her bureau. It is important to her to keep the apartment neat because "people find neatness, rather than sloppiness, attractive."

Shelly's car is in good working condition, and the body has had a recent paint job. She keeps her car clean, both inside and out. She has waxed it numerous times. Once a year she takes it to the Shine Factory and has it thoroughly cleaned and Scotch Guarded. She likes the look of her car, but often wishes it were a two-door car rather than a four-door. "Two-door cars are sportier and more appealing."

Shelly is careful not to smoke or drink excessively in the presence of others, because "this can turn people off." She realizes these are bad habits and tries to limit herself. She smokes approximately ten cigarettes a day. She never smokes in the presence of her relatives, because some of them would find this repulsive. In order to maintain an image of attractive innocence she lets her family believe that she doesn't smoke or drink.

Shelly very seldom uses foul language, unless she is quite angry or upset. She considers bad language offensive, and that it leads others to find you unattractive. Even when she is upset she uses some reserve in her choice of swearwords.

Gossip is another unattractive trait which Shelly tries to avoid. She sees this as a bad habit which causes others to want to gossip about you. However she has a tough time avoiding it. "I like to know what is going on." Her one weakness is talking about one of her roommates with the other roommates. But she does not want to be known as a gossip and this helps her talk less about others. "Knowing I have this weakness helps me fix it."

Shelly prefers the summer months when she gets a nice tan. She uses a sunscreen lotion with SPF 8 in order to prevent damage to her skin which could produce wrinkles and cancer. In order to maintain her tan over the winter Shelly started going to a tanning salon. However, she found this rather costly and recently stopped going. She then tried a Vichy (sunless) self-tanning lotion. This helped her look tanned, but she found the lotion made her face greasy, which detracted from her goal of looking attractive.

Shelly always tries new products and ideas in her efforts to look attractive. "I enjoy experimenting with new makeup, but I never try anything too exotic or wild." Shelly describes her look as "not all natural beauty; it has to be worked at a bit." [#2380]

Trying to look bigger

Appearance is the most important factor in determining which males and females get together. I don't think this is shallow; it's simply the way things are. However, no one will admit it. They say things like "I don't care what you look like. If you can talk and you've got a great personality, you're great." Bullshit! How are you ever going to find out that I have a personality and can talk if I look like hell's creation? Only if my appearance is acceptable to you will you give me a chance to talk to you and reveal my personality.

My problem is that I am a twenty-year-old male, stand six feet one inch tall, and weigh only 150 pounds. In other words, I am skinny. The reason this is a problem is that girls prefer big males. Generally I can score, or get together sexually, with a female if I can sit down and talk to her or get her to sit down and talk to me. But I could get together with better quality females if I was larger and more muscular. I don't think being skinny is the only reason I haven't been able to get together with certain girls, but I think it has often been a factor because appearances matter a lot. I score, but I see real winners go for males who are bigger than I am. Typically guys who are big and muscular go out with the most popular and best-looking girls. Looking bigger is just another trait that makes you more attractive than others. Perhaps girls want someone who looks like he will be able to defend them. I don't know. Although the main reason I would like to look bigger is that I would be considered more attractive, there are also certain jobs I might apply for which are closed to males who aren't big enough, such as a bouncer at a club.

The fact I am skinny has been hammered home time and again over the years. In junior high and high school anybody who was real skinny was always picked on. Kids would only start a fight with someone they thought they could beat up. Because of my build I was repeatedly beaten up. Also, people frequently made comments about how thin I was. For example, my grandparents have always been on my back to gain more weight. In contrast, my parents never said anything, because they realized it would give me a complex. However, my girlfriends' parents usually make comments, such as "Boy, have you lost a lot of weight since winter," which is an awful thing to say to someone who is concerned about not looking skinny. I had a friend in my homeroom class in high school who was tall and real skinny too, and we used to always talk about our problem. The biggest joke when we ran into each other was to say, "Wow! Haven't seen you in a long time. Are you losing weight?" We considered this the very worst thing that could be said to us. If anyone else ever said it we would write them off and just walk away.

In order to appear bigger than I really am, I have developed a number of techniques which I use regularly. I have put all of them into practice. Try them out; they all work.

If you want to look larger, the most important consideration is your clothes. My primary technique is to wear two or more layers of clothes so that my upper body appears larger. Thus in winter I usually wear a shirt with a sweater over it. However, I have at times worn shirts with a sweater or sweatshirt underneath for added bulk. In winter I normally wear a sports coat with a winter coat over it. When I don't wear my sports coat I wear four or five layers of clothes, including two or three jackets in denim and other light materials instead of a single heavy jacket, because several layers together make you look thicker. I also buy flannel and velour shirts because of their thickness.

Trying to look bigger

When buying shirts, jackets, and sports coats, I make sure the sleeves are just a little bit long. Nothing looks worse than drawing attention to your skinny hands and wrists by wearing sleeves which are too short. If my shirt sleeves are too short, I roll them up, but leave them far enough down so that they cover my elbows and a little bit of my forearms. This way people won't see how bony your elbows are and your forearms will look thicker.

It is very important to have the top half of your body look as wide as possible. Therefore, what you wear on top should be short and not extend below your waist. Otherwise, your top half will look longer, narrower, and skinnier. I always tuck my sweater into my pants rather than let it hang beneath my waist. Sports coats and jackets are great for making your shoulders look wider, but I try to buy those that end no lower than the belt loops on my pants. Also wearing shirts with collars detracts from the thinness and length of your neck. Moreover, the collars should extend to the side rather than down. In the case of striped shirts the stripes should be horizontal rather than vertical. The more your clothes take a direction at right angles to your height, the wider you look.

In order to have your top half look as wide as possible, you want your lower half to look narrow. Therefore it is best to wear fairly tight jeans which accentuate what you have, instead of bulky pants. Rugby pants make a person look square, and because they make you look thicker through the bottom, you usually have to wear a sweater to compensate. It looks ridiculous to have a thicker bottom half than top half.

It is important that your clothes fit and not be too large. If they are too big they will hang on you and people will wonder just where you are located and may well underestimate your size. In addition, dark clothes make you look skinny and light-colored clothes make you look larger. Practically my whole wardrobe consists of light-colored clothes.

Sports clothes pose some difficulties. When playing soccer, I always wear sweatpants rather than shorts so no one will see how skinny my legs are. However, if you wear a sweatshirt and sweatpants together it is difficult to have your top half look wider than your bottom half. The only way to achieve this is to wear more than one sweatshirt or to wear your sweatshirt with the inside, or fuzzy side, turned out to emphasize your top.

There are also certain techniques that can be used for your body. My hands are long and thin, or what I believe are called "pianist's hands," and I make sure my nails are short at all times. Long nails make your hands look twice as long, twice as thin, and twice as feminine. People who have skinny necks should let their hair grow around their neck. This allows people to focus on more than your neck. If you have a skinny face, never grow a beard, because it makes your face look longer. On the other hand, a mustache will make your face look much wider.

There are also postures I use to look less skinny. If you use only the top part of your lungs to breathe, your chest looks almost twenty-five percent fuller and bigger. This technique is no good if you are about to talk to someone because you can't get enough air to breathe. However, it is great if you want people to notice you and not think you are incredibly skinny. Another technique is to apply downward pressure on your shoulders with your shoulder muscles. This makes your chest look fuller and causes the muscles which run from your neck to the tip of your shoulders to be more prominent. This is hard to keep up because it strains the muscles. However, for a quick walk through a crowd, it works great. When stretching, never raise your arms above your head. This makes your rib cage stick out and your chest disappear. Instead, always stretch downwards. This makes your chest look fuller and emphasizes your shoulder muscles. The one thing you must never do when sleeping with a female is put your hands behind your head. With your arms raised, the female can count every single one of your ribs. Also, your underwear will slip off your hip bones.

There are important seasonal differences in the techniques I use. In winter I wear about five layers of clothes and look much bigger. As a result winter is my best season for picking up girls. Summer, on the other hand, can be very embarrassing, especially the first time I go to the beach with a female, because I am just down to the raw. I use several techniques at the beach, in addition to breathing out of the top of my chest and forcing my shoulders down. When I lie down on a towel I make sure I lie on my stomach, so that my rib cage and hip bones are hidden. If I have to lie on my back, I try to use a pillow, so that my head is raised and my ribs and hip bones don't show. If I have to get up and move around, I do so with confidence and pride. If you walk around with a caved-in chest feeling skinny, you are going to look gross. But if you try to give the impression that you look OK, people will see you as looking OK. It is also very important to have a good tan before you go to the beach, even if you have to sunbathe in solitude to get it. I refuse to go to the beach if I don't have a good tan. I think a tan makes you look bigger. Also, if you don't have a tan people will assume you don't come to the beach very often. Then they will say, "Oh, I can see why. It's because he is skinny." But if you arrive with a nice tan, people will notice it and conclude you go to the beach a lot, and not think about you being skinny. This may sound ridiculous, but believe me, it's true.

In talking to people I also try to cover up the fact I am so skinny. For example, I really weigh 150 pounds. But if someone asks about my weight, I say 160 or 165. Most people don't have any idea how much you are supposed to weigh based on how you look. I can get away with saying 165 because I am tall. If people say, "Wow! You're pretty skinny," I say something like "Yeah, but I'm tall," or "Yeah, but I don't have an ounce of fat on me. It's all muscle," or "I'd rather look the way I do, than fat. Because at least I'm in shape." Most people think you are in better shape if you are skinny rather than fat. Sometimes I also mention the good points of being thin, such as not getting high blood pressure.

Ideally I would like to be 180 pounds and have the additional weight on my chest and shoulders. If you lift weights you can gain muscle and look bulkier. Although I've started lifting weights many times, I've quit just as often. I'll do it for a month, not see any progress, and say, "Forget it." It's no fun; it's work. You've got to work out so long before you see any change and it just doesn't seem to be worth it. But if I wasn't scoring, I'd be one of the biggest, most muscular guys around. However, I do score enough to make me happy, and it makes all the difference. #2381

Facilities

Many people acquire facilities which increase the likelihood of obtaining sex and relationships. The most popular items are a car for dating and parking and an apartment for privacy. In addition, people use their facilities in ways to increase the possibility of obtaining sex.

When my Moroccan roommate invites a date over to our apartment, he tells me well in advance so I can plan to be absent. He creates the atmosphere he wants by wearing his Moroccan robes, fixing a Moroccan meal for his date, and playing music for her on his lute. #2382

It is important to make physical advances in a natural way. When I set up the living room in my apartment, I only put in couches. I didn't use any easy chairs, because they allow a date or visitor to sit off by herself and it's hard to make advances. Couches on the other hand allow me to sit next to someone and make physical contact easily. Another thing I do is put my TV and VCR in the bedroom, where the only place to sit is on the bed. Therefore if someone watches TV or a video with me, we have to lie next to each other, which makes it much easier to get physically involved. #2383

Roommates use prearranged signals to let each other know they are in bed with someone and don't want to be disturbed. The signal might be a towel hung on the doorknob or a pair of shoes placed outside the door. Sometimes people try to be less obvious, and use a signal such as placing their coat on a certain chair. However, this usually proves too subtle for the roommate, who forgets to look for the signal and walks in on the couple. #2384

I saw a real hunk when I was driving downtown. Then I drove around the block to find him again. I even tried speaking to him, but forgot my car window was up. #2385

I'm originally from Vietnam, where it is often difficult to find a private place for sex. Most people do not have cars or their own apartment. Instead they live with other family members. Often they wait until their relatives are asleep, in another room, or gone from the house. Many families use the lower floor of their house for living and the upper floor for storage. Once I was helping out my husband's parents and entered the adjoining house, which belonged to my husband's uncle. At the bottom of the stairs which led to the upper floor I saw my husband's shoes and someone else's. I climbed the stairs and found my husband and a distant relative of his having sex. She was using a tin bowl turned upside down as a cushion for her rear. His uncle's family was downstairs in the kitchen where they could pretend they didn't see them use the stairs. #2386

Sex in cars

Cars provide a degree of privacy and comfort which enables people to use them for sexual activity. For those who do not have sufficient privacy where they live, a car can be their primary location for engaging in sex. This includes those who are living with their parents, those who are engaged in affairs, and those who don't want roommates or apartment mates to know who they are involved with or what they are doing.

Attitudes vary considerably toward having sex in a car. Both of the following statements were made by women. "Having sex in a car is more exciting and adds to the act. There's a feeling of suspense, because you never know if you are going to get caught. Bedrooms are so boring. I like the sense of adventure, and the carefree, spontaneous feeling you get when you do it in a car." "Having sex in a car has to be the tackiest thing in the world. It seems so cheap. There's no romance about it; it's having sex, not making love. It's just 'Slam! Bam! Thank you, ma'am.' Even when I've done it with someone I've gone out with for a long time, I feel like a whore afterwards. Now I just refuse to do it. It's too hard on my self-esteem, and I can't respect myself afterwards."

One of the biggest problems when parking is finding a good location. The primary objective is to find a secluded place which is out of sight of other people. One can spend an inordinate amount of time looking for likely roads to pull off on, and doubling back to investigate them to see if they are acceptable. Side roads can prove unacceptable for a variety of reasons, including the fact one or more houses are located on them, your car can still be seen from the main road, and their condition is too poor to drive on. The problems of finding a good location are illustrated in the following cases. "My girlfriend and I decided we wanted to park. We drove to an area near Charlottetown where my girlfriend used to live because we figured she might recognize a good place to go. First we drove to the end of one major road, but there was nowhere to go that was out of sight, and besides there was a house nearby. Then we went down this long dirt road, but there were a lot of occupied cottages at the end of the road and cars were continuing to use it. Then as we were driving around we passed this sign advertising lots for future cottages next to a two-track road leading into a wooded area. So we doubled back to check it out. There was a farmhouse next to the woods with several cars in front of it. We decided to take a chance that people at the farmhouse wouldn't bother about us, and drove into the woods. It worked out fine, but because the farmhouse was nearby we only took our clothes partially off. I think we were lucky to find a place so quickly." "Having sex in a car isn't as spontaneous as it sounds. It isn't easy to locate a place which is private and off the beaten track, and it's even harder to find in winter when many side roads are snowed in. Once you find a place and are all set to go, you pray someone else won't come there too." "It's so much easier to have sex in your car if you live in the country, rather than in a town or city. In the country, it's much less difficult to find a secluded area where no one goes. But if you find a secluded spot in the city, you can just bet a lot of other people have found it too."

"I'd just met this girl and was taking her home. She seemed willing, so I decided to take her parking. I don't go in for public parking, so I pulled down a dirt road into a field. We stayed for a couple of hours and had a great time, and I was feeling pretty good. But when I went to leave, the car wouldn't budge. It was stuck solid. We had to walk two miles to get a farmer to pull us out. Man, I learned never to go parking down muddy Island roads in the spring." "My girl and I went for a weekend to Cape Breton. When we were driving home on our last day we decided we wanted to find a place where we could park and have sex. We spent over an hour looking for a good place, but there was something wrong with every place we checked out. We'd just about given up when we discovered a rock quarry and we drove in and parked the car there."

Some areas, such as public parks, become well known as places to go parking and can attract many cars at the same time. This creates additional problems, such as recognition by others that you are there. "Jodi and Mark were parking one night at Victoria Park and Randy recognized their car and walked over to chat. He tapped on the window, opened the door, and Jodi and Mark fell out on the ground." Even if people don't disturb you, they often mention to others that they saw you there. "Sue was at the park Friday night with her boyfriend. Over breakfast the next morning her brother casually mentioned seeing her boyfriend's car at the park. Sue's parents were none too pleased and wouldn't allow her to go out that night." Car windows also make it easy to see inside. "Becky was at the drive-in movie with her boyfriend when a van pulled in next to them. Becky said, 'I swear they spent more time looking at us than at the movie. They had a great view too. Their van was so high they could see right down into the car. We tried to ignore them, but it was hard. We hadn't planned on watching the movie, but that's what we ended up doing.'" Another problem with going to popular parking areas is that one can get blocked in by other cars. People are usually reticent to disturb others who are parking in order to ask them to move. "We were at the park and couldn't get our car out because of all the other cars. We ended up sitting there for two hours. I got in shit the next day because it was so late when I got home. But it was worth it, if you know what I mean. We even went back." Still another problem with public areas is regular visits by the police. "We were parked over at the agricultural research center and just starting to get into it when the cops came along and flashed their lights into the car. They told us we'd have to leave. I was really scared they would ask my name. My father would have grounded me for life. That was the last time I went parking where the cops might be."

Sex in cars

All sorts of questions and difficulties arise when you park. For example, should you leave the windows closed to keep the mosquitoes out, or should you keep them open so the car won't become oppressively hot? Should you take certain precautions, like turn the car around first so you can drive forward if you want to leave quickly, and should you lock the doors so no one can open them from the outside? Should you take your clothes off, or leave them partially on in case someone else comes along? Should you leave the radio on to help the mood? Sometimes the songs they play deal with teenage pregnancy or loose women and can put a damper on your activities. You also have to watch what you say. You don't want to mention being in the same spot before with someone else.

There are also various problems associated with the fact one has to keep the car dark so others don't notice the car and don't see what you are doing inside. "Jeannie and Dean were at the drive-in movie and things became pretty heavy. When Jeannie got home her parents were still up. However, once in the house she realized her shirt was on inside out. She says, 'I was hoping like hell they wouldn't notice. It was so dark in the car, I couldn't see when I put my shirt back on. That will never happen again. Now I always make Dean turn on the dome light so I can check that my clothes are on right.'" One problem is that it is easy to misplace items in the dark. "I had this girl out over the weekend. She was extremely friendly, if you know what I mean, and we had a great time. When I went to take my mother to town the next day, she found a pair of pantyhose in the car. I had to do some fast talking to get out of that one. But I also learned to check the car after a date." "I lost my earring, so I called up the man to let him know. He checked his car carefully so his wife wouldn't find it."

There are numerous structural problems when one tries to have sex in a car. For example, the seat is usually too short to stretch out on, and what space there is is severely limited by objects such as the steering wheel, armrests, seat-belt buckles, and controls and dividers between the seats. "The manufacturers sure make it hard to have sex in their cars. Like who the hell came up with the idea of bucket seats? Now some cars have them in the rear too. Whatever happened to those nice wide bench seats cars used to have? Those were made to make out on. With these new seats it's difficult just to hold a girl's hand, and if you want to do more, you risk bodily injury." "The car adds a lot to the act. There's not much room. So you have to be inventive to do it in the room you have. It's great, and it never gets boring." "Carl and his girlfriend were at a party and decided to drive a little bit away from the house to park. When they were getting into it, Carl's knee struck the horn and the horn got stuck. Carl said, 'Everyone came running from the house over to the car. They all seemed to think it was pretty funny. Take my advice, when you go parking get in the back seat away from the horn.'" Sports cars are particularly cramped for space. "I have a Trans Am, and it's kind of hard to get comfortable in. You're either banging your head on the window or smashing your knee on the dash. You spend so much time and effort trying to get into a comfortable position that by the time you do you're too tired to do anything. The bumps and bruises don't help the mood any. It's really bad for the love life." The cramped quarters also make it much more difficult to deal with clothes and to get them off and back on. "Tom and Peggy were parking at Beach Point, and Tom had on a fisherman-knit sweater and Peggy was wearing a cluster ring. Peggy put her hand under Tom's sweater and her ring snagged on it. Peggy was too embarrassed to tell Tom, and she tugged her hand to get the ring loose. She ended up damaging the sweater."

One way in which people handle the limitations of cars is through the use of vehicles which make it easier to engage in sex. "With a car I never know whether to stay in the front or to move to the back seat. Then if you want to move to the back, do you climb over the front seat or do you get out of the car and enter through the rear door? I've solved the problem by buying a truck. It has a nice wide bench seat which doesn't require any decisions. It's my perfect uncomplicated lovemobile." Vans are considered to be ideal vehicles for engaging in sex and carry nicknames like shaggin' wagons, humpmobiles, and lovemobiles, although such names are also used for large cars. Vans have become associated with sexual behavior to such an extent, that a male who arrives in one risks making a bad impression on the girl's parents. They may assume he is after one thing only, and conclude he is unsuitable for their daughter.

Another solution to the problems of having sex in cars is to use the car to go where one can have sex outdoors. "My girlfriend and I have never had sex in my car, because we've always found a good place to do it outside. We've done it in a secluded campsite on a blanket next to the car, and we've driven to isolated beaches. Once we had sex while my girlfriend leaned against the outside of the car."

When one obtains access to private areas, such as apartments, and as one becomes older, the desire to have sex in cars often wanes. "When I was in high school, if I wanted to have sex with my boyfriend, it usually had to be in his car. We just had no place else to go. But once we both started university, we didn't need the car anymore. We each had our own place, and it always seemed that one or the other was available anytime we needed it." "I found that getting older took all the fun out of having sex in a car. When I was sixteen I thought it was great. But as I got older I started to think it was a cheap way to get thrills. I mean if you want it that bad, you should be able to come up with the cash for a motel room. Like my girlfriend keeps saying, 'We aren't kids anymore, and we shouldn't act like we are.'" "Having sex in a car used to be exciting. But as you become older, it kind of loses its appeal. It just doesn't seem appropriate anymore." #2387

Alcohol

Alcohol is a very important facilitator in seeking sex and relationships. People drink in order to feel confident enough to speak to strangers and to make physical advances. Alcohol enables people to overcome concerns about being rejected or hurting their reputations. It enables people to override their fears of rejection, criticism, and embarrassment. Alcohol is called "liquid courage." Alcohol also provides a convenient excuse for acting however one wants.

People like to have a good time. They enjoy socializing, and drinking makes this a lot easier. Clubs are so popular because men want to meet women and vice versa. Alcohol is a catalyst in this social interaction. "People who normally would never talk to someone sober have no problem talking to that person when they are drinking. In general, people who are drinking are less inhibited, more relaxed, and braver." "Some of the most introverted people become the loudest people at parties. Alcohol lets them let go of their fears so they can say and do whatever they want." "I don't even like the taste of alcohol. But I'm normally shy, and liquor liberates me." "Alcohol has the magical ability to free people of their inhibitions, and this is the reason its use is so widespread. I usually have three or four beer, dance, and have lots of fun. The amount of fun I have is proportional to the amount of beer I drink. Alcohol helps me loosen up and break the ice with other people." "At parties in rural communities when the girls become drunk they dance together until the guys get drunk and dance with them. Any guy who dances before he is drunk becomes the laughing stock of the evening." "It's easier to find someone to make out with and get laid when you're drunk." "One of our neighbors, Mrs. Smith, drinks at parties, picnics, and social visits. I feel really sorry for her family because she has embarrassed her husband and children so many times. My parents had a barbecue this last summer and invited all the neighbors. Mrs. Smith was so drunk she ran around the entire afternoon flirting with all the husbands. When Mr. Smith tried to take her home she threw her drink in his face." Some people also think that alcohol improves sexual performance. "Alcohol helps you get rid of your sexual inhibitions." "I'd like to go to bed with her when she's half loaded." #2388

In high school I and others would drink before the dances. Most people said they drank because it was cool, but we all know they did it so they could get up enough gall to dance and to ask others to dance. That's why I drank. However, at the last dance of the year my girlfriend and I decided we wouldn't drink beforehand. It was a disaster. Not only did we not get up to dance, but we left about twenty minutes after we walked in the door. I was ashamed of myself, because I couldn't go out and have a good time without using alcohol. #2389

I first recognized the ability of alcohol to change people's behavior in the seventh grade. I was at a school dance with two of my friends. The girls were dancing and the guys were standing against the wall. My friends and I were too shy to ask the girls to dance, which was pretty normal. The next night there was a party at a friend's house. There were no parents around and we were drinking beer all night. The same two friends, who had been too shy to ask the girls to dance the night before, were now asking girls to go upstairs to the bedroom with them. The only thing that could have changed their behavior was the beer. Alcohol let them do what they only thought of doing before. Since then I have continued to see people use alcohol to give them the confidence to do stuff they couldn't normally do. And it's true about me too. My behavior changes when I drink. I do things I wouldn't normally do. #2390

Many people believe that in order to have a good time, they have to drink. They find a party, dance, or club very boring if they aren't drinking. They depend on alcohol in order to talk to strangers, dance, and clown about, and if they don't do these things they don't have fun. "If you aren't drunk or feeling good you can't have a really good time." "If you don't get wasted, your weekend is very boring." "It's no fun to go to a party if you aren't plastered." "Some girls and guys will have as many as twelve beer before a party or dance. Then they can let themselves go and have a great time. Some won't even consider going to a dance unless they are drunk, because they'll find it boring and no fun." "Alcohol is hard to turn down because going to a party or dance is a lot more fun when you're trashed. I'm shy and hate going to parties where I don't know a lot of people. But if I'm drunk I don't feel out of place and can always talk to strangers and make friends. I'm much more comfortable. A lot of my friends feel the same way. No one wants to be sober." "People think that if they don't drink they'll have a lousy time. They believe if they're sober they will lack the nerve to do something crazy because they'll be worried that others will think they are assholes. They know if they do drink, they can do what they feel like to make the evening a success because they won't have to worry what others think." "I asked two guys, 'How was the club last night?' One said, 'The club was the shits.' The other said, 'I really had a good time.' Then the first one explained, 'Yeah, you enjoyed it. But you were drunk and I was not.'" #2391

People use alcohol to override their anxieties and gain confidence in a variety of situations. "My middle-aged brother doesn't feel comfortable talking in front of others. He's not unfriendly; just shy. Whenever my family visits him, all he usually says is 'Hi!' or 'How are you?' But at Christmastime, when there's alcohol around and he's drinking, he'll sit and talk about family and sports and news." "My brother once had to fly to Toronto. But he was so scared of flying he wouldn't get on the plane until he was three-quarters corked. It was quite funny." "Once in high school at the winter carnival a group of students had to do a comedy act in front of the whole school. The only way they were able to get enough confidence to do this was to drink beforehand. To my surprise they won first place. I've also seen high-school cheerleaders use alcohol to get enough confidence to perform at their first few games." "We were practicing to give a public demonstration of different Latin dances. Two of the Mexican women joked that they would have to have three tequilas each beforehand to have enough courage to do their dance number." "I am one of the six contestants for Ms. Gay Atlantic Canada. Someone in the audience asked me how long it took me to prepare for the pageant. I told them, 'I started planning my music numbers and dresses a year ago. But tonight it only took a couple of hours to put on my makeup and get dressed before the show. I also needed three or four stiff drinks beforehand, because I was quite nervous.'" #2392

Efforts to obtain sex

Some people think when they are buzzed or drunk they become a better, friendlier, more outgoing person, and that they become more attractive to the opposite sex. Therefore they think they have to drink in order to show their better, more attractive self to others. One girl told me, "When I'm drunk people I barely know will treat me like their best friend in the world. Guys who never looked twice at me in school will ask me to dance and pay all sorts of attention to me." Another girl is normally very shy and doesn't have many friends. She feels she likes herself better after she has had something to drink. She adds, "I love going to the clubs and drinking. I talk and laugh and dance with people I don't even know. Definitely not something I would do if I wasn't drinking. I make so many friends. But I won't go unless I've been drinking." A middle-aged man stated, "When I'm drinking I'm more mellow and I'm nicer." I was also talking to a guy who thinks girls find him irresistible when he's drinking. He said that when he's sober he gets nervous around girls and they think he's "uncool," or immature, because he stammers and sweats, but when he's drinking or drunk he feels more relaxed and the girls see him for the hot guy he really is. I think he really believes this because he'd been drinking and was already quite happy, and as he was telling me this he had his arm around my shoulders. Later he tried to talk me into going for a drive with him. [#2393]

Underage drinking is not only widespread in country communities on Prince Edward Island, it is also widely accepted by adults. The legal age for drinking is currently nineteen. However, children in my community take their first drink at the age of twelve or thirteen. Children are curious about the taste and effects and want to find out what their parents, older siblings, and family friends are experiencing. One thirteen-year-old said, "Everyone in my family drinks, except my mom. So it was always around and I wanted to see what it tasted like." Children are able to get liquor by a variety of means, such as stealing it from their parents, or getting an older relative or friend to buy it for them. They also have little trouble finding a place to drink. A group may go off on "a fishing trip" or "a bike ride." My cousin said two of the boys in her eighth-grade class stole a pint of their father's moonshine and took off on a bike ride. They got drunk and decided to race their bikes down a hill. One boy rolled his bike and scraped his face and arms badly. They didn't want their parents to find out they were drinking, so they stayed away from home until they sobered up. Incidents like this are common, and it is very rare that parents find out what is going on.

Alcohol

Common locations for underage drinking are dances, parties, hockey games, and the woods. A community teen dance is a prime location to see underage drinking. I have attended these dances and my brother is going to them now. Teens arrive at the dance at about nine forty-five at night and form groups in the parking lot. Everyone stays outside to drink until about ten thirty. This is not done secretly. Chaperones are outside watching the teens, and the teens walk around with liquor in their hands, drinking and chug-a-lugging most of their alcohol, not caring who sees them. And why would they care? The chaperones never say a word. When teens go into the dance they are never checked for liquor and most of them carry it with them. My brother reports that at the dance two weeks ago guys and girls were drinking when they were on the dance floor and they mixed drinks at the tables along the walls. Occasionally a bouncer would take a beer or pint away from them, but for the most part there was no interference. Those who were really drunk were falling on the floor and running into people, and the bathrooms were filled with people throwing up. But none of these got into any trouble with the bouncers. It is unlikely the bouncers care as long as no one gets hurt. The police are rarely called to the dances unless a huge fight breaks out. Even if they come and give out a few illegal-possession fines, it is not a big deal. I know one sixteen-year-old who was fined for illegal possession of alcohol at a dance and bragged to everyone that he had gotten a fine the weekend before too. House parties are different from dances because there are no adults present to watch over you. Last weekend I was at a house party. People played drinking games, danced, and chatted with friends. Such parties are ideal for underage drinkers because they don't have to worry about being caught and they don't have to rush when they drink.

Younger drinkers, twelve-through-sixteen-year-olds, behave differently than older drinkers, or seventeen-and-eighteen-year-olds. Younger drinkers often brag about how much alcohol they've consumed. At a party one tenth-grade girl came up to me and said, "I am so plastered. I drank six beer and half a pint!" Often this is exaggerated. At the same house party a fifteen-year-old told me he had drunk a quart by himself, when actually he had given about half of it away. This age group is more likely to make fools of themselves when they are drunk. When I picked up my brother after a teen dance there was a bunch of fifteen-year-old girls running around screaming and singing. They would never do this if they weren't drinking. The guys were going around looking for liquor or offering drinks to the older kids in an attempt to befriend them.

When teenagers are seventeen or eighteen they don't view themselves as "minors" anymore. Most people this age have been drinking for at least four years, so it doesn't seem like such a big thing anymore. Many in this group can now get into the liquor stores and bars, because they look nineteen or older, so they don't have to go overboard every time they drink. At parties they can sit back and enjoy their drink instead of trying to gulp it down before someone discovers them. It is also more common for them to share their drinks with their friends and not hoard it all for themselves.

When girls drink they tend to be more emotional than usual. On many occasions I have seen a girl crying over something unimportant, such as someone who doesn't like her or the fact she has spilled a beer. When guys drink many of them seem to be constantly ready for a fight. They feel they are ten feet tall and bulletproof. Little things set them off, such as a guy they don't like, looking at them the wrong way. Both sexes become more outgoing. Girls become more talkative and straightforward while guys become more carefree and willing to do embarrassing things they don't usually do, like dance.

Most adults accept that teenagers drink and do so at a very young age. They pay little heed to underage drinking and do not see it as a problem. They often remember that they were drinking at that age too. Many parents feel it would be useless to try to stop their children from drinking. One mother in my community told me, "There's nothing I can do about it. If he wants to drink, he'll drink." Another family allows their teenager and her friends to drink at their house, because "We'd rather they drink here and are safe, than have them drive around all over the countryside." Children usually start drinking in front of their parents when they are about sixteen or seventeen. Some parents find it funny when their kids come home after they have been drinking. One girl told me, "Mom was still up when I got home. When she saw me she laughed and said, 'You look in pretty rough shape. You'll be feeling it tomorrow.'" Some parents even tease their kids about their hangovers. At many family activities, such as weddings and birthdays, older relatives give their younger relatives liquor and seem to get a kick out of seeing them drink. It is also very common for teenagers to drink with adults and share booze with them at public events, such as ballgames, hockey games, and community functions. Many teenage males find summer and part-time work on farms, in fishing boats, in the woods, and in sawmills. These jobs are particularly demanding during hot weather, and in the middle of the day or at the end of it workers are usually rewarded with a cold beer. One man expressed the local attitude when he said, "If you are old enough to do a good day's work, then you are old enough to take a drink." I heard one teen complain last summer that after putting in the hay in the heat for a couple of hours, the workers were given nothing to eat or drink. His father replied, "If he does that again, just go in his fridge and grab a beer."

There are exceptions to practically all of these observations. There are parents who do not tolerate their children drinking, and if their children are caught, they are grounded or lose some privilege. There are also many teenagers who barely drink or who do not drink at all. I know of a couple of boys who are now sixteen and have never taken a drink. But despite these exceptions, the majority of teenagers do drink and most adults accept this. #2394

There are lots of ways to get alcohol when you are too young to buy it legally in the liquor stores. You often have a sibling or a friend who is old enough to buy it. In addition, some of your underage friends look old enough so that no one asks them for identification if they enter a liquor store. Also, if you don't have a means to get alcohol this week-end, it is likely one of your friends has a way. "By grades eleven and twelve we could usually get in and out of the liquor store without being asked for identification. We went to one store which was less likely to ask for an ID. I don't think what I did was unusual, because when I was in the liquor store I usually saw some of my classmates there too." As they approach the legal age, which is nineteen at the moment, many kids have fake ID cards which state they are nineteen or older.

Another technique is to ask an adult you don't know to buy the alcohol for you. Kids hang out near liquor store entrances and ask people to buy liquor for them. Most adults drank when they were underage and some are sympathetic to these requests. "On a Friday or Saturday night it isn't uncommon to see two or three carloads of high-school students waiting outside the village liquor store for someone to go in for them. They usually ask guys in their twenties and thirties and men over sixty. They believe the men don't care who they are buying for. Even if the person they ask has just left the liquor store, most of the time he will go right back in for another order. Men who buy for teens say, 'When I was young I needed someone to go in for me. I'd always be pissed off if someone, especially a young guy, said no,' and 'It does-n't take anything out of me. It's their money.' Recently an unmarked police car parked outside the liquor store and gave out fines to those caught buying liquor for minors. This didn't have much effect because nothing has changed since then." Sometimes kids pay someone older to buy their liquor for them. "I watched a group of five fifteen-year-olds, both girls and guys, walk to the liquor store a half hour before it closed. One of the boys stood outside the door and asked people who were entering to buy liquor for him. He even offered to pay them to do so. Finally one man went in for him and returned with eighteen beer and a pint of rum. The teens took the liquor and went to drink it behind the mall." However, certain difficulties may arise. "I'm never going to get a stranger to buy my alcohol for me again. My friends and I put our money together and came up with $34 for alcohol. We found a guy in the mall who said he'd buy it for us in the liquor store, but as soon as our backs were turned he bought the alcohol and ran. We were so mad we just had to get drunk. So I called a taxi and the driver went in for us. Sometimes I just wish I was legal so I wouldn't have to go through this hassle." [2395]

Tactics

People employ various strategies and tactics which increase the likelihood they will make sexual contacts and establish relationships with others. When people are in the presence of one or more acceptable partners they frequently show signs of interest and availability, and employ various techniques to encourage cooperation.

I know how to play the game. All it is is a game. It's the chase you desire. No one wants to be restricted to just one girl. Ask anybody. Over time you feel the old leash. All the pleasure that comes from wanting someone? It's really the challenge of trying to get that chick who is just out of your reach. It's like a sport. It's like hunting for that perfect prize. Sure you feel like you really want her at the time. But when it's all said and done, you know it's the chase. [2396]

Some guys use various lines to encourage their dates and girlfriends to have sex with them. These include "What do you mean you've never had sex before?" "What's wrong with you?" "You really don't know what you're missing," "Come on, you'll love it," "Everyone is doing it," "Oh, yeah. You get me all worked up, and then you leave me," and "If you really care about me, you'll do it." [2397]

I go to parties alone, because the guys who hang out together don't get any hay on their forks. Parties are great. I start by asking a girl an innocent question, such as "Hello, having a good time tonight?" I give her the bait, tease her a bit, and wait until she bites. I like to keep the girl wondering how interested I am. Later on I may approach again and ask if she'd like to take a walk or go somewhere else. Your approaches at a party are not usually noticed by others there. Therefore it is possible to make casts to several different girls and you can usually catch one of them. #2398

I live in a coed university dorm and am a member of a varsity team. I find the best places to meet girls are the corridors and the TV room of the dorm. When I see an attractive girl walking in the corridor or watching TV late at night, I usually stop and talk to her. I put my arm around her while we are talking. Usually one thing leads to another and soon I invite her up to my room or to visit me in the near future. When I see a nice-looking girl walking down the corridor I usually slap her on the ass and say something suggestive. Sometimes they insult me, but then again, sometimes they don't. It is the girls who giggle and laugh and say nothing that I really go after. When they give me the eye, I know it's time to move in. #2399

I'm in my mid-forties and I find it is just so easy to pick up women for sex. Sometimes I have to tell myself not to pick up anyone because I've had a hard week at work and want to go home early. Males frequently ask how I am so successful, but I don't tell them because I don't want the competition.

I like to make contact in unorthodox places, like coffee shops, flea markets, Laundromats, supermarkets, and churches. I also eat out every night, which brings me into contact with many women. I don't pick up much in bars. When I do go to a bar, I like to go out on Sunday, Monday, and Tuesday nights when there aren't many people. I go early before the masses arrive. At that time there is no entrance charge, no crowd, no smoke, and no loud music. You can actually hold a conversation and hear what the other person says. I often go to a hotel or motel bar, and I meet women who are lonely, some of whom are traveling. Trying to pick women up in a busy bar is often a waste of time. When people are drinking women have their protective shields up. Also, there are too many other players, or fellow predators, in bars.

I'm always networking, or meeting women for the future. I meet countless women everywhere I go. I approach them as harmless and just a friend, instead of a predator. You have to throw your bread upon the waters, just like a salesman passing out business cards. I sow more than I reap. It's hit and miss, and sometimes it works. Often it is just a matter of time before you get opportunities to have sex with some of them. I like to have a period of time pass between my initial contact and a later meeting. Often the longer this interval, the better, and it can be a matter of months. This period gives women time to decide I'm not going to hassle or threaten them. Then when we meet again they define me as safe and they feel comfortable with me. Sometimes they say, "Oh, I know you."

Presentation is everything and you need an image. People do judge a book by its cover. I wear trendy clothes. People consider me exceptionally outgoing, friendly, pleasant, relaxed, and easygoing. I also joke around. Women want to be entertained, and I always entertain them. It is very important to like yourself because this overflows to liking the woman.

I look for a woman whose image interests me. When it does, I make contact and see how the woman responds. I show a woman I'm interested by looking at her and by speaking to her. But I never embarrass her by staring. You can usually tell in moments if there is any response. I go down the friendship trail. I try to be friends and act friendly and considerate. I think you have to be the first to make a donation by flashing your personality and volunteering your friendship. Also, I always let her add to the conversation. I show I am infatuated with her by asking her about herself, and by listening carefully to what she says and by commenting on it. Women will prolong a conversation indefinitely when you show you are genuinely interested in her and what she says. It is intoxicating to a woman to be wanted. Women want to be loved; physically, spiritually, and emotionally. When you continue to show interest she may even begin to doubt her relationship with her existing partner. I find the two things women hate are to be treated badly and to be ignored. I take a laissez-faire approach. When I talk to a woman I use neutral vocabulary and never use sexual words or refer to sex. I never, never bring up sex, even if we've been friends for an hour or two. Most women, no matter what their background or profession, want to go to bed, but they will proceed at their own rate. They may be ready in an hour, or they may be ready in a week or more. You have to respect this rate. They have a comfort level and have to feel the situation is safe and discreet. Often if the woman isn't responsive it is because the environment isn't comfortable for her. Maybe her boyfriend or husband is present. Maybe her girlfriends are there and she is afraid they'll talk. I don't assume that she isn't interested in me. Instead, I assume that the time and place may not be right for her. I try to create a level of comfort for her. I've slept with girls I never thought I had a hope in hell getting together with. Some are millionaires. One thing, no matter what happens, I never get angry. If you get angry you will alienate the woman. If you don't get angry, she may decide to come through at a future time, either five minutes or five months later.

In order for a woman to feel comfortable with you, you have to remove her fears. One of her fears is how you perceive her. She doesn't want you to view her and treat her like a female in heat. She doesn't want to hear, "Hey, baby! Show me your tits." Instead, you need to communicate that you view her and will treat her with complete respect. I do this by having a friendly conversation with her. Another fear is that you will make her wish she'd never met you, because you may badger, hassle, abuse, or violate her. She doesn't want the evening to turn into a nightmare. One way I remove this fear is by not asking for her phone number or where she lives. Instead, I give her my phone number and invite her to visit me. This gives her more control over what happens. I do my best to appear nonthreatening and to help her feel comfortable. For example, last night I was in a bar and a nicely-dressed woman entered and said, "I'm waiting for someone." This was a fib, but it gave her an excuse to be there. She looked around the bar and sat in a booth by herself. She seemed aloof and guarded. I got ready to leave and stopped by her booth and said, "I'm on my way out the door. This place is too noisy for me. Can I sit down for five minutes?" I was telling her I wasn't going to hassle her. I would only be there for five minutes, and I was leaving anyway. Her whole demeanor changed and I could see her relax. I have women tell me, "You seem like a nice guy," which is a good indication that they feel comfortable with me. They pick up on my attitude and recognize that they will be in control of the situation. If you can remove a woman's fears, you can remove her panties.

Sex is in the mind. Even if you say hello you are engaging in verbal foreplay. Everything is an invitation to have sex, but you can't present it that way. The way a woman responds to what you say indicates her interest in having sex with you. You give her openings and let her decide how to pursue them. For example, all women want to be desired. So I will tell her, "You're very desirable." If she says, "My husband tells me that all the time," I know this is going nowhere. But if she says, "I feel the same way about you," I know I am halfway there. I let the woman choose where to take things. If I sense an interest, then I know to pursue things. I may suggest, "Would you like to continue this somewhere more comfortable?" Or if we are alone I will lean close to her. If she leans backwards or crosses her arms in front of her then I know she is not ready yet. But if she doesn't move away I know a kiss may be in order. I initiate the contact and then respond to her lead. I'm flexible. I'm like a salesman. I want the sale, but it is the customer's game, so I have to let the customer set the pace and make the decision. Women often want to help us seduce them.

I'll illustrate this with an actual case. One sunny day I enter a coffee shop and see an attractive woman writing poetry. I give her a big smile and say, "Great day!" I'm making contact. Then I sit at a nearby table and read my newspaper and drink my coffee. I'm at my table for half an hour. I'm not being aggressive, I'm not hassling her, and she doesn't know where I stand. I want her to think I am just friendly and not a threat. Then I get ready to leave. I ask her, "Are you a poet?" "Yes," she says, "would you like to read a page?" She is allowing me to pursue her. I sit down, read her poem, and talk to her about it. Then I say, "This is out of the blue, but I'm going to the beach today. Would you like to go? I'm harmless. I could read more of your poetry." I'm giving her an opening. "Beach sounds good to me," she says. She is making another positive response. I have no desire to go to the beach, but I'd be willing to go in order to get to know this girl. When we get in my car I say, "I have to go home and get a towel and shorts, and then we can swing by your place." When we arrive at my place, I ask, "Do you want to come in and get a cool drink?" She accepts. Inside I open the fridge and say, "We have orange juice and we have wine." She takes the wine. If she had taken the orange juice it would indicate we were going to the beach. We sit on the sofa drinking the wine and I move in closer to her and she doesn't withdraw. We start kissing and ninety minutes after I first saw her in the coffee shop we are in bed. This ninety minutes includes the thirty minutes I spent reading my newspaper.

I want the woman to have a good sexual experience. That way she'll come back for a repeat performance. I can delay and have my orgasm any time; it only takes a minute. But I ask the woman to let me know what she wants. Does she want it hard, easy, slow, or fast? I want her to tell me if what we are doing is uncomfortable for her. I say something funny, and get her laughing. She doesn't want to talk about world events. She wants me to talk about her all night and tell her how wonderful she smells and tastes. Afterwards, I don't run off. I like to hang around and have a conversation with her. As a result, I get great compliments from the women. The majority return, and I'm usually the one who breaks the relationship.

You have to be sensitive to what women want. Some women want just a one-night stand with no names mentioned. Some want a regularly scheduled meeting lasting several years. And still others want a permanent relationship. Many married women want some adventure. They may feel something is missing in their lives. Women frequently tell me, "You're so much fun in bed. I don't have this at home," or "I can't believe how exciting sex can be." Often they have everything else, such as a very successful husband and a high standard of living. Some women, on the other hand, just want a revenge fuck to get back at their husband. They are angry or resentful because of a problem in their marriage. One thing, I refuse to have anything to do with a married woman's children. Perhaps the woman asks me to join her in a setting where her children are present. I get mad at women who do this, because children need to be protected. Also, I very much want to avoid husbands. It is no fun to be in bed with a married woman and hear someone call out, "Hi, honey, I'm home," because he forgot to take his lunch with him that day.

I would estimate that about half of my sexual contacts are with single women who have never been married. Almost a quarter are with married women currently living with their husbands. Roughly another quarter are with separated and divorced women. And about five percent are with lesbians, who often say, "I can't believe I'm doing this with a man." The great majority of my contacts are with local women. Only about twenty percent are with tourists and others visiting Prince Edward Island. This would be higher if the tourist season lasted more than a couple of months.

When I get together with a woman I make a decision. I may decide this is for sex alone. When this is the case, sometimes after we have sex I can't wait to get out of the room. Or I may decide that this woman could be the one. Later I find that she isn't. Most of my relationships last no more than two or three weeks. Great sex wears off sooner or later, and I lose interest. Someone new is very stimulating until she isn't new anymore. As they say, familiarity breeds contempt. Also, regardless of their beauty, wealth, race, culture, or religion, women start wanting you to get your ass out of bed and fix their breakfast and take out the garbage. When I want to terminate a relationship some women get upset. They may say that I've used them and they try to make me feel guilty. I tell them, "I thought this could last. I thought we might have worked out." [#2400]

Clubs

Tactics in clubs are discussed under the following topics:

Getting into clubs
Guys and girls go to clubs for different reasons
Importance of looking attractive
Categories of girls and guys in a club
Male and female interaction
Efforts to pick up others
Dancing
Alcohol
Protecting reputations
Picking up drunk girls
Females exploiting the situation
A disheartening experience for many
Finding a serious relationship
Cars, last dances, leaving together, and drives home

Getting into clubs

The legal age for drinking used to be eighteen and is currently nineteen. Therefore you can't get into clubs and lounges until you can prove you are old enough to drink. Lots of underage kids want to get in as soon as possible, because clubs are a primary location for meeting members of the opposite sex. When there is a question whether a person is old enough to be admitted, the bouncer at the club entrance asks to see an ID, or identification card, with the person's age and picture. There are a number of techniques that those who are underage use to get in. One is to look and act older than you are and just strut in and hope you won't be stopped. Another technique is to get together with one or more older people and walk in with them. As one male explained, "I'm still underage, but I go out drinking with my older friends. They don't know that I'm only seventeen. Since I've never been asked for an ID it's really easy to get away with it." A simple way to get in is to know the bouncer and hope he will let you in. This often works, but not always. Another technique is for someone who is already in the club to open the back door when no one is looking and let in those waiting outside. I know of a couple of occasions when this has worked. This is risky because when a person is caught doing this he is barred from the club for at least six months. However, the best and most popular way for someone underage to get into clubs is to get fake identification cards. As one guy said, "If you have a piece of plastic that looks anywhere close to what you look like, you're in for sure." One of the cheapest ways to get an ID is to find someone old enough who looks roughly like you, perhaps a relative or a friend, and borrow their card, or else have them claim their card is lost and pay $15 or so for a replacement, and let you keep and use the original. You can also buy a fake ID. A person who makes them for others explained, "The way I make them is to take someone's driving license who is of age, cut out their picture, then take your picture out of your license and place it in theirs. Then I have it laminated over." The best fake IDs I have ever seen were fake driving licenses. A group of my friends had them made. The licenses stated their birthdays were a year earlier than they actually were, which made my friends a year older. These were very well done and the only way you could tell they were fake was to hold one up beside a real one in good lighting. The green in the background was a little lighter in the fakes. If you're caught using a fake ID you may be embarrassed and you could be in a lot of trouble and face criminal charges.

When you see someone in a club today, you assume they are nineteen or older. This was the case when I met my girlfriend in a club, but later I found out she was only eighteen. That was over a year ago, and even though she is nineteen now, she no longer goes to clubs. She says, "It was more exciting to see if I could get in with my fake ID than it is to be up dancing and have drunk guys make fools of themselves. I find the whole atmosphere cheesy." #2401

It is the responsibility of bar employees to check identification at the door. When someone looks like they are under nineteen you ask them for an ID. If they are old enough they have no trouble showing it to you. When they are not old enough you get a big performance of bullshit. "But I'm old enough. You don't believe me? See this person knows me. Tell him." Usually they appear very nervous and ask stupid questions. Some resort to crying and carrying on while others give up the battle and go somewhere else. When you ask for an ID, there are those who hand it over willingly and cheerfully, those who complain, and those who don't say anything. Some guys get angry or embarrassed because you think they don't look old enough to be a man. On the other hand, some females feel complimented that they look younger than they actually are. #2402

Efforts to obtain sex

Guys and girls go to clubs for different reasons

Guys and girls go to clubs and bars for different reasons. Girls go to clubs to socialize, dance, and find someone for a permanent relationship. They go to see their friends and if they are lucky they will meet a nice guy. Girls seem to think that perhaps some guy is there looking for the same thing they are. It is theoretically possible, but odds are against it. Girls love to dance, and dancing attracts the attention of men. There is nothing like a girl who can dance. It lets girls show off their bodies, their clothes, and their coordination. Most men, on the other hand, don't like to dance unless they are drunk. Only when men are drunk do they actually feel like they can dance. But girls don't go to clubs to drink; they go to socialize.

Men go to clubs for two reasons; to drink and to pick up girls. While girls use dance as a means to socialize, we use drinking. Drinking encourages camaraderie among friends. We use it as an excuse to clown around and blow off steam. Men often go out for the sheer pleasure of getting drunk, without worrying about who is watching them or what people think. Bars are always hot and overcrowded and drinking is the only thing that makes them tolerable. Drinking also serves as a crutch for socializing with girls. For many guys alcohol is almost essential for communicating with the opposite sex. It acts as a confidence booster for many quiet guys who would never approach a girl without it. Actually, much of the time it backfires, and drinking clouds our judgment. There is a fine line between drinking for confidence and drinking to get drunk. Many who try to maintain this separation are unsuccessful.

Most guys do not go to bars seeking meaningful relationships. They are usually looking for cheap and dirty one-night stands, something that will mean nothing in the morning. Guys say things like "I want to get some tail," "I want to get banged," or "Let's get blued, screwed, and tattooed." Guys hope and strive for the most attractive girl available and rarely succeed. Nevertheless we keep trying night after night, weekend after weekend. Why do we act this way? Maybe it's because we are afraid of commitment, or maybe we have a girlfriend, or maybe it's because we are just plain horny.

Not all girls are looking for a mate. Some go for the same reason males go, which is for immediate satisfaction. These girls are definitely in the minority, but they are very popular. They act more straightforward and display more confidence, which makes them more approachable.

They often initiate conversations and drop hints. Sometimes they drink excessively so they will be less inhibited and say what they want.

Not all guys are looking for a one-night stand. One guy explained, "One-night stands are no good, period. They are too demeaning. I feel too guilty afterwards, and I'm also concerned about AIDS. Casual sex doesn't appeal to me. When I go to a club, I'm looking for a good-looking girl with a nice personality." There are guys who hope to meet that girl they can form a lasting relationship with. Some even succeed. Some guys remain sober and try to put their best foot forward. However, they are definitely in the minority.

The different orientations of girls and guys are illustrated in their preparation before they go out. Girls start preparing early. They spend an hour or two showering, putting on makeup, and trying on and borrowing clothes. They call each other to decide where they are going and to make sure that they aren't wearing identical clothing and that their clothing doesn't clash. They meet together at an apartment or house and have one or two drinks. They gossip about other girls and certain guys, and they leave for the club fairly early. In contrast, men start by having a few beer in the late afternoon or evening. They decide spontaneously to go out later. They go home, have a quick shower, and put on some clothes. Friends phone and you tell them to come over and pick up a case of beer on the way. You talk mostly about sports and which girls are hot, and you abuse each other to no end. The stereo blasts away so loudly that you need to scream in order to be heard. You drink until the last beer is gone from the fridge, and you often call a cab before you are ready to go. You arrive at a club in time for a couple of beer and hopefully you get lucky. Although both guys and girls want to find someone of the opposite sex, they do so for different reasons. [#2403]

Importance of looking attractive

How good you look is extremely important in attracting others. Those who are attractive get lots of interest, but those who are unattractive get just about none. "If you don't have a good-looking face, you've got nothing." "Appearance isn't everything, and people say, 'Don't judge a book by its cover.' But I want to see a good cover before I read the inside of a book. I'm attracted by outside appearance, and then I get to know what's inside." "I find the more attractive a guy is the less he has in personality. The face is what attracts me though, nothing else." "Usually when I go out to clubs I'm lucky if I see one or two girls who are really cute. When I see one I want to keep looking at her. In fact it is difficult to stop. Often I move somewhere else so I can get a better look at her and can see her from another angle. The other girls either look so ordinary or so unattractive that I don't bother looking at them. I couldn't get interested in them if you paid me." "A guy would rather ask a pretty girl to dance, even if she has the worst personality in the world, before he'd ask a girl with a great personality who isn't very pretty." "Cute guys catch my eye. I always check stock at the clubs trying to find a nice-looking guy." "When a guy is attractive, I want to talk to him and get to know him." "Attractiveness is the first thing you notice. You don't look at the ugly guys. An attractive guy makes me nervous. He is so good looking that you don't want to say something that will make you appear stupid or make him reject you." "There are some guys who can pick up two or three girls a night if they want to. A friend of mine, Donald, is quite good looking. One night within a four-hour period at a club, I saw five different girls put the moves on him."

Many people admire and even envy those who are attractive. Those who are most attractive tend to be very popular. "I find that unattractive women are intimidated by attractive women. They will agree with statements made by attractive women and accommodate them. I was at a dance and the women's washroom contained only one sink and one mirror, and there were a number of girls lined up to use them. Unattractive girls didn't use the mirror, spent less time at it, or moved out of the way for the attractive girls. The attractive girls spent more time in front of the mirror fixing their hair and their makeup, and also engaged in displays. For example, two very attractive girls stood at the mirror discussing all the boys they had danced with. Their discussion was quite loud and was obviously for the benefit of the other girls in the room rather than for each other."

Many think that a person who is going with someone good looking is lucky and must have something on the ball, and they tend to look up to the person. Some people want to be seen with good-looking people. "One night at a bar a girl who is a friend of mine was hanging around a good-looking guy that she doesn't really like. I asked her why and she said, 'It's good for me to be seen with a good-looking guy. The other girls will think I'm really with it.'"

Some people reject the idea of being very attractive. "I know a lot of nice people that aren't the most beautiful people to look at, but I'll tell you this, their character and personality beats the hell out of any fantastic-looking person I've ever met." "I don't think I would like to be a really gorgeous girl. A lot of pretty girls get hassled by guys coming on to them and stuff. Who needs that?" "I wouldn't want to be a gorgeous guy because girls would be drooling all over the place; looking at me with sly, sexy glances; and giggling to their friends. Frankly that turns me off. I like girls who are reasonably good looking with a good head on their shoulders. The hell with trying to go out with the nicest-looking girl you can find in order to gain status with the crowd." [2404]

Categories of girls and guys in a club

I find you can arrange most of the single girls and the single guys in the club I go to into three groups of each sex. The first category of girls are those who mingle and dance a lot. They are dressed in the latest styles. They make frequent trips to the washroom back and forth past the bar where the jocks sit. They are loud and showy, giggle, and act like stereotyped females. The second category are those who are out for a night on the town with the other girls. They are casually dressed and drink and smoke more than the girls in the first category. They tend to party only among themselves, dance in a group, and gossip about the other girls or about the hunky guys. They often do not stay all evening, because they are barhopping. The third category are the less fortunate girls, who are unattractive or overweight. They have long faces and sit glued to their chairs all night together with their friends. Some do not drink and some drink a lot. They are usually not well dressed and they seem to wear clothes which do not really suit them. They are very quiet and watch everyone the way people watch a television program.

The first category of guys are those who are good looking and popular, and sit or stand around the bar looking over the club or talking among themselves. They walk around and mingle a lot. Some are more confident and sit alone or talk to others occasionally, but look like they don't really have to. Others are less confident and seem to talk all the time, both to males and females. Males in this category tend to dance only in the later part of the evening, say from about midnight on. When they dance they tend to be self-contained, or cool, and very casual. The second category of males are the less popular ones, who aren't good looking and don't play sports. They seem to look at the guys around the bar with awe. They like looking at the good-looking and showy girls, but seldom dance with them or take them home. Instead, they are more likely to dance with the casually-dressed girls, and are more likely to get turned down. Their dancing is similar to that of the showy girls and can be wild and attention getting. These guys are more likely to get drunk. The third category of guys are those who seldom go out, know very few other people, and stick with those they came with. They appear very shy and rarely ask someone to dance. They are often very polite to the waitresses and those around them, but some go to the other extreme. They tend to drink very little. All three categories of guys dress very casually. Very few males dress up.

There are also various exceptions to these categories. There are some younger people who remain by themselves. Most of these are males. Some appear very lonely and radiate negative vibes, while others seem to prefer to be alone. There are also couples, who spend most or all of their time together. There are a few older men, who tend to drink a considerable amount. Some are alone and seem very lonely, but make no attempt to talk to anyone. Others try to hustle the young girls and can make a nuisance of themselves. They are almost always shot down, or rejected, and are even made fun of. There is also a group of middle-aged women who drink expensive drinks and smoke. They are dressed very stylishly, but seem out of place. They try to hustle the younger guys, and are less discreet about this than the younger women are. #2405

Male and female interaction

One of the most important locations where young single males and females make contact is at clubs and lounges. There are a variety of clubs in Charlottetown and Summerside, as well as one or two clubs in various towns around Prince Edward Island. My observations are based on the behavior of girls between the ages of seventeen and twenty-one. The legal age for drinking and admission to clubs is either eighteen or nineteen, depending on current laws.

The first step for a girl is getting ready to go clubbing. This is very important, because a girl never knows when she might see an interesting guy she will want to impress. A girl will spend an eternity picking out the right clothes. She wants to attract a guy's attention, while not looking sleazy. After she has changed her mind about her clothes two or three times, she will iron what she has selected to make sure it appears perfect. Then she'll have her shower or bath. Afterwards she puts on powder and proceeds to work on her hair. It has to be perfect, or she will wet it again and redry it. Some girls are really fanatical about how their hair looks. I know one girl who washes her hair when she gets up in the morning, washes it again if she was very hot or sweaty during the day, and then washes it a third time before she goes out to a club. Under no circumstances would a girl allow herself to be seen at a club if her hair were not washed. Once her hair is perfect and she is all dressed, the girl must do her makeup. This is a very slow job for most girls, as everything must appear perfect. A girl will usually spend about three times the amount of time she really needs to get ready, and then frequently complain about how terrible she looks.

After a girl is ready, it is usually too early to go out, so she will call up one of her friends to gossip for a while. Some girls will talk for ages on the phone. I am one, and I ended up getting my own private phone because my parents complained none of their friends could ever get through on the family phone. When girls talk on the phone before they go to a club, they often talk about who they hope to see there and what happened the last time they went out.

When a group of girls arrives at a club, they have a good look around to check out what's available. They'll point out all the "possibilities" to their friends so they can voice their opinions too. A couple of nights ago I went out with a friend of mine I hadn't seen in a long time, and when we got to the club she saw a guy she thought was just gorgeous. "Look! Look! Look!" she exclaimed. "What?" I asked. "Did you see him?" "Who?" "The guy that just walked in." "No, why? Was he cute?" "Cute isn't the word to describe him. He was gorgeous. And the nice set of buns on him. OOOOWEEEE! I'm in love." Now most girls wouldn't go to this extreme, but they would make a comment if they saw someone they found interesting.

Conversation between two girls is usually about some guy. They talk about how much they would like to go out with him and ways to attract his attention, or else they analyze their relationship with a guy they are seeing at the time. Many girls make comments about girls they see with a guy they like or they used to go out with. I've often heard comments like "Did you see who Jim is with? Isn't that the one who had a baby last year?" or "See that nice-looking guy over there? What's he doing with a slut like Mary?" It isn't often that a single girl makes a nice comment about a girl who is with a cute guy. The single girl doesn't like competition.

Quite often single girls are attracted to the bouncers at the clubs. A lot of girls will make up any excuse to talk to them, and get to know them on a first-name basis. A friend of mine used to go to the clubs all the time and every time I talked to her she seemed to like a different bouncer. Once she decided she liked a bouncer who I knew already had a girlfriend, and when I talked to her a few days later she said she didn't like him anymore. I asked why and she replied, "Well, I didn't really like him all that much to begin with. And anyway, he's not my type." She wouldn't admit that he was satisfied with his girlfriend and wasn't interested in my friend at all. A lot of people don't like to admit they have been rejected or defeated when it comes to romance.

The girls' washroom is an interesting place to be in a club. Girls go to the washroom together. "Since I can remember, if I was going to the washroom I always asked someone to accompany me. If I couldn't find a willing partner, I wouldn't go. It's just not proper for a girl to go alone." "I know guys laugh when girls go to the bathroom together. I just hate going through the crowds and walking to the bathroom by myself. Also, I would have no one to talk to if I went there alone." "Guys don't understand why a girl can't go to the washroom by herself. Little do they realize girls go to the washroom to talk about the guys." "If one of us has to use the washroom, we usually all go. There's always something to do; fix your hair or put on some makeup. I enjoy getting away from the crowd to get a chance to talk to the girls alone. We like to know how each other is doing guy-wise." "The washroom is where the girls refresh their smiles and talk about the guys who looked at them and the ones they danced with." "They should change the name from washroom to gossip room. I go there just to gossip. If I have something to say to my friends about the guys at the bar or other hot gossip, I have a conference in the bathroom. It's a great place to find out what's going on." You can hear just about anything and everything. Anytime you go in you will see hordes of girls fixing their makeup and hair and talking about the latest gossip. This can range from "Where did you go last night?" to "Did you know Nancy is three months pregnant?" to "She's too fat to wear that outfit." It seems every time you go in you hear the same old comments, just with different names filled in. Some girls have their makeup caked on so thick, they must use a jackhammer to get it off at night.

When a girl finally gets asked to dance by a guy she thinks is cute, she'll make small talk about something she thinks is appropriate. Whatever she talks about, it must be interesting without being too intellectual or too boring. While they are dancing, the girl will decide whether or not she's interested in the guy. If she is, she'll hope that he'll ask her for another dance or sit at her table. If she isn't interested, she'll think of a way to get rid of him if he seems interested in her. She'll say something polite so she doesn't seem too ignorant (rude), but she won't let him get the idea she is interested.

Clubs

It is important that a girl not get too drunk at a club. It looks bad to guys that don't know her. It's all right if it's a special occasion like a birthday, but she still shouldn't drink too much. Under no circumstances should she make a bad impression on nice-looking guys who might be interested in her if she hadn't made a fool of herself.

When a guy and a girl finally hit it off and make plans to see each other, often their plans involve clubbing. However, at clubs they don't really get to spend a lot of time together just by themselves. If either used to frequent clubs, the other party may get jealous of all their friends of the opposite sex. This can cause a problem in a newly formed relationship, but is less a problem after they get to know each other.

If the relationship works out, then eventually the couple will tend to get away from clubbing. They will do other things and only go to a club occasionally. However, if a couple really aren't well suited for each other, they will be more likely to go to clubs, where they have friends they can talk to. Eventually when they break up, both parties are likely to be back in the clubs and the cycle will repeat itself. [#2406]

Females often arrive at the club in groups and enter the club immediately. Many guys arrive alone. Some guys wait outside for their friends to arrive. They may finish a bottle of beer or liquor, or get a good look at the arriving females, so they can "check out the stock" and see which ones they are interested in. Early at night you can usually walk right into a club when you arrive. But later at night on Fridays and Saturdays there is often a line of people waiting outside for available space in the club. You can wait as long as an hour to get in. Males in the line usually talk to their friends and verbally abuse each other in a joking manner. They often use this opportunity to look over the females. A few drink their own booze so they can get a good buzz on beforehand and not have to buy as much expensive alcohol in the club. Females are usually quieter and satisfied talking with their friends. They talk about social events and mentally compare themselves to the other girls. "Often it can be more fun in the line than inside the club."

When people enter the club some put on displays so they will be noticed. Girls may talk loudly or make a fuss over meeting a friend. Others parade around while pretending to be unable to find a seat they like. They flaunt their clothes and bodies whenever they can find a legitimate reason to do so. "A club is a fashion show, and the women feel they compete with each other for recognition." "Some females do a great deal of displaying for males when they enter the club. They treat the club as a runway or catwalk to show off their clothes. For some dressing up means undressing. Small tank tops, short tight skirts, and tight jeans are common." "The more a girl is dressed up, the more she will get up and walk around, talking to people she knows or wandering back and forth to the washroom." "A club is the only place I can get dressed up and really strut my stuff. Sure it's kind of a meat market, but you have to look your best if you want to meet guys and get asked to dance." "I find my friends can be really shallow. Like if we're going out to a club everyone tries to look better than everyone else. I just find it really annoying." Some settle down after a display, but others continue their displays. "I get attention by talking to everyone I know in the club and by trying to be the life of the party." "If I'm trying to meet a guy I go sit near him or I talk to his friends. I laugh and make it look like I'm having a real good time." People also try to attract attention by dancing differently and better than everyone else on the dance floor. A girl who really moves will be noticed much more than a girl who hardly moves. Males use various techniques to attract attention. I asked one guy why he always arrived late in the evening, and he said, "I'd rather keep the girls waiting. This way all the girls want you that much more when you finally arrive." Other guys may stand or sit where they can be easily seen by all the females, or else they are somewhat noisy. "Males tend to become boisterous to get attention." "The only way I get attention is by verbally abusing people. For example, I'll say, 'Look at that thing trying to dance.'" Occasionally a male will try to be noticed by starting a fight and establishing how masculine he is. In a club everyone notices everybody and everything.

Many males prefer to stand at the bar, which is sometimes called "stud row." When a male is single or by himself he often prefers to be at the bar because this location provides many benefits. He can get his drinks faster, he can talk to his male friends, and he can watch sports on the TV near the bar. Males usually talk about drinking, sex, sports, cars, and fighting. When they see an attractive girl, guys may comment, "Nice ass," "What a piece," or "I'd like to get down on her." Males do their best to look cool. "Guys drink with the hope alcohol will give them a macho image so they can impress the women." "Through their walk, stance, and clothes, males show they feel it is essential to fit in. Being a jock and acting really cool ensures you fit in. Males who stand out from the crowd do not fit in. Fitting in is very important for both sexes. In order to have a good time you must be comfortable and feel like you are part of the crowd." Males at the bar do not look as isolated or conspicuous as they would sitting alone at a table. But also standing at the bar allows the male to see the entire club, or "check out the crowd," and spot any friends and interesting females. "Certain males are regulars, and most regulars come to the bar four to six times a week. Regulars in the bar where I work are hardened and callous individuals both in personality and appearance. The word 'veterans' would be a better description. They have a tough-guy attitude, and their behavior, dress, and talk support this. They drink a fair amount. Many regulars deliver long-winded, exaggerated stories about themselves to bartenders and bouncers. Regulars have a special territorial spot which they occupy after they enter the club. These are established through years of devoted attendance and no one else can occupy them. Unfortunately many of these spots interfere with the operation of the bar because they are in the aisles or in the way of the waitresses. The boss wants us to keep the aisles clear, and this includes regulars. Asking them to move is a thankless task and meets a response like 'Fuck off!' or 'Take a walk, asshole!' Regulars can constitute twenty-five to forty percent of the clientele in a bar and greatly affect the bar's image." Hanging around the bar allows the males to be seen by others in the club. The bar is often crowded with males. In contrast, girls prefer to sit at a table with their friends. "The girls are usually the ones sitting down, and the men stand at the bar. It's like cattle in a stall and the men are the buyers." A few females may hang around the bar after buying a drink in order to talk to particular males. "Girls who sit or stand at the bar are sometimes looked on as tramps."

Many males regularly travel with one or more friends. "I go to a club with another guy almost every evening for a couple of beer. When you are recognized as a regular in a club you get special service. We get waited on before others, we don't have to stand in line and wait when the club is full, and bouncers put cute girls at our table when all the tables are taken. My friend and I realized we needed a way to communicate without spoiling the other person's chances when he was talking to a girl. We use signals for 'getting a beer,' 'need to take a leak,' 'cute girl,' and so on. We also have an unspoken rule that what we do stays between us. Neither of us tells stories, true or not, about our escapades to others. We certainly don't want any stories to go back to our girlfriends."

Males sometimes discuss the possibility of "getting" specific girls. They try to determine if a girl is single and a possible pickup. "When you see two girls choose a table with four seats you know they hope guys will sit down with them." Usually males will attempt to talk to a female at her table and then may ask her to dance. If a male fails, a friend of his may try too. If the friend fails too, a group of males may decide the female is not single or is not interested. Normally the males use various "lines" in order to be accepted by the girls. "Have I seen you here before?" and "Do you come here often?" are common. A friend of mine uses various approaches and lines until he finds one that works. Once I listened to him talk to two very religious girls that he had never seen before. He used one line after another. He began by expressing an interest in religion. Then he flattered the girls. Next he convinced one of the girls that he was in a Bible class with her when they were very young, which was completely untrue. He succeeded in taking the two girls out. I have seen others succeed through persistence. A guy I had never seen before came over, sat in an empty chair next to me, and started to talk to me. I wondered why he would do this. A moment later he moved another seat over to talk to a girl he was interested in. She didn't want anything to do with him. But because he stayed there she agreed to dance with him to get rid of him. This just encouraged him and he ended up going home with her. Other males feign an interest in the girl. "One of our group is a womanizer. The rest of us sit back, watch, and laugh as he smiles at a girl and shows deep concern with what she is saying in order to work on her." Many males are too shy to do these things. Some males never make a move to pick up a girl and always go home alone. For example, one guy I've seen around the clubs over the past year is always by himself and just stands at the bar. He makes no attempt to socialize with others. The only time he leaves the bar is to go to the washroom for twenty to thirty minutes. People say he does this to kill time and make it look like he is with a girl while he is away from the bar. He always arrives and leaves the bar by himself.

Females generally prefer to wait until the male initiates contact. Often a female is interested in a guy but he is not aware of her interest. When this is the case the female may initiate contact. However, even when she already knows him and approaches him she has usually waited for him to make the first move. Many attractive females sit at their seats all night and wait for guys to ask them to dance. They know that there are always a certain number of males who will approach them. So for them it is just a matter of waiting until the right guy comes along.

Eye contact is very important. "When you walk into a bar or lounge you look to see which girls are by themselves and which ones are glancing or staring at you. Then you just approach them, sit down and buy them a drink or two, and give them an open ear and a warm heart. Once you gain their confidence the rest is easy."

Often people already know others in the club, because they have worked together, attended school together, or regularly see each other in the club. Many people socialize and stop at various tables to talk to others, particularly toward the end of the evening. Often they find out if there are any parties being held after the club closes, or make plans to go get something to eat later.

Some males do not approach females until the bar or club is about to close. This frequently occurs when the guy is looking for a one-night stand. Some guys say, "Getting attached early prevents you from choosing the best women at the end of the night." Many guys ask girls to dance the last few dances in hope of picking them up. These dances are typically slow ones. Many females complain, "Guys are all alike. They won't ask you to dance all night long. But they expect us to dance the waltzes with them at the end of the night so they can take us home." Other males wait until closing time and then offer a female a drive home in the hope of getting lucky. Some females are open to these advances and do not seem to mind them. Others are cautious of them but take them in stride. "What else can you do about guys putting the rush on you who are only looking for a one-night stand?" Other females reject these advances totally. "Often guys at the bar try to decide which one of the females they will try to take home with them. At the end of one Saturday night I watched a guy who had been standing around the bar approach a girl who was about to leave with her friends. He hadn't made any contact with this girl during the night, and now he asked her bluntly if she would like to go home with him. The look on the girl's face was quite something. She gave him one of the dirtiest looks I've ever seen and said, 'I don't even know you, and I have a boyfriend anyway. So will you please leave me alone!' The guy looked quite embarrassed." When women make advances to men at the end of the night, a larger proportion are accepted by the males.

Usually there are several bouncers at a club. They check IDs at the entrance to make sure people are old enough to buy liquor, collect entrance charges, help you find a table to sit at sometimes, and control disturbances, such as fights. "Working in a club as a bouncer is a two-faced business. Everyone is your buddy if you are lenient with them. But if you try to keep some order they can easily consider you a bastard. One night I let about six guys go through the line-up because they were celebrating a birthday. Oh, I was a great guy then. But when the birthday boy got too drunk, I had to put him out. They didn't think I was so great after that." "Guys and girls will be friendly to you when they enter the club, but if you see them in town the next day they hardly know you. They are only nice because they want something from you. A male friend of mine always tries to break in line. When I tell him he can't, he isn't my friend anymore. One girl named Tania is real nice to me when she wants me to find her a seat. But if I don't do it right away she gets angry. When I do get her the seat she is sweet again for about thirty seconds." Patrons also comment on the bouncers. "I usually go to one particular bar. A couple of the doormen are good heads, but most of them are assholes. The good heads know me and they let me in without having to wait in line. The assholes know me too, but don't let me in, so I have to wait a long time." "The bouncers are usually big guys who play or used to play a contact sport. They walk around with their chests out like proud roosters. They only pick on the smaller guys, I guess to show their authority." "I find the bouncers are generally very nice and polite. But once I watched a bouncer throw a guy who was drunk down the stairs. It was clear he didn't care if he injured the guy." "I often see one or two fights a night. The last one I saw was between two males who were interested in the same female. The female used this to her advantage to get free drinks. She tried to avoid each male while she talked to the other. Finally one male hit the other and a fight broke out. The bouncer showed up and kicked both males out. When there's a fight the fighters are usually barred from the club for a specific amount of time. A major factor in determining how long you are barred is how you act when the bouncer interferes. If you continue fighting or hit the bouncer, you may be barred for weeks, months, years, or life." According to a bouncer, "A lot of guys who fight in clubs have false courage. Fighting shows they are tough and this is their means of gaining status. However, they'll fight inside the club, but not outside. For example, one guy is named Matthew. He is nineteen years old and no bigger than a minute. He always tries to get something going. He knows he won't get hurt because I and the other bouncers will break it up. But when he is outside, he is like an alter boy. At the end of all this foolishness we had to bar him." #2407

Most people go to clubs on the weekend to have a good time with their friends. "A club can be a place to have a real good time. I go there, my girlfriends all go there, we have practically grown up there. It is like our second home." However, most also hope to meet someone for sex or a relationship. "A club is where the desire for a relationship meets the desire for sex." "Many of my male friends feel they have to score. They think, 'I have to get it or the weekend is ruined.' For them going to a club is like going to a grocery store where they can pick and choose what they like."

People do a number of things to meet or pick up someone at a club. They usually put on attractive clothes, and apply perfume, cologne, or after-shave. Often the males try to look macho by leaving the top buttons of their shirts open to expose their chest. The women wear eye-catching clothes, ranging from preppy to sexy. They often wear shorter skirts, tops which reveal more cleavage, and more makeup than they do during the day. "It's important to catch the eye of the guy you want to be with. Don't men like a sexy woman?"

When a male or a female sees someone they find attractive in the club they ask their friends if they know whether the person is single or going with someone and what else they know about the person. "It is important to find out exactly what the guy is all about. You have to size up your situation before you make a move." "If I'm interested in a girl I ask my friends about her and she asks her friends about me. Maybe I'll find out she has a kid or has been in a mental ward, and she'll find out I'm divorced and have a problem with alcohol." "When a guy sees a girl he considers pretty and would like to be seen with, he asks his friends what they know about her. He especially wants to learn how 'easy' she is. 'There's no sense wasting your evening on a girl who doesn't fuck.'"

Girls in clubs often try to sit in the right places where guys can easily see them and ask them to dance. Many girls will sit at tables near the dance floor in clear view of the guys at the bar. They also try to sit at tables by the walkways rather than out of the way. Girls usually pick out who they want to meet and position themselves so he has to walk by her to get to the bar or bathroom. They also try to find someone they can go talk to who is near their target. "Those who go out every weekend seem to have their favorite tables and you often see them at the same tables week after week. Many come early to make sure they get their favorite table before someone else does, especially if this is a table where they have had a good time before. They may also choose a particular table if they know that some of their friends or someone they are interested in usually sits in that area. All this makes it fairly easy to predict who will be sitting where."

Often one follows a person or walks somewhere in the club in order to catch their attention. "When girls want to meet or pick up a guy, they may try to walk by him to get him to notice them, and some make multiple trips to the washroom." "Many females will follow a male around wherever he goes. They may be quite obvious or very sly about this. I watched one girl follow a guy the entire evening. When he went to the bar to get a drink, she went too. When he ventured out on the dance floor she managed to bump into him there." "You have to walk around to get noticed. And you have to be sure to make eye contact. If there is any reaction at all then you've got it made." "We call this slutting. If I want a certain woman I will slut around a few times to make sure I can get her."

"Meeting people is not as difficult as you think if you use the proper approaches. Just standing around gives those who want to meet you the opportunity. I've seen my friends picked up by guys who started chatting with them while we were waiting in the line to get inside. If you go in a group, often someone in the group knows the person you want to meet or will help you figure out how. If the club is crowded, you are constantly being jostled, because others want to get by you. This is one of your best opportunities to meet people, because you can bump into those you want to meet."

People stare or smile at someone they are interested in and hope this will be reciprocated. Depending on the guy, he will either stare openly at a girl or avert his eyes when he sees her looking his way. "It is often amusing watching guys trying to put the moves on a girl. Most guys follow a pattern. He watches you for a while and perhaps says something to one of his buddies. Then he gets up and mingles a bit, especially if he knows someone at a table relatively close to your own. He maneuvers himself into your line of sight. He will sit and chat there for a while while facing you and he'll occasionally glance at you. If he catches your eye and the look lingers he will try to give you his most dazzling smile. A little later he will make his way over and ask you to dance. Then he will strike up a conversation and offer to buy you a drink." "When the guy's stare is too intense, the girl often becomes uncomfortable. If she isn't interested, she will try ignoring him and if this doesn't work, she may move elsewhere. She will only return to her original chair if she sees the guy is gone or is interested in someone else." When a girl is interested in the guy who is staring at her, she will encourage him by smiling and staring back.

If a girl is interested in a guy she may try to get him to notice her. "The whole trick is to make eye contact with him." "First I let him know I'm interested by letting him catch me looking at him. Then if he's interested he'll come and find me." "If the opportunity arises a girl will start a conversation with the guy, but she doesn't want him to know she is interested. During the evening she will walk around the area he is in. If he smiles or shows an interest in her she will go talk to him again." "When I see an attractive guy, I try different things. First I go to the same area he is in. Then I try to get eye contact. But I'm too scared to stare at him and I would never talk to him first. I try to get a friend to talk to him. Then I go up and join them and attempt to get a conversation going with him." A girl will sometimes dance with a guy she isn't interested in for a couple of dances to try to get the guy she is interested in to notice her.

Often if a guy sees a girl he wants to meet, he keeps his eye on her and watches for the right opportunity to ask her to dance. Guys don't want to walk all the way across the club to ask a girl to dance. If she says yes, that's fine. But if she says no, then he has to walk all the way back and everyone knows he was turned down. "If she's near a walkway and says no I can just keep on walking and people will think I stopped to say hi." Most males wait until a girl is alone before they ask her to dance. They seldom ask her when she is surrounded by her friends, because they don't want others to witness their difficulties and possible failure. The fewer people who see him rejected, the better. "I was never asked to dance when I was surrounded by friends. But when I was alone I was approached by several different males and asked to dance." Once a guy decides to ask a girl to dance, he tries to make it look like he just stopped to talk, so others in the club won't know if he is shot down (rejected). "If she doesn't want to dance, great, but other girls don't want someone else's rejects." "No one wants to look like they have to settle for sloppy seconds." Sometimes you see a guy ask every girl at a table to dance, and they all turn him down. If a girl refuses to dance or accept a drink she indicates she isn't interested. "Girls are more likely to be asked by and to accept a dance with a guy they already know. About eighty percent of the time I'm asked to dance, it is by someone I already know." Alcohol provides the self-confidence that most people need to make approaches, and helps cushion the blow if rejected. Many people drink to get buzzed for this reason.

If the girl agrees to dance, a guy starts the process of figuring her out. The two usually exchange names while they dance. After dancing for a while they will go their separate ways unless they can find something they are both interested in talking about. "If the girl considers the guy weird, she will leave the dance floor at the end of the dance. She will be polite and return to her friends, rather than continue talking to him. If she sees him heading in her direction again she will pretend she doesn't see him or she'll get up calmly and walk in the opposite direction. She gets really embarrassed when the guy is drunk and won't leave her alone. She hurriedly makes an excuse to leave, because she hates being in a situation she can't control." "The dance floor is where a girl really decides whether she's going home with you." "The girl knows within seconds if she will leave with you. You just have to find out what she's decided. If she wants to sit down after a couple of dances, you know you don't have a chance. But if she is eager to stay and dance you know you have a shot." If two people are interested enough in each other to have a few dances, the guy may ask the girl back to a table for a drink. It is up to the guy to use his technique to get her alone, such as buying her a drink and going to a quieter part of the bar. If he doesn't offer to buy her a drink he appears stingy. Males try to talk to the girl. The girl will usually start to wonder if the guy is really interested in getting to know her, or if he just wants to pick someone up for the night. "A lot of girls travel in pairs and so do guys. Usually your buddy will ask one of two girls to dance and you ask the other one. After a couple of dances you usually go back to your original seat. You wait until a slow dance comes on and ask them to dance again. You then make yourself at home at their table. This is a very effective method of picking up girls." Conversation is usually limited to general topics. If a third party tries to join in the conversation the person is likely to receive a minimal response. "I get pissed off when I'm working on a girl and someone interrupts me."

Girls and guys differ in the way they flirt, and everyone has their own style. "Usually a girl uses lots of eye contact and touching, giggles and laughs a lot, and shows off her body. Occasionally she flips her hair, and sometimes she leans against the guy. Guys tend to stand there and soak it all in, and act more cool about the whole thing. They smile and stuff, and make a little response here and there. Sometimes guys do that fake 'punch you in the arm' thing, or make some funny little sexual remark. But they don't throw their hair around or giggle the way girls do, so no one really thinks they are flirting back. Normally when people flirt, there isn't much conversation going on."

Once they meet the person they are interested in, people try to indicate their intentions and determine whether the interest is mutual. As the evening progresses they sit or dance closely. Most girls prefer to have the guy make the first move. Guys attempt to get physical by

Clubs

talking to the girl, getting to know her, making eye contact, and touching her. People often touch the other person casually, perhaps using their hand to brush the other's arm, or they stand close to them. From there a person may put their arm around the other person's waist or shoulders. Males often attempt to hold and caress the girl's hand or to dance closely to discover if the girl is interested. Dancing, and slow dancing in particular, helps establish what is expected. "I can tell a lot from dancing. If she likes to be real close I know she's hooked. Then I make moves like holding her tight, and slowly caressing her neck. But I don't kiss in public." If a guy doesn't make the first move, the girl may, perhaps by touching the guy while making eye contact, resting her head on him when they are slow dancing, or giving him a kiss when he doesn't expect it. "I always flirt a little by touching his arm or leg. That lets him know I might want to be more than a friend."

As the night progresses one person will often ask the other if he or she would like to go somewhere else to talk, but talk is not what is in mind. If and when a guy asks a girl to leave with him is a judgment call. "If she says yes, you're set." "At the end of the evening he will offer to drive you home and hope you will ask him in." Girls like to wait until the end of the night to leave with a guy so they won't be as conspicuous. "A girl has to watch out that guys don't start talking about her." "If she is nice looking the guy tries to let everyone notice his accomplishment. On the other hand, if the girl is ugly, the most important thing is to make sure others don't see him leave with her or find out about it. Otherwise they won't let him forget it. Guys do things like tell the girl, 'I have to use the bathroom. I'll meet you outside in five minutes.' Or as my friend says, 'If you are caught pig fucking, make sure you can claim you were drunk.'" #2408

Efforts to pick up others

People attempt to strike up a conversation in order to meet someone. For example, at a stand-up bar someone may say, "It's really hot in here, eh?" or "There's a pretty good crowd here tonight." The conversation usually continues from there. Believe it or not, some people still use the line, "Haven't I met you somewhere before?" One night at a bar this guy came up to me and said, "Hi! Didn't I meet you before at a party?" I said no. I knew I had never seen this guy before, and I said it must have been someone else. But he insisted it was me, so I asked him where the party was. He said he couldn't quite remember, but it was somewhere in Summerside. I never once went to a party in Summerside, so I told him it wasn't me. Then he asked if I had a sister who looked like me, because she may have been the one he met. I told him my sister never went to any parties in Summerside either. He was just trying to start a conversation. Another girl observed, "I get some strange lines at times. Usually they tell me how much they like tall girls with long legs. Did you ever see a tall girl with short legs? They also ask me if I have a steady boyfriend, and if I'm not seeing anybody at the time, I'll let them buy me a drink."

Some people get a friend to make contact with someone they are interested in. One night in a bar I was heading back to my table when this guy I didn't know stopped me and said, "My friend is in love with you." His friend was sitting across the table. The guy who stopped me, Jerry, introduced himself, asked my name, and then introduced his friend, Ed. I returned to my table and a little while later Ed came over and asked me to dance. While we were up dancing Ed asked what Jerry had said to me, but I didn't tell him. I don't know if Ed really didn't know, or if they planned it as a way to make contact.

Many guys seem primarily interested in conversation. But others are just interested in a pickup. Jill was at a stand-up bar waiting for her friends to arrive when a guy she didn't know came over and stood beside her. After a few minutes he turned to her and said, "We might as well be talking as holding up the wall." What followed was the typical "What's your name?" "Where are you from?" "What do you do?" and so on. After about ten minutes the guy's eye contact became very intense, and he started playing with the hairs on his chest. Jill became pretty uncomfortable. She decided to leave but didn't want to appear rude by just walking away. So she said she had to go to the washroom. After she went to the washroom, she stayed upstairs to wait for her friends. Another night, Klara was sitting at a table in a bar and a guy she didn't know came over, said "Hi!" and started to rub her back with his hand. She got so mad, she turned on him and said, "I don't think I know you!" The guy got the message. Some guys are not the least bit discreet. One night I was heading for the washroom when a guy said to me, "Wanna come home with me tonight?" I gave him a strong look and kept on going. Girls comment on the situation. "Most guys are insecure. They think they have to prove something to their friends as well as to themselves. Perhaps they think they are studs, although any girl with half a brain can see right through them. A shy guy will usually have a friend act as an intermediary. That's nice. An aggressive guy is a turnoff." "Guys hit on a girl either because they genuinely like the girl, or because they are sex-crazed perverts." [#2409]

Many guys use pickup lines when they approach a girl they don't know. Often they rehearse what they are going to say before they make their approach. There are the old standards, such as "Hi! Haven't I seen you before?" "Hell-o! Don't I know you from somewhere?" "Are you all alone?" and "May I sit down here?" There are the cute lines. "You without me, honey, is like cornflakes without milk." There are the obvious fabrications. "My aunt died and left me six million dollars provided I marry by tomorrow. Can I buy you a drink?" There is the use of obvious flattery. "As soon as I walked in I noticed a shimmering light. Your very presence brings a sense of awe to the place." There are also denials to disarm the girl. "I don't want you to think I'm hitting on you. I just think you are an interesting person and I'd like to get to know you better." One can also compliment the girl. "You look beautiful this evening," "I love your perfume," or "You're a good dancer." "It is better to compliment her than to use a line. Make her feel good and that she is attractive. That way she's more likely to accept you."

First impressions are of BIG importance. Many girls are turned off by a tacky pickup line. Most guys stress that you must let the girl know you are truly interested in her, and avoid any indication that you see her as just another easy pickup. Often a guy can tell if the girl thinks he is just out for a good time and sex. In such cases lines are often avoided. The simpler the contact, the better, such as "Hi! Would you like to dance?" "My name is _____ ," or "Could I buy you a drink?" Many feel it is better to have a good personality and be oneself than to use a line. As one guy stated, "No lines! Any guy who uses lines is a jerk."

But when they think the girl is ready or easy, guys are more likely to be direct and get right to the point. "If the girl is a sleaze I simply say, 'Hey, look, we're both interested in the same thing. So let's quit beating around the bush and get to it.'" "I was dancing with a girl who said, 'I like the way you move.' I told her, 'If you like the way I move on the dance floor, you should see how I move in bed.'" [#2410]

When you go to a club with a group of male friends you try to maintain your individual status. Often we have a few (beer) on the way there, creating a good drinking foundation for the remainder of the night. When we arrive our egos are super-inflated. We are very careful not to do something to destroy this feeling, such as asking a girl to dance and getting turned down. As the night progresses each of us picks out girls we are interested in. We also consider carefully what to do when we ask one to dance and she refuses. "If she says no, do I suddenly return to our table, become two inches tall, and face a pack of wolves who will pounce on me with unbearable laughter?" One solution is to go to the washroom and get sidetracked on the way when I innocently ask "Miss Right" to dance. But even this tactic will not escape the watchful eyes of your friends. Whatever tactic is used, the decision is usually to wager all your pride on one girl. Then you have to fabricate an appropriate line. The usual question, "Would you like to dance?" normally does not work. Perhaps something more interesting, such as "Hi! I represent the National Tulip Growers Association of Holland," followed by an in-depth review of your financial and family status, and ending with the question, "Would you like to receive maximum entertainment by having a dance together?" If properly executed, something like this is often successful. A dance with "Miss Right" scores valuable points with your friends, who are bewildered by your success. #2411

The guys who don't want to accept no for an answer can be a royal pain. No matter what excuse you give them they won't leave you alone. Even if you tell them you have a boyfriend or are engaged to be married it isn't good enough. "Some guys are OK. They just ask you if you want to dance and it's up to you. Other guys are just jerks. They think if they snap their fingers you'll jump in their arms. They figure that's what you want anyway, so they can't understand why you turn them down. Sometimes telling them to fuck off is being too polite." "A whole group of us were in a bar when one of those snap-your-fingers types came over and asked me to dance. I told him, 'No. I have a boyfriend.' He wanted to know who my boyfriend was and told me he was going to beat the shit out of him. When I wouldn't tell him he said I was lying and he wouldn't leave me alone for the rest of the night. I finally told the bouncer about him and the asshole was thrown out." #2412

People who pick up others or who let themselves get picked up do so for various reasons. For some alcohol gets the best of them. Others just do it for something to do, or to have fun. Some have a desire for sex while others hope it will develop into a relationship. "Whether they're trying to find a relationship, or they're just out for a piece of skin, there's someone there for everyone. Bars aim to please all." "For those who are interested in one-night stands, picking up is not that hard if they try long enough. There are some males and females who are simply sluts and everyone knows it by the way they act, talk, and dress. Females hang on guy after guy. They often dress provocatively and show off their features for all to see. Before long they end up leaving with a guy who is usually wasted. Males will behave much the same way, although they dress no differently than the other males. They will often bounce around flirting with different girls trying the latest in pickup lines, until they are either successful or they decide to leave." "A lot of one-night stands develop out of the couple's desire to have a little fun, no strings attached. People don't really want to go home after the bars close because they're having too much fun. So they find someone of the opposite sex to have fun with. After the bars close there is often a party at someone's house. This gives them the perfect opportunity to pick up someone. They talk, get to know each other a little bit, and with any luck end up together. The next day it is all forgotten. It was just something to do at the time."

"Guys are easy to meet because they are all looking for the same thing. When I see an attractive guy I want to meet I'll go up to the bar beside him and wink at him or start talking to him. Guys are easy to pick up in bars, because they are drinking, partying, and horny. Just smile, talk to them, and you've usually got them. They will even buy you drinks and try to get you drunk so they can fuck you. When you tell them you have your own place they are game to go back with you." "When I go drinking with my friends, I usually seem to be able to get a guy to come back to my apartment. I rarely hear from him again. But then I like to have sex, so it doesn't really bother me." "A female friend of mine is notorious for picking up guys when she gets a few drinks in her. One time she pointed at her crotch and said, 'As long as I have one of these, I can get one of those,' and she pointed at my crotch. She's aggressive. She takes a step and then leaps at you. Basically her approach is 'take me home and fuck me all night.' She always gets what she wants."

"When I see an attractive guy, the first thing that comes to mind is if he is any good at sex, and I start fantasizing about taking him to a remote area and letting the fun begin. I try to make eye contact and I smile at him. If he smiles back I figure he's interested and I strike up a conversation. This usually works, because guys want to meet girls. I try to see if he is looking at my body, and if he is, I try to show it off a little more. I use all the body language I can, because guys get turned on by physical attraction before anything else. If I'm at a bar, I try to get close to him, touch him, and get him alone to talk to. Then if I can take him home, I do so."

"I don't usually go on dates as such. I'm more prone to just go to a club and pick up a girl. I just want someone to be with that night." "If I pick up a girl in a club then I have just one thing on my mind. Yes sir!" "I like the idea of going out somewhere and ending up going home with a beautiful blonde. Although they are not all beautiful blondes, are they?" "Most girls you pick up aren't the kind you'd take home to meet Mom." "Sometimes I pick up girls and sometimes girls pick me up. Whatever the case it doesn't usually develop into a relationship. I don't want to get tied down. That's why I'm in the bar in the first place. I don't have a girl holding me down and I don't really want one." "I don't want a relationship, just a good time. If I see a nice-looking girl I'll go over and introduce myself, maybe buy her a drink, and ask what she's doing later. If she comes with me, that's great. If not, I'll find someone else. It's as easy as that." "Some guys view picking up girls for sex as a sport. This is the case with two of my friends, Keith and Barry. Keith singles out a girl and starts an intelligent conversation with her. He spends long periods of time talking intimately with her at a secluded table, before leaving for his place or hers. My other friend, Barry, prefers to work the room and uses humor, facial expressions, and physical movements to flirt with as many girls as possible. He bounces through a bar striking up a conversation with almost every girl there. He often nudges them and asks, 'How youuuu doin?' Sometimes he intentionally bumps into a girl and greets her with a warm smile. After he connects with a girl, they go off somewhere private. Both Keith and Barry succeed in taking a girl home almost every night they go out. Otherwise they feel their night out is not complete. They are not very concerned about the quality of the girls and say that alcohol lowers their standards. Often the girls they meet are just as interested in finding a sexual partner." #2413

I went with two other girls to a club in Charlottetown. They had already made it clear they were interested in catching a guy. As soon as we got to the club the two girls went into action. After they sat down they took a good look around. When they spotted an interesting specimen they nudged each other and began. At all times they tried to appear like they were having the time of their lives; laughing happily, clapping along with the beat, and never letting an anxious expression cross their faces. All the while they would eye the dance floor and then eye the guy they were interested in. They did not stop as the evening wore on. By eleven thirty I was ready to go home, but they said we should stay a while longer because it was getting late and the guys who weren't with anyone would now make their moves. However, no one approached. On the way home they joked that we should all join a convent, where it wouldn't matter that none of us had a man. #2414

I went clubbing with a group of female friends, who spent more than an hour beforehand working on their clothes, hair, and makeup. They didn't want to get to the club until eleven o'clock at night, because "the good-looking guys don't show up before then." Once there the girls walked around the various floors of the club to see which males were there. They chose a table upstairs where most of the males were located, and a table next to the dance floor and nearest the door, where most of the traffic was. One of the girls saw a male she liked and continued to stare at him. She got her friends to go dance with her next to him, but this led nowhere. Then another girl saw a guy she considered "drop-dead gorgeous," and had the waitress deliver a beer to his table. He came over to thank her, asked her to dance, and we didn't see her again until the next afternoon. Another girl drank one drink after another because she feels she is at her best and has no problem meeting males when she's drunk. Alcohol makes her giggle and talk nonstop. Later she "accidentally" bumped into a guy she had her eye on, apologized, talked to him, and was last seen dancing with him. The two remaining girls walked around the upstairs floor hoping to see a promising male. One saw her ex-boyfriend and sent her friend over to find out if he was available. Her friend returned and reported, "He has a girlfriend. But don't worry (about his knowing why I asked), because I never mentioned your name." The girl became pretty discouraged, and went to the bar to get a drink. When she returned, her friend had been asked by someone to dance. After she finished her drink, she took a taxi home alone. #2415

Some girls get their friends to help them get together with a guy. They may get their friend to call the guy up and find out what he thinks about the girl who is interested in him, or learn what he is doing that weekend and where he will be. "A group of us girls were getting ready to go out to a club. Caroline begged Kim to call up the guy Caroline is interested in. Kim agreed and during the conversation asked him, 'Are you going out tonight?' and 'Where are you going?' She added, 'Caroline and I are going to Dave's Club tonight. What about you?'" Often girls stick together for mutual support. "When I want to meet guys, I like to be with my friends. I feel more self-assured and confident, because I don't have to deal with a one-on-one situation." "People think you are a real slut if you go by yourself, and guys think you want to get picked up. It just saves a lot of hassle going with a couple of friends, and it's more fun that way anyway." In a club some girls will get a friend to go over to a guy they are attracted to and suggest that he ask the girl to dance because she thinks he is awfully cute. "When some guy catches my eye I ask my friends if any of them know who he is. If one of them knows him, I hint I would like to meet him. Usually we both go up to him and she talks to him for a few minutes and introduces me. If he seems interested I let him take things from there. It usually works out well." But friends can also go overboard. "My friends went too far when they found out I liked a certain guy. They pushed me into him and told him I wanted to have his children. I could have died!" #2416

Some girls take a direct approach. "When I see a man I'm attracted to, I go up to him, introduce myself, and start a conversation with him." "Sometimes if I see someone I want to meet in a bar, and I'm drinking, I'll go right up to him and say something. Pretty bold, isn't it? I guess that's just the way I am. I do my own dirty work." "I don't care what the other girls say about me. They're just jealous because they don't get as many guys as me. I don't see what's wrong with asking a guy to dance, especially if you like him." "Some girls just walk up to a guy and ask, 'Do you want to dance?' They tell me, 'If you're going to pick up a guy, who cares what it looks like, just as long as you accomplish it. Just go ahead and go for it.'"

But most girls don't want to be this direct. "If I want to pick up someone I try to be as discreet as possible. I hate the thought that people are watching me look foolish. Many girls feel like I do, and would prefer for the guy to make the move." "I'd feel cheap and easy if I went up to a guy and introduced myself. I'm afraid that's what he'd think of me, and I'm really not like that. I'd rather have the guy come to meet me." #2417

Sometimes when I'm out drinking with a group of my girlfriends we have contests over asking guys to dance. One night two of the girls, Marjorie and Judy, started a good-looking-guy contest. The loser would have to buy the winner a beer. The two girls both agreed on Bill. Both girls asked Bill to dance and paid considerable attention to him, while laughing at each other. Eventually Judy lost interest in the game and Marjorie was declared the winner. Later Marjorie got a ride home with Bill, something she does not normally do. The next day she said, "I don't believe I did that. I'm never drinking again." Another night Marjorie and Betty decided to play a point game based on asking the biggest losers in the club to dance. Each guy was assigned so many points and if a contestant could get him to dance with her, she was awarded that many points. The first girl who reached forty-five points would be the winner. The only girl who actually played the game was Betty, who asked two guys to dance. While she was up dancing Marjorie and Helen stood at the bar laughing. Neither of them had any intention of playing the game. Instead, they wanted to see Betty make a fool of herself. When Betty returned from the dance floor, the others made all kinds of sarcastic remarks like "He was cute," "You can really dance," and "Did you see him dance?" One of the two guys was impressed that Betty had asked him to dance and came over and asked her for a "waltz," or slow dance. She politely refused, saying that she had a boyfriend and felt she shouldn't waltz with anyone else. The man returned to the bar and Marjorie and Helen, who were trying to hide their amusement, burst into laughter. #2418

I went over to Halifax with two of my male friends, Dwight and Joe. We are all interested in picking up girls, but we go about it differently. When we got to Halifax we decided to do some shopping for clothes. Dwight flirted constantly with the female clerks and tried anything to get to know them. Joe, on the other hand, was more interested in getting new clothes. But when we went into a music store Joe thought the young clerk was cute. As we left the store, he said, "Did you see her? She was looking at me! She wants me, big time!" He thinks whenever a girl looks at him she's madly in love with him. But instead of pursuing her, he usually clams up. Next we went to a restaurant. All three of us liked the waitress, who was just awesome looking. Dwight tried playing his "stupid tourist" role to get a conversation going with her, but she left to do something else.

Then we went and bought some beer, because Joe always drinks before going out to clubs. We took the beer back to the hotel and watched a hockey game on TV. I don't know why it is, but every time we get together we argue over who controls the remote and the TV. Dwight and Joe swapped a couple of stories about previous sexual encounters. Dwight told us about the time he drove a couple of girls home and one of them screwed him in the car. Joe said he ran into a girl he knew from school one night in a club. He was hungry and they walked over to get a sub, but instead they went behind a building and had sex. "All I wanted was to buy a sub and go home to bed. I didn't even feel like doing it." By now he was getting pretty loaded. After all this typical guy talk I asked them to describe their ideal woman. Dwight said he wanted a girl with nice eyes, a beautiful smile, nice cheekbones, and a firm butt. She should also be tall and have long legs. He said she has to look nice, but also have a great personality. Joe said pretty much the same thing, but added he likes blondes who play hard to get. He was referring to a girl he liked who used to live in his neighborhood.

We then left for a nightclub which was in walking distance, so we wouldn't have to pay cab fare. We sat and drank at a table in the back of the club for an hour or more until more people arrived. The waitress was very attractive and very friendly and she had quite a conversation with us. After we'd had a few drinks we started to mingle with the crowd. Dwight went off on his own, and I didn't see him for another hour. Joe and I didn't seem to find any interesting women. Then Joe came up with a brilliant idea. He said that the last time we were at this club he met these girls he could have picked up. At the time he was sitting on a bench downstairs in front of the washrooms. I wanted to see this work, so we went downstairs and sat on a bench in front of the washrooms, and began talking about TV programs. A couple of minutes later three girls walked by and looked at us. Then they went upstairs. Joe said the girls were looking at him. Just to get him going, I argued that they weren't. Then the alcohol had its effect and he had to use the washroom. While he was in the men's room the three girls came back downstairs. Joe came out of the washroom and started talking to them. The girls began picking on us for staying on the bench. We talked a bit and then headed our separate ways. Half an hour later we went downstairs again and I sat on the bench while Joe was in the men's room. The three girls came by again and this time one of them, who was attractive and slim, sat down beside me and we began to talk. She wanted to know what I was doing after the bar closed. I was drunk and somewhat shocked by her question. Just then Joe returned and sat down beside her. She didn't talk to him, but when she left to go upstairs, as usual Joe said she wanted him. I told him the real story and Joe tried to get me to go after her. I didn't want to, because I have a different personality than Joe. I'm interested in this girl at home and I'm scared to do anything stupid in case it ever got back to her and ruined my chances. Also, compared to other guys my age, I'm the biggest chicken in the world. I didn't know what to do or say to the girl who talked to me. Joe said I was as pathetic as he is when it comes to trying to pick up women. I realized that Joe gets just as nervous as I do in this situation. That ended my night of trying to pick up girls. Joe, however, kept on trying, but was unsuccessful.

We decided to go back upstairs. We met Dwight and he looked like he wasn't having a good time. I asked him why he was in a bad mood and he said he just didn't feel like meeting any women. I told him he should use positive thinking and go for it. Immediately Dwight's attitude changed. He started talking to a couple of girls and then noticed another girl off to the side. He went over to talk to her, but she could only speak French. Dwight doesn't speak French so two of the girl's friends came over to interpret. It was easy to see a bond was forming between Dwight and the girl, who was from Quebec. Even though they couldn't really understand each other, they got along really well, and talked together for the rest of the night. Joe said it wasn't fair that Dwight was picking up, because Dwight had been sooking earlier and didn't deserve to pick up. Joe got really envious and attempted to pick up our waitress. The line he used was "You must have to meet certain requirements to work here. You all have to be beautiful." The waitress smiled and started paying attention to him. But Joe didn't want to pursue her any further. I never did find out why he didn't go after her.

At closing time, we met up with Dwight and his little French girl, who were saying goodbye. All of a sudden she gave him the longest French kiss of his life. They seemed to be tongue tied for several minutes. Joe yelled out, "Good God! She's sucking his face off!" Then the girl left with her friends. Dwight said she wants to see him again and he's planning to return to Halifax every weekend she is there. I thought about my friends and realized that Dwight goes off by himself and is more direct in his approaches to picking up. He is actually quite the charmer. Joe, on the other hand, sticks with the people he goes out with and is more indirect in his approaches to girls. He can be direct if he has been drinking or if someone he knows is talking to a girl he wants to meet.

When the club closed we went to the Subway up the street to get some food. Inside we saw some girls we had met at the bar. I talked to one of them but didn't want to go with her. Then Joe, Dwight, and I went back to our room and sat around chatting for a while. Dwight said he was in love with the girl from Quebec. She was all he could talk about. I asked, "Why didn't you take her back to the room then?" "She isn't like that. She is too nice of a girl to have just a one-night stand with." Joe said, "You bonehead! Don't you realize you'll probably never see her again?" Dwight just laughed and said he was going to be back in Halifax soon. Then Joe began to ridicule me. He said I could have picked up too, but I was too shy to do anything. I laughed at him and said at least someone was interested in me. He got a bit ticked off and said he could have had any girl he wanted. Then he made some excuses why he hadn't.

At three thirty in the morning we went to bed. I had one bed to myself and the other two shared the other bed in the room. I started to laugh and the others wanted to know what was so funny. I said for two guys who were going to pick up women, they didn't do so good, and now they had to resort to sleeping together instead. They laughed and began to crack homosexual jokes. #2419

Some customers make sexual overtures toward the staff at a bar or club hoping they are sexually available. I work as a waitress in a bar and frequently have to deal with suggestive comments and behavior from guys. Because the men are interested in picking someone up, some make comments like "Where's the night going to lead you, baby?" "Is it hot in here, or is it just you?" "Will you marry me?" and "I want to have your children." If a waitress asks, "Would you like something?" the man may respond, "Yeah, but not from the bar." Men often talk to each other about the waitresses. One night when I was just starting my shift I saw two men at the bar chuckling and nodding their heads toward me, and then one said to the other, "Yeah, well I'd bet she'd be good at that." I insisted they tell me what they had said, but they claimed they weren't talking about me, even though I was the only woman present. The regulars know I won't let anyone get away with abusing me. Alcohol makes the situation worse, because when men drink they are less inhibited. Last weekend a female bartender was serving a man drinks through the night and the two were getting along great. All of a sudden the man started to loudly call her "Slut!" "Bitch!" and "Whore!" The bouncer rushed over and told the man he would have to shut up or leave. He offered the man coffee, instead of liquor, and the man angrily accepted. But when he was brought the hot coffee the man tried to throw it at the female bartender. He was immediately escorted outside. Other waitresses have told me of instances when guys have put their arm around them, lifted up their skirts, poked at their breasts, pinched their asses, or kissed them on the cheek. When men do these things they are often putting on a show in front of their friends. Some men think because they tip you or give you large tips they are entitled to certain liberties. One man kept giving me a $10 tip every time I brought him a beer. As the night progressed he became very friendly and started coming on to me. I finally told him I wasn't a prostitute and if he thought he was buying me with his tips I would gladly give his money back. He left the bar in a huff. Another problem is the men who stare at you continuously and make you feel very uncomfortable. You feel their stares are actually undressing you. One night it was so obvious that two men were staring at me that the other staff made jokes about it. Waitresses commonly complain about this. One told me she was so intently watched that by the end of the evening she was scared to walk to her car by herself. I have even heard cases of waitresses actually calling the police because they were scared to death. When waitresses are abused in these ways they feel the men have no respect for them. It makes you feel very dirty. Some waitresses run to the washroom or even out the door in tears. Men are not the only ones who act this way in a bar. Some women make comments about the male staff or directly to them, such as "Look at that piece of meat!" and "Your feet are awfully long. You know what that means, don't you?" (This is the idea that the length of a man's feet indicates the length of his penis.) #2420

Dancing

If the dance floor is empty it is always the females who will be the first to dance. Females in general are better dancers and seem very comfortable dancing while others watch them. Some girls use the dance floor to flaunt their body to the crowd. Many girls dance with other girls because they are simply having fun. When it comes to dancing, males stand out like a sore thumb. For some reason males just are not built to dance. Often males will dance only if they are really wasted and don't know any better.

Often the girls get out on the dance floor and dance together, while the guys stand around and look to see if there is a particular girl they want to pursue. When a guy sees one he stares at her. The girl usually notices this; if not, her friends make her aware of it. If she likes what she sees she looks back and smiles. Sometimes a guy wanders out on the floor and joins a group of girls who are dancing together. If he is acceptable they usually invite him to stay, and he may end up getting to know one of the girls.

Usually there are more females than males on the dance floor. A primary reason for this is that pairs and groups of females often dance together, but males do not dance with other males unless one or more females are dancing with them. Females and males dance differently. When females dance they move their hips and their feet, they shift their weight from one foot to the other, they move their shoulders up and down, and they move their hands and arms; all to the beat of the music. Males are stiffer, move their feet and arms, and with few exceptions do not move their hips. Some males just shuffle their feet back and forth. None of the males dance as flexibly as the females. Few males are comfortable dancing and many keep a frozen expression on their face. Males prefer to be noticed for how cool they look standing against the bar rather than for their skills at dancing. They dance in order to get time alone with a girl or in order to impress one. #2421

When I ask women why they like going to clubs, the number-one reason they give is so they can dance. However, I have never heard a guy say he is going to a club in order to dance. Some guys admit they go just to pick up girls, but they know if any girl heard them say this their chances of succeeding would be nil. This is because girls are looking for a guy who's in it for the long haul. Many guys don't like to dance, and are only willing to dance after they have been drinking. Girls love to dance and love to see guys make the effort to dance with them. If a guy meets a girl he had better be prepared to dance because the girl is going to want to. Therefore even if a guy doesn't like to dance he is practically forced to if he wants to meet any girls or get their phone numbers. One guy stated, "I never go to a bar to dance. Sure, if there is a girl there that I want to pick up for later, then I'll dance with her to keep her happy. But I usually don't dance at all." Another said, "Males should wear little signs that say, 'Will dance for sex.'"

Music on the dance floor is so loud that it is almost impossible to talk to the person you are dancing with. Often you have to scream at each other to be heard. The dance floor is seldom crowded before eleven thirty. After that crowds start rolling in and liquor begins to show its effects. During the peak hours from midnight until two in the morning when the club closes, there is hardly enough room on the dance floor to move, not to mention dance. #2422

Girls like to be seen up on the dance floor dancing with guys as much as possible, because this makes them look popular to the other girls in the club. If a girl is dancing with someone who knows how to dance, the other girls wish they were dancing with the same guy. I am a guy and I consider myself a good dancer. So when I get to a club I dance the first couple of times with a girl I know who is also a good dancer. That way other girls I don't know will see how well I dance. Then when I ask other girls to dance, most will dance with me. I'm careful not to drink too much because alcohol affects your balance when you dance. Often there will be two or three girls sitting at a table together and one of the girls will never be asked to dance. A girl who doesn't get asked to dance is an excellent target. Often she will get up and dance with you and frequently go home with you just to show her friends she can be successful too. #2423

Alcohol

During the night behavior in a club changes according to how much alcohol people have consumed. Early in the evening there is little movement around the club and few people dance. As the evening continues, things begin to pick up. People who are seated together may shout, talk, or laugh; others get up to dance; and many move around the club talking to friends and strangers. The atmosphere in the club becomes much more lively as the night proceeds, and many people open up and become more friendly. As the drinks keep coming, people's fears disappear. They don't worry whether they'll be rejected or hurt their reputation. Some people continue to sit and drink, and others seem to want to put on a show. A few couples get into heated arguments, and occasionally a fight starts between two guys. Others are very interested in watching what happens.

"People feel that drinking puts them in a festive mood. They don't start partying until they've had a few drinks. If you go to a bar early enough you can sense the general atmosphere of a calm before the storm. The doors of the bar usually open around nine o'clock at night and people come in and sit around talking and drinking. By eleven o'clock people have gotten in two hours of drinking and it is time to party. Once they've had a few drinks, they don't care what type of music is playing; it's time to dance." "Those in the club reach their limit or exceed it, and you see a side of them you haven't seen before. I could count on my hands the number of people who remain sober." #2424

Most males and females are shy about making social and physical advances. Alcohol is commonly used and is frequently mentioned by both guys and girls as one of the best ways of breaking the ice. Alcohol allows people to loosen up and become more forward. Many people rely on alcohol in order to feel confident enough to approach strangers, talk to them, ask them to dance, dance, show affection, and become sexually involved. "The girls I know all do things when they've been drinking that they would lack the confidence to do if they were sober. This includes talking to complete strangers, getting up to dance when no one else is dancing, telling other people exactly what they feel or think of them, and making passes at guys." "I have a problem meeting and talking to people. But give me one or two drinks and I will talk to just about anyone about just about anything. However, if I don't have anything to drink, I will just sit there and look stupid." "I don't have to drink to meet guys, but it makes it a lot easier. When I drink I'm not nervous about what I say to them. But I don't get drunk, just feeling good, because it looks skanky to get loaded." "When I have a few drinks in me, it is so much easier to go up and talk to guys I wouldn't normally have the courage to speak to. When I'm drinking I don't think about such things as what if he brushes me off or what if he thinks I'm too pushy. I just go right up and say something." "I always drink when I pick up guys, because if I get turned down I won't care and I won't lose my confidence. I just go to another guy." "I know several guys, and not one of them will go up and talk to a girl in a lounge unless he is half sloshed." "I watched a group of male friends, and like most guys they began the night slowly. They joked and talked about work and commented on certain women who walked by. Although they all noticed the girls, none of them had the guts to approach them yet. One stated to me that as soon as he had a few more drinks in him he would go talk to one of them. I couldn't say anything, because I'm the same way. It is rather pathetic that we can only approach girls after we are half drunk." "Some guys are very shy when it comes to meeting girls. There are guys who can't even look a female in the face to say hello. I have seen these same guys all over women after a few drinks. I asked one bashful male what his technique is for picking up girls. 'First and foremost,' he replied, 'I have a few beer. This helps release tension, makes me feel more relaxed, and makes the night flow better. After a few drinks my dialogue is a lot smoother. I develop a nonchalant attitude, so if I don't score it's the lady's loss.'" "I watched Harold, a quiet and shy guy, change after he'd had a few drinks. He became very confident and started charming the girls sitting at our table. Harold said, 'Gee! You look nice tonight,' 'Is that a new hairdo?' 'Lovely blouse,' 'You're looking good!' 'Nice perfume you're wearing,' and 'You sure are an awfully good dancer.'

What surprised me is that he asked the girl next to us to dance. I knew that Harold liked this girl, but he was too shy to even talk to her when he was sober. The next day I asked him why he hadn't talked to the girl before, and he said he needed a few drinks first to get up his nerve. It paid off, because they are going out now." "Most males I've observed drink up a storm in order to gain confidence. But all a girl needs is one or two drinks. Some girls even order a drink and just leave it sitting in front of them and then let loose. Everything is excused if you are drinking, even if you aren't drunk but everyone thinks you are." One female stated, "Because my friends drink when we get together, I need to drink too so I can behave the same way they do. If I stay sober, I feel out of place and don't enjoy doing the same things my friends are doing." "When I go out it's with the intention of having fun and meeting women. Last time I was at a bar checking out the scenery I met this lady. She was fairly good looking and carried herself in a flirtatious, sexy manner. So we had a semi-hot conversation in which I paid her some of the usual compliments, such as 'You're looking good tonight,' 'What I would do to have you for a night,' and various other lines. She wasn't just a good listener, because she responded with a few comments of her own, including 'You're gorgeous,' and 'I like the way you move.' This made me feel good. She seemed nice enough, and because I'm not a one-night-stand man, I set up a date with her for the next day. The next day I continued giving her well-deserved compliments, but she just listened and blushed. I thought to myself, 'What happened to the sexy, outspoken lady I ran into last night?' Then I realized, it was the alcohol that made the difference in her behavior. Women gain so much more confidence after a few drinks." "If I'm sober I think twice about getting up to dance because I worry that everyone is watching me or they'll think I'm a rotten dancer. But if I've had something to drink I don't think twice about getting up because I don't care whether anyone is watching me and I don't give a damn what they think of my dancing. Because I get to dance and don't worry about anything, I have a good time." "Alcohol can transform the shyest person into a social butterfly. One guy I know refuses to go out on the dance floor until he is completely drunk. But once he's drunk he has the confidence to approach females and dance as wildly as he wants without caring what others think of him. This is quite common. Few males will go out on the dance floor without having some drinks to loosen them up. Also, many people enjoy participating in karaoke, but refuse to go out on the stage if they're sober." Many people start drinking before they go out to a club in order that they will feel confident enough once they are there to make advances to the opposite sex. "Most men feel it is necessary to drink before going out to a club or lounge. As a male, I can relate to this. I can't speak for every guy, but most of us feel we can interact and feel more comfortable around others if we have a few drinks in us." One female stated, "I would never even dream of entering a club unless I was toasted. If I don't want to drink, then I stay at home. Some of my fondest memories are the ones where I am drunk." People also use recreational drugs to loosen up, become uninhibited, and have a good time. "Often you can smell grass outside the club and also when you walk past the men's washroom. Some guys wait until they feel the effects before they'll get up to dance."

One of the most common changes in a person's behavior produced by alcohol is that the person becomes more outgoing. "I'm very shy. If I were to go out to a club and stay sober, I would never ask any girl to dance, even my own sister." "I can always tell when a girl's had a few drinks. All of a sudden she seems so damned happy to see me. She may have seen me two hours before when she first walked in sober, and not looked twice, but now that she's had a drink she's happy to see everyone, especially guys." "I use alcohol to give me courage to ask a guy to dance or to start a conversation with him. I'm a fairly shy person and I find it difficult to do this on my own. If you can't socialize or start conversations with strangers people will think you are stuck-up, antisocial, or weird, and nobody wants to be thought of that way. I want to be accepted and fit in with the crowd. Alcohol gives me the courage to socialize, so I feel I do fit in and am accepted. Alcohol makes me feel relaxed and less nervous. It seems to take away any fears I have. I feel at ease with myself and others and I feel liked and accepted." "Alcohol makes people think 'I don't care,' or 'I can do that. No problem.' One night I watched a friend who was drinking get shot down five times when he approached girls, and it didn't seem to bother him at all. He just laughed it off." "I couldn't believe my friend was the same person, because the liquor completely altered her personality. She is usually quiet and shy. But here she was latching on to every guy who walked by her. And the way she was dancing; I just pretended I didn't know her." "I hate being around people who are drunk, especially if I am sober. They're always falling all over you and hugging and kissing you, whether they know you or not." "Alcohol makes me more easygoing, so I enjoy myself better and feel a lot more confident in myself. Talking to girls is easier and I talk more openly. I don't care what they think. It is easier to cut through all the bullshit when trying to pick up a girl if you're both under the influence of alcohol. If she's drunk you can tell whether or not she's interested." "For some reason when I'm drunk I want to have sex. I have no idea why, it just seems like a natural thing to do. It seems like every time I am drinking, I end up wanting to go home with someone. Go figure." "Males think when you combine alcohol with sex you double the pleasure. When men are drinking they will make several passes at women at a party or in a club. They are looking for sexual pleasure. Women tend to reject these passes. But if the women are drinking they may eventually 'go for it.' Females need alcohol to be willing to engage in sex. Alcohol makes men more confident and aggressive. Alcohol makes women more vulnerable and willing." "I leave girls who are sober alone, because I'll have a better chance of picking up a girl who is a bit tipsy." "When I'm drinking and I'm with a really gorgeous girl, all I can think about is how I can get her home with me. I know I'm not the only guy who does this. There are even a lot of girls who try to take the guys home with them. All a guy has to do is make the girl feel good about herself. The more I drink, the easier it is to do this. If one girl doesn't like it, it's no big deal. There's always one that does." "When you are trying to pick up girls, it's OK to get feeling good, but only up to the point where you might start slurring or stumbling. Girls get really turned off if you can't talk to them coherently. Also, if you are really drunk a girl will think the only reason you are talking to her is because you want to take her home."

Some people become too forward when they drink. "I was sitting in the lounge watching people when a young male, clearly intoxicated, came over and asked me to dance. I politely said, 'No, thanks.' But he wouldn't listen to me and continued to ask me to dance. When I continued to refuse, he informed me, 'I don't bite.' I still refused. He grabbed me by the arm and tried to pull me onto the dance floor. But I resisted and he didn't get very far. At this point he slammed his fists on a table, sending a number of drinks flying, and walked away, leaving me extremely disgusted." "I met a middle-aged truck driver who said he couldn't wait until he started to feel good so he could get up the nerve to ask a girl to dance. As he drank he became louder, told funny jokes, and became the center of attention. Before long he was talking to girls and dancing. When he returned to his seat he gave the waitress a very hard time and repeatedly tried to grab her. Then he tried to pick up every girl near him in tasteless ways. He would grab girls in various places and clown around. Women became tired of his Russian (rushing) hands and Roman (roaming) fingers and left his table. But one girl stayed with him." "I was sitting with a guy who was quite nice until he started to drink. Then he became so confident that he thought he was God's gift to women. He repeatedly said girls were winking at him, and he began to abuse the girls seated at the next table. Then he went over to a couple and told the girl to come with a real man and just leave the pussy there. This didn't go over well and he ended up in a fight. I last saw him fighting with two police officers." "A friend of mine got completely wasted when she went clubbing. She saw a guy she thought was totally gorgeous. She chased him all night and made herself look like an idiot. All his friends abused him and now he won't even look at her. She would have had a chance with him, but she blew it." "Some individuals use the straight-out approach. They will be drinking and walk up to a person and ask her or him, 'Will you come home with me?' They may get slapped, told off, or just be left standing there looking like a fool. But sometimes it actually works. People who are good at this report there is a certain type of person who has 'the look,' and if you spot this look you are as good as in the sack."

Alcohol can easily be blamed if things do not work out well or if others criticize one's behavior. You can always excuse yourself by saying you had too much to drink. People use the excuses, "I was drunk and didn't know what I was doing," and "I was drunk and he (she) took advantage of me." Knowing they can use alcohol as an excuse frees people to act out. "I can act whatever way I want when I drink. Alcohol gives me the excuse to let loose and not have to think about my actions. Normally I'd be judged by my friends, but my friends don't blame me because they know my actions are caused by the alcohol." "I have a very hard time talking to girls, except when I'm drinking. Then I talk to many girls and dance with them. One of my favorite expressions is 'It doesn't matter what I say to her, because I'm drunk.'" "I was sitting in a bar with some friends and a guy I know came over to chat. While we were talking I noticed a girl constantly staring at him and giving him the eye. I brought this to his attention, of course, and told him he seemed to have an admirer. He looked at her, she smiled, and he said 'Hi!' and winked at her. He then turned to me and said, 'That girl is poison. Trust me, she's poison.' I asked why he had said hello and winked if she was poison. He explained, 'Well, I was with her one night, and I think she's looking for more. I'm trying to keep my distance because she just doesn't turn my crank. Besides, I was drunk that night.' Later on that evening I saw him talking to her several times. Even more interestingly, I saw them leave the bar together when the bar closed. I saw him again the next day and asked him, 'Why did you leave with that girl last night? I thought you didn't like her.' He replied, 'Please don't remind me. I've got to stay out of that booze. It ruins my common sense.'" "Women also use alcohol as an excuse for acting foolish or sleazy, even when they drink very little. They fake their condition and blame it on alcohol if anything embarrassing happens." A female said, "I become a different person when I drink. Alcohol gives me confidence to do crazy things I wouldn't dream of doing sober. I don't have a lot of guts, and I don't want people to think I'm stupid. So I drink. That way I can use alcohol as an excuse if I do something really out to lunch, or really embarrassing."

Alcohol also helps to remove inhibitions about sex. "When a person has had a few drinks others can usually detect it. This is especially true with girls. They become more giggly, energetic, and sociable. Guys seem to stick to these girls like glue, for they know they will be easy pickups. With guys it's harder to tell if they've been drinking, unless they're falling all over the place. They usually just stand around, whether they're drinking or not." "As the night gets later and as women consume more alcohol they are much more willing to express themselves sexually. Some women try to pick up different men, and you see women frequently kissing them. Many women dance with other women, sometimes in erotic ways, even though their sexual interest lies with the men at the bar. They are liberated by the alcohol." "When I'm looking for a girl to pick up I watch and see which girls are tipping back the most booze and which ones have to visit the little girls' room most frequently." "Lori is a very nice and proper girl, but when she gets a few drinks in her, she changes. She gets up on the dance floor and dances like she's a movie star, and hugs the guys she dances with. She talks to the fellows while sitting on their knees. She also talks dirty, which she doesn't do when she's sober." "When I drink I'm not as shy around guys and am actually more aggressive. I'm not as nervous about what the guy wants, and I can't say no as easily." "I will admit, when I'm drinking I tend to do a lot more if I like the guy enough." "When I'm drunk guys take advantage of me, tell me a lot of bullshit, and use me." "Drinking plays a major role in picking up people in clubs. People who are drinking are more sociable, less inhibited, and more easily sexually aroused than when they are sober. Alcohol seems to stimulate the hormones and gives you the need to cuddle. Some people don't even think of going home with someone until they start to drink." "If I don't drink, I'm fine. But as soon as I get a few drinks in me the girls look so much better. Almost every time I go to a bar and drink I end up picking up a girl." "I wish I had never gotten drunk last night. I'm such a flirt when I'm drinking and I just ruined a great friendship because of it. How could I be so foolish and stupid? I'm never going to be able to look at my friend Dennis again." "I was completely tanked one night and ended up going home with some guy and making a huge mistake. First of all, we didn't use any protection, which was really stupid. Secondly, he turned out to be sixteen years old, or five years younger than me." "Last Friday Robert and I decided to get drunk. That afternoon we drank a two-four (a case of twenty-four beer), a bottle of Kahlua (coffee liqueur), and I don't know how much rum. I vaguely remember going to a lounge, dirty dancing, and picking up a not-so-good-looking girl. I can't remember any details like who I saw, talked to, or anything like that. But anyway I woke up Saturday completely naked on a pullout bed. I didn't have a scrap on, not even a bedsheet, and there were four girls in the room. They were all dressed and kind of laughing at me. Talk about mortifying." People may also use alcohol to try to remove another person's inhibitions about sex. "When I'm out at a club talking to a woman, I buy her as much liquor as she'll drink. Then I tell her about the three children I have to take care of and how lonely I am. It spears her heart. When she feels sorry for me, she's more likely to take me home for the night."

Alcohol and sex can be used as a means to fulfill other needs, such as seeking attention. "Sally is one of the quieter members of our group. She goes about her business without disturbing anyone, and people find it difficult to get to know her. Sally went to a club with us and after she had had about nine beer she became very 'touchy' with everyone and kept going around telling everyone that she loved them. She dirty danced with all the guys and even led a few to think she was going home with them. She put on a little dance show for her new boyfriends, challenged them to drinking contests, and repeatedly gave them affectionate touches, such as hugs and little pecks on the cheek. All of this was accompanied with provocative body movements. As a result she accumulated numerous invitations to spend the night with different males. But she didn't respond to any of these invitations. She just liked the attention she was getting, and used the alcohol as an excuse for her behavior. Sally said, 'I don't know what I do to provoke all these guys when I drink. I think all they are after is one thing. Well, they are not going to take advantage of me when I'm drunk. They can take some other girl home. All I want to do is have a good time. I don't drink very much, and it doesn't take much until I'm feeling tipsy. I kind of like the attention. I don't get it when I'm sober, so why not flirt a bit when I'm drunk. Everybody does it. And hey, it's what's expected.'"

Clubs

There are also people who do not become more sociable when they are drinking. Some become depressed. One woman stated, "When I drink I get depressed. I always think that drinking will let me loosen up, but the opposite occurs. Instead of loosening up my spirits, it loosens up my heartache." "Sometimes when a person is drinking all it takes is one rejection to make them sook and go off to a corner somewhere and want to be alone." "I was drinking with several girlfriends at a club. One girlfriend, Emily, saw a guy she liked dancing with another girl. Emily got very upset and started crying. Then she ran out of the club. We went after her and found her standing by our car making herself sick. We tried to help her into the car but she pushed us away. She said, 'I'm sick of everyone, even you guys.' She cried all the way home." Others become more aggressive when they drink. "I can't tell you how many times I've gotten into a scrap trying to protect my woman. It seems like every guy in the bar is trying to pick her up even though they know she's taken." People also become more cocky and say what is on their mind. "Man, when I get drinking, it just seems like I totally loosen up. I don't think about what I am saying or doing. If someone pisses me off I let them know. If I were sober it would take a lot more to get me to say something." Others become more biting. "I go out with a bunch of friends, we get hammered, and we don't have a care in the world. I'm a very sarcastic person, and when I get alcohol in me, I become much worse. I know some people don't like my sense of humor when I'm drunk, but hey, these are the same people who don't like me much when I'm sober either."

The drunker people become, the more money they tend to spend. Although some people are very careful with their money, even when they are drunk, there are more people who seem to spend it freely. Not only do people buy drink after drink for themselves and their friends, they even buy drinks for strangers. "I watched a guy at the bar buy about eight drinks for everyone around him. When he asked, 'Who wants a drink,' I said, 'Sure, I'll take one,' just to see what would happen. I'd never even met the guy, and he bought me one too. He didn't even try to talk to me. He just handed me the drink and said, 'Have a good night.'" "Countless times I've seen both guys and girls stumble up to the bank machine in the bar to get more cash. One young man was visibly troubled when the machine was out of service. He went to the other bank machine, but it was out of service too. When he complained his words were heavily slurred. He then went into the restaurant area and convinced the cashier to let him take money from the bank debit machine to pay for drinks and to let him take out some cash too. He was getting very frustrated by all the trouble he was having, so he took out an additional fifty dollars. One thing is for sure. If he consumed fifty dollars more alcohol, he would be in a lot of trouble."

Some people do not use alcohol to become confident. There are those who don't like to drink. "I usually order orange juice or a coke for something to drink. Sometimes I start off with a single drink of alcohol and then switch to something nonalcoholic. I don't like to drink because I always want to be in control of what I do. I never find it easy to ask a girl to dance or to try to start a conversation, but I know if I don't try I'll be really annoyed with myself. So I make myself do it. Rejection is no fun, because who wants to accept the evidence that someone you find attractive considers you unattractive or undesirable? I wish I were outgoing and cheerful in clubs, because it would make it much easier to meet girls. But unfortunately, I'm not that way. Instead, most of the time I just sit there like a bump on a log. And I'm sure that after I'm turned down for a dance I look pretty discouraged." There are those who are very sociable without alcohol. "One guy, who was sober, was the most confident person I saw in the club. He simply didn't care what people thought of him. He danced around, sang, chatted with everyone, and approached women like he had nothing to lose. Any guy can tell you this takes guts. I couldn't help but admire the guy. When I talked to him he told me he never drank, didn't need to, and wasn't about to start. It was good to see that not everyone needs alcohol to socialize with people they don't know. But most guys are not this way, because they feel more comfortable after a few drinks. When I'm sober I would never think of going up to a girl I've never met and starting a conversation." Some individuals reject alcohol as a means of finding someone. "There is no way a girl can have a meaningful relationship with a guy if she has to get a buzz on before she can talk to him." There are also individuals who just like to drink, but do not need to in order to socialize. "No, I don't have to drink to meet guys. I go out to drink, not to meet guys. I can talk to them sober. I just like to drink and guys happen to be there." #2425

On Friday night I went to a club with four of my friends; Bobby, Daryl, Jim, and Mike, who range in age from twenty through twenty-six. When we entered the club at nine o'clock that night none of us had had anything to drink. Just inside the entrance we looked around the club. The club was about half full. We stood fairly close together and after a quick discussion agreed upon a suitable table. The tables we considered were along the edges of the club and provided a good view of the door and the people in the club. The feeling I picked up was that the group didn't like standing there with people looking at them.

After we sat down we didn't say much, except to comment on where the good-looking women were located around the club. The waitress arrived and we all ordered beer. Once we had our drinks our attention shifted from others in the club to each other. We talked about sports, a local hockey team, individual players, and the coach. The waitress returned, and everyone except me ordered another beer. I had to stay sober in order to drive the group home. Those who still had beer in their glass quickly finished it off. It had only been fifteen minutes since we had placed our first order. Bobby went over and talked to a few friends. The group noticed where he went, but didn't comment. Then conversation switched to taking ski trips. Mike was going skiing in Quebec. His main goals were to get drunk and pick up women. By now Bobby had returned, and he told us about his ski trip two years before and emphasized how many single women were at the resort.

By now it was almost ten o'clock. We were out of beer and trying to find our waitress. As our glasses ran dry attention switched back to what was happening in the club. The club had filled up. I would estimate the ratio of men to women at about forty to sixty, and there were roughly two hundred people in the club. Most people were in groups of two to six members of the same sex. The remaining twenty percent or so were couples or mixed groups of males and females. Most people were eighteen through twenty-four years old. Daryl became impatient waiting for the waitress and went to the bar and bought us a round. The waitress returned and we ordered an additional round. Mike and Daryl were the fastest drinkers. However, the others speeded up their drinking until they had caught up. Mike, Jim, and Daryl discussed women. Mike mentioned the names of a couple of women he had picked up recently. Both Jim and Daryl called them down. One was referred to as "a dog," and the other as "nice ass, but ugly."

By now it was eleven o'clock. All four guys were drinking their sixth beer. Mike and Daryl, and to a lesser extent Jim, were showing the effects of the alcohol. Bobby was harder to judge. The group's attention was mainly on the dance floor. Only a few comments were made, usually about a specific girl or to point out a common friend in the crowd. Bobby went off again to talk to a friend. He seemed to know more people than the others did. A few people stopped by our table and said things like "What's going on?" "How ya been?" "Hi! What's new?"

and "Have you seen ____ ?" The only one who had a female stop by was Jim. They talked for a few minutes exchanging greetings and asking what each other had been up to. After she left no one mentioned her until Jim brought her up. Mike said, "She's half decent looking." The rest of the group merely seemed curious and everyone watched the girl go back to her seat. Mike mentioned that there were two other girls sitting with her.

By midnight two more beer had been ordered. Jim declined the last order and was the first to break the practice of everyone drinking at the same pace. Mike was becoming increasingly drunk. For the past half-hour Mike had been suggesting we go ask someone to dance. It seemed to me he was debating over whether to ask someone himself. Bobby, however, was the first to act. He just got up without a comment. A few minutes later Mike saw Bobby and a girl headed for the dance floor and stated, "There goes Bobby. Don't know how he does it." Mike then began again to try to get the rest of us to ask someone. No one seemed interested. However, I noticed all the guys started drinking faster. Jim said he was going to the washroom and I noticed that on his return he stopped and talked to the girl who had come by our table earlier to talk to him. After they talked for about five minutes, they got up and danced. Mike noticed this. Not to be outdone, Mike got up and asked a very pretty girl to dance. However, she refused. Mike, on his way back, asked another girl and she accepted. Bobby was also on the move. However, he just seemed to be talking to friends. Daryl, who was left at the table with me, began talking about Mike and saying he was pretty drunk. All the time he talked to me his eyes kept wandering over the crowd. But he made no move to get up.

Mike returned to the table at the end of the song and immediately began to talk about the girl he had danced with, saying how much he wanted to take her back to his place. Jim was still up dancing and Bobby had returned. Bobby said that Mike should "go for it." Mike, however, began to talk to me. The last two "waltzes" (slow songs) were being played and the evening was drawing to a close. Mike took a gulp of his drink and said, "It's now or never," and went over to ask the girl he had danced with for another dance. She accepted. Bobby got up and went to talk to a girl. Daryl and I were left at our table. It was the last dance. Daryl tried to decide whether to ask someone to dance. He was clearly scared the girls would say no. He quickly finished his drink and went to ask a girl he knew. She accepted. Finally the music stopped, signaling the end of the evening. All four guys returned to the table shortly afterwards. Bobby announced he was going to a girl's place for a few more drinks. He didn't invite the rest of us. After he left, Mike best summed up the feeling of the group by saying, "Jesus, he's lucky. I don't know how he does it." It was one thirty in the morning and we decided it was time to leave. Jim finished off what was left of his drink and everyone went home.

What was noteworthy was that alcohol increased everyone's confidence. None of the group even tried to meet the opposite sex until they were fully drunk. Even then, before a move was made, an extra-long drink was taken for fortification. I think alcohol made them less self-conscious and reduced their fear of rejection. [#2426]

Protecting reputations

Nightclubs are often thought of as pickup joints, and many people assume that the only reason single people go to clubs is to find some "meat," or "skin." Many girls I know want to make clear this is not the reason they go. Therefore they do several things to protect their reputations. One thing a girl does not want to do is walk into a club alone. When she is alone people think she is just there to get picked up. One friend of mine worked late and the people she wanted to go out with were already in the club. She hated the idea of entering alone, so she asked me to meet her downstairs at the door so we could walk in together. It is amazing the lengths people will go to in order that others do not get the wrong impression. Another thing girls will do is leave with the same people they come with. Some girls would never leave a bar with a guy if she didn't go there with him. It doesn't take long for word to get around town about who left with whom. Many girls leave the bar before the last "waltzes" are played. The last waltzes, or slow dances, are when those who are trying to pick up someone move in for the kill. When girls remain in the club and a guy asks them to dance during the last few slow dances, they often refuse. One night I was at a local bar with my friend Jill when the last waltz was played. A guy we didn't know came over and asked Jill to dance. She said, "No thanks." But he was quite persistent and asked her, "Why not?" Jill told him, "I've been sitting here most of the night and not once did you come over to ask me to dance a fast song. Now you just expect me to get up and waltz the last waltz with you. You just think you are too good to dance with me." The guy said he understood why she refused him. While they were discussing this the bar finished playing the last waltz and then put on a fast song to finish up the night. Jill asked the guy to dance and they have since become good friends. Jill and other girls don't want people to assume they are getting picked up. They want to protect their reputations. #2427

People in a club notice just about everything, often recognize the people there, and would love to possess a juicy piece of gossip that they could tell others in order to get attention for themselves. "I know people who go to the club just to get information so they can gossip about it. They want to see who leaves with whom. They want to know which girls are picked up and which guys are cheating on their girlfriends and wives." "I work in a club, and the next day my girlfriend knows everything that happened to me during the night. Her friends give her a full report. She knows who I was talking to, what girl had her arm around me, and so on."

Often when people connect with someone in a club and want to get together they don't want others to know this. Therefore they don't want others to see them leaving together. "Eddie is married and his wife works night shifts. Eddie arrives at the club about ten o'clock at night and stays until closing time, but he leaves earlier if he can pick up a girl. This is a small town and he could easily get caught. So he usually tells the girl the color of his car and tells her he will meet her outside in five minutes because he has to go down the street first and pick up a couple of joints." Sometimes a girl is out with one or more friends and meets a guy she likes, but doesn't want her friends to know she is going to get together with him. Often she arranges to leave the club separately or to meet him later. "I was dancing with a girl and asked if I could walk her home. She said no because she was with her girlfriend. I had already put her glasses in my pocket, because she was very attractive without them. I told her if she wanted her glasses back I would drop them off later at her place. She left the club soon afterwards with her friend, and I went by her place half an hour later." "One night my husband was out of town and I went out to a club with my sister. I met this guy, we danced, and he wanted to get together. When I told him I was married, he said he was engaged. We arranged to meet after my sister drove me back to my apartment, because I didn't want her to know what I was doing." #2428

Picking up drunk girls

I work at a large club, and the staff are familiar with a certain type of male who arrives just after we stop charging a cover charge at fifteen minutes before we close. We close at two o'clock in the morning. These males are normally quite sober and scan the crowd for drunk females, approach those they find attractive, and frequently ask them, "Do you want to get a pizza?" I have seen this work on several occasions. But once I saw this technique backfire. The male made his move on a female on the dance floor. He worked his way through the crowd and snuggled up to the female, who was quite drunk. He matched her dance steps and she didn't seem to mind. Then her female friends arrived back from the cloakroom carrying her coat, and they ignored the male. The male put his arm around the female, and she turned and loudly objected to his advances. There was a chorus of shouts and insults from the female's friends. As the bouncers approached through the crowd, the most outspoken of her friends picked up a beer bottle and smashed it over the male's head. The male was left with his face bleeding while the females disappeared into the crowd. [#2429]

Females exploiting the situation

Because most guys want to pick up a girl, the females are in a position of power. "Girls often take advantage of guys who are willing to buy drinks for them. I noticed several girls who flirt with guys for the sole purpose of getting drinks. One would go up to a guy, flirt heavily with him, and as a result the guy would be more than ready to buy her drinks. After he bought her one, she would say something like 'I'll be right back' or 'I'll talk to you later' and leave. After I watched this happen several times I asked one of the girls, 'So, are you using him for drinks?' At first she was a bit defensive, but when she realized I wasn't angry she said, 'Well, I might as well. It's so easy.'" "Most girls drink draft beer when they have to buy it themselves. They tell me, 'We don't really like the taste. But, oh well, it's really the only thing we can afford that gets us drunk.' But when guys buy them drinks they switch to expensive and tasty mixed drinks, like Blue Lagoons. When I ask why they are no longer drinking draft, they say, 'Hey, if the guys fall for it and buy it, why not take it.'"

Often I see girls toying with guys. "Some girls flirt and come on to guys to see how many offers they can get." "I know two girls who come into town together at least twice a month. One is twenty years old and unemployed. The other is eighteen and in grade twelve. When they are present the boys are just hopping. The two girls really cock-tease. They wear short dresses and are extremely friendly. They dance really sexy and turn the guys on. But they won't slow dance or accept a date with any of them. They really get off on teasing the guys." "I watched this girl meet this guy on the dance floor and keep him there all night. The guy obviously thought he had found a girl. But at the end of the night she told him she was leaving with her friends. The guy was quite angry she wasn't leaving with him." "It isn't hard to find some guys pissed off after a club closes. They have spent all night with a particular girl talking, dancing, buying her drinks, the whole bit. But when it is time to go home she gives him the cold shoulder and leaves. He thinks he wasted his time and money and walks around swearing. Sometimes he tries to pick up any girl who walks by, but this usually fails." [#2430]

A disheartening experience for many

I think for most people the club scene is a disheartening experience. Women spend an incredible amount of time and energy trying to look as attractive as possible. Then few men show an interest in them or ask them to dance, and the men that do they aren't interested in. "I find that a great many single women admit they aren't having a good time and in general are bored to tears. They want to dance but aren't being asked. As a result they spend the entire evening in their chairs, drinking and looking downhearted." None of the girls sitting in a group at a table may be asked to dance during the night. "When you go to a club with another single woman, it is an unnerving experience. It can be very depressing." "If I don't get up to dance during the evening, I get depressed." "It's very annoying when a good song comes on. I really want to dance, and there's a group of guys just sitting there, but none of them ask me to dance." "If no one asks you to dance, or if you have to sit all alone while your friends are up dancing, the evening can be disappointing and even humiliating." "Lots of girls are just dying to get up and dance, but when a guy asks them, they refuse. Maybe the guy doesn't fit their image of a hunk." "The most popular girls are those who are prettiest and those with money who can afford to look nice. People like me don't have a chance here against that competition. I've never met any really nice guys at a club. They're here looking for one thing. I hate the way women are regarded as objects in a place like this." "Many people look bored with the whole scene. Some people never get out of their seats all night except to go to the washroom." "The only people who seem to have any fun at all are the couples and groups who are up on the dance floor a great deal."

Clubs are dark and you can't see people very clearly. Sometimes they are crowded and hot. They are often filled with smoke, and if you don't smoke it can be quite unpleasant. Also, the music is usually so loud it is hard to hear what people say. The club doesn't start getting busy until after eleven o'clock or midnight. If you've already had a busy day or if you're a morning person, by this time you're ready to go to bed, not party. It's hard to be bright-eyed and bushy-tailed when you're tired and sleepy.

If you go by yourself, the club can be a lonely place. It's no fun being alone. But if you go with friends, you spend your time with your friends, instead of contacting people you are interested in. It's hard to approach strangers and it's hard dealing with rejection. Lots of guys sit or stand around and never approach a girl. Although they want to have a good time and hope to get lucky, they rarely do. Another problem is men find a small percentage of the women attractive, and the women find a small percentage of the men attractive. It isn't easy to find someone that you find attractive who also finds you attractive. I think the club scene works for people who are quite outgoing. They are personable, charming, and confident, and they are very successful in meeting people. But few people are this way. Most people just sit there and hope things will work out. They find security in holding their drink, smoking, or talking to their friends. "Many guys are shy and sit there and watch the action around them. They spend most of the evening with a drink in their hand watching various girls. The second they notice that a girl sees them staring at her, they look away as quickly as possible." "I'm not very good at meeting guys because I don't have much self-confidence. You need to be talkative to get guys to like you." It helps when people know a lot of other people there, but often they don't. "If you go to a club by yourself, and you aren't outgoing, you'll probably end up sitting by yourself, and you'll probably leave early. Perhaps you'll pretend you are waiting for someone, or you'll hope someone will come over and talk to you. If you do come back, you'll make sure you come with other people."

Occasionally you find someone attractive who's willing to talk to you, but odds are they're a kook. Their outlook and approach to life is so different from your own that it is difficult to hold a conversation with them. When you leave with someone, often one or the other of you decides you aren't actually interested in getting physically involved or in getting together again. Only a small percentage of the people in the club connect with someone they want to be with. It happens, but it can take a lot of nights of hanging around the clubs before it does. [#2431]

Finding a serious relationship

Many people who go to clubs hope to find a partner for a serious relationship. Clubs and bars are one of the few places where you can count on finding a large number of available males and females who are single. But do people establish good relationships with someone they meet in a bar or club? You often hear, "You can't find a relationship in a bar," and "No successful relationship begins in a bar. Too many women try too hard to find a boyfriend there. Go to church or the Laundromat if you want to find someone to date." However, some people actually do find a relationship in a club. "I was slightly drunk, met a girl and danced with her, then took her home and we had sex. Afterwards we continued to talk to each other and went out a few times. We've been going steady now for the past six months." "I seldom go out, but one night I did and got a little tipsy. This one guy interested me and I went over and asked him to dance. It was the beginning of a true romance, and we are planning to get married in a few months." "One night I went out to a bar. I wasn't expecting anything, but then I met Wade. I couldn't believe how well we got along and how many common interests we had. We got together that night, he called me the next day to ask me out, and the rest is history. We'll be celebrating our second anniversary together next month." "I met my husband in a club. I made it a rule never to go home with someone I met in a club, but that night I broke my rule. We've been together almost thirty years now." "Although lots of guys are interested in picking up girls for sex, I think in most cases if a guy found a nice girl he really liked he would want to settle down." At the opposite pole there are those who say they wouldn't even consider a serious relationship with someone they met in a bar or picked up and had sex with. "Guys go to bars for two reasons; to get drunk and to get lucky. I never go to a bar to find a relationship. I go to pick up a girl and have a little fun; that's all. I don't think I'd ever have a relationship with someone I met in a bar." "I picked up a girl who was totally wasted, took her home, and had sex with her. I realized how easy she was and decided she wasn't the type of girl I want a serious relationship with." #2432

Cars, last dances, leaving together, and drives home

Some guys try to lure girls to their cars. They use various baits and say things like, "I got a new car. Come on out and see what you think of it," and "Did you hear his new hit single? It's really good. I have the tape in my car. Do you want to go hear it?" One night it was really hot in the bar, and Tammy was up dancing with a guy she'd just met. He asked if she wanted to go outside to get some air. Once outside he said, "I wonder where the boys parked my car?" He told her his friends had borrowed his car but he wasn't sure where they'd left it. He asked if she'd mind if they looked for it. When they got to the car he asked if she'd like to get inside. She said no and walked back to the bar. These approaches sound less direct than "Would you like to come out to my car and make out?" When an indirect approach succeeds, both parties can pretend that things just happened and no one was picked up.

The last "waltz" at the bar is when many guys make their move. It's interesting to sit and watch people trying to find someone to dance the last waltz with. Some circle through the bar like predators looking for prey. Danielle had just started going to bars and didn't know the implications of the last waltz. When this guy asked her she said yes. While they were waltzing he pulled her closer and began rubbing her back. She got mad and pushed him away and walked off the dance floor. When a guy you don't know asks you to dance the last waltz, it's best to say no, unless you want him to think you want to get picked up.

If you've been dancing or talking with a guy, at the end of the night he will probably ask for your phone number so you can go out together on a future date, or else he will ask if you'd like a drive home. When a guy asks to drive a girl home the first night he meets her, most girls assume he just wants to pick her up for the night. Some girls are inexperienced and don't realize this. Kelly had just started going to bars. One night she met Angus, who was several years older than her. He seemed very nice and a perfect gentleman. They danced quite a lot and when he asked if she would like a drive, Kelly accepted. On the way home Angus asked if she'd like to go to his place to watch some videos. She felt he was such a nice guy she couldn't imagine him putting the moves on her. She thought they would just watch videos, talk, and get to know each other better. Once there she learned he had something else in mind and she got upset and asked him to drive her home. He dropped her off and said he would phone to ask her out, but he never did. Kelly now thinks that guys automatically expect girls to go to bed with them when they drive them home. #2433

When a girl leaves a club with a guy most people assume that the guy will bang her. Sometimes this is the case, but often it is not. The two may just be friends, and may even have arrived together. They may be leaving to get something to eat, or to go to another club. One may give the other a ride home and nothing more. Even if they are interested in each other, they may talk or neck but not go all the way on their first encounter. "It's too bad you hurt your reputation if you leave a bar with a guy. Maybe you want a ride home because all your friends have already left. I saw one couple leave together, and then later saw them at a different bar. I myself have left with a guy I've just met, and he just gave me a ride home. I hope that didn't hurt my reputation." #2434

Getting drives home with a member of the opposite sex is an intricate issue. Often guys want to drive a girl home that they have met at a club, dance, or party, but don't know how the girl will react. If the girl isn't interested, she will refuse. "Reg, a guy I knew from school, asked if he could drive me home from a dance. His request seemed kind of funny, so I said, 'No thank you.' My friends expected me to go with them." Similarly, a girl may want a guy to ask her home, but not want to seem too forward by suggesting it. She may drop a hint, such as "I wonder if my ride is still here?" or "I think my ride is drunk." Hints usually work, but the girl doesn't want the guy to get the wrong idea and think she is "looking for action." When the guy wants to go parking he may use suggestions to see how the girl reacts. Even if a girl accepts a drive, she may not want to park. "Leonard drove me home from the bar last night. I knew he wanted to park, but I really didn't want to. So when he started hinting around, I simply told him I was tired and was expected home at a certain time. He looked a little disappointed, but didn't seem angry." On the other hand, if the girl wants to park and the guy doesn't take the initiative, the girl has to be careful that she doesn't look like she is "easy" or "looking for it." "Colin asked if he could drive me home from the dance. I liked him, so I said sure. We were almost at my house and he hadn't said anything. So I began to talk about things I knew he was interested in, and he talked too. Then Colin asked if I had to be home right away, and we took a drive out to the point to 'talk' some more." When a girl drives a guy home that she is interested in, she doesn't want to seem too forward by saying, "Well, what do you want to do?" or "Where do you want to go?" Often the guy takes the initiative and asks questions, makes a joke, or uses gestures to suggest they go parking, such as "Do you want to take a drive out by the water?" "I drove a guy I really liked home one night. He was at a dance with a group of his friends, and we had talked and danced all night. So naturally I asked him if he needed a ride home. I couldn't believe it, but while I was driving he slid across the seat and whispered something in my ear I would rather not discuss. Anyway, we took a drive down to the beach, and that's all I'm going to say." In some cases, if the girl knows the guy really well, she will let him drive her car so he can make the first move. When the couple parks they try to find an out-of-the-way place where they are totally alone. They do not want to be embarrassed by being seen by other couples or being disturbed by the police. #2435

Feelings which encourage people to obtain sex

The primary feeling which encourages people to obtain sex is pleasure and the desire for pleasure.

Sex is fun. #2436

I think if anything in the world is underrated, it's sex. The pleasure is so intense. Often when I have sex I think to myself, "How come I didn't remember just how great this is?" #2437

My definition of a good time is to party, get wasted, and get laid. #2438

Having a good time and having sex are one and the same thing. I enjoy sex very much. It's always my main priority during an evening. #2439

I have sex with any guy I go out with more than once, because I don't have the willpower to say no. I enjoy sex, and so do my boyfriends. I see doing it as telling someone I love them. #2440

Some women are not very excitable in bed. But even bad sex is better than no sex at all. #2441

When certain locations of the genitals or nipples are properly stimulated, people experience pleasurable sensations which dominate their attention. When one is correctly stimulated by another person the sensations are more stimulating than when one stimulates oneself. When one stimulates oneself, sensations are less exciting. One's mind has to focus on carrying out the actions to stimulate oneself, and therefore the mind can not focus completely on enjoying the sensations. This stimulation, whether produced by another person or oneself, often produces an increase in tension which culminates in orgasm. One's breathing is coordinated with the sensations of pleasure. One produces exhalations, i.e., relaxations, of breath which coincide with feelings of pleasure and with spasms during orgasm. Sexual activity often includes "heavy breathing." During sexual activity one tenses one's legs, buttocks, back, and stomach, so that when one achieves orgasm one releases all of this tension together and experiences a greater amount of pleasure. People attempt to manage their tension in order to experience as strong an orgasm, or as big a release of tension, as possible. The stronger the orgasm, the more pleasure they experience. The pleasure people receive from an orgasm is of short duration, normally only seconds long. In order to experience this pleasure again, people must achieve another orgasm.

Because of the pleasure people experience with sex, they seek opportunities to engage in sexual activity. When people consider what they would like to be doing, obtaining pleasure from sex frequently occurs to them. One reason why sexual pleasure is frequently considered is that there are a limited number of alternative sources of pleasure available to people. These alternatives consist of positive reactions and various forms of stimulation, such as humor, music, movies, gambling, and pleasant tastes from food and drink. People are tantalized by experiences which anticipate or are associated with sexual pleasure. Thus they are interested in people who wear clothing which reveals their bodies, pictures of physically attractive individuals, pornography, and strip shows. Such things produce sexual desire.

> The guys in my apartment like to sit and look at pornographic magazines. Even though they have girlfriends, they never tire of looking at the girls in these magazines. They borrow the magazines from guys in other apartments and loan their own magazines to them. [#2442]

> In a strip club with table or lap dances, many men who pay for a dance continue paying for more than one dance. They seek to prolong the sexual experience by buying more dances. Customers are not allowed to have sex with the dancer or to masturbate, so they can not reach orgasm. [#2443]

Interest and desire

Males and females are interested in learning about and experiencing sex, starting at an early age. They do so in a variety of ways.

I learned about sex when I was five or six. I couldn't sleep one night because I had a terrible cough. So I went to wake up my mom. I heard groaning from the bedroom, but I went in anyway. Well, when I opened the door, there were my parents, totally naked and doing the nasty as hard as they could. I was totally shocked, and so were my parents. I don't think they wanted me to find out about sex that way. #2444

When I was in the sixth grade there was a girl who had a reputation for taking her clothes off for anyone. I walked home from school with her one day to see if she really would, and she did. Many of my friends would invite her to their parties so she would take off her clothes for them. #2445

My girlfriends told me everything I needed to know about sex. If Mom or Dad had told me, they probably wouldn't have gone into the detail that my friends did. In school we watched a few good films about sex in a sex education class and then we took it from there. Once I got a guy in bed with me, I let nature take its course and soon we were making love. It took a few minutes to get it right because we were so nervous. Once we had explored each other's body and learned where things were, it didn't take us long at all. #2446

I learned about sex the hard way when I got pregnant. The facts of life really hit me in the face. Sex was never discussed at home and I had to pick it up on the streets. I was so naïve I thought if you had a bath after intercourse you couldn't get pregnant. I know it sounds dumb, but it's true. #2447

Interest in sex may be focused on a specific person, or it can be a generalized desire for sex, such as "feeling horny" or "wanting to get laid."

If you're human, you get the urge for sex. #2448

Girl watching is a favorite activity of males. The only time I watch girls is all the time. It doesn't matter what time of year it is. In the summer we watch girls in their shorts and tube tops. In the winter we watch them in their tight jeans. It is impossible to talk to some males when girls walk by, because they are so busy watching the girls. Girls react in various ways when they see you watching them. Many ignore you. Some smile and stop and talk to you.

To be a successful girl watcher, you need to follow certain guidelines. One, never stare, because the girl will consider you a pervert. Two, never stare at a particular part of a girl's body, because it makes the girl uneasy. Three, don't whistle, because it is immature. Four, keep all remarks to yourself. Five, do it alone, because no two males have the same tastes, and another male will distract you. Six, if you want peace in your life, don't let your girlfriend or wife see you watching other females. #2449

I am surprised that about half the girls I talk to think that female sex urges are as strong as the male's. Although males may not understand females, it's also obvious that females don't understand that the only thing guys think about is sex. #2450

I can't remember a day in which I don't repeatedly think about having sex. I'm always glancing at women and watching those I find physically attractive. When I'm in a large group I sometimes count how many of the women present I find attractive enough to go to bed with. #2451

"When I look at an attractive guy, I think about taking his clothes off to see what he looks like. I wonder if he is looking at me and thinking the same thing." "Usually when I'm with my boyfriend I don't even look at other guys with sexual interest. But one day there was this gorgeous guy that I just kept staring at. I couldn't help myself; he was gorgeous. He was playing the drums, which is always a turn-on for me, even though he didn't know what he was doing. But I couldn't help staring at his huge dark-brown eyes, his perfectly shaped nose, his high cheekbones, the way he held his mouth, everything about this boy's face. I was completely mesmerized. When he stood up there was much more to look at. His entire frame was really beautiful. His broad shoulders, his toned body, the tightness of his butt, the size of his hands, the treasure trail on his stomach, everything about this boy was beautiful. I felt foolish watching him with such awe and attraction. I also knew if I wanted to have a relationship with him, at least a brief one, I could, but I do have a boyfriend. Once I realized I would get myself in trouble if I continued watching him, I started to watch his friend instead. His friend had an appealing laugh and hypnotizing eyes. but he also had a long body which I could never be attracted to, and he was very hairy, which is a major turnoff for me." #2452

I find tight-assed jeans make nearly any guy look good. #2453

This winter we have had a number of snowstorms and a very large accumulation of snow. Because of the weight of the snow, it is being shoveled off the tops of some houses and buildings to prevent roof damage. I work in a government office building and the women in my office stand at the windows watching the men shovel snow off a shorter building next door. They comment, "Wow! Look at the ass on that one," and "Come on over to my place, baby. I'll let you shovel my roof." #2454

Girl watching is a dangerous activity, and you can easily be injured. You can be looking at a girl and walk into another person, who may get mad at you. If you are going up the stairs and watching the girl just ahead of you, you can forget where to put your feet and fall, sometimes into the back of the girl. I know several guys who have done this, myself included. One of my friends was walking on the beach, watching a girl walk by, when he stepped right into a hole in the sand. He snapped his leg and the girl had to come over and help him. A fifty-year-old man reported, "It was the first sunny day of summer. All I'd seen since the first of the year were girls in jeans and slacks. But there ahead of me was a girl in shorts and a T-shirt. As she walked I watched her rear and drove into the car ahead of me." If you are walking with your girlfriend, and turn your head to watch a nice girl go by, you can get an elbow in the stomach. Those are just a few of the ways girl watching can be risky for guys.

Girls watch guys too, because regardless of their age, you hear them giggle and laugh when a guy walks by. And girls can injure themselves too. My sister secretly liked this guy and went to see him referee at the rink. Before the game she told her friends that it would be just her luck to get hit by the hockey puck and this guy would have to come over to retrieve it. Well that's what happened. The puck hit her on the leg. The guy came over, my sister was quite embarrassed, and she stood up to get the puck. But when she stood up her purse fell over and the contents spilled everywhere. She reached down to get the puck and when she stood back up she hit her head on the boards. These things happen when you have your mind on someone else. #2455

Feelings which encourage people to obtain sex

Sometimes you are alone with a girl you wouldn't look twice at, get the urge for sex, and make a pass. This has happened to me with girls that I find so unattractive, I wouldn't want anyone else to know I even thought of having sex with them. #2456

Over time one's sexual interest in a specific person or one's general desire for sex changes.

Sometimes I see a woman I find so exceptionally attractive I can't take my eyes off her. I'll even go out of my way to walk near her to get a better look. For months afterwards I'll watch her whenever I have a chance. But after a period of time has passed, when I see her again I don't find her all that attractive. I even wonder why I found her so striking in the first place. Maybe I've just gotten used to her looks and she doesn't stand out anymore. #2457

There are a variety of factors which affect sexual interest. These include availability of a partner, novelty, revealing clothes, and conflicting demands for one's time and attention.

When I see an attractive prostitute on the street, I immediately start thinking of having sex with her. I notice attractive girls all the time, but my sexual interest isn't as strong. Just knowing the prostitute is immediately available seems to make the difference. #2458

Sex is a real turn-on with a brand new partner. It's different and really exciting, and both of us usually reach orgasm several times. Another turn-on is trying a new position with my girlfriend or having sex in an unfamiliar place. If you are outdoors at the beach or in the woods, you have to make sure others don't see you and you have to be pretty adaptable to new "furniture." It's different, and it's just great. #2459

My appetite for sex really goes up when I'm rested and don't have a lot else on my mind. A vacation away from home is perfect, because there is no way I can do the things I ought to be doing at home, so I don't have to devote my time to my regular routines. #2460

Sexual interest may be depressed as a result of fatigue, a loss of novelty as one continues to have sex with the same partner, a lack of interest by

268

one's partner, and a preoccupation with other matters, such as the need to satisfy other feelings. In certain circumstances sex is not pleasurable. This occurs when one is not physically stimulated; has no interest in having sex with the other person; is too tired; or becomes fatigued while stimulating the other person, which normally occurs only if one is not being stimulated too at the same time. Interest is also constrained by factors which occur in connection with sexual activity. These include relaxation and sleepiness after orgasm, and soreness (physical discomfort) from continued sex.

A desire for sex often outweighs other considerations. Thus a desire for pleasure through sex causes people to break commitments of sexual exclusiveness with another person as well as vows of celibacy. If people do not have ready access to partners who are socially defined as suitable, a desire for sex encourages them to establish sexual relationships with partners who are socially defined as unsuitable. This helps explain instances of incest, affairs with married individuals, relationships between partners who differ considerably in age, and homosexuality in prisons.

A desire for sex can also cause one to act contrary to the wishes of the other party. Thus one may continue to make overtures and may even use force to get one's way.

> The problem is you are never sure what a girl means when she says she isn't interested in getting physically involved. Does she mean she positively does not want to have sex? Or does she mean she is willing to go along with you if you persist? Perhaps she isn't ready now, but will be later in the evening. Maybe she doesn't want to appear too easy, or maybe she doesn't want to blame herself afterwards. In any case, if you don't keep trying, you'll never know. #2461

> I knew Kenny for over a year and we started dating. On our fourth date Kenny started to get a little pushy over sex. I told him I had no intention of having sex with him, and he became very angry with me. He started to get violent and told me I owed it to him after all the nice places he had taken me to. I was very frightened and screamed out loud. Kenny let go of me and I ran out of his apartment and all the way back to my own apartment half a mile away. I haven't spoken to Kenny since. I distrust all men. #2462

Feelings which encourage people to obtain sex

My roommate raped his date. I thought he had more brains than that, and more morals too. When I asked him about it, he said, "A man's gotta do what a man's gotta do." #2463

It was our first date and he was a few years older than me. I bought a new outfit and had my hair done. He repeatedly told me how pretty I looked and what a good time we were going to have. When we got to the party someone handed me a beer. During the night I had another beer and another one until I realized I was drunk. My date was kissing me and I liked it, but I wanted to sleep. I was asleep for a while, but there was something heavy on me and I woke up. My date was on top raping me. I started to cry and yelled at him, but he didn't stop. Ever since, I haven't been able to trust males. #2464

Things just got out of hand. I was teasing him, and I guess he couldn't handle it when I said no. He forced me and I guess I deserved it. I see him now and then, and when I do I just shake like crazy out of fear. #2465

One afternoon I gave a male friend of mine a ride home. He lived in the country, and on the way he kept saying I should come in and meet his mother. I was in a bit of a rush and kept trying to put him off, but he insisted she really wanted to meet me. When we got to his house there was no car in the driveway. He said I had to come inside and he took my car keys. I started to feel there is something very wrong here, but I couldn't get it straight in my head what it was. I couldn't leave and I followed him into the house. When we got inside I realized there was no mother and he had no intention of giving me back my keys. I demanded my keys, told him what I thought of him, and grabbed for the keys. We got into a wrestling match which quickly turned into a violent attempt at rape. I'm not sure how I got the keys, but I remember driving away with tears streaming down my face. There's nothing worse than being trapped by someone you like and trust. I'm scared of everyone now. I hardly go out, and only in crowds. I also don't drive guys home alone anymore. #2466

One time I went over to the apartment of my friend's boyfriend. There were just a few of us sitting around watching a movie. My friend had a headache and went to her boyfriend's room to sleep. After a while he went to join her, and they both fell asleep. They were on the other side of a really big apartment. Then the boyfriend's roommate came over and sat beside me. I only knew him to say hi to, but in a matter of seconds he was all over me. I told him, "Fuck off, creep!" But he picked me up, dragged me to his room, hit me on the side of my head, and raped me. My friend couldn't hear me scream, and didn't hear me crying until she found me. I'll never forget that, and it took me a long time to deal with it. Today, if I feel uncomfortable around a guy, I just get up and leave. No question. #2467

In addition to a desire for pleasure, there are other reasons which can underlie a desire for sex with a person. These include curiosity about sex, a desire for positive reactions from others, a conscious attempt to produce children, and an effort to maintain or improve one's self-image.

It is important for me to have a sexual encounter, and I'm curious what it would be like. When the guys in my dorm talk about their sexual experiences, I feel uncomfortable, because I've never had one. The guys ridicule me, insult my manhood, and tell me, "Scott, you've got to get yourself a woman." I think I'll be better accepted by the guys once I've had a sexual experience. #2468

Guys like to brag, and they're always trying to outdo each other. When you get a bunch of guys living together like we are, things tend to get competitive. Sex is just another thing to compete over. #2469

A guy who gets girls easily is looked up to by other guys. It's sort of a power trip, I guess. Everyone wants to be looked up to. #2470

I couldn't stand the fact I was the only virgin among my friends. So I had sex with the first male who looked promising, even though I hardly knew him. #2471

The students I know in high school don't worry at all about getting a sexual disease. All they are concerned with is losing their virginity so they can't be made fun of. #2472

I'm having a contest with my friend from high school to see which one of us can sleep with the most guys during our first year of university. So far I'm ahead. This is April, and I've been to bed with over thirty-five guys since September. #2473

I had an acting teacher who was just beautiful to look at. One weekend when her husband was out of town, things sort of developed and we ended up in bed together. Afterwards I felt so good about myself. I never thought I could attract someone that beautiful. [#2474]

Sexual fantasies

A significant proportion of human fantasies involve sexual activity. Female fantasies often have romantic themes and frequently take place in natural settings.

I start thinking about a particular movie star, whom I would love to meet. He takes me out to dinner at a fancy restaurant and afterwards to the most beautiful hotel, where he makes love to me. [#2475]

The man of my dreams and I go on a picnic. We find a beautiful field in the middle of nowhere. We spread out a blanket and lie together admiring the beauty of the scene and listening to the peaceful sounds. We smell the flowers and hear birds singing in the distance. It is an extremely hot day and both of us are covered with sweat. Then rain starts to fall cooling off our bodies. Each of us peels the soaking clothes off the other. We slowly kiss each other all over. Then we do the deed and it is the most amazing experience of my life. [#2476]

We are on a vacant beach in the middle of the night. The moon is full and the sky is filled with stars. We hold each other and hear the waves pounding against the nearby rocks. We feed each other chocolate-covered strawberries and drink a bottle of sparkling champagne. Then we move where the waves meet the beach. We make love in synch with the pounding waves until we both explode. Then we hold each other tightly as the sun starts to rise. [#2477]

I go to the gym to work out, and there I meet the most beautiful guy in the world. After we finish our exercise, we go into the sauna. We are sweating a lot, and a sweaty male is a real turn-on for me. He makes love to me in the sauna. [#2478]

I wake up in the middle of the night and see my boyfriend masturbating. I start masturbating along with him and we both climax at the same time. Then we make love until the sun comes up. [#2479]

I am hiking in the mountains with the most beautiful man in the world. As we hike we flirt with each other in a sexual way. We discover a waterfall and I walk through it into a small cave. I think I am alone and take off my clothes. When I start to wash them I feel the touch of a hand on my back. I turn and see my hiking partner standing there naked. I stand up and throw myself into his arms. We kiss passionately. He slowly journeys down my body with his kisses and makes me shiver with goose bumps. I return the favor. When the two of us can no longer contain ourselves, I climb on to give him the ride of his life. #2480

The most beautiful guy in the world and I are in a giant store which is closed. We gather all the fur coats and pile them in the middle of the floor. Then we make love on this soft, sweet bed of fur. #2481

We are at a whirlpool which is surrounded by candles. We start to massage each other to set the mood. Then we perform oral sex and the excitement builds. We spread whipped cream over each other's body and slowly lick it off. Then we have sex in every position possible and maybe make up a few of our own. #2482

Male fantasies are more likely to involve a variety of sex acts and multiple partners. Sometimes women take the initiative in male fantasies. For the most part, romance is unimportant. Male fantasies often take place in public settings, rather than natural ones.

I think about this really attractive girl I've seen. We are both nude on a bed. I explore her body and go down on her. Then she goes down on me. I fuck her in several positions while she plays with my nipples. #2483

I'm lying in bed with my girlfriend. After she falls asleep, I start rubbing and kissing her whole body. Then I climb on top of her and slowly start to make love. Things start to get really hot and she wakes up and realizes it wasn't a dream. We both come harder than we ever have before. #2484

I take a girl out to dinner at a fancy restaurant. During dinner she gets so horny she pretends to drop something and crawls under the table. She gives me head while I finish eating my T-bone steak and Caesar salad. #2485

I am in a dental chair. I wake up from the anesthetic and the blond secretary is riding me. #2486

I am playing hockey, and during a timeout a girl gives me head under the stands. It is very risky and exciting. #2487

I am on a crowded bus. A good-looking stranger walks up to me and doesn't say a word. She just looks down, unzips my pants, pulls my Barbie out, and plays with it until I get hard. She is wearing a mini-skirt and doesn't have any underwear on. Then she climbs on and starts to ride me like crazy while screaming out loud. People look at us, but we don't care. When we finish she hops off me, and I never see her again. #2488

I am speeding down the highway. I look in my rearview mirror and see a police car chasing me. I pull over to the side of the road really pissed off. While I am reaching in the glove compartment to get my registration papers, I feel a hand grab my cock. I am bewildered and look up and see the officer has me by the dick. She has dark hair and huge tits. She yells for the other officer to come assist her. A hot blonde with a really short skirt approaches the car. The two of them pull me out of the car and give me a body search. One of them handcuffs my hands behind my back. They slowly take off my clothes. One gives me head while the other fingers herself on the hood of my car. Then I fuck them both like crazy. #2489

I am in my girlfriend's bedroom and we start getting it on. Her mother comes in the room and wants to know what is happening. Halfway through my girlfriend's explanation, her mother takes off her clothes and joins us. Then the fun starts. #2490

I would love to have sex with a girl doggy style. While we are in this position I pull her ponytail with one hand and spank her ass with the other. She barks out my name to show I am her master. #2491

Functions of obtaining sex

The feeling of pleasure encourages sexual intercourse between males and females and frequently brings about reproduction. In fact, reproduction is the primary function of sexual feelings.

> Sex is a wonderful activity. Not only does it feel great, but you get children to carry on your name. #2492

People are much more likely to reproduce because their desire for pleasure encourages them to engage in sex. A desire for sexual pleasure promotes reproduction by overriding various obstacles, such as ignorance concerning the causes of reproduction or a desire not to reproduce.

In order to obtain pleasure, people tend to maintain contact with those who provide them with sex. As a result of maintaining contact they receive additional resources from their partner and provide their partner with additional resources. Such resources may include food, money, positive reactions, help, and protection. In addition, sexual partners are likely to produce offspring together. When they maintain sexual contact with their partner, they usually maintain more contact with their offspring. When they maintain contact with their offspring, they are more likely to provide the offspring with resources. The additional resources that partners provide each other may also be shared with their offspring.

In sum, sexual contact between adults leads to the production of offspring and the provision of additional resources to the adults and the offspring.

Constraints

The pleasure that people receive from sex promotes both interest in and desire for sexual contacts and gratification. However, there are other feelings and various cultural models which restrain and prevent sexual contacts. The other feelings include fear of a) rejection, b) criticism, c) embarrassment, d) guilt, and e) loss of resources. The cultural models specify proper and improper behavior. These psychological and cultural forces serve as constraints which limit sexual contacts and behavior.

Other feelings

People do not want to experience rejection, criticism, embarrassment, or guilt, because they hurt. People fear this hurt and try to avoid it. They frequently do not pursue sexual relationships they are interested in because they think they would experience this hurt. Fear of experiencing hurt has a strong influence on the nature and frequency of the sexual contacts people have with each other. Rejection, criticism, embarrassment, and guilt are dealt with in Volume One of this series. People also do not want to lose resources, and fear (anxiety) often prevents them from taking risks through sexual contacts which could cause them to lose resources. Taking precautions (avoiding risks) is dealt with in Volume Two of this series.

Self-confidence is one of the biggest factors in one's success in getting together with people for sex and relationships. Very few people are confident enough to deal easily with people they hardly know at all. But those who are seem to be extraordinarily successful compared to those who aren't. Because most of us are scared to say Boo! those who are confident and bold have practically the whole field to themselves. Take two of my female friends who wanted a date for the upcoming Winter Carnival Ball. One of the two, Tracy, never ceases to amaze me. I watched her one night when she asked a friend of mine the name of a guy who was standing by the bar. She learned that his name was Percy and that was all she needed to know. Not two minutes later, when Percy walked past us on his way back to his own table, Tracy stuck her foot out and practically tripped him. Then she proceeded to introduce herself. "Hi, Percy! You don't know me. My name's Tracy. But I saw you up at the bar and you look to be a decent-enough fellow. I was wondering if you'd like to go to the Winter Carnival Ball with me, if you're not already going that is? Tickets and drinks are on me, OK?" Others, like my friend Sonya, have to be constantly prodded by their friends or they would never ask anyone. Sonya spent two hours one evening talking to the guy she wanted to ask to the dance. But she wasn't getting any closer to the topic, even though we kept making faces at her, jabbing her, and telling her to hurry up. The two talked about the weather, their courses, the price of their drinks, their professors, and even their pets. But they took forever to bring up Winter Carnival. "Have you gone to any of the winter events yet?" Sonya finally asked. "No," said Roy, "I've had to work at my job a couple of nights, so my week's been pretty busy. Have you?" "Oh yes, and I'm going again tomorrow night," she answered. "Are you going to the Ball?" asked Roy. "No, but I'd like to," said Sonya. "Yeah, so would I." "So how about it if we go together?" asked Sonya. "Sure, that's a great idea. Let's," stated Roy. After Roy left, we told Sonya, "See how easy that was." But Sonya didn't think it was easy at all. Most of us are much more like Sonya than we are like Tracy. #2493

Girls expect guys to make the first move, but this is usually hard for guys. If the girl shows she isn't interested, guys feel disappointed, hurt, and humiliated. Girls often feel frustrated because guys are reticent to approach them. However, guys fear rejection more than they fear anything. Because they have been rejected in the past, guys often want a sign the girl is interested before they make a move. "It's really hard to speak to a strange girl you find attractive. I find if I go over and stand or sit next to a girl I'm interested in, I have to try to speak to her right away. If I don't, the longer I stay there without speaking, the harder it is to ever speak to her. The longer I am there, the more self-conscious I become, and the more I want to just play it safe and sip my drink and look straight ahead and not say anything. I think I'm scared she's going to react in a negative way to me. Odds are she won't be interested in me, and she may feel I'm bothering her." "Nobody wants to be shot down when they ask a girl to dance. If one girl at a table rejects you, all the girls at the table will too." "They're real bitches! It takes a lot of guts to go over and ask one of them to dance and if you get turned down, you can hear them laughing among themselves when you walk away. That can hurt a lot, man. I don't need that shit. It's hard enough to ask in the first place." "A guy is nervous about asking a girl to dance because he may be refused, which would embarrass him in front of his friends. Most guys try to drink enough to no longer care what others think about them." "I love watching a guy come on to a girl. It's funny as hell, especially when he gets turned down." "When guys ask girls to dance, being rejected can be a real ego deflater. If one of my buddies asks a girl to dance the rest of us are intent on grading his success. When he is turned down he tries to pretend nothing has happened and nonchalantly heads back to our table. The rest of us are in hysterics, even though this has happened to all of us on various occasions." "I never thought about the guy's feelings. Thinking back, I must have made a lot of guys feel pretty stupid because I never cared how harsh I was turning them down, and there were certain guys that you always turned down."

Constraints

"Guys respond in various ways when they ask a girl to dance and are rejected. Many don't say anything and return to the bar or their buddies to nurse their wounded ego. A guy may comment to his friend, 'She was really ugly anyway.' Others try to hurt the girl back for embarrassing and humiliating them. Thus some may retort, 'That's OK. It's only 'cause I felt sorry for you,' or 'So I guess a blow job's out of the question?' One guy walked by a woman who had refused him earlier and commented, 'Nice face. You want a banana?' A few try to put a guilt trip on the girl after they are refused and walk away with a comment like 'That's the story of my life.'" #2494

When there's a coed dance, the shoe is on the other foot, and girls have to ask the guys out. Girls now have all the anxieties about looking foolish and getting rejected. Often they develop various methods of handling the situation. "When there's a coed dance, it's common to enter the hall of a girls' dorm and see half a dozen girls talking and laughing together about who they want to ask. They often do so in a group to give each other support. The usual practice that I've seen is for a friend of the girl to call the guy up and pretend to be the girl who wants to go with that guy. The friend invites the guy as though she is the other girl she claims to be. This way the girl who wants to ask him out doesn't have to deal with him directly and can only be rejected second-hand." "I had to ask a guy to go with me since I wanted to have a date for the Winter Carnival Ball. But I was so worried about being turned down that I took all kinds of precautions. I ran around asking questions about a whole lot of guys to see who had a girlfriend and who didn't. I would find a guy who wasn't going out with anyone, and I would make sure he was a fairly nice fellow. Then I would get some of my friends to ask some of his friends if he was already going to the dance. If he wasn't, I would get them to find out why. And if there wasn't a real reason why he wasn't going, I would find out if he'd like to go. If so, then I'd arrange to 'bump into him' sometime and ask him if he wanted to go. There was nothing to it, as long as I knew he wanted to go." #2495

One of the best ways you can indicate you are interested in a man is to look directly at him. Many men feel if a woman looks his way and keeps looking she is making contact in a strong and seductive way. However, even though this may seem like a simple gesture, many women shy away from it because they don't feel secure enough for direct eye contact. When the man starts to look back, they look away. This is not restricted to women, because many males are equally shy and look away if a woman looks at them. #2496

I'm not against sex, and there's lots of pressure to have it. My room-mates all seem to do it, and sometimes I get curious. But I'm just too afraid of the disappointment my parents would feel if they ever found out, and believe me they would somehow. I'm terrified of getting close to a guy, because of the way my parents would react if I ever got pregnant. I'd feel I let them down. #2497

There are a hundred reasons why you don't want to cheat on your wife. The main one is you can destroy your relationship and really hurt the person who cares the most for you and also does the most for you. People always talk, so she is likely to find out. Also, you could give her a sexual disease, or even AIDS. Can you imagine how guilty you would feel about that? #2498

Cultural models

There are widely accepted cultural models of proper and improper behavior which have a great deal of influence over sexual contacts. These models often determine whether or not one pursues a sexual contact, who one pursues the contact with, when and where one does so, and how one goes about it. These models are reinforced by criticism, punishments, and rewards. Failure to heed cultural models and to take proper precautions so that one does not violate them can result in injury to oneself and loss of resources.

Each person formulates numerous models to help him satisfy his feelings. These models enable the person to understand phenomena, predict events and responses, and act appropriately. Individuals formulate their own models, adopt the models of others, and modify models, in order to satisfy their own feelings and needs. Cultural models originate as personal models, and later are shared by two or more people. Individuals use criticism and resources to get others to adopt their personal models. People adopt the models of other individuals in order to get a share of their resources, to avoid criticism and other punishments, and because they believe they will find the models useful. Once a person's models are adopted by other people they become cultural models. The more people there are who adopt a specific model, the greater its cultural presence and impact. (See the chapter on Establishing Consistency in a later volume.)

Individual members of various species formulate their own models and learn models from one another. Human language has enabled humans to communicate their models in greater detail than other species can. This is because human words are more specific than animal sounds. As a result humans have more rules for proper and improper behavior than do other species. Consequently humans exert more control over the efforts of their individuals to satisfy their feelings than do other species.

Human cultural models exert a great deal of control over individual efforts to obtain sexual pleasure. These models differ from one culture to another and from one subculture to another. They specify a) which sexual phenomena are proper concerns for females, b) which sexual phenomena are proper concerns for males, c) what is proper and improper female behavior, and d) what is proper and improper male behavior.

What is striking about many of these models is how simplistic they are. Normally they are recognized, taught, and enforced like religious commandments with little or no variation permitted for differences in personality or circumstances. The implication of this is that "Humans produce simple models for human minds." It suggests that humans are too simple minded to be able to deal with anything more sophisticated.

A number of these cultural models are discussed below under the following topics:

Male and female taboos
A female should not appear promiscuous
    Keeping a good reputation
    Risking pregnancy
    Embarrassing purchases
A male should not appear effeminate
    Showing affection and concern
    Henpecked
Gays in town
Double standards

Male and female taboos

In rural Prince Edward Island men and women have their separate sexual concerns which for the most part are not revealed to members of the opposite sex nor are they discussed openly with them. There are strong feelings of privacy and secrecy tied to these topics. Although they may be talked about among members of the same sex or between a husband and wife, they are not considered fit topics for a mixed group of outsiders.

One topic which is the province of males is sexual intercourse, and this includes the practice of breeding animals. As a female child growing up on a farm, I never understood why neighbors would arrive with a cow on a rope, disappear into the barn, and emerge sometime later with the cow struggling and mooing. My parents warned me severely that I was not to go into the barn at such times. Often I was not even allowed outside. Several years later, I discovered that the neighbor was bringing his cow for breeding purposes. So much for learning the facts of life naturally if you live on a farm.

This spring a neighbor arrived with his cow to be bred at my brother's farm. Unlike past years, however, he brought his entire family with him. No one was terribly surprised when he allowed his three sons, aged ten to fourteen, to accompany him to the field. However, we were all very much surprised when his wife and seven-year-old daughter joined him there to watch the breeding process. My brother's wife was extremely angry that the neighbor's wife was interested in the procedure and especially upset that the little girl was subjected to "the performance." My brother agreed it was terrible. Everyone, male and female, that my brother's wife reported the incident to was equally angry. They said it was obvious the neighbor and his wife knew very little. People were more critical of the wife. "If he doesn't know the difference, you'd think she would." Members of my family said that if Mom were still alive she would have chased the neighbor. Indeed we felt insulted by this ignorant action on the neighbor's part. But for some reason he did not seem to realize he had done anything wrong. He was an Islander who had moved to Ontario for several years and then returned to Prince Edward Island. Obviously, he had been "away" too long.

The whole issue of menstruation is considered the province of women and is not discussed in front of men and children. Words used for menstruation include "period," "that other," "the curse," and "trake." Trake refers to any strange illness such as a virus or flu. Words used by women outside our community include "sickness," "the flowers," "the visitor," "monthly blues," or some name, such as "George" or "Mrs. Murphy." For example, "Mrs. Murphy's here this week." When you use a word for menstruation, other women know immediately what you are talking about. Men probably know also, but if they overhear it they have enough sense not to intrude on the conversation. Mothers clearly don't want their small children to know they are menstruating. The kids would be interested and their mothers would be embarrassed talking about it.

Many forms of everyday behavior are commonly stopped during menstruation. These include sexual intercourse, swimming, bathing, and washing one's hair. You are considered to be weaker when you are having your period and therefore more susceptible to colds. Colds are considered to be the very worst thing to get during your period, and if you get wet you are thought to be more likely to catch a cold. It is also believed that other physical problems both before and during your period are related to menstruation. Therefore, if you break out in a rash, have a fainting spell, experience severe headaches or nausea, or develop some other problem, it is all viewed as part of your period, even if it occurs a week prior to the beginning of menstrual flow. Many women will say, "Anything at all is possible with that trake." Some women keep their daughters home from school or church on the first day of their period in case they get weak (feel faint). They explain to others that "Mary won't be going to school today. She has the flu." As a result many girls feel they are much more delicate at this time of the month and tend to be idle.

It is considered very important that others, particularly males, not know you are menstruating. When I was living at home, I wasn't allowed to go to church on Sunday morning if my period had started. Mom would tell others, including my father, that I had the flu or a headache. Dad would say, "She was alright last night." But he must have understood, because he would never come upstairs to see me at these times, which he would always do if I was really sick. If I were to go to church it was feared that I might get weak or a stain might seep through my clothes and everyone would know. I was never supposed to wear light-colored clothes when I was menstruating because of the possibility of a stain showing. I can remember arguing with Mom when my period was practically over, "Can I please wear this dress?" which was light colored. "No, no," Mom would insist. Many girls are obsessed with the fear that a stain will show and others can tell. I also know several teenage girls who wear close-fitting jeans and won't wear large-size sanitary napkins because they are afraid the shape will show through their jeans. As a result they wear the small "mini" pads and are forced to change them every half-hour or so. Such techniques are relatively successful in hiding menstruation. One girl I know thinks that her brothers, whom she grew up with, never even realized such a thing occurred. However, attempts to hide menstruation add to feelings of embarrassment associated with it.

Another subject which is considered the exclusive domain of females is pregnancy. The word pregnant is seldom used. Instead women will say someone is "expecting," "going on a trip," "in the family way," "ready to go anytime," or "has a bun in the oven." If a child overhears and asks where she is going, he is likely to be quickly told to be quiet and mind his own business.

A woman who talks in mixed company about a topic like menstruation or pregnancy is considered "mouthy" or "flip" and to be showing off. One does hear such topics mentioned publicly by women when younger couples are together. But there is a big difference between mentioning these subjects and going on about them, which is viewed as bad taste. Nevertheless, older women tend to be shocked by any reference to them in the presence of men. One couple moved to our community from Ontario. The wife seemed very outspoken because she always brought up topics such as sex, pregnancy, labor, and so on in mixed company. On one occasion several women were talking unfavorably about this habit of hers and one said, "I hate that kind of talk. That damn thing should know better. Who wants to listen to that?" I have never heard sexual intercourse discussed in a mixed group nor have I ever heard women discuss it with each other. Similarly, a woman who dares to breast-feed a baby in mixed company is said to be making a spectacle of herself. These behaviors seem to violate standards of basic decency, and the woman who engages in them risks her reputation. #2499

A female should not appear promiscuous

Females markedly restrict their behavior in order that they do not appear promiscuous. They restrict what they wear, how they sit and stand, where they go, how they act, who they talk to, and what they say. They not only carefully control their own behavior in order that they do not appear sexually available, but they constantly monitor that of other females. A variety of terms and expressions are used for girls and women who are not properly restrictive. These include loose, easy, ready, fast, hot, bold, cheap, wild, keen, savage, slut, sleaze, whore, tramp, skank, hussy, floozie, strumpet, tart, sleazebag, riptear, "not a nice girl," "likes to get around," "a run around," "is looking for it," "a good time," "has a reputation," "has a bad reputation," and "is quite the rig." The assumption normally made is that a female who shows signs of being sexually available is actually promiscuous.

Individual females who look or act promiscuous are a popular topic in female conversations. (The great majority of the quotes in this section, *A female should not appear promiscuous*, are from females. An asterisk is placed after each quote by a male.)

> I was sitting with three of my friends; Carol, Janet, and Tammy. At one point Carol smiled sweetly at a passerby and they exchanged hellos. As soon as she was past us Carol started smirking. Carol looked like she would burst and couldn't get it out fast enough, "See that girl I just said hello to? Quick, look, the blonde with the blue jeans and white jacket. Well, I guess she's quite the girl. Wayne said that Ritchie told him on Friday night she was with four guys, and they all took turns with her, several times. I guess she just doesn't get tired, if you know what I mean?" Janet asked what the girl's name was. Carol replied, "I can't remember. I heard it, but you know me and names. I guess she's a slut anyway." Tammy expressed disbelief over the story. "I swear to God, Tammy, the girl's a tramp. Ask Wayne. I'm going to try to find out who the guys are." All three, Carol, Janet, and Tammy, got excited trying to guess who the four males were. #2500

Many females express very negative feelings about women they consider loose, or promiscuous.

> To me a loose girl doesn't have much respect for herself. She goes around using her body and her actions to attract guys. She tries to tell guys she is available to them. In other words, she is sleazy. #2501

> A loose woman is sexually permissive in her actions and has no set standards as to who her sexual partner is. If someone were to call me loose, I would slap her face, and then feel very hurt and examine my actions to see why I was called that. #2502

A female should not appear promiscuous

She is out to get it when she can, as much as she can, and to get it with as many men as possible. The only difference between a sleazy woman and a prostitute is that a prostitute charges a dollar value for her services. #2503

There's this girl, Terri, who socializes occasionally with my sister and her friends. Terri makes no bones about being interested in sleeping with a number of guys. One of her friends has a boyfriend and Terri says she would just love to get the boyfriend for a night. Now my sister and I think this is just the most disgusting thing in the world. The other girls say things behind her back, like "You know who she was out with last night? Oh, it just makes me sick." It is really strange to me that Terri would do this and feel this way. I think it's really weird. She's fat and homely and I think her friends laugh at her. They think it's the only reason guys take her out. 2504

Some people are completely disgusted when they see certain forms of sexual behavior in animals. For example, a male dog may try to mate with another kind of animal, such as a cat. This can be compared to the human practice of having various sexual partners. In both instances sexual desires are satisfied by unnatural and unacceptable means. When you look at it, what is worse, a human seeking various partners simply for the purpose of having cheap sex, or an unthinking dog who knows nothing about morals fulfilling its needs with an equally uncivilized cat? #2505

Women's morals are equated with their sexual availability. A woman who is believed promiscuous is seen to be lacking in morals and respect for herself.

A slut is someone who doesn't care who she jumps in bed with. She has no respect for herself or others. #2506

A loose girl has no self-respect or self-morals. She doesn't mind flaunting her body in front of males. A loose girl disgusts me. Some girls even do it with guys who are married or going steady. They seem to make it a game. But in the end they lose the remainder of their self-respect and don't gain a thing. Loose girls are tramps. #2507

Constraints

It is recognized that someone who appears to be loose will seriously damage her social standing.

A woman shouldn't appear loose because she'll get a bad reputation. Even if she isn't loose but her appearance and actions show she is, she may be classified that way. #2508

Women and teenage girls who are viewed as loose often find themselves the subject of a lot of gossip and speculation. People assume that if they dress and act this way openly, then just imagine what they are like behind the scenes. #2509

Some girls get off on letting other people know what they're like. I think they want to have people think they are bad, so they make it super-obvious that's what they are like. On the other hand, if you are discreet, but go around with all the guys, a lot of people are still going to find out. If you act like a tramp, you are going to get the reputation of one no matter how you go about it. #2510

Loss of reputation is believed to be permanent.

Once you acquire the reputation of being loose, it is virtually impossible to get beyond it. #2511

There are two main types of girls; girls that do and will, and girls that don't and won't. #2512

There are two types of women; ladies and tramps.* #2513

Once a woman gets a bad reputation she can never get her name re-established. She will never be free because people will always be talking about her. And men will always be at her doorstep badgering her to go out, so they can take advantage of her. #2514

Girls who have bad reputations often get nicknames and some people continue to refer to them by these nicknames for the rest of their lives. Examples might include "wild child," "easy does it," "hot to trot," and "the peanut-butter girls." The last example implies that their legs are easy to spread. #2515

A female should not appear promiscuous

Therefore it is thought that a person who acts loose is obviously not concerned about the opinions of others.

Sleazes don't seem to care what people think of them. They flaunt themselves around bars or parties and must know what people are saying, but it doesn't stop them one bit. They don't care what either guys or girls say. #2516

A loose woman doesn't care about her reputation or who she has sex with. You never see her with the same guy more than once. These girls don't mind acting this way when they are teenagers or young adults, but as they get older they begin to regret what they did in their younger years. They learn that to forget your own past is one thing, but for someone else to forget your past is quite impossible. #2517

Women do not want the reputation of being promiscuous. As a result they try to avoid behaviors which suggest to others that they are sexually available. In many instances they also try to discourage these behaviors among their own friends and family members. These behaviors involve many factors, including appearance, posture, seeking attention, availability, location, activity, being alone, taking initiatives, dating, and associations with males. Any behavior which indicates or hints that a woman is interested in sex, engages in sex, wants to engage in sex, or might engage in sex is likely to cause her to be viewed as promiscuous. A woman's reputation is based primarily on her perceived sexual availability. The more a woman disassociates herself from sex, the better she protects her reputation. Women engage in considerably less sexual behavior than they would engage in if they did not have to contend with cultural models such as *a female should not be sexually available* and *a female should not appear promiscuous.*

In the past a woman who had premarital sex was considered promiscuous. Today, a promiscuous woman is one who has casual sex with many men. #2518

Most girls say no to pickups when it comes to sex. They may very well want to have sex, but they are reluctant to do so for fear that the guy won't respect them afterwards. #2519

I would sometimes go all the way with a guy, but then I started thinking of what those guys might think of me for doing so. #2520

I think many girls would screw around if they could find ways so it wouldn't hurt their reputations. I know I would have. My girlfriend and I had to find creative ways to have some fun. So we went on trips to try to meet guys off the Island. #2521

Certain appearances are associated with being promiscuous. Many of these have to do with clothing, particularly clothing which is more revealing than the current local fashion. This includes particularly tight clothes that one looks "just poured into," and clothes which otherwise emphasize a woman's body more than is customary.

When I buy clothes, I always consider whether they would make me look loose. #2522

The way women dress can protect or destroy their reputation. If I saw a girl in dress pants and a sweater, and wearing oxfords and very little makeup, I would think she is respectable. But if I saw a girl in jeans that were so tight they looked like they were painted on and a low-cut revealing top, and wearing high heels and lots of makeup, I would assume she is loose. The other night I was talking to a friend in a bar when this girl walked by wearing tight jeans, high heels, and a black tank top that didn't cover much. My friend and I looked at each other and commented that we wouldn't be caught dead wearing that. People get the impression she is easy. I dress the way I do to protect my reputation. #2523

Anna doesn't have a good reputation. She is the type who wears an imitation leather skirt, a tacky blouse cut incredibly low, and the highest spiked heels you can imagine. I'm sure she considers it a nice outfit, but people talk about her. #2524

If a woman wears skintight pants, very low-cut tops, or dresses that have slits, and the slits are cut so high they barely cover anything, she may be on her way to getting a bad reputation. If a woman doesn't wear a bra and bounces around, everyone gets the impression she's trying to strut her stuff and is a slut. #2525

A female should not appear promiscuous

Most loose women dress to suit the part. They wear real low-cut dresses and blouses and make sure all the guys notice what they've got and that it can be theirs if they want it. Many males sit and slobber over women when they see them wear something which exposes their body. #2526

Girls in my group are really terrible about talking about how promiscuous other girls are. If we see a girl with her blouse undone through her third button, we say, "She's looking for a pickup," and "She's really sleazy." #2527

Clothing which is suitable in one setting may not look proper in another. Thus a sweater or dress which is acceptable at a party or lounge might cause someone working in an office to be defined as loose. In addition there are clothes which are considered cheap or garish which can carry this suggestion.

A friend of mine is a middle-aged man working for the government. Referring to a woman who works in his office, he asked me, "Does she strike you as being kind of loose?" "Yes, she does," I said. Well, she is very talky and although she has money for very good clothes, she looks cheap. Her clothes are shiny, or gaudy. My friend says she looks sleek. #2528

There's this woman who goes to card plays. She has a dark tan and always wears hot pink or passionate purple. She never wears inconspicuous clothes like a pastel blouse and jeans. Instead she wears purple shoes, a low-cut blouse, hot-pink pants, a wide black belt, and a pink lipstick that looks slimy. Her hair is teased and looks dyed and she always has a bright bow in it. She is flashy. She also has a shapely figure and her clothes emphasize it. Every time she bends forward the men's eyes almost pop out. But she must be forty because of the bags under her eyes. My friends and I have nicknamed her Kewpie Doll. We never come out and say we wonder who she's sleeping with, but even though it's unspoken, the feeling is definitely there that we think she's sleazy. #2529

A woman is also expected to avoid postures which men might find sexually suggestive.

Women sometimes comment that someone is sitting "just like an old man." This refers to sitting with one's legs spread widely apart when wearing a dress, especially in the presence of males. [#2530]

If a girl crosses her thighs, people who see her say she looks quite ladylike. However, if the same girl sits with her legs spraddled open, people see her as suggestive and loose. [#2531]

About the time I was starting high school, I can remember my mother picking me up on the way I sat, especially if I had shorts on and my legs were outstretched and there were men around. She felt I was sitting unladylike, in an ungraceful manner, and that it wasn't good to do that in front of men. She didn't say I might provoke them, but I think that was her intent. [#2532]

There were three of us girls in my family. When Dad was the only male around, Mom didn't seem to mind if we sat or lay around any way we wanted. But when other males were in the house, Mom didn't want us to lie on the rug to watch TV or sit with our feet on or near our knees. She didn't want us to look like improper girls. [#2533]

It is also considered best not to try to make yourself the center of attention in a mixed group.

Another sign that a person is loose is that she is overly talkative in the company of men. Other women say, "She acts like she knows too much." [#2534]

A person may dress in a certain way and act a certain way too. Then if she talks all the time to boot, you know she's loose. She may monopolize the conversation, act really dumb or giggly, or show an almost phony enthusiasm about everything. One woman who acts too approachable always says things like "That would just be super." [#2535]

We have a friend who is fairly shy and quiet. But after a few drinks at a party, she becomes very outspoken, foolish, and flirts with any male who happens to pay attention to her. She acts sleazy and tries to get people to notice her, which she accomplishes. [#2536]

One night at a party there were some joints being passed around. This one girl was very quiet and not with any guy or dancing. After she smoked some of the stuff she became the life of the party. After the drug wore off she was still the center of attention with the guys. From then on she had quite a reputation for being loose. #2537

It is felt important that a woman not make herself too available to males. Therefore, she is not supposed to associate with males too much. Also, a proper woman does not socialize with a number of different males at the same time.

If a woman spends all her time talking with the men rather than with the women, she will be viewed as loose, whether she talks too much or not. #2538

A girl who dances with numerous partners is tacky. It's easy to tell that she's available. #2539

It looks pretty bad when you see a group of girls and they're eyeing every guy in the club. I mean, who there doesn't know what these girls want? It's pretty obvious. That's how girls get bad reputations. #2540

My sister-in-law works at a tobacco farm. She talks about this one woman who's always hanging around with the men. This woman makes sure she finishes her drill at a certain time when the guys are finishing theirs. The other women always notice. #2541

My mother used to worry about me. Apparently from the time I was quite young, you usually found me around the men. When there's a party or get-together, you normally find the men gathered in one room and the women in another. At our farmhouse the men tended to be in the kitchen and the women in the living room. I would usually be in the kitchen talking to the men. That was what Mom noticed. Also, I often went to horse races and hockey games with my father. I did that a lot. And I loved going to old farm sales, just loved it. A person would be selling off his farm, so they'd be auctioning off everything, from animals to furniture to machinery. It would take a whole afternoon and evening and often the Women's Institute might sell squares and stuff there. And there'd always be the little bit of liquor hidden away in the barn for the men to get at too. And I just loved those things. I loved trundling along with Dad talking to the men. Mom used to comment on it. Her concern was what people would think. Like I don't think she thought I was making myself available, but she thought I might be giving that impression. This distressed my mother a bit. And I'm still the same. I like talking with women too, but I enjoy talking with groups of men. And I've heard other girls say the same thing. They enjoyed listening to what the men had to say. Often it was so much more interesting. #2542

I went to a wedding anniversary in our community. If it had been a party just for younger couples, there would have been more mixing of the sexes. But as it was, the women were all in the living room and the men all out on the back porch. Susan, who is thirty-five years old, and her husband were there from Saskatchewan. Susan joined her husband and the other men on the porch, where the liquor was. She was just having a good time participating in the conversation, drinking, and laughing with the others at any off-color remark. All of the men, whatever their age, kept raising their eyebrows and grinning and chuckling away in reference to Susan. The women in the living room would cast knowing looks at each other when they heard Susan giggling and laughing. Later the men commented she was "a pretty-hot number" and "a pretty-fast mover." Susan was considered quite loose, because she was out there carrying on with the men. #2543

A woman can get a bad name from what she does. It is not hard to get a reputation for being a flirt, or playing up to guys. If she has a lot of guy friends and talks to them a lot, she is classified as a flirt. If she sits on the knee of a male friend while talking to him, a lot of people get the impression she's trying to pick him up, even though they are only good friends. This guy I went with didn't like me talking to other guys, even though I told him they were my very good friends. He told me, and I quote, you can't be friends with guys, because even if you think they are your friends, they just want to get in your pants, unquote. No matter what a girl does she can't win. She always seems to get a bad name one way or another. #2544

It's a shame, but girls and guys can't just be friends. In high school there were about thirty students in the band. We were all friends, not just girls and guys. We'd talk about everything, and sometimes we'd sit on the guys' knees and joke and laugh. But everybody else assumed the worst, and would tell stories about us. Even the teachers. If we were just joking around and the teachers overheard, they'd assume something was going on. One time I was talking to a guy I'd been in class with for six years. He was saying he and a friend had been out of town and went in to use the whirlpool without any clothes on, and found there was a girl in the pool. The teacher wanted to know what we were laughing about, and I said, "Clarence is just telling me about his sexual exploits." The teacher got upset with us. #2545

I work as a bouncer in a club. Some girls are regulars in the club, and even though they are really very nice girls, they eventually get bad names. They're just out all the time. The guys get talking. You know, they wonder why they're out all the time.* #2546

Women are expected to avoid locations where men congregate or engage in male activities.

When I was growing up there was a girl named Pat who was always seen hanging out on the corner or playing street hockey with the guys. She was thought to be a wild and unacceptable playmate for the girls. No respectable girl was about to be seen playing with her. #2547

If I went to the rink and played hockey with other girls, that would be alright. But if I went out on the ice and there were all guys, I'd go home. Because if I played with them I would look loose. It'd be the same thing if they had something like a dance class for guys and I was the only girl. #2548

I can remember one girl I later became good friends with. In high school she would always be tearing off in trucks with boys at noontime. We always thought of her as being wild. And really she was just a kid that loved having a good time. She had a lot of fun, and I don't think she was any looser than we were. #2549

I wouldn't go to a cattle sale. There's nothing there but guys. Yuck. You'd look so – it'd be like thinking you were going to a baby shower and arriving at a stag party. When you think of loose, what kind of woman would feel terribly comfortable sitting among five hundred guys? And watching a bunch of cattle being sold? I wouldn't go there, but my sister-in-law goes to pick up her check. What you do is you take your animal in and you don't have to stay for the show. Come back in the evening or on the next day and get your check. It's OK for my sister-in-law to go in because she doesn't stay. Not only that, but she's married and she doesn't sit around. She just goes to the office and gets the check. But I wouldn't do that. I suppose you could if you took a friend with you and made it clear you were just going to get the check. If you made a point of saying that to the people who mattered, then it'd be OK. These would be men from your region, who otherwise would go home and say, "Guess who I saw at the cattle sale?" And their wives would say, "What a loose outfit, hanging around there." [#2550]

If you went down to the wharf where all the fishermen were hanging around, that would be really bad. What would you be doing there? Maybe if your brother was a fisherman and you just went down to see what he brought in, that would be alright. But not if you were just sauntering around down there. You'd look too available. And you definitely wouldn't go in the bootlegger's. Unless you were loose, I can't think what would take you. There used to be a couple of girls who sat with the football players all the time in the university cafeteria. That was too available. [#2551]

Certain bars and clubs have a bad reputation and respectable women stay away from them. For example, people think that any girl who goes to the clubhouse of the local motorcycle club is a whore. [#2552]

In male hangouts, such as bars and pool halls, it is improper for a female to enter alone. It can even be improper for a female to participate in certain social activities for both sexes by herself.

It's very seldom you see a girl walk into a club by herself. It she does she is labeled a pickup or a tramp, unless she is meeting someone there. If a guy walks into a club alone, which is very common, nobody thinks anything of it. [#2553]

When you walk into a dance or something alone, men consider you a piece of meat, not a single woman who might want to dance. [#2554]

None of the guys I've asked would allow their girlfriends to be seen at a club alone. They also don't like them going with a female friend or in a group of girls because they look like they just want to get picked up. However, "It's OK for single girls to go with their friends." When I asked, the guys said there was nothing wrong with a couple of guys going to a club without their girlfriends, because not as many girls try to pick up guys. [#2555]

A female should not appear promiscuous

I usually feel really stupid sitting at the bar. Look around you. Do you see many other girls? The bar just seems like a place for guys to sit. If a girl sits here she just looks easy, like she's trying to pick up. The only reason I am sitting here now is because I am waiting for my friend and there are no tables free right now. #2556

However, it is often considered acceptable if a female goes with a male escort or is accompanied by one or more female friends. Even in situations where one has a very legitimate reason for being there, another female may be needed for psychological support.

There's a snack bar downtown where they sell newspapers from all over Canada. A couple of times I've gone in there to get a paper. But the first time I went in I didn't know there were only guys there. They were all older guys; senior citizens. Looked like they'd come with the place. Next time I went in there I was with my roommate, Rebecca. I will not go in there alone. I feel uncomfortable, because they all stare at me. #2557

There are other ways one can give the impression one is too available without hanging around males.

We live in Charlottetown, and my mother never wanted me to take walks by myself. She said other people would think I was sleazy. But all I wanted to do was take walks. #2558

Some people consider a woman loose by the way she acts. A woman who walks alone at night in the city is cruising for a bruising. It's almost like she is looking for trouble. #2559

After high school I used to go to dances at a big dance hall in Charlottetown called the Rollaway. If you were one type of girl you stood on one side of the hall, and if you were a different type you stood in another section. The crowd I hung around with looked down on girls who stood in the other section, because they were the fast, or sexually active, girls. #2560

There are certain behaviors associated with males and if a female engages in them she is thought to be promiscuous. These include getting drunk or stoned on drugs, being foul-mouthed, fighting, talking about sexual matters, and telling dirty jokes. A female is more likely to be seen as loose if she does such things in the presence of males.

One way girls lose their reputations is by having big mouths. Girls who are considered ladies are quiet and timid. They know their place in society. But a girl who uses swearwords and foul language gets a bad reputation. Because she's a roughie she's less likely to get a date. #2561

Many guys are turned off by girls who swear a lot. It's alright for guys to swear because that's a man's thing. But when girls swear it just isn't acceptable. It really doesn't sound pretty. No guy wants to date a girl who talks looser than most guys.* #2562

My friend leaves the room when males start telling dirty jokes. A proper lady doesn't revel in dirty jokes in mixed company. I think girls are often embarrassed by them. However, some girls tell them to their girlfriends or close male friends. #2563

A nice girl doesn't talk about her dog being in heat or the fact she drank more beer than anyone else at the party Friday night. Such things are very improper for a lady to discuss, let alone be associated with. #2564

Jean goes out almost every weekend on a drunk with four guys. She doesn't have sexual relations with any of them; she is just one of their best drinking buddies. The guys she drinks with are very popular, but Jean has one of the worst reputations around. As one person commented, "Jean is nothing but a tramp. She never gets around with any girls, so she has to resort to guys. But do you think she minds? No way! She is definitely no lady, that's for sure." #2565

I don't mind seeing a girl out drinking. I'll even buy her a drink. But she should only drink enough to feel good. It's when she's falling-down drunk that it's disgusting. With a guy it's another story. Sometimes it's disgusting if he throws up, but it's not as bad as when a girl does it.* #2566

There is nothing more disgusting than to see two girls fighting. They kick, bite, scratch, punch, and pull hair. You don't see it often, but it does happen. They usually fight over a guy.* #2567

Other actions which are acceptable for males can also carry the suggestion that a female is loose if she engages in them.

A female should not appear promiscuous

I was keeping house for this family with a teenage daughter. The mother was going on vacation and she instructed me, "Now Donna is not allowed to smoke in her room. She's not allowed to smoke anywhere except the living room and then she has to sit by the fireplace so the smoke will go up the chimney. This is because I'm allergic to smoke and it soils the curtains. And furthermore, I've caught her smoking in the street and she is definitely not to smoke outside of this house unless she's in a friend's home. She's not a common street girl, and she should remember that." #2568

Some girls walk around in jeans and denim or leather jackets and act tough. They smoke like a man and talk mean. They also walk like guys. Sometimes it's hard to tell the girls from the guys. They drink and swear and are gall-y, just like some of the guys. It's scary. I'd like girls to act a little more like ladies. At least they should look a little like one.* #2569

Such actions make a girl look tough, or masculine.

There are also clear limits as to how far a female is supposed to go in making overtures to males. Basically she is allowed to act friendly, through looking at a person, smiling, and talking, but limited in what other initiatives she can take without seeming too available.

In clubs guys will approach girls and say hello, use their famous lines, sit down and talk to them, or ask them to go home with them. That's normal. But if a girl goes up to guys she doesn't know and talks to them, when she's out of hearing the guys will say, "God, she's ready," or "She's a whore."* #2570

You can hurt your reputation if you are a flirt or a tease. Even if a girl doesn't go any further, she is going to get a bad reputation. One girl I knew was a flirt and she said that was all she was. But she had one of the worst reputations and every guy around tried to get at her, even though, according to the remarks I often heard, they didn't really like her. #2571

Sometimes you hear the girls talking about their sexual interests among themselves as openly as the guys do. I've been at the canteen of a drive-in movie and heard one girl say, "He's really good looking," and another respond, "I wouldn't mind going to bed with him." "Oh, your hormones," said a third, and all of them laughed. But when the guy they were talking about walked by, they didn't say a word to him. They just giggled and kept it to themselves. Because of what others would think, girls just don't pursue males. In contrast, a guy will say to another male, "She's nice looking. I could handle her," and then often take the initiative and call, "C'mon over," or go speak to her.* #2572

As a result women often develop subtle strategies to promote a relationship with a desirable male.

Traditionally girls have to act demure and ladylike and always wait for males to make the first move. If a girl is interested in a guy she has to let him know in an "innocent" way, so she won't look too bold. Usually this is done with the help of a friend. The friend asks the guy if he is interested in anyone. If he isn't, then the name of the interested girl is casually brought up, as in "So what do you think of Tricia? She's awfully nice, isn't she?" If he doesn't agree, then the plan has failed and the girl is forced to try some other way to get his interest or has to turn her attentions toward someone else. #2573

I conducted a three-year campaign to get together with Professor Cordy. The first day of classes I saw him standing outside the classroom and thought, "Wow! What a handsome man." Then he turned out to be the teacher of my course. In class he frequently talked about three students who had really impressed him with a research project they had done. So I decided I would do a research project too. I spent hours and hours organizing it. But when I took it to him he brushed it aside as trivial. I continued to take his courses and eventually took all of them. Throughout this time I always looked for legitimate reasons to go see him at his office. I can remember once spending the entire morning getting ready to see him. First I had a permanent at the beauty shop. Then because I didn't like it, I reset it myself. And my clothes and makeup took a lot of time too. I had to get my appearance just right, because I didn't want it to look contrived. Finally when I got to the university I was told he was out of town, so all my efforts were wasted. But then one day I lost my notes for his course and went to see him about them. While talking to him I mentioned I was having a bad problem at home. He jumped up to shut the door and I spent two glorious hours telling him all about it. I only mentioned it to get his attention, and I was getting more than I had ever hoped for. This is when he began to know me as a person, because he hadn't even known my last name before. On future visits to his office we talked about my problem and about certain community events I knew about that he was interested in. I should mention that he was married and so was I, and I was involved with other men during this period. Later he offered me a position as a student assistant, and a major reason I took it was to be able to get closer to him. Finally, after about three years we were out looking for wildflowers together and I could tell it was in the bag. But I was no longer really interested, and did nothing to encourage him. #2574

Asking a stranger to dance, asking someone on a date, or initiating and increasing physical intimacy are considered male prerogatives, and improper actions for a decent female.

The dance is coming up next week, and I'd really like this guy to ask me to go, but I don't know if he will. My girlfriends are bugging me to ask him. I don't know; I still don't feel right doing that. They say everyone else is doing it. I'm not sure what I'll do. I don't feel bad talking to guys, you know, calling them. That's only if I know them though. I don't know this other guy very well though. I'm scared of what he may think of me if I ask him. I'll have to think about it. I'll see if he asks me first. #2575

I've been very seriously involved with this man for several years. He is always breaking off because of his wife, but after about a week we're back together again. We just broke up for the tenth time, and I haven't heard from him for days. I feel just sick, and fear I'll never see him again. But I don't want to call him first. I don't want him to think I'm trashy. #2576

Some girls will try to pick up guys at clubs by going up and putting their arm around them. Obviously they're loose. What other interpretation could you make? #2577

One night at a local club, this girl was making quite a spectacle of herself. She was up dancing with this man she had just met that night. She was dancing and rubbing up against him. Then her hands began to roam. She attracted a lot of attention to herself. Men started to talk, because she gave the impression she was an easy score. #2578

Constraints

There are a couple of whores who work in the bank with my wife. My wife and I went to a party for the bank employees, and when my wife was out of the room this girl asked me to dance. I agreed and when we were up dancing this girl put her hand down my pants. The room was dark, but you'd have been able to see if you were near us. If this kind of thing happened in a lounge or on a trip away from home, you'd know you were going to score. But you don't expect it at an office party. Someone told my wife who was dancing with me, and she came right back and cut in.* #2579

Often men feel put off by women who are obvious about taking the initiative.

Women who go around always looking for men often scare men away. Men don't know exactly what to expect from them.* #2580

I often try to avoid such women. They make me nervous. You're not only confused about what they want from you, but you don't know whether they've got a boyfriend. I think loose women are bad news.* #2581

There are girls who hang around with the guys and play football, hockey, and other sports with them. If a girl is seriously into sports and enjoys playing sports with guys, then that's OK. But if she just hangs around and watches us play, and then after we are done comes over and talks to us and flirts, touches, and nags, well, that's pretty scary. I think that's slutty, and I don't like that type at all.* #2582

I very rarely pay attention to a girl who tries to put the moves on me. I know she'll drop whoever she picks up and then just laugh at him. I won't be that poor sucker.* #2583

I personally don't feel too threatened by loose women. They are just out for a good time the same as anyone else. If they feel they have to go looking for it then that is up to them as well. It is just something that is changing with the times, like movies and fast cars. I don't bother with the ones who get around too much. They don't bother me a hell of a lot.* #2584

However, waiting for a male to take the initiative can be a very frustrating experience for a woman.

A female should not appear promiscuous

> I met this nice man and invited him over to my place. But then he spent half the night talking and never made a move. There just aren't any real men anymore. #2585

A woman often cannot be sure to what extent a male is uninterested, shy, scared of rejection, or involved with someone else.

It is also considered bad for a female to date a number of different males at the same time or within a short period of time.

> If you regularly date two different guys at the same time, you'll hurt your reputation. #2586

> If you want a good reputation, you date only one guy at a time. When a girl goes out on a date, it is taken for granted that she is going with the guy. If she decides to have several dates with different guys, she is going to get a bad reputation. People say, "That girl gets around." #2587

> I've seen Jackie go into a club with one guy and leave with another. That kind of thing doesn't help her reputation. #2588

> As I looked closely at the people in the club, I noticed one girl dancing very intimately with a guy. She looked really hammered. This is the third guy I've seen her with in two weekends. #2589

> Mom is always telling me to go out with different guys and not to stick to one. She used to go out with a guy a couple of times, and then if someone else asked her out she would go out with him. But if I went out with a different guy every week and we had fun but nothing happened, I would still be classified as a slut. #2590

> This married man I am involved with saw me out with another man. I was quite upset and felt like a whore. #2591

> Girls talk about those who see a lot of different men. They'll comment, "She changes guys the way most of us change socks," and "She goes through guys the way most girls go through toilet paper." #2592

It is considered very bad for a female to get pregnant if she is not married. This is visible proof that she engages in sexual relations.

When my younger sister told me she was pregnant, she was worried I'd consider her a slut and a whore. My other sister was so stressed by the situation, she developed shingles and gray hair. #2593

I was very popular in high school, but then I got pregnant. I had to drop out before graduation to have my baby. All I did was lose my education, my boyfriend, and my family's trust. I see other girls going to dances and parties with other people, but I'm stuck with a squealing baby that my boyfriend will have nothing to do with. Half the time I feel like a child looking after a child. I'm excluded from all the social activities that a teenage girl should do. My friends' parents tell them to stay away from me because I'm a bad influence. A lot of people look down on me as though I have the plague. My whole reputation has changed from being a goody-goody to a tramp. #2594

Eleven years ago I gave birth to an illegitimate child. Some people still hold it against me, so I would hazard a guess that my reputation isn't very good. This is gradually wearing off, so I think my reputation is getting better. I'm married now and have additional children. #2595

After marriage it is even easier for a woman to appear too available, and therefore promiscuous.

Touching men other than her husband, or even just hanging around them, causes eyebrows to rise. #2596

If someone sees somebody dancing with another man's wife, it's off to the races boys. They're into wife swapping and who knows what else. Things can get blown out of proportion so easy. Especially if the person who sees them doesn't like one of the individuals. #2597

People are likely to wonder about a married woman who has social contacts with men when not accompanied by her husband.

My music teacher and I are really good friends but we never have enough time at our lessons to talk. I keep suggesting that we have a coffee together, but the only time she is willing to get together is when her husband is along too.* #2598

I saw this girl I know at a dance. She's married, but there she was in the midst of a group of guys and she was making faces and flirting. It would be one thing if she was single, but this can't be helping her marriage any. #2599

Such strictures can also apply to an unmarried woman who has a boyfriend or who is living with a man.

If a guy and a girl are going steady, the guy can talk to anyone he wants to. But if the girl talks to a guy she's seen as a run around. #2600

There was a couple who moved into the community who were living together and she had two kids. They were unusually outgoing and friendly. When the man would go away on business trips, she would go to dances with a group of us. And some of the stories you'd hear in the community, you'd have to laugh. That there's this loose woman who's running around; oh, she is really loose. #2601

Often a person who is characterized as being promiscuous is said to show several of the above types of behavior at the same time.

You can tell when a girl is trying to act loose by the way she talks, acts, and by the clothes she wears. #2602

One example of a girl who is loose is someone who walks around with sleazy clothes on and is always giving guys the eye. She tries to be the center of attention. #2603

Diane is loose. Before I ever knew anything about her I thought of her as loose. Because she was loud and she was always talking about being out drinking and always talking about these guys she knew that were her friends, and there seemed to be an inordinate number of them. #2604

Almost any behavior which is out of the ordinary, or is more extreme or different than what other females are doing, can be viewed as showing that a female is sexually available.

It's OK to do wild and crazy things if you are a guy. But if you're a girl you'll definitely be looked down on. #2605

Girls should not make a scene or stand out in a crowd. You don't want people to notice you for being extra loud or obnoxious. Naturally people will talk about "the girl in the bright pink jeans who was screaming and yelling in the Burger King parking lot last Friday night." #2606

Even the tiniest things are noticed. For example, if a girl wears too much makeup one day, then you can be sure that a story will be going around about how she is trying to turn some guy on. The other girls won't think too highly of this. #2607

Most women are very much interested in avoiding the impression that they might be promiscuous.

There are not many girls that act sleazy because they know that people will talk about them and become disrespectful toward them. #2608

When you're a girl, you're looked down on if you have sex. It's kind of unfair really, but even other girls will call you a slut if it gets around you have sex frequently. Most girls don't talk about their experiences very much. When they do it's usually only with their closest friends. #2609

I work in a clothing shop. We carry a line of off-the-shoulder tops, which come in various designs including low necklines or open and net backs. Women are quite enthusiastic about them and frequently exclaim how much they like them. However, they are very poor sellers because they are designed to be worn without a bra. Even women who don't need a bra won't go without one because of what others might think. #2610

Whether they're promiscuous or not, some women look this way in their behavior with males. So other women try violently not to appear this way. They are very careful not to dress too seductively or to flirt too much. They play it coy or aloof with the men to a degree. And that always tended to interest the men more anyway. Girls who are more aloof may have been involved sexually with just as many males, but they don't want that impression left with everyone else. #2611

I went to the ten-year reunion of my high school class with my husband. After I introduced my husband to several guys at the bar I walked over to see two or three girls from my class who were sitting together. I wasn't even seated before this particular girl said, "I just finished saying isn't that typical of her over there talking to all the boys." She meant me, and I was just so insulted. Because this came from a girl who had chased boys incessantly. I had liked boys too, but there was no way I was quite as blatant as she was. And I thought, well if you didn't ruin my night right off the bat. [#2612]

When I was a young girl I was taught what to do and what not to do. I may not have lived totally up to my parents' expectations, but at least I don't strut around so that everyone knows about me. I also don't go chasing all the guys. They'll come to me if they want to ask me out. [#2613]

Women do not want to be thought of in sexual terms, and generally go to considerable lengths to disassociate themselves from any suggestion of sex.

I've found that girls don't want you to compliment them in sexual terms. I once told a girl that she had on a really sexy sweater. And she did. It made her just look great. The sweater wasn't at all risqué. In fact it was conservative. But it fit very nicely and did show the shape of her ample bust to full advantage. However, it was clear that my comment bothered her, and she asked what I meant. Another time a girl was standing at a vending machine, when a guy came up and grabbed her around the waist. She laughed and playfully pushed him away. When he saw her studying her hair and outfit in the reflection on the machine, he told her, "You look hot today." You could see the compliment made her uncomfortable.* [#2614]

If you leave a bar with a guy you've just met there, you'll get a bad reputation. People assume one thing and one thing only. They think you're going to his place or your place to have sex. [#2615]

I have found that women really do not want others to know they engage in sex. Even though there was no danger of us being disturbed, one woman insisted on leaving her clothes half on so she could get dressed really quickly if anyone came around. Another time a woman and I were on the bed when we suddenly heard someone approaching our locked door. Even though we had no intention of answering the door, the woman leapt straight up in the air. It was like a reflex action.* [#2616]

Constraints

I've been seeing Alice for two years now and she still doesn't want anyone to know that we sleep together. It's so bad that she won't even come into the bedroom with me when someone else is around, in case they think we are doing something. We always have to wait until no one else is in the apartment except us. It's so stupid. Like who is really going to care what we do? But I have to go along with Alice's paranoid ways or she'll cut off my balls!* #2617

Males who share an apartment or a room in a dormitory often develop signals so they can let their roommate know they want some privacy when they have sex with a girl. "My roommate and I cover up for each other. We'll hang a white towel on the doorknob of our room. That way no one walks in on us. Also, this notifies my roommate to tell anyone who asks, including my girlfriend, that I'm not at home."* "My roommate and I talk in code. We wink at each other a lot when we have a girl over, and the other person knows to leave. It's no trouble getting privacy to be with a girl."* Females, on the other hand, are much more private and usually don't want their roommate to know they are having sex with a guy. "When I want a male friend to come over, I make sure my roommate is on a date or at least out for a couple of hours. I don't want her to know who I fool around with and besides it's none of her business. I avoid making excuses to my roommate by phoning guys to come over when my roommate isn't at home." "Only my closest friend knows what I do. First of all, I don't do anything in my room. My roommate doesn't bring guys over, so I shouldn't either. Instead, I take a guy over to my closest friend's place, and she has a single room which we use." #2618

In high school we never knew which girls were sexually involved. Girls who were having intercourse with guys kept this information to themselves. If others had known, such girls would have been branded loose. It was years later that my best girlfriend told me she had been sexually active in high school, had gotten pregnant, and had to travel elsewhere to get an abortion. Even though we were extremely close at the time, I had had no idea any of this was going on. #2619

If you want to get closer to the truth about a person's sexual experiences you often have to apply the rule of three. When a woman tells you about her experiences, multiply what she says by three. When a man tells you about his experiences, divide what he says by three.* #2620

306

A female should not appear promiscuous

Women are often very embarrassed in situations where people may suspect they are engaging in sexual activity.

You're respected if you don't sleep with a guy unless you've gone out with him for a long time. Even then you can't be flagrant about it. You know, you can't let other people know about it. #2621

My girlfriends and I didn't have enough guts to go to the doctor by ourselves to get a prescription for birth-control pills. So we made all our appointments together. #2622

I live in a house with other males, and my girlfriend is frequently over. When we have been fooling around in my bedroom, we have to walk past other males in the house to get to the front door. I go to kiss her good night, but she leaves the house and yard so quickly she is practically running.* #2623

A girl and her date, who are both close friends of mine, needed a place to have sex, and came over to my apartment to use my bedroom. When they arrived we spent an hour or so joking around and getting stoned together. Then they entered the bedroom. I was in the next room when they went to leave. The guy came in and said goodbye, but the girl left very quietly without even acknowledging I was there and waited for the guy outside. I think she was too embarrassed over the situation to speak to me.* #2624

It bothers me to wear the same dress home the next morning that I had on when I left home the night before. I worry the neighbors will notice and realize I was gone all night. #2625

I like to spend the night with my boyfriend at his apartment. The problem is that his landlord lives in the same apartment house and knows who I am. Normally I won't stay overnight unless I know the landlord is out of town. If the landlord has been away and returns during the night, I'll get up even if it is two or three o'clock in the morning and go back to my own place. That way the landlord can't assume I've been up to anything. When I do stay overnight, I park my car elsewhere in the neighborhood so the landlord won't see it. The next morning I try to make sure the coast is clear and leave as quickly as possible. I just hate to go out that door in the morning, because I'd feel so ashamed if the

307

landlord saw me leaving. I don't want him to think I'm not a respectable woman. Once I could have died, because he saw me leaving and asked if I wanted a ride to work. I had to tell him my car was around the corner. I also won't stay when my boyfriend has one of his friends coming by early the next morning who might get the idea I slept over. I really wish my boyfriend lived someplace else where the landlord wasn't on the premises. [#2626]

I live in a duplex and won't make love to my boyfriend there. The bedrooms of the two halves of the duplex are right next to each other, and the other family might hear us. [#2627]

Often single women hide the fact they are using birth-control pills or they tell others they are using the pills to regulate menstruation or clear up acne. And in certain cases, a young woman who is upset over menstrual difficulties or facial acne will not consider taking birth-control pills to clear up the problem, because of the sexual association that the pills carry. After having sexual relations with a new partner, many women seek to make clear to the man that they have done this with very few other males.

I went to visit a girl I know at a dorm. When I went in the room I saw a package of birth-control pills lying on her dresser. She snatched them up, told me she used them to help her plants grow, and proceeded to give one to a plant.* [#2628]

This woman's husband had had a vasectomy. After the woman separated from her husband she decided to have a tubal ligation, and the staff at the hospital couldn't stop talking about it. Why should she have it done, now that she's single? As long as she wasn't married it meant she must be screwing around. My friend, who is separated and is known at the hospital, won't consider having her tubal ligation done here. The OR (operating room) list is sent around the hospital, and the staff would notice her name immediately and discuss why she's doing it. She'll have it done in Halifax (Nova Scotia) instead. [#2629]

I've been really scared I'm pregnant. But I won't go to a doctor to get a pregnancy test. He'd send it to the lab with my name on it and the lab workers would see my name and talk. [#2630]

A female should not appear promiscuous

In order to keep all signs of their sexuality from public knowledge, women are very sensitive over males discussing sexual experiences with them with others.

> A sure way for a girl to lose her reputation is to have guys talk about having sex with her. A guy may say, "I got more off Tammy in one night than I did with Caroline in a week." Some guys say such things to get back at a girl for rejecting their sexual advances. Whatever his reason, he gains status among his male friends for his sexual success.* #2631

> When your name is mentioned in the locker rooms of the hockey or soccer teams, you can rest assured your reputation is being shot to hell. Guys talk about the girls they pick up. It's a big thing when a guy picks up a girl with a reputation for being "hard to get." He is applauded or given a slap on the back by the other guys. Then the details begin about how far he got with her. Locker rooms have the dirt on most of the girls on campus.* #2632

In cases when a female learns that a male has told others about his sexual relations with her, she often sunders the relationship.

Women do not limit themselves to monitoring their own behavior. They also make frequent attempts to correct other females whose behavior might be considered loose. Within the family repeated efforts are made by older females to ensure that younger females do not make an improper impression. Younger females are told, "Nice girls don't do that."

> Our family was up at my grandmother's this weekend. I was talking with the men in the living room. I am already engaged to be married, but my grandmother called me in the kitchen to be with the other women. #2633

> My daughter attends university. She had a favorite nightshirt which she always wore at home. But it was worn out and quite revealing. I didn't like her wearing it, so unknown to her I threw it out. #2634

> What would upset my mom the most is if I started running around with lots of men. But I'm not a whore. #2635

Females also take an active interest in the impression their friends give to others.

Constraints

When Sylvia broke up with her boyfriend, she started dating a number of guys at the same time. She was afraid to let herself get too close to anyone again. But there were problems. Sometimes a couple of guys would want a date with her on the same night. Also, her friends began to tell her that dating like that didn't look very good for her reputation. Sylvia knew she had nothing to hide, but agreed that other people might not think so. #2636

If a girl went to a party and saw one of her friends acting loose, she'd probably tell her to smarten up and stop acting that way. If the girl didn't stop then her friend would likely tell everyone else not to pay attention to her and to ignore her. #2637

Efforts are made to change the behavior of women who could have an undesirable influence over female children.

Members of the local ballet association sought to get the school's only ballet teacher to wear a brassiere under her leotard. They felt she was setting a bad example for her young students. #2638

The local figure-skating club was composed of a large number of girls of various ages and a few adults. An adult member who wore revealing sweaters was told by a female member of the club executive, "You should wear a brassiere when you skate in our skating club. Some of the little girls might get upset." #2639

Most of the concern over promiscuous women is expressed by other women.

Most girls are able to detect someone who acts sleazy. If they start a conversation with her, they notice she always talks about the guys she has been with and the ones she wants to go out with. #2640

It is women who usually notice that another woman is sitting improperly or spending too much time with the men. The interesting thing is that most of the talk is by the other women. Men rarely comment that a particular woman is behaving in a loose manner. #2641

Women can even blame loose women for society's ills.

A female should not appear promiscuous

It's unfortunate that the ordinary women of the world have to be here simply to worship the males and bow to their every need. If men don't like how they're treated, they know there are lots of loose women out there on the prowl they can run to for sexual fulfillment. This is always held over the head of an ordinary woman, who feels compelled to satisfy the sexual desires of her male. Without loose women there would be a lot less violence and divorce cases. Loose women are a menace to society and to pure, true love. #2642

At times concern about women who appear sexually available seems motivated by jealousy or by anxiety over losing a male.

Amy is very popular with the guys at my high school. She is blonde and almost everything any girl would want to be. The guys give her most of their attention and almost every other girl at school hates her. They strike back by spreading rumors about her. Some say her pants are far too tight, and that she is so fat her pants couldn't be anything but tight. Others say she is trying to steal their boyfriends. #2643

Quite often it is girls who are bothered by loose women. They are usually the ones who point them out at bars and parties. It's truly as though they are jealous. Maybe they try to mark such women so the guys will pay less attention to them. This is quite often the case with girls who don't get asked to dance as much as others. If they see a girl dancing with a lot of different guys they often start talking about her. Yet the girl may not even have asked any of the males to dance.* #2644

I find girls with boyfriends are especially mistrustful of girls who may be loose. #2645

Whenever one of those women comes around my boyfriend, I see red. She won't add him to her list if I can help it. #2646

That bitch! She can't get a date on her own, so she has to ask someone to take her out. Well, she better just stay away from my boyfriend! #2647

When I was living in a motel, the man and woman who lived upstairs had a fight because he had been sitting next to this woman who was considered loose. The woman upstairs got really mad and said, "That woman thinks she can have just anybody she wants." "I don't care," said the man. "Well, you'd better care, and not sit there again." #2648

311

Other factors can be involved.

> Some females identify others as sleazy in order to direct attention away from themselves. By attacking such behavior they indicate that they would never engage in it themselves. One girl got drunk during a beach party and went nude bathing with a guy she was interested in. The next day she was highly critical of a girl for wearing a skimpy bikini at the party. Another girl puts down anyone who has sex before marriage and states she would never do so herself. But she flaunts herself in clubs, leaves the clubs with different guys, and her male friends describe their sexual activities with her in great detail. #2649

A variety of reasons are offered by females as to why some women act loose. The reasons they suggest include attempts to win attention, gain acceptance, get a boyfriend, or reject a strict family and church upbringing. Other reasons they mention are that the girl no longer cares after breaking up with a male, is trying to get back at the male, has learned to enjoy sex at an early age, or is putting into practice the sexual freedom and assertiveness advocated by the women's liberation movement.

A number of consequences are believed to befall the woman who acquires a reputation for being loose. A primary one is that she will not attract desirable males.

> If you use sexual attraction to try to pick up a guy, he gets the wrong impression. He tells all his friends and you get a bad name. Then all these gross guys try to pick you up. #2650

> Once a woman gets branded as easy, she will never find a nice guy to go out with. If a man hears she is a slut he will take her out just to find out what he can get from her. Even if he doesn't get anywhere he won't admit this. He is out to prove how masculine he is and is concerned with what the other guys will say. So he'll tell the guys the opposite of what happened, and the other guys who are trying to prove themselves will ask her out. Respectable guys won't ask her out because if they do the respectable girls won't go out with them anymore. The girls would think these guys are just like the rest of the jerks. #2651

> Girls who dress like sleazes and get around with a lot of guys are usually the most insecure. You can pick them out in a crowd with

their cheap-looking hairdos and clothes. They probably think these things make them pretty because that's how the girls around them dress. They always look cheap. If they could only realize they are pretty underneath the makeup and high heels. They are trying to prove something, either to themselves or to the world, I don't know. They never get the nice guys. They get the disrespectful ones who abuse them. You know, the greasy, gross type. Not the kind of guy you'd take home to meet your parents. I've always thought they must have a low self-concept, because they seem to think they can't do any better than these guys. I feel sorry for them. [#2652]

There are a few girls who are sluts who bop every guy they can get their hands on. I know one girl who is doing it with my friend. She is also doing it with almost everyone else. The only reason my friend is doing it with her is because she's there and she likes to fool around.* [#2653]

Whenever I feel like sex, I call Ann, because she never says no. Also, she doesn't expect anything in return. But I wouldn't go out with a girl like Ann. Ann's nice, but she goes out with too many guys. I'd want someone who knows the meaning of faithful. Besides, Ann doesn't have the best reputation in the world.* [#2654]

There is the common concern that a guy never knows what he'll catch from a loose woman. This talk is sometimes a joke, but usually a guy means it when he says it. There are lots of nice girls a guy can take out without having to worry about what he'll catch.* [#2655]

There are always exceptions to the rule. I've seen a few nice guys go out with girls with bad reputations. Many people are just happy that they have someone. But this usually happens with a guy who has low self-esteem. [#2656]

Another consequence mentioned is the greater likelihood a girl who is considered loose will be raped. This idea helps explain why some women who are raped hold themselves responsible. They think they must have done something, perhaps through their dress or behavior, which suggests they are loose and this brought about the rape. This is similar to the reaction by heterosexual men who are approached by homosexual men and wonder what about their appearance or behavior suggests that they are homosexual too.

If a woman appears loose she is more susceptible to rape. The woman's clothes and actions make it appear like she's asking for something, and she may get it in the form of brutality. #2657

A girl that makes several passes at different guys and acts available may get herself in very deep trouble. If one of the guys should take her up on her actions she may be hurt badly. Some guys who don't think much of a girl may molest her or seduce her against her will. This could occur if the guy is drinking or on drugs. Most guys have sense enough not to do this to a girl because they know they can get in very serious trouble with the law. #2658

Another consequence is that the girl who is labeled loose will not have friends.

A woman who appears loose doesn't have very many close friends. No one wants to be seen with her because they might also get the reputation of being loose. Only the males say they are her friends. But are they really? #2659

Loose girls are avoided by girls who do not wish to be called loose. As a result, they find they are accepted only by the boys, which reinforces the idea they are loose. #2660

Although Prince Edward Island doesn't have that many loose women, those who are are always being talked about. Those who hang around with a loose woman may pick up a bad name. Often a loose woman doesn't have a best friend, nor can she keep her friends long. However, loose women do seem to get along well with other women who are also loose. #2661

I was shopping when Heather, a girl I knew from high school, came over to talk to me. I felt so embarrassed I almost died. Heather doesn't have a good reputation. She has had three children and hasn't been married, and she uses bad language and she smells. I didn't know what to do. She was so loud I'm sure everyone in the store heard her cursing. I'm glad nobody I know walked by and saw me talking to her. I don't want people to know I know her. #2662

Jane and Margaret were best friends for many years and practically grew up together. When they began going to parties and dances Margaret hung out with a tough crowd. Jane didn't like this but didn't want to end their friendship. Margaret began to get quite a bad reputation. She drank excessively and was considered easy by the guys. Jane realized that her own reputation was at risk. People assumed that because the two were best friends, Jane was probably just like Margaret. Jane developed uneasy feelings about the friendship and she stopped going to dances and parties with Margaret. Soon they no longer kept in touch. They still talk to each other when they meet, but neither makes an effort to see the other. [#2663]

Diane moved into an apartment with Kelly and Melissa. Diane is in her early twenties and Kelly and Melissa are in their late twenties. Diane soon realized that Kelly has a bad reputation for picking up guys at a bar and bringing them back to the apartment for the night. Diane says, "Kelly always drinks before she goes out and then drinks more when she gets to the bar. By the middle of the night she's wasted and is looking for someone to pick up for the night. I don't know how many guys she has brought back to the apartment since I moved in, but there's been quite a few. I hope people don't think I'm like her just because I live with her." Diane is afraid that her reputation may be damaged. Diane and Melissa plan to ask Kelly to leave if she doesn't change her behavior. [#2664]

I would never go to bars every weekend to pick up guys like some girls I know. I think they are sluts. Girls like that have no pride in themselves. I won't even speak to them, because people will think I'm one too. [#2665]

Other consequences mentioned that may befall a loose woman are that she will be rejected by her parents, no one will want to hire her for a good job, people will not treat her seriously in community affairs, and no one will want their children around her because she may be a bad influence on them.

The concerns expressed by women are in certain respects legitimate, because the behaviors associated in people's minds with being loose actually do evoke sexual interest on the part of males. A woman who acts overly friendly, is known to use contraceptives, has her blouse half unbuttoned, wears a T-shirt without a bra, or has on shorts which do not fully cover her buttocks can elicit a strong physical interest from males.

Occasionally I've seen girls acting in ways that I've found quite arousing. One girl was seated in a bus. She was wearing a skirt and was slouched down with her legs wide apart. Another was walking along the street and the slit in her skirt was almost all the way up her thigh. Another time was at a bootlegger's where this girl was drinking and hugging and kissing a number of guys. And a fourth time the girl was so stoned she kept dropping her eating utensils. I find I get an immediate sexual interest in such girls, and often kick myself later for not trying to pick them up.* #2666

A man on our construction crew told us he went in a trailer and found this girl we know having sex with his friend. The next time I saw the girl at a lounge I viewed her with much more sexual interest than I had before.* #2667

While I was sitting in a coffee shop during a recent trip to Montreal I saw two women necking with each other. I found this so erotic, and I fell in love with both of them. I drank cup after cup of coffee as I continued to watch them and got quite an erection.* #2668

When you are at a club, many males and females think they can pick out the girls who are using contraceptives, such as birth-control pills. You can tell by the way the girls dress and socialize. Such girls are more outgoing than other girls, and they usually flirt from table to table. They are likely to be labeled sluts or whores by girls who are not using contraceptives. Girls who don't use contraceptives know what the typical guys want, and don't appreciate getting less attention than girls who do use them. Girls who use contraceptives aren't as moralistic as other girls about the whole idea of sex. They are easier to pick up and are much more willing to engage in a one-night stand. This helps explain the stereotype that girls on the pill are very active sexually. When a guy finds out that a girl he is going out with is on the pill, he will start to press harder for sex. However, I have heard of a few guys who have broken up with their girlfriends after they learned they were on the pill. I guess they assumed the girls were whores and must have slept with guys all over town.* #2669

The woman who wants to avoid more sexual interest than customary from males, may do well to avoid the behaviors associated with appearing loose. For the same reason, the woman who successfully hides signs of engaging in sexual activity is less likely to attract purely sexual interest from males.

A female should not appear promiscuous

It is equally important for her to keep other women from considering her loose or sexually experienced, because they would communicate their opinions of her behavior to everyone else.

It is believed legitimate for females to try to attract desirable males through devoting attention to their clothes, face, tan, figure, weight, hair, and personality. However, this often fails to achieve the desired result, which is to attract the males one wants to attract. At the same time, it is considered illegitimate to use behavior which is felt to indicate sexual availability. Appearances and actions which draw attention to a woman's sexuality are likely to attract purely sexual interest, rather than "honorable" reactions from males which will lead to a committed relationship. For the female who wants to attract males, being labeled a whore by men and women alike is a high price to pay, and is normally sufficient threat to keep her behavior within standard limits.

Envy plays an important role in this. Attention from males is a limited resource. Females who get attention from males and from desirable males produce envy in females who are not getting this attention. A primary way in which females express their envy is to state that the females who get this attention are using sexual means to get it, by acting too available or loose. It is much easier to attribute the attention that another female is getting to foul play, i.e., using sex to get it, than it is to admit that males consider the other female more attractive and desirable than they do you. The strongest attack that females can mount against another female is to claim she is promiscuous, which is the worst thing that can be said about a female in the competition for male attention. It is interesting that many of the ways in which a female is likely to get herself labeled promiscuous have nothing to do with sex, but have everything to do with getting attention from males. Examples include drawing attention to herself, being the center of attention in a mixed group, associating with males, hanging out with a group of males, or going to locations where males congregate. The more successful a female is in getting attention from males, the more likely she is to be attacked for being promiscuous. This is the case if she is asked to dance or asked on dates by a number of males within a short period of time.

> I have a reputation of being a slut, and it worries me. I go out on weekends and have a few drinks and tend to get a bit friendly. Other girls are always giving me dirty looks, like I'm trying to steal their

boyfriends. They don't understand that it's my nature to be friendly to males. They think I'm flirting and slutty, but I never go home with and sleep with anyone. They think because I'm always talking, joking, and dancing with guys that I'm a whore. #2670

It's the guys' fault that women are so catty. When your back is turned guys start drooling over some other girl. What else can you do but compare yourself to her? It gives women some consolation to rip her guts out and spread them around for everyone to see. Nine times out of ten she's some sleaze who will go to bed with a guy on a first date. #2671

(See the chapter on envy, Trying To Get What Others Have, in Volume Two.)

Women carry a set of models of proper and improper female behavior. These include the models that it is bad for a woman to have a variety of sexual partners, recreational sex is bad, sex is acceptable only within a committed relationship, and sexual activity should be kept secret. Females judge themselves and other females in terms of these models. As a result they view promiscuous women, sexual displays by women, public sex, sex with multiple partners, pornography, prostitution, and the exposure of children to sexual knowledge and experience very harshly. Females are disturbed and disgusted by such things and feel a moral duty to eradicate them by whatever means available, including legislation and criminal punishments. This erophobia is the female equivalent of male homophobia.

Benefits and costs

Females should not appear promiscuous is a dominant societal model which provides certain advantages and disadvantages. A primary benefit of this model to females is that it restricts the availability of sex for males. Females avoid appearing promiscuous by limiting and hiding their sexual behavior. A reduction in the supply of a resource raises the value of that resource. With less sex available, the amount of sex that each woman provides acquires greater value. Many women are only willing to provide males with sex within a committed relationship. If a male wishes to have sex with such a woman he has to appear willing to establish a committed relationship with her. Most men obtain the majority of their sex from their mate in a committed relationship. Another advantage of this model to females is that when females avoid the appearance of being sexually available, the attentions they attract from males are less likely to be purely sexual interest, and are more likely to lead to a committed relationship. In other words, adherence to this model helps to avoid males who are only interested in sex. Committed relationships provide women and their off-spring with more resources, including food, shelter, money, help, protection, and positive reactions. An additional advantage of the model is that any measures which help restrict sexual activity to committed relation-ships also help limit the spread of sexual diseases. The fewer sexual part-ners that people have, the less likely they are to contact and disseminate sexual diseases.

This model also produces a variety of costs. One is that it reduces the amount of sexual contact females have with different partners and the amount of sexual pleasure that females receive. Females also have to devote considerable time and energy hiding their sexual behavior from others. As a result they can not discuss their sexual experiences with most other people, or openly obtain contraceptives. In addition, the sexual con-tacts they do have can produce problems for females in regard to their self-image. For example, "Am I a bad girl?" There are also a great many restrictions on women as to what they can wear, say, and do in order that they do not appear promiscuous. There are certain limits as to where a female can go and what she can do when she is not accompanied by another person. Adherence to these restrictions is costly in time and energy. Females also have to markedly restrict their contact with males and male activities, as well as limit their use of certain sources of stimulation used by males, such as alcohol and recreational drugs. Females have to adopt a passive approach to males, and allow men to initiate most social contacts and physical involvement. Females can not explore relationships with a number of different males at the same time. Social contact with other males is even more restricted when a female is already in a committed relationship. Deviation from the model can produce permanent destruc-tion of a female's reputation, as well as rejection by other women and the community, and result in males viewing her as a sex object and unsuitable for a committed relationship. An additional societal cost is that most sexual behavior is hidden and sex outside a committed relationship is treated as dirty and bad.

Keeping a good reputation

Here in Charlottetown, I have an absolutely snow-white reputation. I have carefully guarded my reputation and I'm really quite proud of that. There is no one here who has known me sexually, so they can't talk to their buddies about what a good lay I was, or whatever. I have no worries whatsoever that someone can put dirt on me, and I can walk anywhere in town and hold my head up. It's really nice to know you don't have to worry about the guys standing on the corner winking to their friends that you are one of the ladies they've had.

There were so few guys I went to bed with while I was at the local university, that I have absolutely nothing to worry about. They weren't Islanders, and they moved back home after university. Now I didn't do this intentionally; it just happened. Other guys I've been sexually involved with also live in other provinces, so I have a very pure reputation here. I would probably have gone to bed with a lot more guys, just for the fun of it, if I hadn't been living where everyone knows what's going on.

Having a good reputation is very important here. You do not want to become known as a slut, because people will have no respect for you. In a small community such as this, everybody knows everybody. If you are a professional woman, as I am, it is important not to be known as a sleaze. Otherwise, other professionals might not respect me and value my opinions as a professional. I consider myself to have a lot of self-worth. If you have respect for yourself you watch your reputation.

Girls who go to clubs and pick up a guy for a one-night stand are classed as trash right off. If people think you've slept with a variety of different guys, you're automatically labeled a whore, and you can't escape that reputation. If they know you've been with this one, this one, and this one, you're dead. It's as simple as that. It's an absolute no-no. This isn't a problem if you're going steady with a guy. You are going together and there's a commitment. People assume you are having a sexual relationship; what else are you going to be doing when you're going with somebody? However, because the relationship is seen as legitimate, people ignore the sexual aspect of it and don't think about it. The ideal is marriage, where everyone just expects you'll be having sex. However, when you are in a committed relationship, such as going steady, living common law, or married, you aren't supposed to fool around with anyone else. Otherwise, you can get a pretty lousy reputation and your relationship can be ruined.

A girl, therefore, has to be very careful if she wants to protect her reputation and also get involved in any sexual activity other than in a committed relationship. There are a variety of things she can do. One, she can try to be very discreet about her sexual activity with men who live here. Two, she can have relationships with men who are only temporarily on Prince Edward Island, such as tourists and traveling salesmen. Or, three, she can have her sex outside the province, such as when she leaves for a professional meeting or shopping trip, when she visits friends and relatives elsewhere, or when she goes on a vacation. Going off the Island to have a good time enables a woman to keep a good reputation. The Island is so small and so many people know you that anything you do here becomes public knowledge. You do not want others to think you sleep around, because they'd lose respect for you. I would rather die than have others think I'm loose. If anyone ever called me loose, I'd ram it down their throat. If I want to have a good time, I'll find guys who aren't from here to have it with.

There are certain things a girl can do if she wants to have sex with people who live here. Sometimes a girl can go places where she isn't known. I never go to the Royal Canadian Legion in Charlottetown, but one night I did so with a girlfriend. I met this guy and ended up going back to his apartment. I figured it was alright because I wasn't planning to go back to the Legion again. Sometime afterwards I saw the guy downtown. I crossed the street so he wouldn't have an opportunity to recognize me. Also, if a girl meets a guy in a club and doesn't want others to know they are leaving together, she can arrange to leave separately. The two people can agree to meet outside or plan to get together later someplace else. This is a good idea when a girl is with other girls, because they can be terrible about ruining a girl's reputation. Another thing is to only get involved with guys that one is sure won't talk to others. Girls tell each other which males talk about their sexual exploits. One guy where I work has a big mouth. If he went to bed with a girl, he'd make sure everyone knew the next day. Whereas another guy whose office is near mine would never say a word. A gentleman never tells, and a girl really appreciates that. Another thing is to get involved with a married man. He certainly has good reason not to broadcast his experiences with you to others. I was involved with a married guy once, but it's an awful situation, because you always come second relative to the wife. #2672

Risking pregnancy

Every year many teenage girls get pregnant. It is so common that when people hear that a teenage girl is getting married, they assume she is pregnant. Many pregnant teenagers, however, do not get a fast trip to the alter. Instead, they end up alone with a baby, give it up for adoption, or decide to get an abortion.

When people learn that a girl is pregnant, one of the most common reactions is to blame her for not taking proper precautions. I could not begin to count the number of times I've heard friends and their parents sitting around saying such things as "I couldn't believe it when I learned Nancy is pregnant. You'd think she'd have had enough sense to at least get him to use some kind of protection," "Now, if her mother had taken her in and put her on the pill, none of this would have happened," and "I think it's absolutely ridiculous. All these young girls running around pregnant when they have all those pills and contraceptives to prevent it."

The problem for young women is that many people have the attitude that an unmarried girl who takes the pill must be promiscuous. Many people don't think this, but enough do to create real difficulties for someone seeking protection. One guy I know had gone with a girl for some time. When he learned her doctor had put her on the pill, he demanded to know where she was all the time and would sometimes accuse her of lying to him. He drove her so crazy with this, she finally broke up with him. When I asked why he constantly bugged her, he said, "When you give girls the pill, they take it as an invitation to take all the liberties they want. They just start running around with everyone." Many think that a girl's behavior changes when she uses protection. A common male attitude is that a girl who takes the pill is an easy pickup. One guy said, "Look, if she's on the pill she has to be fairly easy. Why else would she take it?" This attitude is not limited to males. I was told about a girl at a party who went around telling everyone to watch their boyfriends around this other girl. When asked why, the girl said, "Didn't you know? She takes the pill!" I've seen this sort of thing happen myself. A bunch of us were out, and a friend of mine said she had just started taking the pill. Another girl in our group just looked at her and said right out, "I never thought you were like that." Not everyone thinks this way. Some guys couldn't care less, and others even encourage their girlfriends to get protection. Yet a substantial number of people believe that only one kind of girl uses protection.

Some of the people who argue that there is no excuse for girls to become pregnant with all the protection available, are the same ones who think that only sleazes take the pill. Many of the parents I know who are quick to say a pregnant girl should have taken precautions, would get very upset if they were to learn that their own daughter was on the pill. They seem to feel that only bad girls need to take precautions, and their own daughter is clearly not "one of those."

One girl I know had been going out with the same guy for two years. Her father became worried something might happen between the couple and there would be an unpleasant surprise. Therefore he had his wife suggest to the daughter that if she thought anything might happen, she should tell them so they could take her to the doctor to get protection. The girl, of course, was too embarrassed to say anything, and so the matter was dropped. Shortly thereafter the girl developed severe cramps and her mother took her to the hospital. The doctor said it wasn't serious and prescribed the pill, which he thought would probably help. When the girl got home her father wanted to know what the doctor said, and she told him and what he had given her. Her father went crazy. He took the pills away and called the doctor. He started yelling at him and demanded to know if he was insinuating his daughter was a slut, or if he just tried to pawn the pill off on all the teenage girls. The doctor explained that the pill was commonly used for a variety of types of medical problems, and they used an alternative only if the pill didn't work or if the dosage was too high. When her father finished talking on the phone he called his daughter into the room and made her swear never to tell anybody she was on the pill. Then he drove her crazy over the next few weeks. Every time she went out with her boyfriend he wanted to know where they were going, how long they were staying, and who was going with them. The only reason I can see why her father would first encourage her to get protection, and then throw a fit when she did get it, is that he also holds this attitude that only bad girls use protection.

An additional factor is that many family doctors do not like to prescribe birth-control pills for young girls. One hears of high-school-age girls who have gone to their doctor to get the pill and have been refused. Some doctors have acquired bad reputations in the community because they are known to prescribe the pill to young girls. Certainly doctors do not want parents angry at them. The fact that girls thirteen and younger are engaging in sex is ignored.

Sex and sexual precautions are difficult subjects for many females to deal with. However, it certainly doesn't help that many people hold the attitude that girls who do take precautions must be bad girls. I know of girls who have refused to take the pill when their doctor prescribed it because they say that they aren't sleazes. I think that this public attitude is a major reason why many girls never take precautions and therefore eventually become pregnant. Most girls will go and get some kind of protection secretly and hope and pray that nobody finds out. But there are others who would rather run the risk of getting pregnant, than take the risk of having their reputations ruined because others find out they are using protection. I asked one girl who was five months pregnant why she didn't use any protection. She replied, "I wanted to take the pill because my boyfriend and I were taking a few chances, you know. I made my own appointment to get it. Then one night I was at a club and looking for something in my purse, when my package of pills fell out. One of the girls at my table saw it and within a week everybody knew. I was so embarrassed that I stopped taking the pill and this is what happened." #2673

Embarrassing purchases

There are a number of items which people want or need to buy, but in many cases are reticent to get. Such purchases can easily generate gossip about the person and may therefore affect the person's reputation within the community. However, much of the discomfort exists whether or not others recognize the individual making the purchase, because people do not like to have others know they use or need certain products.

One such item is contraceptives. In small rural towns and villages there is usually only one pharmacy and the pharmacist and clerks know the residents personally. Even in the greater Charlottetown area, where there are at least eight drug stores, many people from Charlottetown and nearby communities are known or remembered by the staff. Teenagers and unmarried adults are especially likely to stimulate gossip if they purchase contraceptives. Several high-school students in an Island town with a population of about 1500 have told me they definitely would not buy contraceptives at the local drugstore. "It would be all over town in no time. Mom would probably get a phone call within an hour. They even talk about the married people who buy them, so imagine what they'd say about one of us." A male university student said, "There's only one pharmacy where I live and the pharmacist has worked there a very long time and knows everyone. Guys have asked me to buy condoms for them, because they are too embarrassed to face the pharmacist. They tell me, 'You wouldn't be talked about. Everyone knows you wouldn't do something like that.' I tell them, 'You're crazy if you think I'm going in there.' I have a reputation to maintain and I certainly wouldn't want to ruin it for a few people who just want to have some fun. News gets around fast, and whether it's right or wrong, it usually has a few things added or taken out by the time the wrong person gets wind of it." People are just as concerned that other customers will see what they are doing. According to a male, "One day I went into the drugstore and ran into some neighbors. It took me an hour and a half to buy a package of three rubbers without anyone seeing me."

I myself am an adult female and when I am in a drugstore looking for something like shampoo or toothpaste, I sometimes find myself standing in front of the female contraceptives. I move away as fast as possible, so no one will associate them with me. If someone came into the store who knew me, they would know I'm not married and would wonder what I was doing there. Many women dislike intensely to have other people know they are buying contraceptives, even if the other people do not know them. One young woman reported, "The other day I went to buy a box of rubbers. It had to be the hardest thing I ever did. I was even more embarrassed by the fact I didn't have a clue what type to buy and there are so many different sizes, shapes, and colors. I felt stupid." Another young woman I know said she quit going to one pharmacy in Charlottetown because they made such a big production of filling her prescription for birth-control pills. Then she got really upset with the next pharmacy because they would bring the pills out from behind the counter and put them in a bag in front of other people standing there. The woman is much happier now because they started putting the pills into a case with a Japanese design on it and the case is all anyone sees handed back and forth.

Many people are also quite hesitant to go into a store to purchase sex magazines. These are magazines with nude pictures of females, like *Playboy* and *Penthouse*, or nude pictures of males, such as *Playgirl*. A young man said, "If I'm looking at the skin magazines and anyone else comes nearby I pretend I'm looking at something else, like *Road & Track* or *Popular Mechanics*." One middle-aged man told me, "I make no bones about the fact I read them. But there's no way I'd be seen buying one. I read the ones my boys bring home." I am quite sure many people feel the same way. One high-school girl who knew very little about male anatomy decided to get a *Playgirl* magazine to learn more about it.

However, she told me if she went to buy a copy in the local town, her mother would definitely be informed. Therefore, I asked a middle-aged friend of mine to buy it for me in Charlottetown so I could give it to her. But he said, "Look, I wouldn't go in and be seen buying a *Playboy*, so I definitely won't be seen buying a *Playgirl*." People who saw him purchase a copy of *Playgirl* would wonder whether he is homosexual. I know for certain I myself would not go in a store on Prince Edward Island and buy a sex magazine. In fact I have never been in a store on Prince Edward Island when someone actually bought one. When I lived in Toronto it was common to see a group of men in a store looking at the centerfolds of these magazines and discussing their merits. I have never seen such an occurrence on Prince Edward Island, although I'm told it happens.

A similar problem occurs when people want to rent adult, or X-rated, videos. Several video rental stores in Charlottetown have a separate room or section where they display these films, and one store even has a back entrance and parking lot so people can enter out of sight. One man said, "I always wait until no other customers are present in the store before I enter the adult room. I have to hope no one will be around later to see me leave. I won't take the adult videos up to the checkout counter until no other customers are around. Also, I'm careful about who is working behind the checkout counter. There are a lot of people that you don't recognize who know exactly who you are. In one store, I don't mind so much renting from the owner, but I won't rent these videos if the owner's wife is working that night. There's also the problem of other people entering the adult room and seeing me there. There are some junior people where I work and I definitely would not want them telling everyone else they saw me in the room. Occasionally I even see a woman there, but I'd guess only about one in ten customers is a woman. There's even a problem playing the videos. I live in an apartment house and I keep the volume low so neighbors won't hear the heavy breathing and graphic conversations in the films. I certainly wouldn't want them to know what I'm watching."

Women are also embarrassed to buy items associated with menstruation. Although I don't mind buying such products, I hate having to stand in line holding on to them. If I'm buying a bunch of stuff, they are the last item I pick up, and I sure don't stand around. I want to get them and get out of the store, because I don't like having people see me with them. It makes me uncomfortable, which is really crazy. When my best friend buys menstrual pads, she gets this gigantic box of forty-eight or so, which really bugs me. It's cheaper, but I wouldn't consider doing this myself because it's so noticeable, and I don't like being there when she's doing it either. I heard of an instance recently when the clerk at a store apologized for not having a brown paper bag which would hide the fact the woman had bought menstrual pads. The clerk used two plastic bags to try to make the box inside harder to see.

Women are often even more uncomfortable about such purchases when men can see what they are buying. Most females I know feel very ill at ease when they want to buy menstrual pads and the clerk is male. Recently I was at a friend's house and she and her mother were arguing over who was going to go to the pharmacy in the local town to buy menstrual pads for the mother. The daughter, Patricia, said she wouldn't go because Kent, who is in his late twenties, works in the drugstore and she wasn't going to go buy menstrual pads with him there. Her mother said, "I don't want to go either for the same reason." So they argued and argued. I think if there had only been girls working at the drugstore there wouldn't have been this hesitation to go. Anyway the mother eventually went herself and purchased the big pack of forty-eight or sixty. But as she did so, Kent asked her, "Expecting a flood?" The mother replied, "I don't know, you'll have to ask Patricia." The mother is very naughty, but that's the kind of thing Patricia would do to her mother. When Patricia heard about this she told me she was never so embarrassed in her life. She claimed she would never go into that drugstore again, nor did she ever want to see Kent again either. I couldn't get over Kent saying that, especially to the mother. However, I could see him doing it to Patricia, because he's her age. But after this I never bought anything like menstrual pads in that drugstore again. I wouldn't want Kent saying anything like that to me. I would just die. Kent's brother works with me, and I could see Kent going home and telling his brother, "Guess what she came in and bought today?" And his brother would probably mention it to me in front of others. Women are not the only ones who feel embarrassed when they buy sexual items from the opposite sex. A male reported, "I definitely would not go in a drugstore to buy condoms if I had to deal with a female employee."

Males are embarrassed to buy female products for women for fear of being considered either effeminate or henpecked. Products in this category include menstrual pads and tampons, bobby pins, cosmetics, and female articles of clothing. Some males absolutely refuse to pick up such items for their wives when they go to the store.

Many people are embarrassed to buy solutions for body or head lice, because they are concerned with what the pharmacy staff will think of them, whether or not they know them. No one wants to be thought of as dirty, and I'm sure that half the discomfort of lice lies in getting up the courage to get the disinfectant.

Some people also do not want to be seen buying liquor. For example, one married woman won't go in the liquor store because she is too scared and embarrassed. She says, "There might be someone in there who'd recognize me. Dad is very strict. If he ever found out, he'd give me hell." As for myself, I definitely do not like to be seen entering and leaving a liquor store. I try to spend as little time in the store as possible, and while inside I try not to look directly at people because they might recognize me. If I spot someone I know, I try to stay away from the part of the store where they are. I would respond if they said hello, but I wouldn't be the first to speak. I don't want people to think I drink, and if they don't see me there they can't tell on me. I'm willing to go in to get a bottle of a liqueur. But I hate picking up a bottle of hard liquor or a case of beer for my brother, and I certainly don't want anyone to see me carrying it outside. A close female friend of mine always asks to have the beer she buys put in a bag. The clerk has told her, "It looks like a case of beer, dear, whether it's in a bag or not." Although she will carry it out to her car, she wouldn't walk home with it. Some people also try to hide the fact they are carrying liquor when they take it from their car into their house.

Worry that the staff at a store will talk about you if you do make such a purchase is not an idle concern. A friend of mine works as a clerk at a grocery store in Charlottetown which also sells magazines. She remembers those who purchase sex magazines and often points them out to me on the street. She makes comments like "There's that fellow who used to buy all the dirty magazines. And I don't mean *Playboy* or *Penthouse*. I mean the real dirty ones," and "That's the fellow who tried to steal the dirty magazine at the store, but the owner caught him," and "That fellow used to come into the store to look at the dirty magazines. He just ignored the *No Loitering* sign. He would stand there and read them, and let me tell you they had a noticeable effect on him (an erection)." She reports it is often a matter of conversation among the staff of the store when someone buys such magazines. "Isn't it awful, him buying those magazines and his wife so nice. I feel so sorry for her, being stuck with the likes of him." It is reasonable to assume that many people who work in other retail outlets discuss their customers in similar fashion.

As a result of possible embarrassment or damage to their reputations, people adopt a number of strategies when they want or need such products. One strategy is simply to do without. A female high-school student who became pregnant told me that she and her boyfriend would have used contraceptives if they didn't have to buy them locally, "But I wouldn't ask for them (at the local pharmacy) and neither would he. Everyone would talk." On the basis of what I've heard, I would say this is a common reason for unwanted pregnancies. Other people try to find substitutes for what they need so they won't have to go in a store. I know of a case where a middle-aged farmer contacted crab lice. Although he lived in the country, he still wouldn't buy medication in one of the drugstores in Charlottetown for fear he might be recognized. Therefore he used a disinfectant for animals that he had in the barn together with a flea spray for pets that he got from a friend.

Another thing that people do is travel away from their local area to make the purchase. I would guess that many Catholic couples in the country who use birth-control materials buy them at a pharmacy in Charlottetown or Summerside where they are not known. I have heard of people traveling to distant liquor stores to make purchases if they are worried someone from their church might see them entering or leaving the local liquor store. If I absolutely had to purchase a sex magazine, I would go to a store where no one knew me, even if it meant driving a considerable distance. Even then, I would probably make some excuse, like "This is for my brother." Others also resort to claiming that they are buying the article for someone else.

Occasionally people try to hide what they are buying from others. Recently, I drove into the parking lot of a pharmacy in Charlottetown at the same time as another couple. The man stayed in the car and the woman and I entered the store and both of us headed for the pharmacist's counter. The woman had this paper bag folded up as tiny as possible clasped in her hands. She pushed it over to the druggist and mumbled something. I think she thought I knew what she asked for because she seemed very uncomfortable and just fidgeted the whole time she waited for her order. I felt so embarrassed, because she obviously didn't want anybody to know what she was getting. I don't know what she wanted, but I assume it was contraceptives. One male I know will buy such items only at the pharmacist's counter, so he won't have to take the chance of being seen by other customers at the front counter of the store. He said, "Once I went in a drugstore where I didn't know anyone to buy contraceptives. A female customer was waiting at the pharmacist's counter to get a prescription filled. I waited and waited, and the lady was still there. Finally I wasn't going to wait anymore. I said, 'Fuck it,' and took them up to the clerk at the front counter. It's funny though, I never look at the person I'm buying them from." Occasionally people ask close friends who have previously purchased such articles just where in the store they are located, so they won't have to ask a clerk to help them find them. Sometimes people also try to make the object they are buying seem less conspicuous by buying other articles at the same time. "I went to the drugstore the other day to buy rubbers, and because I didn't want anyone to notice, I bought about thirty dollars worth of other shit. But when I went to the cashier, she smiled and winked. I just about slid under the fucking counter. The witch got me but good."

Another strategy is to get someone who is less concerned about public appearances to buy the item for you. I have had a friend go in and buy a bottle of liquor for me. The same friend also purchased the *Playgirl* magazine for me and says he has bought crab-lice medication for a number of people who were too embarrassed to go in the store for it. If I had lice or something, I'd get my cousin to go get the stuff for me. She just wouldn't care. And she'd probably say something to the druggist like "Got to get this mess cleaned up." She can handle it, and she'd make a joke out of it. The rest of us would be skulking around, but she'd just go in, pick it up, and buy it. I can't think of anyone else I'd ask to do it. I wouldn't ask my two best friends, because they'd refuse. One young man said that when he was fourteen the sixteen-year-old boys would tip him a dollar to buy contraceptives for them. A Baptist director of a nursing home asked a counselor to buy liquor for one of the patients, who needed it for medical reasons. He gave the counselor the money and asked her to hand the liquor to the nurse. The director didn't want to touch the liquor or have anything to do with it. I have also heard of a politician in Charlottetown who has his friend buy liquor for him in Summerside. Even though the politician doesn't try to hide the fact he serves liquor in his home, he doesn't want to be seen buying it.

Another technique is simply to steal what you want rather than face the staff of the store. One man said, "I thought I had contacted crab lice a second time. But when I went to the drugstore, the same clerk was working at the cash register who was there before when I bought the medication. If some other clerk had been working, I'd have paid for it. But it was just too embarrassing to have this one know I needed it a second time. So I put the bottle in my pocket and left the store."

Most people do not want to look bad in the eyes of others, and go to great lengths to avoid having people think or say negative things about them. Consequently they are quite apprehensive when it is necessary to engage in a public act, such as making a purchase in a store, which could be given a very negative interpretation. People also frequently feel embarrassed when they make such purchases in stores outside of the province, where they are sure no one knows them. They do not want to be thought poorly of by other people, even if the people are strangers. #2674

A male should not appear effeminate

Males are very much concerned that they not appear effeminate. They carefully monitor their own behavior for any signs that might be considered feminine, and they avoid behaviors which in their own minds or in the minds of others are associated with being less than masculine. If they are considered unquestionably masculine, others look up to them, treat them with respect, and seek to associate with them. On the other hand, if they are considered effeminate, their reputation is destroyed and they are subject to avoidance, exclusion, laughter, ridicule, and sometimes violence.

To a considerable extent male concern with not appearing effeminate is based on the belief that a male with feminine traits is homosexual, which is one of the most negative things that can be said of a male.

> One of the worst things you can be accused of is being queer. Guys will say this about you if you walk or talk the wrong way. #2675

The numerous terms which are used to refer to homosexuals are also applied to males with feminine traits. These include fruit, fairy, gay, queer, fag, faggot, queen, fruitcake, pansy, and fifi. Sometimes the words sissy, wimp, pussy, and momma's boy are also used. This notion of homosexuality is not restricted to effeminate behavior, because when other forms of unconventional behavior are encountered in a male, one of the most common interpretations is that the male is homosexual.

Acting masculine

Most males desire to appear to be clearly male, and avoid all feminine appearances. There are numerous traits associated with being masculine which are related to an individual's mannerisms, appearance, activities,

331

possessions, occupations, and participation in male groups. By revealing such traits males affirm that they are masculine and not effeminate.

A male is expected to be tough. He should be able to endure hardships without complaining. He should not show fear of anyone or anything.

> Males try to hide their fears. They think it isn't cool to be afraid. They won't admit being scared of something, and they don't want to look chicken. A friend of mine hates to take a girl to a horror film, because she jumps at every little thing, and this embarrasses him. #2676

A male should be willing to take physical risks, for example, by riding a motorcycle or drag racing.

> Some males won't wear seat belts in cars, because they consider them suitable only for women and wimps. #2677

A male should be able to support and protect himself, his family, and his property. He should be definite and sure of himself; be independent of others, especially women; and stand by his friends when the going gets rough. A man should be the master of his own destiny.

A male should be strong. Maleness is associated with a large, muscular build; the bigger, the better. Many males, particularly those in their teens and twenties, work out with weights to increase the size and strength of their muscles. Some spend extra time at exercise in the spring so they will look better during the summer months, when they will be outdoors and at the beach. Some males who lift weights use steroids to speed up the process of muscle growth, even though they are aware of the health problems associated with steroids. Males with muscular builds frequently draw attention to this by wearing clothes which reveal their bodies or the outlines of their bodies. Thus many wear shorts, bathing trunks, T-shirts, shirts with no sleeves, skintight shirts, or no shirt at all.

> Summer gives guys the chance to sport the muscles they've been working on over the winter months. One place they go is the Exhibition, or yearly fair. Some try to hit the pounding block with a sledgehammer with as much force as they can. They show off their muscles and frequently miss the block altogether. If they do hit it hard enough to ring the bell, they win a cigar. Then they spend the rest of the night

walking around the fairgrounds with the cigar hanging out of their mouth. #2678

Certain clothing is considered typically masculine. This includes jeans and sturdy boots which are associated with physical work and working outdoors. Other typically male items are leather jackets; shirts and jackets decorated with the emblem of a gymnasium, sports team, or type of motorcycle; and caps with company logos. Males tend to wear conservative colors, such as browns, blues, blacks, grays, and tans.

A male is also expected to be competent. He should be willing to take risks and be successful when he does so. He should also show good judgment and not get the worst of a business deal. He should achieve a top position in his career as well as financial success. He should be a self-made man. Ideally, he should own or run a large operation, the larger and more successful the better. He should acquire the biggest and best equipment and facilities, such as the fishing boat with the biggest engine or the largest and latest farm equipment. And he should own large desirable possessions, such as an expensive and showy car, house, and/or boat. Operating large vehicles and machinery is seen as particularly masculine. A male should also be assertive, competitive, and decisive. He should be able to take charge, know what to do, and succeed.

Males are expected to better other males and defeat them. In contrast, when a male is victorious over a female, whether it is at sports or on an examination, it proves nothing, because his opponent is "just a woman." However, losing to a female can be a major humiliation. One of the worst things a male can do is allow a female to take control of his life, tell him what he can and cannot do, and treat him like a child. A male who is henpecked, or who allows a female to "wrap him around her little finger," shows weakness of character and is considered deficient in masculinity. As a result he suffers considerable loss of face in the eyes of the other males and is likely to be severely teased or ridiculed by them.

Jobs which are based on physical exertion, strength, and endurance are typically male occupations. This is even more the case when the work takes place outdoors. In such occupations males frequently compete with each other.

I often work loading the potato boats that come to town in fall and winter. A bag of potatoes weighs 110 pounds, and a crate 120 pounds.

> We load them in the cargo holds and the job is physically demanding. Some of the bigger, stronger guys compete to show how many crates they can carry and how high they can stack them. Some guys try to prove they are tough and manly by showing how long they can continue working. Those who quit early or can't keep up the pace are considered wimps and are not included when the next work crew is selected. When teased about being wimps, some workers unload the next few pallets of crates by themselves to prove their toughness. I have even seen them do this at the end of twelve hours of work. [#2679]

Part of being male is that one does not mind getting dirty while engaged in physical work. Therefore a scruffy appearance contributes to a male image.

A male is expected to be physically active, and most males participate in sports. Males normally have a strong interest in watching sports events and are knowledgeable about them. Some sports, however, are considered more masculine than others. These are sports in which males pit their strength and toughness directly against other males. Sports which involve rough physical contact and violence, such as hockey, football, Rugby, and boxing are ideal in this regard.

> In high school my teenage friends equated being good in a tough sport, such as hockey or football, with being masculine. Many of my teammates in these sports held the idea that the more physical abuse you could take, the more you were a man. [#2680]

> Males are expected to be physically aggressive in hockey and football. It is important for a player to "have guts," "never back down from a fight," and "never give up." A successful male must strive for strength and speed, show coolness under pressure, work with the team, be willing to risk violence, and have a desire to win. [#2681]

Sports without physical contact, such as tennis and curling, are considered less masculine.

Certain activities and possessions are considered masculine, and the extent to which one is associated with them indicates the degree of one's masculinity. Such activities include hunting, fishing, and trapping; gambling; and doing construction and repair work on one's house and car. Male possessions include trucks, jeeps, motorcycles, guns, knives, and weight-lifting equipment.

When males pick books to read and films to see, they usually prefer those that involve action and violent threats. They like adventure, war, exploration, treasure hunting, police, crime, westerns, science fiction, thrillers, spies, villains, horror, monsters, sex, racing, hunting, nature, sports, and competition. In contrast, females tend to prefer books, TV programs, and films which deal with romantic relationships between males and females. These are called romances, soap operas, and chick flicks. #2682

Aggression and violence are strongly associated with males.

When I was in high school, we would hang out in small groups of three or so males. We talked mostly about sports such as football and hockey. We also talked about "doing up" cars, fighting, and wanting to kick somebody's head in. We reacted negatively to anything that wasn't manly. Occasionally we shoved and pushed each other around to establish who was tougher and to be looked up to. We acted aggressive in order to let others know just how tough, strong, and masculine we were. #2683

Girls rarely fight, but it's common among guys. During my last year in high school almost every dance concluded with a fistfight between two or more males. #2684

Some males react violently in certain situations.

When my brother's girlfriend broke up with him, he put his fist through the wall in his room. #2685

I watched how people react to having to wait in the emergency room of the hospital. Several females seemed flustered and some searched through their purses. The two males, however, were more expressive. They would groan aloud with pain, hit the wall with their fists, demand the whereabouts of the doctor, and curse the hospital. #2686

Males are more likely than females to take their anger out on someone or something. A male friend of mine locked himself out of his house, got a little frustrated, and kicked out one of the door panels. #2687

Males are also more likely to engage in willful destruction of property than are females.

Males should be willing to fight when challenged, provoked, or if their masculinity is questioned.

> Numerous fights at teen dances are caused by young males threatening each other. Sometimes they just want to give their masculinity a boost by proving they are good, tough fighters. Often fights between males start because one of them calls the other a sissy, wimp, fruit, faggot, or some other term which questions or puts down the other's masculinity. #2688

> If someone called me a fruit to my face, or even behind my back, I'd beat the shit right out of him. #2689

> It isn't very manly for a male to show he's scared. Danny is twenty-one years old and much smaller than the guy who picked a fight with him. Danny bravely wouldn't back down, even though he thought he would lose, which he did. Afterwards, Danny said, "Of course I was scared. That big SOB was twice the size of me!" #2690

Another male trait is consuming alcohol. Alcohol is a man's drink, and the better a man can deal with it, the more masculine he is. Beer, straight liquor, and moonshine are all considered masculine drinks. Cocktails, on the other hand, are considered more suitable for females.

> I work in a bar, and males and females order different drinks. Girls will order beer and shots, as do the guys, but many order "girl drinks." A girl drink is a cocktail, cooler, or fancy shooter, which is colorful and sweet. Girls tell me they prefer sweeter drinks that hide the taste of alcohol. Guys would never order such a drink in front of others. They might order an occasional shooter, but never a girl drink. Guys drink beer or shots of rum, vodka, or rye. Anything else is pushing the boundaries of what is acceptable for males to drink in a bar. #2691

A male is expected to be able to consume large amounts of alcohol and show little reaction. Passing out or getting sick reflects poorly on a male's ability to "hold his liquor."

A male should not appear effeminate

To some people being masculine means being able to drink a six pack of beer and a pint of rum without blinking an eye. [#2692]

I have seen drinking competitions to determine who is "the best man" in the group. They drink until only one person is left standing, and he wins the honor. Sometimes this is carried over into a fight to establish "a best man," who is the last one standing at the end of a brawl. [#2693]

Smoking tobacco and using recreational drugs are also activities which are considered masculine.

There are a variety of other traits which are associated with males and being masculine. Thus a male should maintain a calm and cool exterior, not show emotions, and never cry.

When my brother and I were in grade school, two of the kids we played with were killed in an accident. I'm a girl and I cried. My brother did nothing but mow the lawn. I can't see how mowing the lawn could make him feel any better. He was always like that. Guys have such hang-ups about crying. They are so self-conscious. [#2694]

A male should be relatively silent, have a deep voice, and say something significant when he talks. He should have a firm handshake. A male is also expected to be successful in attracting good-looking females, to have an interest in physical involvements and recreational sex, and to be sexually successful; the more women and the better looking they are the better.

When I was younger, my parents showed an immediate interest in any girl they saw me with. They would ask me about her and encourage me to ask her out. I guess they were probably worried about me because I never had any girlfriends. Maybe they figured I was gay or something. [#2695]

A male should acquire an attractive girlfriend or wife, the more attractive the better. He should father children, preferably males. It is necessary that a male have his own vehicle, such as a car, truck, or motorcycle, and show mastery in driving. For some males having a powerful and fast vehicle and driving fast are also important. Males are more likely than females to drive with one hand and rest the other arm on the window frame or along the top of the next seat. They are less likely to wear seat belts and safety helmets than are females. Having a beard or mustache, and appearing unshaven, are also masculine characteristics. Spitting and getting tattoos are predominantly male activities, even though most people consider them undesirable. Swearing and using "strong" swear words and phrases are also viewed primarily as a male activity.

> My boyfriend swears all the time. I finally told him not to swear around me because it makes me uncomfortable. I also found myself using words I never would have used if I hadn't been around him. [2696]

Another masculine trait is participation in all-male groups. Many males get together at regular intervals for the purpose of playing a sport, drinking, or playing poker.

> Members in the male group I hang around with are roughly twenty years old. We work together and play on the same hockey, baseball, and football teams. We also play cards at a friend's house and are great drinking buddies. My group and other groups I know have a rough-and-ready camaraderie. When we go to a hockey game or out to a club, we tell jokes, describe the movies we've seen, and discuss girls. We argue constantly among ourselves. At clubs we try to gain each other's respect by talking to attractive girls, and by getting drunk and making abusive remarks. Top priority is given to picking up an attractive girl. A male who does so is looked up to and anything he says tends to be listened to by the others. Sometimes a member of our group informs a female that he already has enough friends and what he wants is a sexual partner and nothing else. We also consider it important that the other males know, "I'm not letting that girl wrap me around her little finger." [2697]

> A group of us get together over the lunch hour in the local rink to play hockey. Those playing range in age from sixteen to over fifty. Although which players come to play changes somewhat from year to year, some have been coming for over ten years. The group is quite diverse and includes administrators, lawyers, professors, businessmen, police officers, and various students. Although there is a pool of about fifty guys who play at one time or another, there are usually only about ten players present on a particular day. What I really enjoy is the interaction between the guys. We are familiar with each other's style of play and get

a lot of pleasure from outmaneuvering each other on the ice. We really like to tease one another about our play and anything else we think of. Most of us have been given nicknames by the others. Lots of the ribbing takes place in the dressing room before and after our play. The other day a player was there with his son, and someone said the boy looked a lot like one of the other players. Then someone else added, "Come to think of it, he looks a little like all of us." #2698

The activities which males and females engage in with the opposite sex are often different from the activities they engage in with members of their own sex. The following two statements are from males.

There's a lot of difference in the things I do with my male friends and my female friends. I wouldn't go to a nice restaurant with a male friend, and I wouldn't go to a pool hall with any of my female friends. #2699

You do different things with guys than you do with girls. There are some bars that I go to with guy friends that I wouldn't go to with a girl. #2700

The next statement is from a female.

When I'm with a friend, what we do depends on whether my friend is a girl or a guy. I like to go shopping with girls, which I wouldn't think of doing with a guy. I'd rather go driving or biking with a guy. #2701

It is interesting to note how males describe other males they consider masculine.

Allan comes from a family of six children. His parents brought him up with the idea that boys played baseball and football, were tough and masculine, and had nothing in common with girls. Boys in his family played together while the girls learned how to bake from their mother or played with each other. Now Allan is in his last year in high school and on the football team. He is popular with girls and always acts like a man. He is strong and a good sport, has good manners, and would stand up to anyone who would call him anything other than a man. #2702

Rick comes from a financially successful family. He has four sisters, and is the only boy and the youngest child. His father has always stressed that acting like a man is very important. Rick is very protective of his sisters. Recently his father became quite sick and Rick has had to manage the family business and take care of his mother and sisters. Because of the way he was brought up, he has been able to take on this responsibility without difficulty. #2703

Frank is a soldier in the army. He is not very smart, but the men look up to him because of the way he handles himself. Frank is one tough customer. The way he walks and talks leaves no doubt he is a man in every way. The men all want to be just like him and would follow him anywhere. #2704

Effeminate signs

At the same time that males seek to act masculine, they try to avoid behavior which is associated with females and acting feminine. If a male does engage in behavior associated with females, he immediately places himself in danger of being considered effeminate. It is as though the safest strategy for a male concerned with protecting his reputation is to act the opposite of females.

There are numerous traits associated with females. These include being gentle and passive; being physically small and weak; needing physical protection; being physically and psychologically dependent on others; getting visibly upset; being unsure, flighty, and fickle; displaying emotions; crying; being sensitive; acting effervescent and bouncy; being talkative; being excitable; screaming or shrieking; and gossiping and saying catty things about others. Males who reveal these traits are more likely to be seen as effeminate. It is also considered effeminate when males use certain "female" words, such as lovely, darling, sweet, adorable, enchanting, gorgeous, and cuddly.

I work at a day-care center and we have a blind boy of five named Michael there. The children at the center act more gentle with him than they do with each other. When Michael cries, they'll ask, "Is the baby hurt?" The other day a four-year-old boy asked me if Michael is a boy or a girl. Now he knows damn well what Michael is, but I asked him what he thought, and he said Michael couldn't be a boy because he acts like a girl. Michael isn't rough and tough like the other boys.

A male should not appear effeminate

When Michael gets mad, he doesn't throw a block at a wall or punch it like the other boys. Instead, he cries. #2705

When girls are happy about something they are more expressive than guys. The girls I know are louder and jump around, laugh, and never shut up. #2706

Sometimes when something sad happens in a movie, like a good character dies, you see females with tears streaming down their faces. Guys may feel sad when they see the same scene, but they aren't going to cry. #2707

Wimps are found all over the world in all levels of society. If you want to see a wimp, go to any library and look for a person with his face in a book studying his little head off from morning to night. Although a library or video arcade is a sure place to locate wimps, you can find them practically everywhere. Wimps come in all shapes and sizes. They are usually too fat or too skinny. They are found as far from the sporting field or hockey rink as possible. They don't go in for sports because they find them too violent. The only way a wimp becomes familiar with a sport is by reading about it. Wimps don't dress to fit the times, and many wear a pair of coke-bottle glasses that they frequently drop and smash.

Most wimps are very smart. They are usually teachers' pets, because they sit up front and make good marks. However, wimps are unpredictable, because they are either very vocal or very quiet in class. All day long you see them all over campus, but after the library closes you'll be lucky to see any at all. At the same time wimps don't have a clue about what is going on around them. They are really naïve about the world and don't stray too far from their parents for fear they'll go hungry or lack a comfortable place to sleep at night. One wimp I know went out west for a job which paid two thousand a month. But he had to live in the bush and couldn't handle being away from home. After one month he returned. Wimps stay much to themselves and are very protective. I think they are afraid someone is going to hurt them or damage what they have. They were likely pampered at home and taught to be careful of themselves and their possessions.

Wimps do not fit in properly in university. They have a limited social life because they are afraid to speak up and join in conversations. They stand back and let the good-looking jocks rule the talk. They don't show any school spirit because they are afraid to make their presence known. They never sit through a cold hockey game or cheer the soccer team on. Instead, wimps prefer the company of other wimps. They may get involved in the school newspaper where they can remain behind the scenes.

Many wimps have girlfriends, and these girls are half the cause why wimps are what they are. Their girlfriends are much like themselves. They aren't involved in sports or music and they are rarely seen in a club. Some say the girls are too scared to go out with a real man. I think they like being a second mother for a wimp.

Some wimps can handle a few drinks, but not many at a time. When a wimp drinks he usually takes lots of trips to the bathroom to be sick. Wimps never smoke drugs, because drugs are bad, and a wimp wouldn't dare do anything bad. If a fight breaks out anywhere near wimps, they run away. They would never try to defend themselves. They couldn't anyway, because their bodies wouldn't let them. They don't even know what a barbell or a bench press is.

Many guys tease wimps, make fun of them, and call them names, such as nerd, idiot, spa, mama's boy, and teacher's pet. Some guys bump into wimps when they leave the library with an arm load of books. The wimp stumbles and the books crash to the floor. Then the bully laughs at the wimp and tries to get him to fight. But the wimp picks up his books and walks away.

Despite all this, society needs wimps. Wimps serve as ego builders for others. If you want to impress a girl, all you have to do is point at the nearest wimp and start making comparisons between him and you. #2708

Having a pronounced concern with physical appearance, particularly with one's face, hair, clothes, or weight is considered a female trait. Clothes are very often used as a means of identifying femininity in a male. Bright colors and colors such as pink, orange, mauve, or lime green; materials such as silk, satin, lace, and fur; frilly designs; or outfits which are highly color coordinated can cause the masculinity of a male to be questioned.

Really bright clothes are considered a giveaway the person is gay. People say, "Look at that guy. What nerve. Can you imagine, red pants and yellow shoes? He's got to be gay." #2709

A male should not appear effeminate

When I was in high school, I would regularly wear some article of clothing that was pink. People assume this color is for females only, and I was forever being harassed about it. Both the students and teachers felt it wasn't a proper color for "a real man." #2710

Whenever I see a guy with a pink or lavender sweater on, I wonder if maybe he doesn't know how feminine the colors are and that others might think he's gay. I always wonder if I should mention it to him, but then I think I would look stupid because maybe he knows and is trying to make a point, like show he's above that kind of thing. #2711

If a guy dresses too well he's considered gay. You don't want to be too perfect in appearance. #2712

Use of a purse, a neck scarf, earrings, or a necklace normally brings uncomplimentary attention to a male, because they are considered female accessories.

Jewelry and neck scarves are considered fruity for males. If a male wore a gold chain and a pink shirt, eyes would pop. Somebody would say, "I wouldn't allow a man on the street looking like that. Someone should tell him what he looks like." #2713

In fact, any unconventional clothing is likely to cause others to question the masculinity of a male.

One sign of a homosexual is white socks and "fruit boots." "Fruit boots" are footwear which are not being worn by the general population. #2714

When males buy and use various items, they are careful that they do not take items designed for females.

I would never buy a shampoo or deodorant designed for women, because they usually have a strong floral scent. I can just imagine walking around all day smelling like a flower. #2715

When I go in a clothing store that sells male and female clothes, I usually ask where the male clothes are. Some of the styles and colors are so similar for the two sexes, I sure wouldn't want to make a mistake. #2716

Physical appearances which do not fit the norm also lay a male open to question. This is true of body build.

> When I first met this middle-aged man I thought for sure he was homosexual. He had a slim build and was mild mannered. However, when I asked a friend about him, she said he was definitely heterosexual, no question about it. #2717

> Guys with skinny bodies are more likely to be labeled gay than are muscular guys. Many males start lifting weights to get rid of a skinny body. Fat guys have a similar problem. A guy who lived up the street from me was big and fat and didn't play many sports. One day he came out to play baseball with us and no one would let him play because we thought he was gay. #2718

Other physical characteristics are also taken into consideration.

> Male fingernails are normally cut all the way back. A friend of mine plays the guitar and keeps his fingernails long. He is a large, muscular guy, but he sometimes gets really odd looks from guys who notice his nails. #2719

There are a variety of mannerisms which are likely to cause a man to be branded as feminine. These include a high voice; a dainty walk; a weak handshake, such as "like a jellyfish;" and various gestures involving limp wrists or very expressive use of the face, head, shoulders, and/or hands.

> This guy in our neighborhood lives alone with his aged mother. He has a really high-pitched voice, and people nickname him Cinderella because of his curly blond hair and his walk. Everyone, including my mother, thinks he is gay. #2720

Certain activities are associated with women. A primary one is housework. Chores such as cooking, cleaning, washing dishes and clothes, and tending to the children are generally considered feminine activities. Males who engage in these activities are considered less masculine.

> One man I know will quite often wash the supper dishes or do a load of laundry on his own initiative. If another male is present, the male is likely to remark, "Gee, you'll make someone a good wife someday,"

or "That's woman's work. Leave it alone," or "Don't be foolish. Let the wife do it. She didn't work all day like you did." [#2721]

I worked at a camp for seven-to-sixteen-year-olds this summer, and it was clear boys didn't like doing the dishes because they considered it a girls' job. When they did the dishes they would often make a mess and have a little water fight. Girls didn't like doing the dishes either, especially if they did them at home, but they didn't make a mess. [#2722]

I know a guy who was trying to quit cigarettes and took up needlepoint to keep his hands busy. Some of his male friends made comments like "How about showing us some pictures of your grandchildren, Granny?" and "How about if you and I get it on tonight, big fella?" The last comment was accompanied by a gesture that implied he was gay. The women on the other hand thought it was great, and some even tried to get their men to take it up as a vast improvement over having them spend their spare time watching TV and drinking beer. This met replies such as "Are you crazy? I wouldn't be caught dead doing that stuff." Despite the comments of his friends, the man continued with the needlepoint. He got very good at it and eventually tried macramé and rug hooking. I must say the boys were impressed when they saw what he produced, especially a hooked rug which one of them tried to buy. [#2723]

Certain activities around the house, such as emptying the garbage, mowing the lawn, washing the car, cutting and stacking wood, painting, and making repairs are considered male tasks.

There are also various interests which are associated with females. These include home furnishing and decorating; reading and literature; shopping; emotional involvements and romance; television soap operas; the rights and welfare of females and children; physical activities involving music, such as figure skating, synchronized swimming, and gymnastics; participating in and observing the performing arts, such as theater, dance, singing, and music; and opposing pornography and recreational sex. Whether or not a male pursues such an interest, and the degree and manner in which he does so, is used as a measure of his masculinity. For example, many females are active and expressive dancers on the dance floor, but few males are. A male who swings or waves his arms in the air, swivels his hips, or jumps around when he is dancing can generate questions about his masculinity.

Constraints

I love to dance and so does my boyfriend. But I won't dance with him in public, because he hops up and down like a Mexican jumping bean. He dances so differently from other males I get really embarrassed. I'm trying to get him to tone it down and try to dance more like a male. #2724

Also, the more a male participates in groups composed predominantly of females, the more his masculinity is subject to question.

In the university cafeteria, it looks bad for a girl to go sit at a table with a bunch of jocks, because she'll look too available. Likewise it looks bad for a guy to sit at a table of girls. He'll be called a fairy. #2725

There are certain sports which are associated with females, and a male who participates in them places his reputation at considerable risk.

In high school guys in masculine sports like hockey and football commonly made derogatory remarks about males who participated in a "woman's" or a "sissy's" sport, such as gymnastics or figure skating. Their attitude was that the only ones in these sports were females and frail boys, but if you were normal you stayed away from them. #2726

A relative of mine is from a small Island town and went into the hockey system. Like lots of kids who aren't that good, he would put on his uniform and end up sitting in the box, game after game after game. He was a real good skater, but I guess he wasn't aggressive enough or he didn't have the hockey moves. Anyway, the coach wouldn't play him. So he got tired of this and asked his parents if he could go to figure skating, and they said fine. He was twelve or thirteen at the time. I thought it was great that he had the courage to go. There was a young man teaching figure skating at the time, and I think that helped. Maybe if there had only been female teachers he wouldn't have gone. But he was mocked by his friends for figure skating and didn't stay with it but a year or two. #2727

Sports which are composed predominantly of females, such as figure skating and ballet, do occasionally have a male or two participating. The great majority of the coaches and teachers in these activities are female and they show little appreciation for the problems of male students, who do not want to look effeminate.

A male should not appear effeminate

In order to obtain a correct position when doing figures, a skating coach will require skaters, both male and female, to keep their wrists bent so that their hands remain at right angles to their forearms. This is a variation of the gesture which is widely used to symbolize male homosexuality. [#2728]

In ballet, teachers expect males to do female steps as part of the class. Many of these steps do not appear particularly feminine by themselves, but there are others that do. For example, bourrées consist of a series of extremely petite, "mincing" steps across the floor. Also, when the teacher goes through the reverence at the end of class which students are required to copy, she usually presents a curtsy and rarely a bow. In both ballet and figure skating, teachers frequently say "Girls!" and "Alright, girls!" to get everyone's attention, even when males are participating in the class. Ballet teachers also tease male participants that they will have to wear a tutu in the public performance put on by the ballet school. [#2729]

The teacher or coach holds complete, unquestioned authority in the studio or rink, and the male student is highly unlikely to break rank. Occasionally when a teacher or coach places a male in an effeminate position, there are other nonparticipating males in the vicinity watching what is going on, which intensifies the embarrassment of the male participants.

Many women are frightened by such things as mice, snakes, spiders, lightning, and the dark. They are also frequently squeamish about blood, guts, and killing.

In one of my university courses we see films on hunting and gathering societies. Whenever there's a scene in which an animal is killed or butchered, the guys don't seem fazed at all. However, something like one-third to one-half of the girls wince or squirm or bow their heads and cover or avert their eyes to avoid watching. [#2730]

A male who shows similar reactions is likely to appear sissy or effeminate to others.

A male who shows a strong interest in schoolwork and intellectual culture, can also be seen as participating in the female world, and therefore effeminate.

Constraints

All through school the girls in my family were expected to make all the good marks, while the guys only had one objective, and that was to make sure they passed. #2731

In a great number of families I'm familiar with, girls are encouraged to study harder in school than are boys. A girl is really encouraged to do her homework, while a boy isn't noticed. It's assumed that boys don't like school as much as girls. Boys who do well in school tend to be those who don't have to study terribly hard. #2732

In school the little boys who cried when they got hurt and weren't as quick to fight would be called sissies. Boys were supposed to be tough, take their bumps and bruises, and beat up the guy who hit them. When I was in school boys wore their hair short or in a brush cut. If a mother sent her son to school in curls, it was noted by some of the bigger boys. I remember also that the little girls would sit around and talk to the teacher more than the boys did. If a boy was a bookworm and stayed in school during recess instead of playing rough games outside with the other boys, he was likely to be considered a sissy. These things were certainly true of one boy I knew. He stayed inside and worked while the other boys were outside. The teacher lived at his house and the boy would walk to school and home again with the teacher. I also remember another boy in high school who was an exceptional student, and worked hard and did extremely well. He would talk to the teachers and wanted their help. He spent so much time doing his schoolwork and practicing his music that he was in poor physical shape and somewhat overweight. He would walk to school and back with girls he had grown up with. The other boys wouldn't talk to the teachers as much. If they did walk home with a girl, it was with their girlfriend, not a group of girls. All the things this boy did were noted by the others. He was considered different by the boys and something of a sissy. Some of the other males in high school were good students, but they weren't considered sissies because they acted more masculine. #2733

A number of men I know feel it is unmanly to discuss such things as films or books. It is much more appropriate for a man to talk about sports or politics or even the weather. One man said to me, "I'm always a little suspicious of guys who talk about movies they've seen or books they've read. Often those guys are fairies." #2734

A male should not appear effeminate

There are a variety of occupations which are held almost exclusively by women, and when men learn that a male holds such a job his masculinity is often questioned. This includes hairdressers, dancers, models, nurses, secretaries, clothes designers, interior decorators, and daycare workers. A male who works as a househusband while his wife holds a regular job, certainly generates questions. Such questions also arise when male students take certain programs of study.

> I feel a great deal of group pressure, especially from my buddies at university. I mean, look at me. Do I look like I'm majoring in Home Economics? I mean, I even play hockey. But I love to cook. So why should I stop just because some screwballs call me a fairy? #2735

Failure to engage in male pursuits or to succeed at them can also cause a male to be seen as effeminate.

> There's a kid in my neighborhood who never plays street hockey or any other contact sport with the other boys his age. They claim it's because he doesn't want to play with them. Instead, he plays with girls his age or with younger kids. The boys look down on him and call him a sissy. #2736

> Among teenagers, any guy who backs down from a fight is looked on as weak or girl-like and is usually considered a wimp or a baby. Such guys are often made into punching bags by other guys who are more physically oriented or better fighters. #2737

> I don't think it is right for a woman to swear. In fact, women who swear really turn me off. Of course it's fine for men. Swearwords are needed in a man's vocabulary to help him express himself. Men who don't swear are fairies. #2738

> Part of this whole macho image is to screw as many women as you can regardless of how many hearts you break doing it. I think wrapped up in this is the idea that if you don't screw a whole lot of women, you must be kind of fruity. #2739

When a male shows incompetence at activities which are traditionally associated with males, he places himself in the only other category, which is the one for females. This is the case if he is a poor driver, unable to hold much liquor, or incapable of building and fixing things and understanding how things work.

There is a real sensitivity to effeminate behavior in males, and people are quick to see "instances" of it and to judge males accordingly.

A fellow female student was telling me that one of her professors is gay. When she went to see him at his office there was a nineteen-or-twenty-year-old male student already there. According to her, this student was blond and had a very pretty face and the professor looked embarrassed when she entered. That's all she used to decide he was gay. Now I know the professor isn't gay, but you can't argue with the local mentality. #2740

My husband and some of his male friends from Quebec sort of hug when they meet. I think that's gorgeous, myself. But I think some people would think it strange. #2741

Communities and regions have their own definitions of effeminate behavior in males based on local norms for men, and this is applied to males from outside the community.

In my home community, there are a number of activities which people consider very effeminate in a male. One is for a male to wear shorts, especially Bermuda shorts with socks. That is looked on as the worst, or absolutely sissiest, thing a man can do. Another thing is for a male to wear a bathrobe. No male in my community would wear a bathrobe, or pajamas, or slippers. Also, most sports other than hockey are looked on as silly, or childish. Take golf. To someone watching on TV, it looks like if you give the ball a good whop, it'll go in the hole anyway. It looks so easy. Yet these golfers get down and smooth the grass and study the ball like they think it is such a big deal. They try to be so precise, you'd think they were building a house. A house would crumble if you didn't put it together right, but really it doesn't make any difference whether you get the ball into the hole or not. Curling is another thing. It looks so silly, men standing out there with these brooms, and then lying down judging the ice. #2742

When I grew up kids thought that when you lit a match and scratched it away from you, you were feminine, but if you scratched it toward you, you were masculine. #2743

A male should not appear effeminate

Different age groups of males also have their own definitions of effeminate behavior.

> My two brothers refuse to wear rugby pants. Rugby pants don't have back pockets and don't require a belt because they have an elastic waist. My brothers say they're for gays. They only want to wear blue denims and plaid jackets. They think it makes them look rough and tough. Also they refuse to wear boxer shorts like Dad wears, and will only wear briefs. #2744

Charges of homosexuality are applied to more than effeminate behavior. Homosexuality is one of the concepts commonly used to explain behavior. Thus it can be used to "understand" any male who acts in an unconventional fashion. It can also be used to attack a male that one envies.

> A friend of mine could easily be nailed as a gay. He wears peppermint-striped shoelaces and a bright blue jacket. Also, when he wears his cowboy boots he tucks his pant legs into the top of the boots. #2745

> When I was in high school, the norm for males was blue jeans, plaid shirts, and sneakers. One guy wore pleated slacks to school, and many guys I hung out with assumed he was a fruit. Whenever he got dates with the prettiest girls in school, guys became much more outspoken about his being queer. #2746

> When I was growing up, if you saw a grown man, say twenty-five or older, riding a bike, he was considered kind of fruity. #2747

> There's a guy down the street who is about fifty years old. He used to coach me at boxing. One day my mother asked me if I thought he might be gay. This is because he has never been married. #2748

The following are examples of males whose behavior is considered effeminate.

> Hank isn't gay, but he walks and talks like a girl and has "weak wrists." He has two older sisters and his mother is the dominant parent. His father is an alcoholic and always runs to Hank's mother for protection.

351

Constraints

Hank has a hard time fitting in with the guys and finding a girlfriend because of his feminine behavior. All the guys make fun of Hank and call him names like Hanky-Panky. #2749

There is this guy who is about twenty-three years old at the food-processing plant where I work. I became aware of him when my friends told me he wasn't normal. Everything about him is somewhat feminine. He walks like a woman, smokes a cigarette like a woman, and even talks in a very feminine tone. He also tends to communicate better with females. Most of the guys at work think he's homosexual. People talk about him behind his back and look down on him. Some of the guys go around imitating his walk or the way he talks. Even though he appears healthy, he asks the boss to give him the easier jobs at the plant. This has lowered people's opinion of him further and they call him a pansy for not doing hard work. I know he isn't homosexual because he has a girlfriend who occasionally picks him up at work. #2750

There's a guy in high school who dresses differently from the other students. They wear rugby pants and K-way jackets, which you pull on over your head. This guy, however, wears cowboy boots and country and western shirts under a leather vest. When he did buy a K-way jacket, he got one that was bright orange, which is a bad color for a male. He's also quite obnoxious in class as a result of trying to run things, and this puts the students and teachers off. When he dances he's wild and he tries to act like he's really into the music. He even says, "I'm really into it." It just turns everybody off. He likes to use big words too, but he often does so incorrectly. Others like to mock him by repeating his errors. He's a tall, muscular guy, but because he acts so different, students think he's gay. They call him "Fag of the Year." #2751

When I first met my boyfriend I thought he was gay because he has a lot of feminine characteristics. To start with there's his appearance. He's skinny and has thin fingers. Most of the guys around here are stocky with thick fingers. The ends of his nails are white because he doesn't cut them all the way back. He's also quite verbal and chatty, which most guys aren't. And when he talks he gestures with his hands, which most guys don't do. As I talked to him about myself, I found he was sensitive to me, empathetic, and supportive. Most males have poor relationship skills and can't deal with these things. #2752

352

A male should not appear effeminate

There's a guy at the office, Greg, who likes to paint and garden. He doesn't impress people as being particularly masculine. He's always late in getting his reports to the secretary, so he asks one of the other employees to type the report for him. He'll plead in a whining voice, "Charlene, will you do something for meeeee?" One day he was going on like this when Charlene was in a bad humor about something else, and she said, "Oh yes, I'll do it. And quit your sooking. I hate men who sook." At this point someone else said, "That's right. Charlene is used to big he-man types. She's not used to this." "That's right, I'm not," agreed Charlene. A lot of people at work think that Greg is gay. Just the fact he has artistic interests is all they base it on. #2753

I had a male instructor once in school who had a real problem with discipline. It was his first year as a teacher, and his problem was he was too kind. But we kept trying to see what we could get away with and how far we could push him. We would just sit and talk among ourselves and he didn't do anything to get us to be quiet. We'd tell him we couldn't do our math or other homework, and instead of realizing we could actually do it, he would go over it again with us. This was a one-room schoolhouse without running water. Every day two kids would have to go get a bucket of water from a neighbor's house, and the task was assigned to two different kids every two weeks. This teacher was tall and gangly, and one time we appointed him to go get the water with the shortest boy in the school. We expected him to refuse, because it was unheard of for a teacher to go get the water and any other teacher would have told us, "That's your job." But he went ahead, and people couldn't believe their eyes seeing this tall man carrying a bucket with this little short fellow for the next two weeks. While he was gone we were left unsupervised. Another chore for students was taking turns washing dishes after our hot meal at noon. Other teachers had never washed the dishes, but we had him doing this too. Also, his hand movements were much more delicate than those of other males. But probably the most sissy thing he did was in regard to mice. There were always mice in the school, and one day he saw a mouse and acted afraid of it. The worst kid in the school then caught the mouse and said, "Look at it, sir." And of course when the poor man shied away from the mouse, the kid ran up to him with it. Instead of standing his ground the teacher ran away from the student, accompanied by gales of laughter from everyone else. It was just pathetic when I think of it now. My face should be red as a beet just talking about it. Years later

I met someone who had him as a teacher the following year in a different one-room school, and she said he was just so strict you would not believe. #2754

Nevertheless, some males, whose traits would normally brand them as effeminate, become accepted as proper males by those who get to know them.

One of the teachers at the local high school is noted for his wild color combinations. He wears bright yellow pants with a red shirt, or orange pants with a purple shirt. Strangely enough, people accept him readily. No one makes any harsh judgments about him on the basis of his clothes. He is a very easygoing, athletic man who tries to have a good time. People generally like him and see him as a lot of fun. Everyone assumes he dresses this way to get attention and it is part of a gag. However, seeing him for the first time can be quite a shock. #2755

Avoiding the label

Most men are concerned that they appear properly masculine. The idea of not appearing effeminate is frequently present in male thinking. Males say to themselves, "I will do this, because it's the way a proper male acts," and "I won't do that, because it's feminine." Being male is a popular topic of discussion among men.

The masculinity and lack of masculinity of other males is one of the most common topics of male gossip. Males discuss this at card games, in bars, and wherever you get a group of guys together. #2756

Most males go to considerable effort to avoid the label they are effeminate.

Once you get the reputation of being gay, you don't lose it. The important thing is not to take the chance of getting the reputation in the first place. #2757

Therefore, males commonly avoid certain tasks which are associated with females. One reason is that males simply do not like to do such tasks. Another reason is that they consider the tasks too feminine and want to protect their self-image and their reputations. One activity which is commonly avoided by males is housework.

My husband doesn't see anything wrong with cooking and washing up. But he hates to do it. So I do it because I don't mind. #2758

In our household the boys don't have to do anything. Since Mom and Dad both work, the girls are expected to cook the supper each night, and make sure the house is kept clean and tidy. There is always a big hullabaloo when we try to get the boys to chip in doing the household chores. It is much easier for the girls to do them than to listen to the boys whine and complain about any little chore they are asked to do. #2759

Who does what around our house is a constant source of arguments. Most guys wouldn't be caught dead hanging clothes out on the line because people would think they are fruits or something. My brother is sixteen and he doesn't know how to make his own bed or how to turn on the washing machine. Heavier tasks are supposedly for guys. Loading wood is for guys to do, dishes are for girls to do, mowing the lawn is for the guys, washing is for the girls, and so on. But how often is this followed? The guys say, "Why can't the girls help with the wood? They can carry the smaller pieces," and "The girls should help when they aren't doing anything, because there really isn't much for them to do around the house." #2760

In one middle-aged couple the wife works outside the house and the husband has a medical condition and stays home. Even though he is physically able to do household chores, he does very little. His wife does the cooking, cleaning, and laundry before and after she goes to work. She accepts this because "He is a terrible cleaner. I'd rather do the job myself." #2761

When Mom was in the hospital and I had to go to school, there were no women left in the house. Dad and my brothers cook for themselves if no one is there to do it for them, but they won't wash dishes. Each time they fixed a meal, they would push the dirty dishes from preceding meals further back on the table. There would be dishes from their first breakfast, second breakfast, tea, lunch, and another tea. And they'd leave their dirty pans on the stove and table. But they'd never run out of dishes or pans because I'd get home eventually and do them. I've never in my life seen Dad with his hands in dishwater. He will get me out of bed to come down and wash a cup for him if there are no clean ones for his tea. Or else you'll see him go out and buy more cups. I can get away with telling him to wash them himself. He just laughs. I'm the only girl and he thinks he's spoiling me. But if Mom were to tell him to do them himself, which she won't, he would get mad and tell her she should wash them right away. #2762

When your wife is pressed for time she's likely to call on you to do just about anything around the house. However, there is a real art to getting out of tasks you don't want to do. For example, you can continue asking just how to do the task or whether you've done it to her satisfaction so you can stop. It gets to be more trouble for her than it's worth. Sometimes I tell her, "Never send a man to do a woman's job." Once we had company coming and my wife gave me a hand mixer to beat the cream for the dessert. I felt it was her fault she wasn't ready because she'd wasted the whole afternoon. I really didn't want to do it and managed to splatter cream all over. I even got some on the walls and ceiling. She never asked me to beat cream again. #2763

Many males also avoid tasks dealing with young children.

My dad and the other farmers in the community would never think of changing diapers. Dad never changed us, he never dressed us, nothing; that was Mom's duty. Now there is a man in our area who does change, diaper, bathe, feed, everything, the baby at their household. He moved here from the United States. They are city people too. What he does is viewed as weird by the other men. The husbands of my friends are younger men, and they are beginning to do dishes and stuff, but I've never seen any of them change diapers. #2764

Many men shy away from chores involving small children. Hospitals are trying to get men more involved with babies now than they used to, but some men view this as sissy. I've been told some men will not go up to the window at the maternity ward and look at a baby after it is born. Various women tell me they don't get help from their husband because he doesn't feel comfortable with a tiny baby, or that he's told them he'll wait until the baby's older before he helps out. #2765

A male should not appear effeminate

In fact, any activity which is associated with women is likely to be avoided by males.

I know a group of guys who tell me they have nothing to do with Christmas shopping. Instead they get their mother or girlfriend to do it for them. "Anyway," one guy said, "shopping is a female's job." [#2766]

Although some men do the family shopping, most men I know view it as women's work. Thus my middle-aged brother will not go in a grocery store and buy groceries unless he absolutely has to. [#2767]

When I worked in a store selling men's clothing, we planned to hold a fashion show. Another guy who worked there said to me, "Don't you think you'll look gay up there modeling clothes?" They wanted him to wear a pair of bright white pants and a pair of blue plastic shoes, but he wouldn't go into the show. [#2768]

Most guys wouldn't be caught dead reading a woman's magazine or a romantic novel. If they do look at one, they make sure there aren't any other males in the vicinity. [#2769]

Males are also careful about the amount of physical contact they have with other males, and the kind of attention they give them.

When males touch another male they make sure they limit it to a handshake or pat on the back. When there is more than this the other male often gets a strange feeling. Once I met a friend I hadn't seen for seven years. He had his arms extended as if to hug me, but I grabbed his hand and just shook it. I found his greeting so super-strange, I watched him for signs of being gay for the rest of the day. When I see males hugging I get a feeling of revulsion. Males also make sure they don't sit too close. Otherwise people would notice. Whenever I go to a club with another male, we usually sit on opposite sides of the table. [#2770]

When I go to a dance with my female friends we all get up to dance together, and lots of other girls do the same thing and nobody thinks anything about it. But you never see two or more guys dancing together. They have to protect their reputation. Guys are afraid others will think they are gay. [#2771]

Constraints

Although girls can say whether or not they consider another girl good looking, guys can't comment on another guy's looks. No guy would ask another if some guy is good looking in the first place, because it would be considered a weird or gay question. When a girl asks a guy if some other guy is attractive, he says, "How would I know?" No self-respecting guy would admit to noticing another guy's looks. Males also don't compliment each other on looks and accomplishments as much as girls do with each other. #2772

I work in a men's clothing store, and salesmen are really uncomfortable when they go to measure a pair of pants that a customer has on which has to be altered. The salesman has to take this measurement along the inseam from crotch to foot. The guy wearing the pants is also some-what nervous about it. I always talk when I do the measurement because it takes my mind and the customer's mind off what I am doing. One day I started selling to a guy who had come in the store. I soon got the im-pression he might be gay because he was acting very feminine, and I left him. Another salesman started waiting on him, and when he had to measure the pants, he decided to simply pin up the guy's cuff and wouldn't touch his inseam. After the customer left, the other salesman was really mad at me for refusing to wait on him. The rest of us thought it was pretty funny. But after thinking it's pretty funny, you realize it's pretty disgusting. #2773

I find when I go in to use the toilet in a public men's room I avoid look-ing at the other males and talking to them if I don't know them. Other-wise they might think I'm gay and trying to pick them up. I think other guys do the same thing and carefully keep their eyes straight ahead when they are using a urinal next to another male. I hear it's really different in a women's room, because women will borrow a comb or cosmetics from strangers and talk about all kinds of things. #2774

It is important for males to avoid physical and emotional closeness with other males.

Female friends and roommates commonly try on and borrow each other's clothes. However, it's very rare for males to do this. Sometimes one brother may borrow an item of clothing from another brother, but male friends and roommates don't do this. Maybe they consider this getting too familiar with the other male or too close to his body. #2775

A male should not appear effeminate

Sometimes I pick up my cat and hug him against my cheek. Because my cat and I are both males, this bothers two middle-aged males I know and they comment on it. I suppose if my cat were female, this would be OK with my friends. #2776

Males do not want other males to think they are weak, soft, vulnerable, or have difficulty coping. They do not want to show that they feel lonely, embarrassed, anxious, afraid, hurt, unhappy, guilty, or in love. Above all, they do not want to cry. Therefore they keep these feelings to themselves. If they reveal these things to anyone it is likely to be a close female friend.

Real guys don't sit around discussing love. #2777

If I were in a room full of guys and one of them started in about how much he loved his mother or his girlfriend or something, I'd think he was queer or something. If he said he loved football or sports or something, that's OK. #2778

My husband would never tell me he loved me in front of other men. #2779

Our father never showed his feelings toward us. He certainly never told us he loved us. #2780

Women talk about their feelings and the psychological impact of what they've gone through all the time. But guys don't. Guys talk about events, but not about the psychological impact these events had on them. They don't talk about their feelings, unless it's how pissed off they are about something. It's like men and women live in two different worlds and talk two different languages. #2781

I don't talk to the other guys about my true feelings, but I will joke around about them just to see how they respond. #2782

There are some things I'd never do with my guy friends that I do with girls, like talk about things that are bothering me. #2783

I have two really good friends, one male and one female, who I call and talk to every once and a while. I trust them because I know what I tell them will be kept between us and I don't have to worry about the rest of the guys finding out. #2784

When I'm emotionally moved by something I read or see in a film or on TV, I don't want others to see this. If my eye or cheek itches during a sad movie, I don't want other people to think I'm wiping a tear away, so I try to make it very obvious I'm scratching an itch. I can feel very sad, but I don't cry. I cried as a kid, but adults said things to me about it, and I don't cry anymore, no matter what happens. One problem I have is if I tell my wife about something that really moved me, my voice often breaks. I'm embarrassed that I don't have better control over my emotions. #2785

Men also frequently avoid gestures and postures which are associated with females. Thus they are not inclined to carry objects like books pressed against their chest, cross their legs at their thighs, or peel a sweater off by crossing their arms and gripping each side by the bottom. Instead, they are likely to carry their books in their hand at their side, sit with a foot or ankle on their other knee, and "drag" or "haul" a sweater off without crossing their arms.

In addition, men avoid certain clothing as well as materials and colors that are closely associated with women.

I was with a man who was shopping for a pair of outdoor boots. When we found a pair in the store he rejected it immediately because the heels were too high and he felt this made the boots look too feminine. But really, the heels were only slightly higher than those on his regular shoes. #2786

Guys won't wear certain clothes because they are afraid of what others might think. Some wouldn't touch a pink shirt or flowery shorts. They say, "Only gays wear that." They maintain their male image by wearing jeans and shirts in regular male colors. #2787

My two brothers won't wear wool sweaters that are red or yellow. This is because they aren't traditional male colors. #2788

I was in a clothing store and a middle-aged man I know was there with his two children. This summer some of the males have started wearing these long shorts with bright, Hawaiian-styled patterns. The man put on a gaudy pair of these shorts in the change booth, stepped out and looked in the mirror, then went back in the booth and took them off.

He wouldn't let his son and daughter see what he looked like with them on. Afterwards he said two separate times, "When I put them on, my hands did this," and he flopped his hands forward in a limp-wrist pose. He was saying he considered the shorts too fruity for him. [#2789]

Many males will purposely avoid locations that have a reputation for being associated with homosexuals. One bar in a hotel in Charlottetown is frequented by the Bohemian set on weekends and by government and professional employees Friday after work. It is also a favorite locale of the gay crowd, and carries this reputation.

There's not one guy I know who'll admit going to that bar. The place is crawling with fruits. Why your reputation is practically ruined if you're seen within a half-mile radius of the place. [#2790]

I was told that none of the men in one government office will go buy a drink in that bar because gays go there. My husband used to work in the bar, and it bothered a friend of ours so much, he used to just be sick when he had to go in to see my husband. [#2791]

I wondered if he was gay because he's a hairdresser. Then I saw him in that bar and my suspicions were confirmed. [#2792]

I went in and ate at this restaurant the other day, and the male waiter kept trying to make eye contact with me. I'm sure he's gay, and I'm staying away from that restaurant from now on. [#2793]

Another area in Charlottetown is known as Dizzy Block. It contains a variety of restaurants and gift shops and after dark is the primary cruising area for homosexuals.

I wasn't positive he was a fruit until the other night. He was walking down by Tom's Café with another guy. They entered the parking lot and got into a car but didn't go anywhere. It was dark but you didn't need a light to see. You knew what was going on. Everyone knows about that parking lot. [#2794]

At night you often see guys in the area standing by themselves in doorways, and other guys driving slow and staring at any males and occasionally honking. When I have to walk through the area after dark, I always walk briskly and keep my eyes straight ahead so no one will make a mistake and think I'm cruising too. One night I arranged to meet a female friend in a restaurant there. Unfortunately the restaurant was closed and I had to wait outside for her to get there. I felt really self-conscious because I thought anyone going by would think I was part of the gay scene too. #2795

Many men hold on to their concept of what is masculine, even when the definition of masculine behavior is in the process of change.

I don't know what's become of this generation. In my day and age a man had a proper haircut; one that would last a while anyhow. None of this running in every couple of weeks to get a centimeter trimmed off here and there. And all the primping and styling going on besides. Why you'd think men nowadays were a bunch of fussy old women. #2796

When I grew up, men didn't wear perfume. Later it became quite the thing to sell men after-shave lotion. I remember one with a masculine name called Hai Karate. But it still seems like perfume to me, and I have no desire to use it. I bet they call it after-shave instead of cologne so men won't reject it. My girlfriend goes on about how she loves a nice scent on a man and occasionally gives me a bottle of after-shave for Christmas. I don't care how many other men wear it, I really don't think she's ever going to get me to budge on this. It's just not something this man does. #2797

People also attempt to make sure that the males they are associated with act properly masculine. This is an important concern of families in raising boys.

My husband wouldn't let our son learn to play the violin. It's because he considers it too sissy. #2798

I was sitting out in the yard with a man and his two children, a boy of six and a half and a girl of seven and a half. We were drinking beer and throwing the bottle caps for the children to catch. The children would retrieve the caps and give them to their father to throw again. The man kept teasing the boy and getting him to try harder than the girl. After a couple of hours of this the boy was really tired. But even though the teasing was getting him down, he kept trying. The next time that he went to give the caps to his father, I took them away from him and he broke into tears. His father called him a crybaby and recited the following poem: "Cry, baby, cry; Stick a finger in your eye; Tell your mommy it was I; Cry, baby, cry." His sister repeated the poem. The boy went over to a tree and stood underneath it with his head down. He wouldn't say a word. Then his father asked him to go get him another beer. The boy did so and his behavior returned to normal. #2799

We bought Paul all the best dump trucks, machine guns, dinky cars, and bows and arrows. You name it, he has it. But what does he do but ignore them all and play with his sister's dolls. Can you believe a son of mine singing a lullaby while he rocks his dolly off to sleep? I mean it's getting to the point where I'm ashamed to let the neighbors in the house. They're already whispering and gossiping about him, and probably waiting to see him go off to school with a dress on. I told my wife the other day that if all this nonsense doesn't stop once and for all, pretty soon I'm going to have to lay a beating on the boy. Course then again, it might be the poor boy is sick. You know what I mean. #2800

Those who are not members of one's family will also sometimes take a hand.

When I was in grade school, there was a guy named Lee who loved to play hopscotch with the girls. The teachers were often heard saying, "Lee, don't be such a sissy! Now, get out there and go play with the boys." #2801

When I was in junior-high school the male coach, who taught physical education, held a meeting with all the male students in the gym. The purpose of the meeting was to warn us about adult males in the community who were trying to make sexual contact with boys. But during his talk the coach said it just made him sick to see a boy in school hold another boy's hand or put his arm around his shoulders. #2802

Family and friends will also seek to protect the reputation of a male they are associated with and to cover up any slips on his part.

I saw Big Ed cry once. Course it was at his momma's funeral. I ain't ever seen it since and I don't expect to neither. He's one mean fella, that guy. #2803

Constraints

If males receive indications that others are viewing their behavior as effeminate, they usually take immediate steps to correct the impression.

I was sitting on the porch one afternoon watching a group of neighborhood kids. A young boy from England had just moved here and was getting an awful teasing about his fancy clothes. Well I guess he finally had enough and ran off home. Next time I saw him he was sporting the neighborhood uniform of scruffy jeans, beat-up sneakers, and a shirt with a number on it, and he had a pack of new friends. Still beats me how he got a pair of jeans in that bad a shape so fast. #2804

When I was in the eleventh grade I went to a dance and my date and I both had on white satin shirts and black velvet vests. After I had been at the dance for about fifteen minutes a guy commented I was a "Disco Joe." Now if a guy were to stand up on the floor and dance like John Travolta in the movie *Saturday Night Fever*, he'd be labeled gay the rest of his life. Although this guy was referring to my clothes, he couldn't have said anything worse, because the implication was I was gay. I took off the vest five minutes later and covered my shirt up with a coat. I was so self-conscious about my appearance I was having a terrible time, and we left shortly thereafter. #2805

Males will sometimes go to great lengths to dispel the rumor they might be gay.

A rumor started going around that a guy in my class in high school was gay. He was six feet two inches tall and weighed 160 pounds. I don't think he had ever hurt anyone in his life. But when he found out about the rumor he started getting drunk and starting fights just to be one of the tough guys. He would come to school with cut hands and black eyes. Eventually the rumor stopped and he stopped fighting. #2806

However, efforts to stop such rumors are not always successful.

When guys in high school found out a rumor was going around about them being gay they would start going out with lots and lots of girls and subtly tell others about their sexual escapades. This often failed to dispel the rumor. After one guy had gone out with one girl for some time, he was still considered gay and she was now considered lesbian.

A male should not appear effeminate

Once the rumor starts, people watch your behavior for any signs which support the idea. They'll pick on anything, such as leaning close to another guy or accidentally bumping into his hand. [#2807]

Because males are so concerned about not appearing effeminate, other males take advantage of the fact to tease them about it.

Once I was at a club and this guy came over and asked me to dance. I was totally disgusted and told him where to go. The other guys with me thought it was the funniest thing. They told everyone they could during the next week about the incident. [#2808]

In high school the guys would get together and play a joke on one of their own crowd. For example, they'd agree, "Let's do it to Doug." Then they'd make up a box and put in fruit, fruitcake, fruit-flavored chewing gum, and anything else associated with fruit. They'd also add things in the colors green and yellow. In high school anyone who wore green and yellow on Thursday was considered a fruit, and when we were growing up I can remember us saying, "Oh, my God. He's got on green and yellow. He must be a fruit." Then the guys would take this box with all this stuff in it and put it in the mailbox at Doug's house. They just did it as a joke. They didn't suspect him of being a homosexual. [#2809]

Several of us guys study together on the second floor of the library. One of our group is a soccer player, so he has his kit bag with him practically every day. The rest of us will hide books on homosexuality in his bag, and then stand at the top of the stairs to watch what happens. Because the books have not been checked out, they set off the alarm when he goes to leave the building. The librarian then insists on check-ing his bag for stolen books and pulls out the ones on homosexuals. The first time this happened he turned quite red and swore to get re-venge on everyone. But he did laugh through the whole ordeal. [#2810]

A frequent form of banter in many male groups is joking around about various members of the group being gay.

Dad finds the way teenagers act today amusing. He can't believe how often they call each other fruits around here. People use the word as much as they use the word hello. Dad will be sitting in McDonald's Restaurant and there'll be a whole bunch of teenagers there. They'll use the word fruit all the time, even among friends just joking around. There's no meaning attached to it, and no one takes offense. However, others will roar the word out at people when they are driving down the road. And if someone gets mad, it's one of the first things they think of calling the other person. Occasionally a guy who's called a fruit responds aggressively. He may come over and say, "Want to step outside?" #2811

One summer one of the construction crews where I worked spent the whole summer pretending to be gay and teasing each other about it. They were all guys in their late teens and early twenties. Some were more into it than others, and they would pretend that the other person was making a welcome pass at them, speak in high voices, and use effeminate gestures. They only carried on this way with the other members of their crew. #2812

Males commonly tell jokes and off-color stories about homosexuals.

This morning on the radio, one of the announcers said, "When I was a child, I never believed in the tooth fairy. That was until I saw my dentist walk." #2813

One of the guys at our poker games really makes great jokes about homosexuals. He'll be dealt a card and say in a very effeminate voice, "That's putting it right in there." The other guys crack up. Or he'll start describing a homosexual party or dance with comments about the bodies, assholes, and vaseline. He's just a howl. #2814

Dealing with effeminate males

Most men are quite careful in their choice of men they associate with. Many are suspicious of strange males until they have been cleared as acceptably masculine.

I belong to this health club and males in the locker room are frequently nude while they are in the process of changing clothes, showering, or using the sauna. Few of the males say much to each other inside and outside of the locker room unless they already know each other. I think it's probably because they are not comfortable talking to strange males. I always wonder whether some male I see there might be gay, and I guess he might be thinking the same thing about me. When I say hello or start a conversation I always keep it short, because I don't want them to think I'm trying to get to know them because I might be gay. Two of the guys there are great friends who arrive together every day and do all their activities like weights, swimming, and saunas together. I wondered about them until one day when one brought his girlfriend along. I think you wonder about solitary males until you see them with a girlfriend or wife. It's like they are guilty until proven innocent. [#2815]

I know males who treat any new male they encounter with extreme caution and a great deal of distrust. They never know who will turn out to be less than masculine. One male I know remarked, "I don't know if he's a fruit or not. I mean he has a steady girlfriend. But he hangs around with that Bobby guy an awful lot, and everyone knows Bobby's a fruit. Just to be on the safe side none of us guys associate with him." [#2816]

Whether or not the other male is effeminate is an important consideration. Males normally avoid other males with effeminate traits. The last thing they want anyone to think is that they might be homosexual too because they have an effeminate associate.

Males react in a variety of ways when they encounter effeminate behavior or homosexuality in males. A common response is surprise or shock.

I was talking to a young fellow in the bar and he said he was just so glad to be back on the Island after a year in Halifax. He had never seen homosexuals in drag before he moved there. The first time he saw two men walk hand in hand down the street in Halifax, he thought he was going to smash up his car. He couldn't believe how blatant they were. [#2817]

I was walking down the main street of Charlottetown one afternoon when I passed two guys walking with their arms around each other's waists. They must have been about twenty years old. I did a real double take and turned around to watch. Guys were calling others to come out of stores to see the couple. Over the next few days I told several people what I'd seen. [#2818]

I was at a place and knew that this one guy there was gay. It freaked me out knowing I was in a place with someone who was actually gay. [#2819]

Often males feel sufficiently disturbed to speak out.

> In male university dorms, the most severe put-downs are of anyone who acts effeminate. #2820

Males frequently want to distance themselves from those they suspect of being homosexuals.

> My feelings about homosexuals are "Stay away!" That's their choice, just as long as they stay away from me. #2821

> One night my friends and I were in a bar where there were many homosexuals. It didn't bother me, but my friends got very uptight and uncomfortable. Some got angry. When they saw two guys kissing, they left immediately. #2822

> One time I was in the whirlpool at the health club. There was a guy sitting next to me who was naked. He started talking about his genitals and I ran out of there as quick as I could. #2823

Most males find the very idea of homosexuality repulsive. When instances of homosexuality are mentioned many males produce a look of disgust on their faces. (Many women react similarly when they encounter pornography, loose women, or recreational sex or when others mention them.) There is also a fear among males that the "gay" male may "try something" with them. When males encounter effeminate males or homosexuals, they sometimes respond violently.

> I was at a party one time and there was a guy there that everyone thought might be gay. After the party continued and people got more and more intoxicated, the real tough guys took him outside and beat him up. There was no reason except that they thought he was gay. #2824

> Last year at harvest time kids in cars threw potatoes at gays in town. I guess that's what they do with their surplus potatoes around here. #2825

When they come in contact with an effeminate male or a homosexual many males seek to reassert their masculinity.

A male should not appear effeminate

Occasionally I've seen a group of guys watching TV when a program on homosexuality comes on. Some of those watching become quite negative toward the gays on the program and curse them. I feel they are trying to assure everyone about their own sexual preference. [#2826]

This guy came to buy drugs from me and I think he knew I'm gay. He was wearing construction boots and baggy jeans. But he had this macho strut and kept spitting. The spitting was disgusting and uncalled for. [#2827]

When approached by a homosexual, a common response is to wonder whether one's appearance is sufficiently masculine.

A friend of mine was propositioned by a gay. For the next week he walked around wondering whether he looked gay or not. He started dressing in scruffy clothes, denims, and anything that made him look tougher. [#2828]

I was at a club over in Halifax the other weekend. There I was minding my own business in the can when this guy came on to me. Well I tell you, by the time I got out of that washroom three different guys had tried to pick me up. I was really getting pissed off at the end of it. Holy shit! I must look like a fruit or something. I tell you if one more had come at me that night, it would have been his life. [#2829]

Many women also avoid males with effeminate traits.

I have this friend who is one of the nicest guys you'd care to meet; some would say too nice. It's not his fault his voice never changed. Still it's kind of amusing. You almost want to ask him if he has ever considered singing soprano in the choir. Then again others would only consider asking him which sissy friend he's meeting later on that night. It's funny, isn't it? Most girls would just never consider going out with a guy that talks really fruity. [#2830]

He is a really nice guy, but he just doesn't turn me on. He is not all that bad looking, but sort of wimpy, so I didn't want to go out with him. It just wouldn't be good for my image if I was seen with a wimp. I know I'm being a bitch, but I can't help it. I just can't bring myself to go out with a guy like that. [#2831]

At the same time many females wish that males shared some of the traits that females value.

> I would like a guy to be kind and considerate and show how he feels. I'd like him to be easy to talk to. I don't think he should act really tough and beat on others, but I don't want him to act too feminine either. Still, he doesn't have to work out every day, talk big, and act like a super-macho man, like a lot of guys do. #2832

> I personally like to see a man who is fashion conscious and well groomed. It adds an extra-sensuous quality to a man. I'd dress a man in bright, tight clothing with short, clean, well-dressed hair. Other women agree with me, because we talk about it at our bridge games. #2833

Acting feminine

Occasionally males are placed in situations where they have to engage in feminine behavior. Often they comply with considerable reticence.

> I don't think females realize the significance of the situations they place men in at times. Not only do they lack empathy for the male, but they often find the situation humorous. My girlfriend always expects me to hold her purse when she puts on a sweater or coat. I often object or try to hold it in an inconspicuous manner, such as tucked under my arm, and I give it back as soon as I can. Sometimes she seems to expect me to hold it as we are walking, but that's too much. I stop and wait for her to take it back. She is amused by this. #2834

> My sister and I were collecting for a charity and went to a home where the woman is crippled with a muscular disease. After the couple gave us some money, the woman asked her son, who is about nineteen years old, to fix her some tea. At first the son pretended he couldn't hear her. She kept asking until it became very obvious and he got up to fix it. He was embarrassed because he had to make the tea in front of us. The woman got mad because her son was really slow about getting it. He got really mad too and banged the teapot down on the stove. #2835

At times males want to engage in activities that are generally associated with females. This includes attending Weight Watchers, bingo games, and figure-skating, dance, and aerobic classes; watching soap operas on television; and watching romantic films. One means of dealing with this situation is to participate in the activity together with one's wife or girlfriend. Males do not find this as uncomfortable as they would if they were attending alone. In addition, a male can always imply that he is attending because his wife prefers having him there or would not go without him.

I know two men who attend the local chapter of Weight Watchers, and they go with their wives. More men should be there, because there are as many overweight men as there are women. But I think they're embarrassed to go because the place is full of women. Not that the women are going to bite them; just that they know few other men will be there. #2836

One day last summer a group of five of us, three guys and two girls, made plans to go play minigolf. Then one of the girls called me and said she couldn't go, because she had forgotten she had to go to a relative's birthday party. I thought, "That's OK, four of us will go." But when I told this to the second girl, she decided she wouldn't go either. She said she was tired, but I think she would have felt uncomfortable being seen as the only girl with a group of guys. She was concerned about her reputation, and didn't want to hang out with an all-male group. Then when the two other guys came over, they decided they didn't want to go. By then I didn't want to go either, because just the three of us guys would have gone together. I thought about it the next day. It was kind of strange because initially we all wanted to go. But none of us guys wanted to go without the girls. I think it was because of how it would look to other people. I try to pretend I really don't care what people think, but part of me does. I know I'd be uncomfortable in a group of three males playing minigolf together. #2837

Many males feel they are so obviously masculine that no one would question their masculinity if they were to do something generally associated with females. Males are all the more likely to assume this when they have a wife or girlfriend. Therefore, they think they can engage in some activity, such as wear a pink sweater or dance flamboyantly, without any repercussions. However, the more openly and the longer they pursue the activity, the more likely they are to encounter comments or reactions questioning their masculinity. This can come as a real surprise to the "deviant" male.

I'm a middle-aged professional man, and because I didn't grow up in Canada, I had never learned to ice skate. My wife and I decided we would learn. So we bought figure skates, joined a local figure-skating club, and practiced regularly. My wife and I would also go to public skates at the local rink. My figure skates were black, the same color as hockey skates, but because I wasn't wearing hockey skates like the other males, I must have stood out like a sore thumb. It didn't matter so much that an occasional male kid would follow behind me with elaborate bent-wrist gestures in an effort to mock me. Besides they would frequently fall flat on their back when they tried a jump or a turn on one foot. What did bother me was that a large group of adolescent males would stand at the edge of the rink and throw ice balls at me as I skated. They were so young I really didn't know how to deal with them. There are all kinds of problems if an adult male slugs a minor. So I stopped going to the public skates. #2838

This twenty-five-year-old guy who was always considered tough and masculine picked up the practice of carrying a purse in Montreal, where he lived for a short while. Actually his "purse" was really just a canvas bag with a shoulder strap. But when he got back to the Island, his friends put so much pressure on him he quit carrying it. It didn't take him long to recognize the change in people's attitudes toward him, and the effect on his reputation. Just for a man to carry his wife's purse in from the car can get rumors started about his supposed sexual perversions. #2839

On occasion some males pretend to be female. A number of males will appear together wearing dresses, cosmetics, and large fake bosoms in a beauty contest or a talent show sponsored by a school or organization. Often the participants are the most popular or athletic males, whose masculinity no one questions. Also, they appear in a group, not as solitary individuals. Events such as these are treated with hilarity by the others present. Some males also dress up as females on Halloween.

I went to this Halloween dance and this very hairy, muscular guy was wearing heels and lingerie. He had on a red, lacy camisole and half slip, and was having a great time dancing with his girlfriend. Every dance or so he would pull down his half slip and wag his rear so everyone could see his matching red panties. #2840

Women do a similar thing when they dress up as a vamp or dance-hall girl on Halloween. By appearing loose, they too are acting out the very thing they spend their lives preventing others from thinking about them.

Benefits and costs

Models enable us to direct our behavior, rather than waste our time and energy in random action. A society, group, or individual can adopt any model, and can replace any model with another one. One can envision a future in which model designers will specify and customize models for societies, groups, and individuals. And one can foresee an education system which teaches a wide variety of models to people in order that they can select those which they think will best enable them to achieve goals, satisfy their feelings, and fulfill their needs.

It is useful, therefore, to consider a dominant model in a society, such as *A male should not appear effeminate*, and identify its advantages and disadvantages. This model provides several benefits. In accordance with this model roughly one-half of the population, the males, are encouraged to fight to physically protect their own public image, or to fight whenever someone wants to fight with them. This preparation for fighting could be useful if males can transfer it and use it to protect themselves and their resources, particularly in face-to-face and hand-to-hand confrontations. In doing so males could also provide protection for their mates and for their offspring. However, if we want to prepare males to fight, why not encourage them to fight when their resources are threatened or when an injustice occurs, rather than when someone calls them effeminate or homosexual? An additional benefit of this model, *A male should not appear effeminate*, is that males are prepared through the medium of team sports to work together in cooperative groups and to struggle against other groups to obtain and defend resources.

There are also a large number of costs in employing this model. This model requires conformity to a single, narrow definition of maleness. A single standard of behavior is recognized, rather than a multitude of alternatives. Alternative activities and occupations are viewed as unmanly and unacceptable, including those which deal with the arts, intellectual pursuits, emotional support, and certain forms of family maintenance, such as childcare, cooking, cleaning, and washing clothes. Males must dedicate considerable time and energy proving that they fit the standard model of masculinity. Standard males depend heavily on the approval of other males, and are discouraged from thinking and acting independently. The emphasis of this model is on physical opposition to others, rather than mental opposition. In fact, mental preparation and independence are not dealt with. This model is highly simplistic. Basically it states that if you do not fit a single standard for males you must be female. Female is the only category offered as an alternative to the standard-male model, and female is equated with male homosexuality. The idea that there could be a variety of alternative models for males is not considered. This model also places the standard male population in opposition to both the female population and the alternative male population. Therefore it pits large segments of the population against each other. For example, the model encourages standard males to persecute and alienate males who engage in any alternative behaviors. No matter what behavior females adopt, males are expected to do the opposite. It is not in the interest of society for males to adopt behaviors which are the opposite of any favorable traits adopted by females. In addition, according to the model it is legitimate for the standard male to be influenced by other males, but not by females. It is also difficult for males to admit weaknesses and limitations. Males are also expected to deny and hide their feelings, with the exception of a) anger, b) aggression, and c) pleasure from sex, alcohol, drugs, and sports. Given that feelings constitute the motivational system of humans, it is ludicrous to adopt a model which suppresses experiencing and expressing feelings. The expression of feelings enables us to communicate our feelings to each other and to respond appropriately. A model which forbids the expression of most feelings removes a very important system of communication. The idea that males do not cry, for example, prevents males from letting others know that they are physically or emotionally hurt. Crying encourages others to feel guilty and a) want to help the person who is hurt, or b) want to stop hurting him. In addition, the denial of feelings prevents males from understanding both human and nonhuman behavior, because this behavior is founded on feelings. It also prevents males from providing others with effective emotional support.

Showing affection and concern

It is easy to design models which would provide more benefits and fewer costs than *A male should not appear effeminate.*

Showing affection and concern

In rural Prince Edward Island adults practically never express affection in front of others. Affection is considered a very private act. People who are dating or having a relationship are affectionate with each other, but they normally do so out of sight of others. In my own family, aside from being affectionate toward children, no one hugs or kisses another person in front of others. In fact, I have never seen my father and mother or my brother and his wife express affection toward each other. It's even hard to think of my relatives that way. I assume they do so privately, but it's just not something one does in front of others.

This also applies to adults outside the family. If you were to go to the door and kiss a friend you hadn't seen in a while, it would be viewed as weird or seedy. It certainly would not be seen as masculine for a male to kiss a female in this situation. In the community where my mother grew up there was a family noted for strange behavior whose name was Kelly. Last year when my mother was very sick and in the hospital, Inez Kelly came to see her. Inez is really old and while she was in the hospital room she kissed my mother. Afterwards my mother said, "Did you see Inez Kelly kissing me? What in the name of God got into Inez Kelly to kiss me?" Also, I can remember going to a wedding anniversary party for my aunt. A number of people were drunk, including my aunt. When she saw this one couple, she ran up to the man, who is in his seventies, said, "Hello, Jim," and kissed him on the cheek. It was so foreign to him, and he was so mixed up, he went outside and didn't come in for supper.

People also react to the amount of affection expressed by non-Islanders. In the soap operas on TV, people are always kissing each other when they arrive and when they leave. I can remember my mother saying, "What is this all about? Everyone running up and kissing each other anyway." Also, our family has a relative from New England. When she comes to visit every summer she always wants to kiss everybody. It is a well-known joke in our family that the men will only shake hands with her. They stand way back and stick out their hand, and my brother is a master at it. Recently I went with a woman from another community to visit some old people. Although they were Islanders, they tended to hug us, which most Islanders wouldn't have done. Afterwards

375

the other woman told me she had just been to Boston, and that people there were always hugging and kissing you. She said, "It's alright Christmas or New Year's, but they go a little too far with it."

In rural Prince Edward Island, publicly showing signs of affection for one's spouse is generally frowned on and indeed mistrusted. Men are normally quite reticent to be too demonstrative toward their wives in public in case the other men laugh at them or the women make them the subject of gossip. When affection is expressed openly, it causes comment. There is a couple who live in a house down the road. When the man comes home from work, his wife runs outside and kisses him in the yard. People talk about it, and say, "What a silly thing," and "Those are the ones to watch." What they mean is that the more a couple put on a big show in public, the more likely they are to be fighting at home. People would say the same thing and laugh about anyone who used words like "dear" or "darling" when talking to their spouse.

At the same time, women in rural areas appear to have a need to show other women that their husband is caring and affectionate toward them. They cannot engage in public demonstrations of affection, because it is frowned upon. Therefore women often try to convey this message by other means. For example, some women I know seem to use their husband's concern for their safety and welfare to indicate the husband's feelings for them. One said, "Bill wouldn't dream of letting me take the car to work on the icy roads this morning. He absolutely insisted he drive me in." Another was discussing church the previous Sunday and said, "It was raining hard when we went in. When church was over the rain had stopped, yet Frank insisted he drive the car around to pick me up. He knows how I hate to get my hair wet. It really wasn't raining, but he wouldn't take no for an answer." Another was quite disappointed her husband neglected to start the car and clear the ice and snow from the car windows for her. "I don't know what he was thinking. I had to put my hands right in the snow, and didn't have gloves on because he normally does it for me. Perhaps he was in a hurry, because he usually looks after it. He doesn't think I should do that kind of thing."

The idea is to make the husband appear to other women as a sensitive, caring individual, while not painting him as seedy. (A "seedy" person is someone who behaves in a strange, extreme way.) Women commonly mention that their husband has done something around the house he doesn't normally do, like cook supper or do the dishes. "I got home at five thirty and Jim had the supper all ready. I was so glad. He said he knew I'd likely be tired after the meeting." Other women point out incidents where the husband put up with something really tedious just so their wife wouldn't have to do it, such as getting the car registered or waiting in line for theater tickets. "He looks after all that for me. He doesn't think it's right for me to have to wait in line. Not that I'd mind, but I'm glad he does it for me." The husband is showing real concern for his wife when he performs a favor for her or does an unpleasant task. Some women illustrate their husband's concern by telling how he keeps his temper when they are present. "Jack was pretty mad when the other driver pulled out in front of us. He really told him off, but at least he didn't hit him. I'm sure if I hadn't been there, there'd have been a fistfight."

Most women delight in relating such stories about their own husband, and some women seem unable to refer to their husbands without recounting such incidents. Such illustrations of feelings on the part of the men are safe to report to others, because they do not paint the man as being seedy or weird. The women are pointing out that although the other women may not see this side of their male, here are examples of his behavior which indicate he is caring and sensitive. In a society in which men are expected to be tough and macho, their males also have some of the other attributes which are valued by women. In recounting such episodes women show they have a good husband and have made a good marriage. Also, every woman places great stock in being able to hold her man and such instances are proof she is doing her job well.

There is another aspect involved in mentioning how caring one's husband is. Such episodes are used by some women to upstage others present by indicating that they have a more caring, sensitive, affectionate, and therefore better husband than the others do. For example, one woman was telling how angry she was at her husband. When it was storming, she started to drive home then decided against it. She phoned her husband, but he was really mad she had delayed and not just come straight home. It seemed to her that her husband was more concerned about the car than he was about her welfare. When the woman told this, another woman spoke up and stated, "Oh, you know, my husband's not like that at all. He'd come get me. He wouldn't even let me drive one day when they announced a storm was expected." This made it appear that the second woman had the much better mate. In another instance, a group of women were talking about how their homes are real bedlam in the morning. They spoke of getting children ready for school, and having to find clothes, pack lunches, wash dishes, and so on. Suddenly one lady said, "Yes, I don't know what I'd do if Jim didn't always make me a coffee in the morning. He always does it, even though he's rushing off to work. He knows I can't function without my coffee, and of course, I don't mind being spoiled." This comment made the others look like they had the short end of the stick, and they could think of nothing to say in response. In another case two women were discussing a death in the community and the necessity of going to the wake. Carol said she couldn't decide whether to go in the afternoon when she'd already be downtown, or to wait for the evening when she could go with her husband but would need a babysitter. Helen replied, "I know a bunch of women are going down this afternoon, but I wouldn't dare go to a wake without my husband. I like to know that if I feel like crying, I have his big shoulder right there for me." By indicating how great her husband was as an emotional support, Helen placed Carol in a weaker position. It appeared it was strictly a matter of convenience whether Carol went with her husband or not. On another occasion, several women were discussing marriage within the British royal family. Someone said all the public attention must create a lot of strain. Then one woman stated, "It's this business of not being able to show any affection in public that would kill me. I couldn't stand not being able to be affectionate in public." No one in the group had ever considered this woman and her spouse to be very affectionate with each other. But what could they say? She might have a much more affectionate marriage than they had, and the women just looked at each other. Efforts to best others are also applied to other aspects of family situations. For example, a woman may be talking to another woman who has no children, and make a point of saying how elated her husband was at the birth of their son. There is no way the woman without children can appear equal in this exchange. In the same sense, married women in the presence of single women always seem to tell stories about how great their husbands are. The single woman is hard put to say something comparable.

Naturally people discuss such comments when the person who made them is not present. "Did you hear Anne this afternoon about not being able to show affection in public? You'd think they were some kind of romantic couple or something. Half the time they're not even speaking. That's the truth. That kind of talk just sickens me." Or, "Remember Louise saying that Jim made her coffee every morning? What a pile of bullshit. She'd say anything to let on they have the perfect marriage." While most women question these comments, it is hard not to feel threatened by them. You know that your husband never makes coffee just for you, while this woman gets her special coffee every morning. In such situations, it is hard not to feel a little left out. When the whole thing is thrashed out with other women, the woman with "all the blessings" is usually treated with suspicion and perhaps a comment is made to belittle the affair, such as "Oh it doesn't hurt me to make my own coffee." But at the time you wonder if perhaps the other woman has the better situation and therefore has been more successful than you.

On the surface, a woman's account of what her husband has done for her might seem unimportant. The reporting is done casually, and no one makes much of the occurrence. Some other topic is being discussed, and the incident revealing the husband's feelings is slipped into the conversation. An outsider might think the incident has nothing to do with what is being discussed, but in fact such incidents of caring are often the hidden agenda, and the matter under discussion is simply the vehicle for their expression. #2841

Henpecked

The issue of whether a man is henpecked is an important one on Prince Edward Island. Often the word "henpecked" is not used. Instead a phrase such as "He's scared of her," or "He hasn't got the dare to open his mouth," is applied. Among themselves, males will sometimes say that another male is "pussy-whipped." No man wants to be considered henpecked. It suggests that the man lets women "walk all over him" or "wrap him around their little finger," and implies he doesn't have the gumption to stand up for himself and is therefore deficient in masculinity. Being thought of as henpecked involves a total loss of face for a man. Women too would not want it thought that their man is henpecked. It implies that the woman is bossy and controlling, has taken charge in the relationship, and that her male is an inferior specimen.

When men appear henpecked they lose a lot of respect in the community and often in their own eyes as well. Therefore, men work hard to avoid being henpecked and to avoid appearing henpecked to other people. Many men will mention situations in which they opposed the wishes of their wife or girlfriend. "You could do a survey of henpecked males just by sitting in church. Watch the guy who follows his wife up the aisle and lets her choose the seat to sit in. He'll let her organize all the kids rather than do it himself. Oh, I've seen that plenty of times. It was tried on me too, but I soon fixed that. Yes sir. I just dropped back a couple of times and she ended up sitting by herself. That ended that, I'll tell you." "I have no interest whatsoever in clothes. Lots of times I mess up and wear things that don't go together. But what the hell, it's me who's wearing them. My wife may buy all my clothes for me, but by God, I'll be damned if I'm going to have her tell me what to wear every day. So, lots of times when she lays clothes out for me I just ignore them. Damned if anyone is going to push me around." Such stories illustrate to the listener that the man is clearly not henpecked. However, often what the man is doing in the stories is dragging his feet, failing to do things properly, and quietly neglecting a task, rather than directly confronting the woman.

When people feel a man is henpecked they respond very critically. Men say, "Oh, yeah, Bill is terrified of Edna. Absolutely terrified," or "Jesus, I'd like to spend a day with his wife. I'd let her know in a hurry who's boss. A few boots in the arse would go a long way." Women say, "You know it's desperate the way Agnes bosses Tom. She just walks on him and he doesn't have the dare to say a word. Not the dare," or "Gail's really bad to Charles. She always tells him what to do, and usually he doesn't go along with it. When his friends come over to drink with him, she'll start scrubbing the floor around their feet. It embarrasses Charles so much, the men usually leave."

Despite this negative reaction, people seem to like to recount instances which reveal that a man is henpecked. "When Jim said he was going to the hockey game with me, you should have heard Sarah. She went on about him being out Monday night, and about her wanting him home to help paint the ceiling. Well, I never heard the like. I'd like to see the woman who would stop me from doing something I want to do. I'd really like to come across her." Although Jim did go to the hockey game, he was shown in a very poor light because Sarah was objecting to what he wanted and doing so in front of another person. At the same time, the person telling the story looked good to his listeners because he completely separated himself from Jim's behavior.

A primary indicator that a male is henpecked is the fact he is unable to participate fully in male activities. A male who can not attend sporting events and watch sports on TV, go drinking or play cards until the early hours of the morning, or take a hunting or fishing trip with his friends is likely to be teased about excessive control by his wife or girlfriend. Sometimes the teasing is limited to the gesture of pretending to wrap something around one's little finger. On other occasions the teasing is more elaborate. "One man who plays in a weekly poker group has the reputation of being henpecked. Before he married he was very independent, a big drinker, always out with different girls, and the envy of his married friends. Then he got married and Wow! what a change. Every week his wife would call the house where they were playing and want to know what time he'd be home. The other players laughed at this and the man was really embarrassed. Finally one of the other guys said, 'I'd like to see my wife call up every weekend to ask when I'll be home. Do you know what I'd tell her? I'd say, "Which day?"' One of the group's favorite pranks is to get one of the other wives to call the man up and pretend she's his wife telling him when to come home. He'll go to the phone, get really embarrassed, and tell the men, 'That's not my wife.' Then the others will say, 'Sure, sure, it's just some woman calling you.' 'I don't know who it was, but it wasn't my wife.' 'Yeah, sure. Who else knew you were here?' His poker buddies constantly tease him about being henpecked, and he always denies it. It's reached the point where if the guy has somewhere else to go on a poker night, such as to a meeting or a sports event, the others say he's just making up an excuse because his wife won't allow him to come to poker. They believe this too; they're not just joking."

When there are indications that a woman controls a man or that a man cannot make his own decisions, he is thought to be henpecked and loses face. If a man has to get his wife's permission to do things, if he makes sure what he does is acceptable to her, or if he has to let her know where he is all the time, he is considered henpecked. For example, a man who had been away from home all day called his wife to tell her that their team had won and what the score was. The other men taunted him, "Aw, checking in are you?" and "Getting your clearance for another hour?" Men also notice a man who is too solicitous of a woman's wishes. If he caters to her desires and whims and does not assert himself or stand up for himself he will be considered henpecked. "A male who is overly submissive to his wife's or girlfriend's every need is henpecked. I'm not trying to say he can't be courteous. He wouldn't be considered henpecked if he holds a door open for her or goes shopping with her." If a woman mothers her man and treats him like a child in front of others, he is considered henpecked. "My wife handed me something to eat and said, 'Did you wash your hands?' Because she said this in front of others I felt humiliated. As soon as we were alone, I told her I didn't appreciate it."

Many men also think that a man must be henpecked if he does chores which are traditionally associated with women, such as cleaning, cooking, and tending to children, or if he turns his masculine responsibilities over to a woman. As a result they are quite reticent to make these exchanges themselves and ridicule those who do. "Robert, a friend of mine, is middle aged and has a wife and two children. I've frequently stayed at his house, and I know the family well. He tells me, 'I take care of the farm, and my wife takes care of the house and the children. I work and make the money to pay the bills, and I don't ask my wife to plant and cultivate, so why should I have to cook or make the beds? I work out on the farm every day, so why should I have to do housework when I come in?' Robert would not be caught dead doing what he calls 'women's work.' He won't vacuum, dust, or even change the garbage bag in the garbage can. He has no idea how to do the laundry or prepare a meal. Making a peanut-butter sandwich seems to be his limit. When his wife can't get home to prepare dinner, arrangements are made so he can eat elsewhere. When he's with his daughter and sees she's messed her pants, he sends her to her mother to get changed. I've told Robert I know plenty of men who do housework. My uncle often vacuums and will get up in the middle of the night to see about the baby. Another man I know washes and irons, and does all the cooking because he doesn't feel his wife is a good enough cook. Robert replies that these men must be henpecked." "My grandfather believes that a man's place is working and earning money, and a woman's place is in the home. He definitely thinks the man should be in command when it comes to dealing with money. When he heard that the wife of one farmer looked after the books on the farm and paid the workers, he concluded she was running the farm. This was clearly wrong to him, because a woman should have nothing to do with handing out farm money. Moreover, he felt the farmer was no man at all to let this happen. He must be henpecked." #2842

Gays in town

It is difficult to categorize gay males in Charlottetown into subgroups. Their common denominator, of course, is their sexual preference. But aside from this they seem to vary in every possible respect. Those who are active range in age from their late teens to their late fifties, and their backgrounds and experiences are quite diverse. All are residents of Prince Edward Island and most were born on the Island. Many have lived practically all their lives on Prince Edward Island, while some have lived various lengths of time in urban areas elsewhere in Canada and in the United States.

Gays in town

Gay males who have spent some time off the Island tend to have a different outlook from gays who have spent practically all of their life here. Living in a larger urban area promotes freedom of expression which is not available in Charlottetown. In cities off the Island there is the opportunity to become submerged in the larger numbers of gays and straights. This is not possible in a community such as Charlottetown where people know each other and each other's business. Although gays who have lived off the Island often return with a more secure and open approach to their own homosexuality, still they know what they are missing and they experience more dissatisfaction and frustration back on the Island than the gays who have always lived here. Not all gays, however, find city life off the Island enjoyable or even tolerable. Some find it difficult to adjust, and complain it was very cold and unfriendly with everyone playing mind games and pulling rip-offs, and a few state, "Everyone I met was weird."

Charlottetown is a very conservative place. As such it stifles minority groups, such as gay males, who wish to lead open lives and express their sexuality. The gay scene in Charlottetown is characterized by a high degree of paranoia and a large number of closet cases. People are quite reticent to declare a nonstandard sexuality for fear of ruining their reputation and being ridiculed and partially ostracized. There are also numerous cases of threats and violence directed against gays on Prince Edward Island.

Another reason why many choose "life in the closet" instead of "coming out" is fear of rejection by other gays. Nothing is more devastating than to be socially or sexually rebuffed by another member of one's minority group. Gay males are not prone to show compassionate understanding for each other. To the contrary, the actions of many support the stereotype that all gays are tacky bitches. This attitude alone goes a long way to undermine the possibility that a true community of homosexuals will ever exist.

In Charlottetown, there is no bar or club which caters exclusively to the gay population. The city is simply too small for such a place to be successful. However, there are several locations which gays frequent. One is the lounge of a local hotel, where the more stouthearted of the gays began to gather. Word of this spread quickly and was even picked up in several international gay directories. However, the clientele at the lounge remains largely heterosexual, and only about fifteen to twenty gay males attend on a regular basis. You can often find several sitting or standing at the bar. Although there are some twenty or more tables in the lounge, I have never seen more than three tables with gays at them in all the years I've been going. Few of the local gay males go there, because they are afraid that if they go they will be identified as gay by the larger community. Because of the bar's reputation, many straight males are even afraid to go for fear of being labeled gay. When an international chain took over ownership of the hotel, it tried to get rid of the gays. One method was having the waitresses in the bar slow down or withhold service to gays. However, this is no longer attempted, and the gays still attend.

Another active place for cruising is the public library. The library is open most days and evenings and provides a legitimate reason for gays to be there. One can always appear to be looking for a book or reading a newspaper or magazine. The benches outside the entrance to the library are also sexual hunting grounds. Gays recognize each other easily through body language and eye contact. There is no difficulty differentiating between the casual glance of the straight male and the longing look of an interested gay. However, having made eye contact, a very high percentage of the gays are unable to proceed further. They give all the signs of wanting to meet the other person, but are afraid to act. Even saying "hello" is impossible, to say nothing of carrying through a full-fledged pickup. I believe this timidity is due more to a fear of rejection than to a fear of acquiring a label of being gay. Some sexual activity takes place in the washrooms of the public library and the hotel. In such situations the public tends to hold all the gays responsible, rather than just the few who participate.

The most notorious cruising area is nicknamed "Dizzy Block," or "The Cabbage Patch." This is a specific city block which is composed of a variety of gift shops, restaurants, offices, and a large parking lot. Several years back queens would congregate in the parking lot to gossip. Most of the action today involves gays driving around and around this and adjacent blocks in their cars. The idea is to follow the car of someone you are interested in and hope he will stop or lead you to someplace private and then stop. Basically it's a game of follow the leader. However, most participants end up quite frustrated, because the great majority are either too inept or too apprehensive to stop. A friend of mine says he hasn't cruised the block in over five years, because, "It isn't worth the effort. They go round and round in circles, too afraid or too stupid to stop the car." Often if they do stop, it is a block away, which doesn't do anyone any good. Gays cruising in cars also honk at solitary males in the area in hope of eliciting interest. The bulk of this activity on "the block" takes place late at night. Some gays wait until all the clubs are closed and everyone else has gone home before they start cruising, and it isn't unusual to see cars circling up until daybreak.

The scene with the cars is very unsatisfactory. Most gay males here live with their parents or their families. Consequently, they are unlikely to invite you to go home with them. Instead they usually want to park and have sex in the car, which precludes the development of a serious romantic relationship. Moreover, they almost always park in a very public location. Recently a high school teacher and his partner were caught by police because they had parked in the major city park. The police don't arrest you if they catch you. Instead they ask to see your IDs, tease you, and send you on your way.

Those who frequent "the block" have been doing so for a number of years and are considered regulars. Regulars frequently attach female names to each other and the names stick. They are terms of endearment, and nothing malicious is meant by them. A few of the names are Susan, Alice, Tammy, and Linda. However, everyone has hopes of finding someone new. When you encounter a friend in the area, the first question is always, "Anything new on the block?" There is little change though, aside from a stray businessman from out of town or the occasional male who decides to finally leave the closet. Most gays like to gossip and brag about their conquests. As a result, when they have a liaison with someone new, they tend to go right out and tell the gays, and straights too, who they have been with.

I have lived in major cities in Canada and the United States and have not seen there the degree of selfishness and disloyalty among gays which exists on Prince Edward Island. I have not had a relationship here, nor have I seen anyone else have one, which lasted any length of time or was based on any depth of feeling. Instead, gays are consumed with envy of one another and constantly gossip about each other in a very vicious way. Even those who are supposedly good friends tear each other to shreds. It is very rare to hear someone stand up for another in his absence. One of the tackiest games I've seen played here I call "fuck up your neighbor." This game consists of interfering in order to prevent other gays from getting together with each other. Thus a gay will drive up behind gays who are meeting and shine his car lights directly on them. In one case a gay called up the police and reported two gays parked in a car. A few nights ago I ran into a friend on Dizzy Block. It was quite late, and while we talked we were watched by a gay in his car in the parking lot. My friend invited me to join him in a toke of hash and we walked to my place. Sure enough, the guy in the car followed along at a crawl all the way there. The next evening I ran into someone who reported the guy in the car had told him what he had seen me do the night before. When gays destroy the privacy of those who are trying to get together, the other gays are much less likely to initiate contacts and pickups.

There is another problem with violence from the straight community. Few gays cruise the vicinity of Dizzy Block on foot anymore, because gays have been beaten up and robbed. In a recent incident a gay male was severely beaten by a group of males. In another incident a gay had his wallet stolen by four males on foot. There are many rednecks around and if you talk to the wrong person you can get physically hurt. One guy cracked my jaw and bragged to others about doing it. He claimed I had been putting the move on him, which I had not. I'm too smart to put the move on someone who's not responsive. Anyway, a couple of my friends went around and talked to him about this. The effects of such attacks on the gay community are devastating. Fearing for their personal safety, gays stay away from Dizzy Block or else remain in their cars so they can escape easier. Even though cars provide the gays with much greater protection, not all gays have a car. However, there are also numerous cases of straight males being beaten up by several males in various parts of the city when they were outside late at night. In addition, there has been at least one instance in which a gay male was picked up and severely beaten by another gay when he was not interested in getting sexually involved.

The most satisfying contacts I've made in Charlottetown have been in situations away from the usual gay haunts. It is very possible to score in almost any of the local bars, provided one doesn't act like a flaming faggot or take an approach that is too forward. There are a lot of bisexual males in town. They maintain their masculine stance with other "jocks," but although they are with girls most of the time, they are also open to encounters with other males. Some gays are able to make contact with bisexual males by being discreet and showing they can be trusted to keep the other's identity private. I am well known to be homosexual, and various bisexuals have been told this. I also keep quiet about who I am with. As a result a bisexual male will occasionally be interested in getting it on with me. For example, I was attending a talent show in a club on a Saturday afternoon recently, and there was a guy at the bar I used to go to school with. I had always wondered whether he was gay, and had tried to pick him up before. We talked together, and when the show ended the guy asked me to come over to his house and see the cupboards he'd spent three hours cleaning. Of course it was just an excuse. We really had fun at his place. However, he made a point of telling me he was ninety-nine percent straight, and only one percent gay. That's what he said, but he was certainly getting into it. It'll probably be another six months before we get together again, if then. He said I wasn't to come on to him, but to wait for him to contact me.

There are certain approaches taken by individual gays who are unwilling to try to deal with the local environment. One approach is to maintain contact with gay areas off the Island. Some frequently travel to Halifax, Toronto, or Montreal either to visit or to seek seasonal or full-time work. Those who do find work often return to Prince Edward Island when they leave their jobs or draw unemployment insurance benefits. Gays in their twenties and thirties who are not married are more likely to seek work in urban areas off the Island. Another common approach is to withdraw almost entirely from gay life. A longtime friend of mine who is about forty years old has adopted this approach. He was always very outgoing and gregarious and spent his time with lots of people. Now he spends most of his time at home in self-imposed confinement and on an occasional Saturday night goes to the hotel lounge. I've seen others undergo this radical change in behavior. Their zest for life has fizzled at an early age, and they have become very passive and complacent. Their lives have become less meaningful and productive, their perspective on the world has become more narrow, and they spend their time with family and a few friends who visit them. [#2843]

Double standards

People are expected to engage in behavior which is appropriate for their sex and to avoid behavior which is inappropriate for their sex. Whenever there are different rules for different groups, double standards are created. When group A is expected to follow rule A, then group B is allowed greater leeway to violate rule A. If children six years old and older are required to go to school, then children younger than six are not required to go to school. If people younger than eighteen years old are not allowed to buy alcohol, then those eighteen and older are allowed to buy alcohol. Therefore, when group A is expected to follow rule A, and group B is expected to follow rule B, then group A is allowed greater leeway to violate rule B, and group B is allowed greater leeway to violate rule A. The same thing happens with the two rules, *A female should not appear promiscuous* and *A male should not appear effeminate.* Females should not appear promiscuous, but males are permitted to appear promiscuous. Males should not appear feminine, but females are permitted to appear masculine.

Females are not supposed to appear promiscuous. However, this rule is relaxed in the case of men. Men do not destroy their reputations if they make themselves the center of attention in a mixed group, if they date a number of different girls within a short period of time, if they are sexually available, if they have sexual relationships with many females, if they let others know they engage in sexual activity, if others know they use contraceptives, if they go topless, if they look at pornography, or if they tell dirty jokes. Moreover, if males do these things they are not ostracized by other males, they do not lose their friends, and they do not destroy their chances of attracting a desirable female.

Males are not supposed to appear effeminate. However, this rule is relaxed in the case of females, who are allowed to engage in many masculine behaviors. Females do not destroy their reputations if they wear shirts, pants, caps, or other male clothing; if they wear colors associated with males, such as blue, gray, brown, and tan; if they wear materials associated with males, such as denim and leather; if they smoke, drink alcohol, use drugs, or swear; if they work in male occupations as doctors, lawyers, politicians, accountants, engineers, or bus drivers; if they join the military or the police; if they use male gestures; if they get angry and violent; if they fail to show emotion; if they endure hardships without complaining; if they do not show fear; if they are not frightened by mice, snakes, spiders, lightning, and the dark; if they are not squeamish about blood, guts, and killing; if they are competent, assertive, competitive, and decisive; if they take risks; if they take charge of their own destiny; if they are strong; if they are physically active and play sports; if they watch sports on television; if they engage in physical work; if they like outdoor activities; if they mow the lawn, wash the car, cut and stack wood, paint the house, or do farm work; if they repair things; if they carry male objects, such as tools; if they are competent drivers; if they hunt or fish; if they gamble; if they dress unconventionally; or if they get a tattoo. In addition, females are permitted to touch, hug, and have eye contact with other females; to wear each other's clothes; and to talk to other females in the bathroom; because these things are not believed to imply that they are sexually interested in other females. Moreover, if they do these things they are not ostracized by other females, they do not lose their friends, and they do not destroy their chances of attracting a desirable male.

Unfortunately, there is little appreciation of the fact that each sex has to cope with a double standard. Instead, each sex envies and resents the privileges of the other sex, and ignores the difficulties the other sex experiences. Females frequently mention the freedoms males have which they do not.

Guys can do anything they please, but most of the time nothing is said about them. No one would believe you anyway. #2844

When I was about sixteen I wanted to stay out as late as my twin brother could. But I had to be home at eleven o'clock, while he got to stay out until twelve or twelve thirty. Whenever I asked my mother why, she always replied, "Well, he's a boy, dear. He can look after himself better than you can." #2845

When I was sixteen there was a big concert in town and everyone was going. I asked Mom if I could go. She refused because it wasn't a good place for a girl. She said all these weird people would be there with drugs and alcohol. I was a little upset, but decided to drop it. Two days later my brother, who is a year younger than me, told me he was going to the concert with all his friends. I went straight to my mother and asked why he was allowed to go and I wasn't. She said it was simply because he was a guy and I was a girl and that spoke for itself. #2846

I wanted to go to Halifax with a bunch of my friends to shop for the day. Mom wouldn't let me because she said if a group of girls drove over for the day they would look easy. Two weeks later my brother, who is two years younger than me, said he was hitchhiking over to Halifax the next day, didn't know how long he was going for, would probably stay with a friend, and would need about fifty dollars. The next day he was on his way with seventy dollars in his pocket. #2847

When I was going to high school the morals of a girl were often the topic of conversation. This was especially so the Monday after a school dance or some other social event. On the tongues of everybody were tidbits of gossip concerning who was with whom and how discreet or indiscreet they were. A minimum amount of time was spent on the discreet couples and much time was spent discussing the really zealous ones. The actions of the boy were almost never questioned. It seems like the girl was actually held responsible for both herself and the boy. #2848

A girl always has to look after her reputation, but a guy can do as he pleases and not worry about what others say about him. When I was in high school there was a party somewhere almost every weekend. The guys who went were considered part of the in-crowd. But the girls who went were labeled wild and loose. #2849

I'm twenty-eight and I live with my girlfriend. My parents have no problem with this. But my sister, who is thirty years old, makes her boy-friend move out of their apartment whenever our parents visit her in Moncton. She says they'd flip if they knew, and I think she's right. #2850

I can't understand why there is so much difference between what guys can do and what girls can do. What would you think if you heard about a girl who went out with a different guy each night? The initial reaction would be "What a slut," "Talk about sleazy," "Holy Shit!" and "How can I get her phone number?" But what if you heard about a guy who went out with a different girl each night? People would say, "Shit, I bet he's busy!" "Sounds like a pretty good head to me," "I wouldn't mind meeting him," and "That's what I call lucky." #2851

No one cares when a guy has a reputation. People say, "Who cares if he sleeps around? It's natural for a guy. If you don't, you aren't a man." But girls are hurt when they have a reputation. No one wants to date "one of those girls." A friend of mine would like to go steady with a guy she and I both know. I asked her, "But why? He takes a different girl home every weekend." "I don't care," she said, "He is so sweet and you know I've always liked him." Now if this were a guy talking about a girl who had a bad reputation because she went home with a different guy every weekend, he wouldn't want to get serious about her. #2852

Girls should be able to sit wherever they want to. There's no rule against it. The double standard really makes me sick. Guys assume I'm either an alcoholic or a slut just because I like to sit at the bar and talk to the female bartender. It's not fair. #2853

Some guys can be such hypocrites. They'll start calling some girl they've slept with a slut. They really have to realize it takes two to have sex. #2854

There is this extreme double standard in society. Males who have sex frequently with different partners are considered "studs," while women who do so are called "sluts." #2855

Guys can say anything they like about their behavior, like in a sense brag about it. But girls can't. Guys talk about it all the time. It's really quite embarrassing sometimes. There probably is a comparable word for males who are loose, but I don't know what it is. #2856

Males are less likely to mention the freedoms which females have that males do not. Males do know that if they complain about not being able to cry, play house or play with dolls, take ballet or figure skating, or wear clothing or colors associated with females, others will seriously question their masculinity.

As a girl I was free to play with trucks and tractors, but my parents wouldn't allow my twin brother to play with dolls. They bought toy vehicles for both of us, but they never bought any typical girl toys for my brother. #2857

I worked as a play supervisor at one of the city parks this past summer. The relationship between the boys and girls who played there was very good and neither sex discriminated against the other to any great extent. When a girl wanted to play football or baseball, no one said anything to her about it. It didn't make the least bit of difference she was a girl. Those with the biggest problem were the boys. They had to watch what they did if there were any other boys around. If a boy were to try to skip rope he would be called a "sissy" or "queer" by his male friends. Being called this was just terrible for a boy. Boys wouldn't consider trying things which would cause them to be embarrassed by the others. Other than this, the children accepted each other for their abilities, and did not make judgments on the basis of whether a child was a girl or a boy. #2858

My great uncle lived with us for a year before he died. My brother, who was eleven years old at the time, bawled at the funeral, and my grandfather took him outside and told him that big boys don't cry. My sister and I were nine and seven years old and we cried just as much, but because we were girls no one thought of telling us not to. #2859

In junior and senior high, males avoid sports like badminton, gymnastics, ballet, and figure skating so they won't be called gay. I remember my mother wanted me to start figure skating to improve my skating ability. I would have nothing to do with it for fear someone would find out and call me gay. #2860

When I was a teenager, any guy who participated in activities which are normally associated with women was considered effeminate or homosexual. This included dancing, singing in a choir, sewing, and doing housework. A few guys in high school had unconventional interests, such as painting and clothes design. The macho guys viewed them as different and didn't know how to react to them. Even neutral activities could get you in trouble. One kid in our neighborhood was ostracized because he was effeminate. This reaction became stronger when he got involved with photography. #2861

I am female and live in a university dorm. One night the girl in the room next to mine wanted to stay with me because some guy was drunk and had passed out on her bed. So she and I shared the bed in my room. We were giggling and carrying on when a male friend of mine walked in and turned on the light. At first he wondered what we were up to, but then he realized what the situation was. Can you just imagine what he would have thought had we been two guys? #2862

It's acceptable for women to enter a man's world to some extent, but men can't enter a woman's world. For instance, people say of a woman who helps her husband with farming or fishing, "What a good wife she is to go out and work with her husband and give him a helping hand." But when a man helps his wife around the house, men are likely to say, "Oh what a pussy he is. Does the farming and the woman's work too. It's not hard to tell who wears the pants in that house." #2863

A female friend of mine was trying to tell me that males and females don't have a double standard, because it's alright for her to wear her husband's pajamas. But do you think her husband could get away with wearing her nightgown and underwear? I'd love to watch other people's faces if he told them he was doing so. #2864

Double standards

Females are amused by the discomfort they cause males when they ask them to hold their purse or buy female items for them at the store. They do not realize this is comparable to the discomfort females would feel if they were asked to stand in a public place holding a condom, to walk topless through a shopping mall, or to tell dirty jokes in front of a mixed group. When females tease heterosexual males about being homosexual, they do not consider that this is comparable to males teasing a woman about being a prostitute. Women want men to talk about their feelings and be willing to cry. Similarly, men should ask women to boast about their sexual experiences and yell sexual words. Conversely, when males put pressure on females to have sex with them when they are not in a committed relationship, it is the equivalent of females putting pressure on males to engage in a sexual relationship with another male. There is enormous resistance because this is the one thing both the female and the male are not supposed to do. The female is not supposed to engage in sex outside of a committed relationship, and the male is not supposed to engage in sex with other males. Similarly, when males display their sexual conquests to other males, they do not consider the significance of this to the women involved. When a male talks about his sexual relations with a specific woman, it is comparable to having a homosexual tell others about his sexual relations with that particular male.

Many females expect males to be both a proper male and a proper female too, and they criticize and reject males who do not succeed at this. Females expect males to act like proper males and be financially successful, protective, confident, and respected by other males. At the same time they expect males to act like proper females and openly express their emotions, such as by crying; to be emotionally supportive; and to help raise the children and do housework. The better a male is at acting like a female, the less likely he is to keep the respect of other males and the less likely other males will be willing to cooperate with him in getting and protecting resources. When a boy is given dolls to play with to develop his feminine nature, it is comparable to giving a girl dildos to play with to develop her masculine nature. Each of these toys will cause the child to be ostracized by members of their own sex. Some females want males to participate in the female activity of exploring and expressing their emotions with their friends, or female bonding. Males do engage in male bonding when they get together with other males to go to a bar or club,

393

or play cards, fish, hunt, play sports, or watch a sporting event. In these settings males frequently drink, tell dirty jokes, talk about sexual exploits and fantasies, and try to pick up women. However, this male bonding is unacceptable to many females, and few males try to get females to participate in this. For the most part males do not expect females to act like both a proper female and a proper male. However, some males do want their wives to obtain jobs outside of the household in order to supplement the family income.

Other constraints

There are also numerous other constraints on an individual's willingness to seek sex with another person. These constraints are based on other feelings and other personal, group, and societal models. They include lack of attraction to the other party; lack of positive response from the other party; fear the other person will tell; concern over damage to one's reputation and resources; potential damage to one's relationship with one's parents, mate, children, or friends; the risk of pregnancy or venereal disease; lack of privacy; moral objections; religious training and models; violation of one's self-image; fear of hurting one's chances of developing a relationship with another person one is more interested in; insufficient recovery from a previous relationship; fatigue; and preoccupation with other matters.

> Sex is a pretty frightening situation. When you come right down to it, who knows what might happen? You not only have to worry about getting pregnant, but also what kind of disease you can get. [#2865]

> Sex is just too dangerous to be promiscuous. Pregnancy and STDs (sexually transmitted diseases) are major risks. I take birth-control pills, and I still use condoms too. [#2866]

> I'm always hearing stories about guys who picked up some girl at the clubs and took her home. I find this disgusting. Most of the time they don't even know each other, but they have sex just the same. I mean what would happen if the girl got pregnant? She'd be having a stranger's baby. [#2867]

I am a virgin and very proud of it, and I plan on staying this way until I am married. I've gone out with my share of guys and know that most guys are out for only one thing. But I have found a very nice guy who isn't like the others. Sometimes he and I talk about sex, but we always conclude it would be better to save it until we have "a license," or get married. If I ever got pregnant I am sure I would kill myself. I love my mother and father and could never face them again after doing such a stupid thing. Sometimes I think I am obsessed with the idea of killing myself if I got pregnant. I figure this is a major reason why I will remain a virgin until I get married. I love life too much to louse it up by getting knocked up. [#2868]

I really have a low opinion of anyone who has sex before marriage. It's disgusting and it's not right. I had this friend I really felt close to. Then I found out she believed in sex before marriage and it totally shattered my image of her. It disturbed me so much, it ruined our friendship. I mean, what guy is going to marry you when he can get all the privileges without a commitment? Besides that, how many diseases are you going to catch? What about AIDS? No thank you! If a guy loves me enough, he'll wait. [#2869]

My boyfriend and I go to the same high school. I've been going out with him for about a year, and we love each other. He loves me too much to do it to me. Sometimes I would like to do it, but I'm afraid it will either turn him off or it will ruin everything we have going. [#2870]

I feel pressured because all the other guys talk about is sex. A few of my buddies razz me about being a virgin, but it doesn't bother me. My religious upbringing tells me premarital sex is wrong, so I'm going to wait until I'm married. What does bother me is that a lot of these guys are giving the rest of us a bad name. Not all guys are just out for sex, but I guess that's what most girls think. [#2871]

I have a lot of female friends who complain to me about how a man can hurt a woman. It makes me think twice before I do something foolish. Besides, if I ever hurt a girl I think my friends would beat the crap out of me. These girls hear all, see all, and know all. Help! [#2872]

I am a born-again Christian, and the Bible tells us that lusting for a woman is a sin. Sex is permitted only after the commitment of marriage. God knows what is best for me and will choose my mate for me.

Sex is a natural part of life as long as God approves of the circumstances in which the act takes place. #2873

Discouraging sex

When one is not interested in sex one can discourage overtures from others by ignoring or rejecting them, or by claiming one is busy, tired, ill, menstruating, or committed to someone else.

I worked at a restaurant last summer and the boss, who is about forty-five, kept trying to get close to me. He'd "accidentally" brush up against me, or reach for something the other side of me and let his hand slip, or shit like that. Once when he did it, I looked him square in the eye and said very firmly I didn't like what he was doing and wanted him to stop. I told him I didn't like being touched like that. It worked, because he left me alone afterwards. #2874

Women have it easy. It's acceptable for them to say no. But the situation is totally different for men, because we are supposed to be sex starved. This girl and I were together and things started to get out of hand. When I stopped, she got really upset and started to rave on that there must be something wrong with her. I tried to explain, and she got really quiet. I never got the opportunity to talk to her again. She must have been mad, because afterwards rumors started flying around that I must be gay. How is a guy supposed to stand up to that? #2875

I usually have to work hard to think up reasons to avoid sex. Recently I've been using menstruation to my advantage. Because it's so messy, it's a real turnoff for my husband. It lasts for four days, but I can have it "last" for eight to ten. When it's over I can always say I've got a female infection. I'm putting what nature gave me to good use. #2876

Pregnancy was my golden opportunity to avoid sex. It was the one time I could control my husband's sexual advances, because Errol didn't know how much discomfort he was causing me. I would carefully explain to him what the doctor had supposedly told me about sex during pregnancy. I stressed that each woman is different, in case Errol learned that someone else continued to have sex during their pregnancy. As my pregnancy advanced, Errol became resigned to the situation. After the baby arrived I needed to heal and nurse the child, so sex was pushed to the back burner for several months. Once you have children you have an easy excuse for avoiding sex. Errol is at work all day and has no idea how much trouble the kids have been. So I can decide whether or not to use being tired as an excuse. But I don't want to use this excuse more than absolutely necessary, because it's like crying wolf. When I really am tired, he won't believe me. #2877

When my husband gets interested and I'm not, I bring up a depressing topic, like world poverty, nuclear war, AIDS, a parent's illness, or over-due bills. It turns his desire into conversation. "Depress your lover" is my motto. #2878

I don't have to dream up excuses when I don't feel like sex with my husband. I just don't bother shaving, and go to bed with stubbly legs and underarms, which turns him off. He lets me read or sleep, whatever I want. #2879

Sometimes I tell my husband, "I'm tired, so buzz off and leave the material alone." It's rude, but it works well. #2880

Other techniques that people use to discourage sex include looking scruffy, eating garlic, and remaining in the vicinity of other people.

I find the easiest way to avoid sex with my boyfriend is to double date with another couple or meet friends at a dance or a barbecue. He is more likely to get sexually aroused when we are alone. Also, he knows that my dad is quite strict. So if things start to get out of hand I tell him I need to get home to meet Dad's curfew. #2881

However, even when people are not interested in sex, they often give in to the other person's desires.

I, and many other women I talk to, consider sexual intercourse ani-malistic. We find kissing and fondling sexy, but we don't enjoy having this thing stuck into our body. We go ahead with it just to please the guy. #2882

If you're going with a guy and you don't have sex when he wants to, you know you won't last long. You'll probably break up. #2883

During the years we've been together my husband and I have learned that our desire for sex is frequently out of synch. It doesn't wax and wane in both of us at the same time. The thing that makes us give in to the other's desire is a fear of cheating. If I'm not in the mood for two nights in a row, I get worried he'll find someone who is, so I succumb. #2884

Excess behavior

Excess behavior is behavior in response to feelings which results in one acting contrary to the purposes the feelings are designed for. As a result, one loses resources rather than gains or protects them. For example, the feeling of pleasure causes people to engage in sex. As a result people reproduce. However, there are many situations in which people waste time and energy seeking pleasure from sex when there is little likelihood of reproduction.

People expend a great deal of time and energy thinking about sex, watching individuals they consider physically attractive, reading about sex, and observing sexual behavior in films and photographs. Very little of this effort leads to reproduction. Also, a desire for sexual pleasure can interfere with efforts to obtain resources.

Many of the university students I know are more interested in sex than they are in their studies. If they took the time they spend thinking about and pursuing members of the opposite sex and spent it on their studies they would be outstanding students. #2885

I've heard that half the searches on the Internet are to visit adult, or pornographic, sites. Some of the provincial governments are trying to prevent their employees from using their computers for this purpose while they are at work. #2886

Because people obtain pleasure from sexual activity, people engage in sex in situations when there is little or no chance of reproduction. This is the case when people masturbate, use sex toys, practice homosexuality, have oral or anal sex, use contraceptives, have sex at a time when there is little chance of fertilization, or engage in sex with individuals who are too young or too old to procreate.

People make associations between a) the pleasure they experience through sex, and b) the stimuli which produce this pleasure or appear to be associated with it. In order to experience sexual pleasure again they often return to the same stimuli. When the pleasure is associated with stimuli other than traditional heterosexual contact, they return to the same stimuli, even when these stimuli are considered deviant by other people.

Society and sex

Sex is a subject of enormous interest. People frequently think and talk about sex, tease their friends about sex, tell "dirty" jokes, read about the sexual adventures of others, and worry about the amount of sex they have and about their sexual performance. Many people dedicate a great deal of time, energy, and expense to obtaining sexual pleasure.

During the normal operation of the society there are countless opportunities for individuals to meet and spend time with potential sexual partners. In addition, the society provides settings, activities, and services which make it easier for people to locate others for sex. These include nightclubs, bars, dances, parties, dating services, personal advertisements in newspapers, escort services, and red-light districts.

Many goods and services have been developed in response to people's interest in sex. A large number of businesses provide products and services to help people appear more attractive to potential and existing sex partners. These include beauty parlors, gyms, clothing and cosmetic stores, dance studios, and tanning salons. In addition, there are sex education classes, books of instruction on sexual technique, and sexual aids. Also, because people are interested in pictures and descriptions of the physical appearance and sexual behavior of other people, such pictures and descriptions are regularly used in television programs, movies, art, novels, biographies, newspapers, magazines, and advertisements to generate interest and sales. Certain individuals become recognized for their sexual appeal and command high salaries for their appearance in films, television programs, and advertisements.

Nevertheless, societies and individuals differ in the degree to which they accept and participate in open consideration and discussion of sex.

The issue of sex education in the local schools has been quite controversial. Some parents feel that sex education should be the sole responsibility of the parents. "The school board is questioning our competence as parents." "I think it is just disgusting how they teach my Janie that stuff on sex. I mean she is only ten years old and if I wanted her to know about sex so soon I would have told her myself. She's just too young to handle it." "I'm the parent and I'm going to dictate when, where, and just how my children are going to learn about sex. If parents want to decide when their children learn about sex at home, the schools should respect our decision. After all, we bring our children into this world and we've earned the right to educate them." "She's my kid and I'm damned if some know-it-all teacher is going to tell her everything she wants to know about sex. AIDS is the most deadly thing out there today, and the schools want to show all the kids how to avoid it and still have sex. My answer is better. I say avoid AIDS by having the decency to abstain from sex until you're married. Maybe they don't give medals to virgins, but at least they'll be around to attend the awards ceremony." "If the schools show them all these safe ways to have sex, kids are going to start doing it as soon as they can. I speak for many parents when I say that I don't want any of my children going out on a date and having sex just because they can get away with it. It's just not right!"

Others feel that there are many advantages to having schools provide sex education. "Sex education should be taught in the schools. The kids are at school most of the time anyway." "Parents can't control what their kids do unless they lock them in the basement. All kids are curious about sex and sexual differences. Kids are having sex, getting pregnant, and catching sexual diseases as early as twelve and thirteen. I don't think you can begin sex education too early. Most parents try to avoid the issue or put off talking about it while their kids get older and older and are more and more likely to engage in sex. Also lots of parents don't have much knowledge about sex because they don't read technical books about it. Teachers who teach sex education know much more about it than most parents. Opposition to sex education is just another form of cultural stupidity." "We feel a great burden has been lifted from our shoulders. It's just too difficult for us to talk about something that we learned about just before we were married." "It's great! Now we don't have to worry about choking on our food some night during dinner when our children decide to ask us about making love." "Thank God for sex-education classes. I hate to think how I would have discussed things like the structure of a woman's or a man's genitals with my children. I feel a lot safer knowing my kids learned about sex from a teacher who could respond objectively to their questions. If one of my kids had asked me how to reach an orgasm, I would have had a heart attack." [2887]

I grew up in Vietnam and there was no mention of sexual intercourse in the family or school system. Instead, a girl is taught to sew and cook. A girl is expected to be a virgin and to learn about sexual matters through intercourse with her husband. Most girls are virgins when they marry. I estimate that between a quarter and a third of the single and married males in my family and in my husband's family are actively pursuing sex with as many girls as they can, and they consider virgins particularly desirable. Most Vietnamese women, both married and unmarried, are not even aware of the possibility of female orgasm or masturbation. Instead, sex is equated with the male orgasm. Oral sex is not imagined, and would be considered deviant and dirty. However, menstruation is mentioned among the women of the family. Females certainly do not want to appear sexually available or experienced. They are expected to be innocent and passive. The worst thing a female can be considered and called is loose; a prostitute; or damaged, used, or worn-out goods. The worst thing a man can be considered is an addicted gambler. An addicted gambler can't be trusted because he is likely to lie to and cheat family members, to borrow money and not repay it, and to become violent. [2888]

Many people are concerned about the degree of explicitness in pictures and descriptions of physical appearance and sexual behavior. Such pictures and descriptions produce various responses, including stimulation, amusement, disinterest, and outrage.

An entire generation of teenagers is being raised on erotic programs that they see on TV every night. Teenagers already have all these unwed pregnancies and abortions. It's not difficult to see what's in their future; sexual abuse and divorce. TV programs have done this to them. [#2889]

When separate shows of male and female "exotic" dancers visited and performed in Charlottetown responses were quite varied. Women stated, "It's grotesque that our Island is infested with such vulgar entertainment," "I wouldn't go see them, because it doesn't turn my crank," "My friends and I waited in line for three hours to get in, and we would do it again. We were quite impressed," and "It's super entertainment. The men dance so well. I wish my husband could dance half as good even with his clothes on." Men stated, "I don't have the urge to go see them peel off their clothes. But it's nice to know if I do, there's a place to go," "The body is supposed to be something to be proud of. No one complains about nude paintings or sculptures, so why make a fuss over exotic dancing," "I went twice, and there's nothing to get excited about. It's no worse than going to a beach. True, the dancers didn't have tops on, but once you've seen one you've seen them all," and "It's a bloody shame. It's not entertainment; it's pornography." [#2890]

In addition, various segments of society concern themselves with individual reproduction, and the willingness of the individual to share resources with sexual partners and offspring. Relatives and nonrelatives frequently exert social pressure on individuals to conform with established norms of reproduction and support. Also, organizations and laws are set up to promote certain ideals regarding birth control, abortion, infanticide, and the support of one's mate and children.

.

ACKNOWLEDGEMENTS

I most sincerely thank the residents of Prince Edward Island for their patience, openness, and cooperation with this research. Hundreds of people have contributed their time and labor. They have provided information about their families, friends, and neighbors, as well as themselves, for the sole purpose of helping to identify types of behavior. Because of the private nature of much of the information, most of those participating have asked that their names not be mentioned. As a result, I am hesitant to mention the few who indicated they do not care whether I use their names. I certainly would not want these few criticized for information that they did not provide. Therefore, my policy is to identify as few names as possible. If, however, someone wishes to have their name mentioned in connection with specific pieces of information that they provided, I will be happy to do so if this book is reprinted, as long as this does not place others in an embarrassing position.

I wish to single out Sharon Myers, who has been an invaluable assistant in collecting case studies for this research. She gathered excellent information, painstakingly placed this within a proper context, helped me understand the significance of the behavior, answered my numerous questions, and patiently corrected me when I was off base. She has made a significant contribution to our understanding of rural life. I can not thank her enough. Many others have worked for me as research assistants during various stages of this study, and their contribution has been enormous. Regrettably, most have requested that I not mention them by name. I very much thank all of these individuals for the care, attention, and interest they have given this project.

I also greatly thank Hoa Huynh and Llewellyn Watson for their patience and cooperation in serving as sounding boards as I have written up my information and developed my ideas. Often they put aside their own work to listen to me. Their thoughtful comments have helped me deal with certain weaknesses in the study, their examples have clarified the subject matter, and their encouragement has boosted my morale.

I very much want to thank Bill Charlesworth for all of his encouragement and intellectual support for this project.

Many other individuals have been extremely helpful in answering specific questions which have arisen during the course of the study. These include Doreley Coll, Satadal Dasgupta, Kay Diviney, Anne Marie Eberhardt, Frank Falvo, Susan Gallant, Egbert Huynh, Joseph Kopachevsky, Frank Ledwell, Brent MacLaine, William Mason, Shannon Murray, Annie Myer, Wayne Peters, John Joe Sark, Barbara Seeber, Charlotte Stewart, Elizabeth Thai, Tien Thai, Linda Trenton, Tom Trenton, Judi Wagner, and David Weale. Thank you very much.

A number of individuals have freely loaned me slides and photographs and have given me a great deal of help understanding their content. Some have also gone to a great deal of trouble to take photographs for me. These include Barbara Currie, Ron Eckroth, Mamdouh Elgharib, Margot Elgharib, Charles Holmes, Hoa Huynh, Thuy Huynh, Vicki Huynh, Amanda MacIntrye, Jean Mitchell, Harold Saint, Charlotte Stewart, Elizabeth Thai, Llewellyn Watson, and Marty Zelenietz. I very much appreciate their help, and know this research would be much poorer without it.

I have also received an enormous amount of technical help. Marc Beland, Dave Cairns, Bruce Ferguson, Nancy Kemp, Scott MacDonald, Evelyn Read, Bonnie Suen, Chris Vessey, and Larry Yeo have provided excellent advice and support with computers and word processing. Donya Beaton, Katie Compton, Shelley Ebbett, Richard Haines, Angela Hughes, and Tom MacDonald have gone far beyond the call of duty and have painstakingly prepared countless outstanding photographs. Glenda Clements-Smith, John Cox, Janos Fedak, Sibyl Frei, Michelle Gauthier, Matthew MacKay, Floyd Trainor, Mary Ada Upstone, and Kent Villard have given me excellent advice and a great deal of help with illustrations, layout, and printing. Mary Ada Upstone has created the very useful maps.

I particularly want to thank my wife, Hoa Huynh, who has given me an enormous amount of help and support. It is not possible to express how much this means. She understands how important it is to me to spend so much time on this project.

Although numerous individuals have given freely of their time and help, limitations in the conduct, analysis, organization, and interpretation of this research must be recognized as my own.

INDEX OF NUMBERED EXAMPLES

This index is designed to help those who have read the text to locate specific examples they want to find again. The numbers below refer to the consecutive numbers which follow the indented quotations in the text.

alcohol (*continued*)

   some people become too forward when drinking, #2425
   ten feet tall and bulletproof, #2394
   those who do not use alcohol to become confident, #2425
   using alcohol as an excuse, #2425
   using alcohol to get confidence to do things, #2392
encourages people to spend more money, #2425
   buying drinks for others, #2425
   girls who get guys to buy them drinks, #2430
and going to clubs, #2293, #2403. *See also* clubs
   drinking in clubs, #2403, #2424, #2425
   five males drinking in a club and wanting to pick up females, #2426
helps one get attention, #2425
influence on a female's behavior at a party, #2536
males being able to drink a large quantity of alcohol, #2692
ordering male versus female drinks in a bar, #2691
they have to drink in order to have a good time, #2391
   if they don't drink things will be boring and no fun and they'll have a lousy time, #2391
   we couldn't have a good time at the dance without drinking, #2389
those who become depressed, more aggressive, or more sarcastic when drinking, #2425
   Mrs. Smith throws her drink in her husband's face when he tries to take her home, #2388
trying to hide purchases of, #2674
underage drinking, #2394
   how minors obtain alcohol, #2287, #2288, #2292, #2394, #2395
   if you are old enough to do a good day's work, then you are old enough to take a drink, #2394
   teenagers drinking at a fast-food restaurant, #2288
   teens looking for a place to drink, #2288
   underage drinking is widespread and widely accepted by adults in rural communities, #2394
   underage teens buying liquor at a shopping mall, #2287, #2288
   underage teens drinking in a shopping mall, #2287
animal breeding, #2499
apartment. *See* landlord
appearance. *See also* attractive; bathroom; dressing up; envy
   having a beautiful appearance, #2302
   trying to not look contrived, #2574
   weight and appearance, #2302
Asian sex centers, #2370
athlete, athletes
   discussing sexual conquests in the locker room, #2632
   drawing attention to themselves in clubs, #2361

competition between women as to whose husband is the most caring, #2841

compliments

girls do not want to be complimented in sexual terms, #2614

condom, condoms

buying, #2674

we would go through twelve in two days, #2276

conductor on a train, sex with the, #2369

confidence. *See* self-confidence

construction crew pretending to be gay, #2812

contraceptives. *See also* birth-control pills; condoms

difficulties buying, #2674

embarrassment associated with buying, #2674

identifying girls in clubs who use, #2669

why people do not want to use, #2673

cool, acting

accepted style of clothes, #2285

at a dance, #2292

when dating, #2297, #2298

in a fast-food restaurant, #2288

it isn't cool to be afraid, #2676

guys want to appear cool, #2283

cops. *See* police

courtship. *See also* clubs; dating; females; males; sex

and alcohol, #2279

at the beach, #2289

at a community dance, #2292

in a community, #2279, #2304

competition for males, #2294

and cruising, #2290

dating, #2297 - #2300

first dates, #2297, #2298

economic factors, #2279

efforts by staff to control romantic physical contact at a roller-skating hall, #2285

at a fast-food restaurant, #2288, #2290

females trying to keep a good reputation, #2279, #2280

and finding a boyfriend, #2294

going to clubs, #2293, #2401 - #2435

at the gym, #2303

illegitimate children, #2279

keeping a relationship together through important social events in school, #2281

living common law, #2279

males making physical advances, #2279

males often show little concern for female feelings, #2279

males trying to have sex with as many girls as possible, #2279, #2280

marriage, #2279

Index of numbered examples

Index of numbered examples

Index of numbered examples

fights at a, #2288, #2290, #2291

teens hanging out at a, #2288, #2290

fat

females dressing in ways which hide weight, #2376

trying to avoid looking fat, #2302, #2303, #2376, #2380

feelings

female versus male willingness to talk about their feelings, #2777 - #2785

female, females. *See also* courtship; double standards; effeminate, males trying not to appear; males; promiscuous, females trying not to appear; sex

are more expressive than guys, #2706

being able to hold their man, #2302, #2841

besting other females, #2841

books and films of interest to, #2682

competing to show that their own husband is more caring, #2841

competition for males, #2294, #2406

don't pursue guys because of what others would think, #2572

embarrassed when others know they are engaged in sex, #2616 - #2618, #2623 - #2627

females do different activities with males than they do with females, #2699, #2701

females looking for the perfect male, #2293, #2296. *See also* dating

girl talk, #2406

hiding sexual activity, #2301. *See also* promiscuous, females trying not to appear

males who are big and muscular go out with the most popular and best-looking girls, #2381

not wanting to be thought of in sexual terms, #2291

ordering "female drinks" in a bar, #2691

pretending they aren't as smart as they are, #2301

pretending they don't play a sport better than the males they are with, #2303

reacting to scenes of animals being killed or butchered, #2730

segregation of the sexes, #2499, #2542, #2543

sexual fantasies, #2475 - #2482

status in university, #2302

taking the initiative asking males out, #2298

taking trips out of town for sex, #2359, #2360

there are three types: greenies, cock-teasers, and loose sluts, #2312

three-year campaign to get together with a professor, #2574

trying to figure males out, #2293

trying to find Mr. Right, #2293

trying to get together with a male in a ladylike fashion, #2573 - #2576

using sex to keep a guy interested in them, #2365

waiting in the emergency room, #2686

fight, fights.

if called effeminate or homosexual, #2688, #2689

in clubs, #2407, #2425

at dances, #2292, #2684, #2688

423

Index of numbered examples

identification. *See* ID
insults, insulted. *See* yelling at people from cars
intramurals, #2303

Kewpie Doll, #2529
kiss, good-night. *See* dating
kissing, #2841

landlord
    not wanting to let boyfriend's landlord know she is spending the night, #2626
library, putting books on homosexuality in a friend's kit bag in the, #2810
lice, difficulties buying products to deal with, #2674
life of the party, girls who are the, #2302
lines used by males to try to get sex, #2397
liquor. *See* alcohol
locker room, male interaction in the, #2815
loose. *See* promiscuous, females not wanting to appear
love. *See also* relationship
    female opinions about, #2293
    giving up on, #2293
    I sleep with lots of guys because I think it will lead to something better. Love, I guess, #2307
    love should exist first, before sex, #2314, #2315
    real guys don't sit around discussing love, #2777 - #2780
    true love, #2296

magazines for women, males do not want to be seen looking at, #2769
male attitude, #2295
male bonding, #2295
males. *See also* clubs; cool; effeminate, males not wanting to appear; females; fights; green; henpecked
    acting tough in high school, #2683
    avoiding "girly stores" in the mall, #2287
    being masculine is equated with being good at a tough sport, #2680
    being physically aggressive in hockey and football, #2681
    dancing conservatively, #2724
    doing tricks and showing off when roller skating, #2285
    establishing "a best man," #2693
    females don't understand that the only thing guys think about is sex, #2450
    fighting, #2684, #2688 - #2690, #2693
    gaining status for their sexual success, #2631, #2632
    guy talk, #2419, #2426
    interest in rough sports, #2683
    kicking out a door panel, #2687
    the male attitude, #2295
    male books and films, #2682

pregnancy, risking, #2673, #2674. *See also* birth-control pills
  the belief that an unmarried girl who takes birth-control pills must be
    promiscuous, #2673
  blaming girls for not using contraceptives, #2673
  female doesn't want to get a pregnancy test because the lab workers will talk,
    #2630
pregnant. *See* pregnancy, risking
prince
  I've kissed many toads, but never my prince, #2293
professor. *See also* graduate school
  a student's three-year campaign to get involved with a, #2574
prom, having a date for the high school, #2281, #2294
promiscuous, females trying not to appear. *See also* females; pregnancy, risking; sex
  behavior which indicates a female is promiscuous
    associating herself with sex
      a female who enjoys dirty jokes in mixed company, #2563
      a female who talks about her dog being in heat or about drinking more
        beer than anyone else, #2564
      nude bathing with a guy, #2649
    associating with many males
      dating many different males, #2851
      dating more than one male at the same time, #2586 - #2592, #2635,
        #2636, #2851
      a female who is present at or participates in male activities, #2542,
        #2547 - #2551
      a girl who dances with numerous partners, #2539, #2644
      a girl who has lots of male friends, #2544, #2604, #2612
      a girl who sits with a bunch of jocks looks too available, #2551
      going into a club with one guy and leaving with another, #2588
      running around with lots of men, #2635, #2636, #2640, #2654, #2672
    being available to males outside her committed relationship
      dancing with a man other than her husband, #2597
      getting together with a male for a coffee when her husband is not
        present, #2598
      hanging around, touching, or flirting with men other than her husband,
        #2596, #2599
      socializing when her husband or partner is not present, #2598, #2601
      talking to guys other than her boyfriend, #2600
    being readily available for sex
      going to bed with a guy on the first date, #2671
      leaving a bar with a guy she has just met there, #2615
      making physical advances toward males, #2577 - #2579, #2666
      Terri wants to sleep with a number of guys and is considered disgusting,
        #2504
      an unmarried girl who takes birth-control pills must be promiscuous,
        #2673

432

Index of numbered examples

spitting in order to look macho when buying drugs from a known homosexual, #2827
sports. *See also* athlete; effeminate, males trying to avoid appearing; gym; hockey;
    males; roller-skating hall
    female and sissy sports, #2726, #2727
    local attitudes toward golf and curling, #2742
    males avoiding certain sports so they won't appear gay, #2860
    not letting a big and fat male play baseball with them, #2718
stealing in order to avoid making an embarrassing purchase, #2674
stimulation
    decline in, #2457
suicide
    hunting incident brought up at a fast-food restaurant, #2291
sunglasses at the beach, #2289
suntan
    getting a tan at the beach, #2289
swearing, #2738
    causes others to find you unattractive, #2380

table and lap dances, #2443
taboos, sexual, #2499
tan. *See* suntan
teacher
    male teacher in a one-room schoolhouse who has discipline problems, #2754
team jackets
    males keeping them on in a fast-food restaurant, #2288
teasing
    males not wanting to be teased by their friends for having sex with an unattractive
      female, #2368
teenager, teenagers. *See also* alcohol; clubs; courtship; pregnancy, risking
    cruising, #2288, #2290, #2291
    at a dance, #2292
    at a fast-food restaurant, #2288
    having friends come to their home, #2287
    at the shopping mall, #2287
    underage teenagers and alcohol, #2287, #2394
    yelling at people from cars, #2290, #2291
Thailand as a sex destination, #2370
thin. *See* skinny
time with the boys, #2295
toads
    I've kissed many toads, but never my prince, #2293
train conductor, sex with the, #2369
trake, #2499
travel, travels
    to Asian centers for sex, #2370

SUBJECT INDEX

See also a) the table of contents and table of detailed contents for the chapter on seeking sex, and b) the index of numbered examples.

Subject index

tension and release, 18 - 19

volume one, 1
volume three, 5
volume two, 3